Reason's Nearest Kin

PHILOSOPHIES OF ARITHMETIC FROM
KANT TO CARNAP

MICHAEL POTTER

OXFORD
UNIVERSITY PRESS

OXFORD
UNIVERSITY PRESS

Great Clarendon Street, Oxford OX2 6DP
Oxford University Press is a department of the University of Oxford.
It furthers the University's objective of excellence in research, scholarship,
and education by publishing worldwide in

Oxford New York

Athens Auckland Bangkok Bogotá Buenos Aires Calcutta
Cape Town Chennai Dar es Salaam Delhi Florence Hong Kong Istanbul
Karachi Kuala Lumpur Madrid Melbourne Mexico City Mumbai
Nairobi Paris São Paulo Singapore Taipei Tokyo Toronto Warsaw

and associated companies in Berlin Ibadan

Oxford is a registered trade mark of Oxford University Press
in the UK and certain other countries

Published in the United States
by Oxford University Press Inc., New York

British Library Cataloguing in Publication Data

Data available

Library of Congress Cataloging in Publication Data

ISBN 0–19–825041–X

10 9 8 7 6 5 4 3 2 1

Typeset by Michael Potter
Printed in Great Britain
on acid-free paper by
Biddles Ltd
Guildford and King's Lynn

REASON'S NEAREST KIN

Preface

If one is to choose a fifty-year period in the history of mathematical philosophy for concentrated study, one hardly needs to apologize for choosing the one that started with the *Grundlagen* in 1884 and finished with *Logische Syntax der Sprache* in 1934. It was a period of exhilarating progress in the subject. Frege, Dedekind, Russell, Wittgenstein, Hilbert, and Carnap produced accounts of arithmetic that were brilliantly innovative both technically and philosophically. All are described here. But all of these authors stood in Kant's shadow, and all of us today stand in Gödel's. So the work of these two authors is discussed as well.

The writing was greatly assisted by two periods of leave, at the Department of Logic and Metaphysics at the University of St. Andrews, and at the Department of Philosophy at Harvard University. I am grateful to Fitzwilliam College for funding the first of these periods, and to the British Academy for funding the second under its Research Leave Scheme. The concluding chapter is based with the Editor's permission on my article in the *Aristotelian Society Supplementary Volume* for 1999. In the course of writing the book I consulted unpublished material in the Modern Research Archives of King's College Cambridge, the Russell Archive at McMaster University, and the Moore Archives at Cambridge University Library. I am grateful for the assistance I received from librarians at all these institutions. The extract from Ramsey's diary quoted here is copyright of the Provost and Fellows of King's College, Cambridge; Russell's letters are quoted by courtesy of the William Ready Division of Archives and Research Collections, McMaster University Library, Hamilton, Ontario; I have been unable to trace the owner of copyright in Whitehead's letters to Russell.

For detailed and perceptive comments on earlier drafts I am very greatly indebted to Alex Oliver, Timothy Smiley, Naomi Goulder, Ian Proops, Charles Parsons, Warren Goldfarb, Steven Gross, Michael Detlefsen, Bob Hanna, and Peter Sullivan. I am sorry that the final version does not do justice to all the points they raised.

M.D.P.

Contents

Introduction

In popular parlance the word 'arithmetic' means the study of calculations involving numbers of all sorts, natural, integral, rational, real, and complex. Mathematicians, on the other hand, often use the word to mean only the study of the properties of the natural (i.e. counting) numbers 0, 1, 2, etc., and that is what we shall mean by it here. The philosophical problems arithmetic poses have been widely studied since the Ancients. Chief among these is that of reconciling its inevitability — the impression we have that it is true no matter what — with its applicability. Both of these features were recognized by Plato: on the one hand he took mathematics to possess not merely human but divine necessity, a property 'of which he who has no use nor any knowledge at all cannot be a god, or demi-god, or hero to mankind, able to take any serious thought or charge of them';[1] but on the other he ridiculed the notion of someone who knows only divine mathematics and does not understand its relationship with applications.[2] Admittedly some have disagreed with Plato's claim that the necessity of arithmetic is not human but divine, but whichever one says creates difficulties: if arithmetic is necessary only for us, then it is presumably applicable not to the world itself but only to our representation of it, in which case it is legitimate to ask in what sense we can really think about the world at all; if, on the other hand, the necessity of arithmetic transcends the accidental features of us humans, that might make its applicability to the world more explicable, but now our knowledge of arithmetic seems problematic. Two questions, then. Can we give an account of arithmetic that does not make it depend for its truth on the way the world is? And if so, what constrains the world to conform to arithmetic?

0.1 Arithmetic

It is common for stories to circulate among English speakers about the linguistic practices of distant peoples, such as that Eskimos have

---

[1] *Laws*, 818. [2] *Philebus*, 62a.

thirty words for snow, or that some primitive tribes have virtually no knowledge of arithmetic. The claim about the Eskimos and their great variety of snow words is, like many of these stories, an invention based on a misunderstanding: at root there are hardly more words for snow in Inuit than there are in English. But the claim about primitive arithmetic is true. Locke[3] mentioned a people he called Tououpinambos, who had no names for numbers above five; the same was true of the Guaranies of South America,[4] the Aranda tribe of Australia, and others. The arithmetic of these peoples is a rather extreme example of what is now called strict finitism, that is to say the doctrine that there are only finitely many natural numbers. We shall write $\mathbf{EA}(N)$ to mean arithmetic restricted to numbers less than N. Restricting arithmetic in this way of course has the awkward consequence that addition and multiplication are not everywhere defined: to restore them as everywhere defined operations we have to add a symbol '∞' (read 'many') to use as the default value in all such cases. The arithmetic of the Guaranies may thus be identified with part of $\mathbf{EA}(5)$. (It is probably not the whole of $\mathbf{EA}(5)$ since it seems unlikely that they had a grasp of multiplication.)

When we remove the restriction that there are only finitely many natural numbers, the core of arithmetic consists of equations and inequations involving addition and multiplication, such as '$7 + 5 = 12$' and '$7+5 \neq 13$'. We shall call this *quantifier-free elementary arithmetic* or $\mathbf{EA}_0$. It is indeed elementary not just in name. It is a complete, decidable first-order theory: there is a mechanical procedure for deciding whether any numerical equation is true or false. This decision procedure is taught to young children all over the globe and encoded in the circuits of every pocket calculator. Even if we extend the range of functions to include not only addition and multiplication but all those functions computable directly by means of an explicit rule (the so-called *primitive recursive* functions), the resulting system of *quantifier-free primitive recursive arithmetic* or $\mathbf{PRA}_0$ is still complete and decidable.

So far we have been discussing only the quantifier-free part of arithmetic. When we allow quantifiers — the universal quantifier '(x)' and the existential quantifier '$(\exists x)$' — into arithmetic, we stop it being mechanically decidable and increase its complexity beyond measure. The caesura here is strikingly sharp: without the universal quantifier arithmetic is a subject for children, lacking mathematical interest; with it we can formulate problems, such as Fermat's (recently solved) and Goldbach's (still unsolved), which are as hard as any in mathematics. Goldbach's problem is indeed a useful one to have in mind throughout. He conjectured in 1742 that every even number > 2 is the sum of two

---

[3] *Essay*, bk. II, ch. xvi, § 6.   [4] Dobrizhoffer, *An account of the Abipones*, 169–71.

primes. This conjecture may be stated in the form $(x)\,f(x) = 0$ where f is a certain primitive recursive function. Because of this Gödel called such propositions of *Goldbach type*, but nowadays they are more usually called Π_1 propositions. Each instance of a Π_1 proposition can be verified or refuted by a mechanical procedure since it is an equation of the form $f(n) = 0$ for some particular primitive recursive function f and number n, and the value of the function for this argument can be calculated explicitly. Goldbach's conjecture has in fact[5] been verified in this way for every even number less than 4×10^{11}. Weaker results than Goldbach's have been proved generally too: for instance, it is known that every even number is the sum of no more than six primes. The truth value of Goldbach's conjecture itself, however, is still not known 250 years after the problem of determining it was first posed. What the history of Goldbach's conjecture illustrates, then, is that general arithmetic (which is usually called number theory) is a rich source of hard and interesting problems.

It is sometimes said (chiefly, it is true, by mathematicians) that the philosophy of mathematics suffers through being practised mainly by philosophers ignorant of higher mathematics. The accusation is that this ignorance forces them to concentrate their attention unduly on the most elementary parts of the subject, quantifier-free arithmetic in particular. It is therefore worth noting that all but one of the philosophers of mathematics whose work we shall be examining in this book were familiar with a substantial amount of the university-level mathematics of their day. Hilbert, Ramsey, Dedekind, and Gödel, of course, were mathematicians of genius. Although Frege is remembered as a logician, his doctoral thesis was on geometry and his employment at the University of Jena throughout his working life was as a mathematician, not a philosopher. Russell was a Wrangler in the Mathematical Tripos at Cambridge before turning to philosophy. Even Kant, who has sometimes been stigmatized as mathematically ignorant, lectured on mathematics at Königsberg for eight years, and when he died his library contained a considerable number of mathematical books, including Newton's *Principia* and Euler's *Mechanica*.[6] Moreover, his pre-critical writings on astronomy and physical geography show him to have been a master of contemporary science. Only of Wittgenstein could it plausibly be argued that he may have been hindered in his discussion of mathematics by ignorance of technicalities. Indeed Ramsey wrote (in a letter of support for Wittgenstein's application for a research grant from Trinity College in 1929) that he had been 'afraid that lack of mathematical knowledge and facility would prove a serious

---

[5] Sinisalo, 'Checking the Goldbach Conjecture up to 4×10^{11}'. [6] Martin, *Arithmetic and Combinatorics*, pp. xx–xxvii.

handicap to [Wittgenstein's] working in' the philosophy of mathematics.[7] So to the extent that the authors I shall be discussing focussed
on simple arithmetic (and the subject matter of this book will lead to
the impression that they did so more than is really the case) it was not
— with the possible exception of Wittgenstein — through ignorance of
other parts of mathematics.

The problem we shall be discussing in the case of arithmetic is in any
event one that arises elsewhere in mathematics too. It is most clearly
expressed with the aid of a distinction between arithmetic proper and
its applications, or, as is sometimes said, between pure and applied
arithmetic. This distinction is common ground among the authors we
shall be discussing and goes back at least to Plato, who called the two
parts 'arithmetic of the academics' and 'arithmetic of the vulgar'.[8] It
is quite hard to define what the distinction amounts to generally, but
easy to draw it in practice: the proposition that $2 + 2 = 4$, for example,
belongs to arithmetic proper, whereas the proposition that two apples
and two oranges make four pieces of fruit is an application of it. The
problem that interests us is thus that of accounting for our knowledge
of arithmetic proper in a manner that explains the relationship between
it and its applications. We can begin to understand this problem better
if we start by considering a few obvious, but obviously flawed, solutions
to it.

0.2 The a priori

Many authors[9] treat the distinction between the necessary and the contingent as logical; and that between the a priori and the a posteriori as
epistemological. In doing so they appeal to a tradition going back to
Aristotle: in addition to the perspectival (epistemological) element in
the notion of truth that consists in *my* grounds for holding a proposition
to be true, this tradition allows room for a non-perspectival (logical)
element that consists in the ultimate ground of its truth. But it is not
intended that a proposition should count as a posteriori merely because
I come to know it empirically: that would make the result of an arithmetical sum a posteriori for me if I worked it out on a calculator or was
told it by a friend. So we might be tempted to say that a proposition is
a priori if it can be known independent of experience. One unfortunate
consequence of defining the notion of the a priori in this way is that

---

[7]In Monk, 270–1. [8]*Philebus*, 56d. [9]e.g. Kripke, *Naming and Necessity*, 34–9.

it renders it parasitic on that of necessity, since we need to say what notion of possibility we mean when we talk of what *can* be known.

This does not, of course, show the epistemological notion of the a priori to be nonsensical. What matters for present purposes is for us to be clear that for some at least of the authors we shall be discussing in this book the distinction between the a priori and the a posteriori is *not* an epistemological one. Russell, for example, thought for a time that logical knowledge is inductive, but continued even then to assert that it is a priori. He could do so without inconsistency only if at that time he explicitly subscribed to a distinction between logical and epistemological grounds for truth, and placed the notion of the a priori on the logical, not the epistemological, side of this divide. Something similar is to be found with Frege, who took the term to refer not to the ground of *our* knowledge of a proposition, but to 'the ultimate ground upon which rests the justification for holding it to be true'.[10]

Reflecting this tradition, then, let us say for the sake of definiteness that a proposition is *a posteriori* if its truth or falsity depends on experience, *a priori* otherwise. When we call a proposition a priori that is not to say that we could know it without having had *any* experience, though: without experience it is hard to conceive that thought would be possible at all. Kant stressed this point at the very beginning of the *Critique*:

There can be no doubt that all our knowledge begins with experience. For how should our faculty of knowledge be awakened into action did not objects affecting our senses ... arouse the activity of our understanding to ... work up the raw material of the sensible impressions into that knowledge of objects which is entitled experience? ... But though all our knowledge begins with experience, it does not follow that it all arises out of experience.[11]

So to say that arithmetic (or mathematics more generally) is a priori is not to claim that a being without any experience at all could be a mathematician: without experience we would, as Frege said, 'be as stupid as stones'.[12] Nor is it to address the possibility that whether mathematics is applicable to the world might depend on how the world is.

Kant took it to be part of what is meant by pure mathematics that it is a priori. He thought that the truths of mathematics cannot be a posteriori

because they carry with them necessity, which cannot be derived from experience. This is true at any rate if we limit the claim to *pure* mathematics, the very concept of which implies that it does not contain empirical, but only a priori knowledge.[13]

[10] *Gl.*, § 3. [11] *KrV*, B1. [12] *Gl.*, § 105 n. [13] *KrV*, B14–5.

Kant's thought here is presumably that we do not take experience to bear on the truth and falsity of the judgements of pure mathematics, in contrast with empirical disciplines such as physics or geography. To see that this is so it is not quite enough, however, merely to note that the method of mathematics is proof whereas the method of physics and geography is observation. What matters is not only how we justify the inferences we draw in mathematical proofs but how we justify the *premisses*; and if these are a posteriori, the conclusions may be so too. But when we consider how the premisses of arguments in pure mathematics are assessed in practice, it is immediately evident that empirical observation is never considered relevant. Indeed, it is quite hard to see how one might construct an experiment that could provide evidence either for *or* against the principle of mathematical induction, for example.

But if anyone were to ask *why* we take pure mathematics to be a priori in this fashion, there is little we could say except that it is part of our understanding of its rôle that it should not be revisable in the light of experience. Anyone who denies this merely 'confuses the applications that can be made of an arithmetical proposition, which often are physical and do presuppose observed facts, with the pure mathematical proposition itself.'[14] Quineans, of course, will take this to indicate an unavoidable relativism to convention in the very notion of the a priori, but it is very far from clear that this need be granted, and it is in any case not a line that will be pursued in this book.

We shall instead simply take it as evident that pure mathematics — pure arithmetic in particular — is a priori. Whether applied mathematics is similarly a priori is more problematic: many parts of it plainly are not, but a case can be made for thinking that applied arithmetic is: we can imagine worlds with a different geometry, but when we try to imagine a world in which two things added to two things do not make four things, 'complete confusion ensues'.[15] It is this thought that gives the problem of reconciling pure with applied mathematics its special urgency in the case of arithmetic.

0.3 Empiricism

The notion of what a proposition is about is a hard one to make precise, and even when we have done so it may not be clear what a particular proposition is about: philosophers are fond of analysing problematic

---

[14]Frege, *Gl.*, § 9.   [15]Ibid., § 14.

propositions so as to show that their content is not what it seems to be. For the moment, though, an informal understanding of the notion will do well enough.

That arithmetic is directly about the physical world is the claim of empiricism, advanced most famously by Mill, who held that the number three is to be identified with all triples of physical things and that $2 + 2 = 4$ is nothing beyond the generalization that any two things added to any other two things make four things. Now Mill himself took this last to be an *empirical* generalization, so that pure arithmetic was a posteriori, a view we have already dismissed, but we cannot refute the notion that *numbers* are empirical simply by invoking this previous conclusion since, as we have already remarked, it is at least arguable that applied arithmetic is a priori: if so, pure arithmetic would also be a priori even if its content were empirical. An a posteriori proposition must plainly have some empirical content — for how could its truth or falsity depend on experience if it said nothing about experience? — but the converse is false, at least on the informal understanding of content that is currently in play, since 'Either it's raining or it isn't' is a priori but apparently has empirical content. This point was made vividly by Frege when he asked

how arithmetic could exist, if we could distinguish nothing whatever by means of our senses, or only three things at most. Now for our knowledge, certainly, of arithmetical propositions and of their applications, such a state of affairs would be somewhat awkward — but would it affect the truth of those propositions? If we call a proposition empirical on the ground that we must have made observations in order to have become conscious of its content, then we are not using the word 'empirical' in the sense in which it is opposed to 'a priori'. We are making a psychological statement, which concerns solely the content of the proposition; the question of its truth is not touched. In this sense, all Münchhausen's tales are empirical too; for certainly all sorts of observations must have been made before they could be invented.[16]

Is it tenable, then, to suppose that numbers are physical? One argument that has been deployed against this view is that if it were correct we could not apply them to what is not physical. According to Husserl the opinion that numbers are physical

is so manifestly false that one can only wonder how a thinker of Mill's rank could be satisfied with it. Two apples might undoubtedly be distinguishable from three apples, but not two judgements from three, two impossibilities from three, etc. Therefore numerical distinctness as such cannot be physical, visible and touchable. The mere mention of physical acts or events, which one can count just as well as physical contents, demolishes Mill's theory.[17]

[16]Ibid., §8. [17]*Philosophie der Arithmetik*, 17.

Many have found this argument convincing. Frege, for example, re-marked that for a property abstracted from physical things to be appli-cable 'to events, to ideas and to concepts ... would be just like speaking of fusible events, or blue ideas, or salty concepts or tough judgements.'[18] This is not, however, a refutation that will convince a thoroughgoing empiricist. The argument is that we could have no reason to apply Mill's empirically derived notion of number to anything non-empirical, and yet that is just what we seem to do: 'number applies itself to men, angels, actions, thoughts — everything that either doth exist or can be imagined.'[19] But the argument depends on the premiss that there is something non-empirical that 'doth exist or can be imagined'. An empiricist can simply deny this premiss — be empiricist, that is to say, about absolutely everything.

A more worrying objection to empiricism is that it cannot justify more than a fragment of arithmetic as it is generally understood and practised. Since we are finite beings, we inevitably experience only finitely many objects. So an arithmetic whose content is based on ex-perience cannot, the objection runs, involve more than finitely many numbers. But what is wrong with that? It is difficult, admittedly, for anyone who has ever counted further than five to believe that the Guara-nies of South America, whose arithmetic was a fragment of $\mathbf{EA}(5)$, had nothing to learn where arithmetic is concerned, but the empiricist po-sition is less extreme: although what the empiricist can justify is still only of the form $\mathbf{EA}(N)$, the value of N is somewhat larger, namely the limit of the size of what we are capable of experiencing. It would, of course, be impossible to specify N precisely, but it might, for instance, be in the region of 10^{80}, which is estimated to be the number of baryons in the observable universe. Since we cannot experience anything bigger than N, we have no use for numbers that large. We therefore cannot argue for anything more than $\mathbf{EA}(N)$ on empirical grounds alone. It is not open to us to avoid this conclusion by arguing that the number of objects in the universe *might* have been greater than N because what might have been must, if we are to respect the empiricist's principles, be explicable in terms of what is. Moreover, if the empirical world is indeed finite, the parts of arithmetic that depend on the infinity of the number sequence are according to the empiricist simply false.

We shall nevertheless pursue empiricism no further here. The reason is that the challenge to philosophers of arithmetic is to explain how what are standardly taken to be arithmetical truths can possess a ne-cessity which empirical generalizations do not share, but nevertheless

---

[18] *Gl.*, § 24.   [19] Locke, *Essay*, bk. II, ch. xvi, § 1.

be applicable in reasoning about the world, and it is manifest that empiricism fails to meet this challenge. This remark will not convince the diehard empiricist, of course, who will simply protest that the original challenge was misconceived, but for the purposes of this book I shall take it that the very deviance of the arithmetic grounded by empiricism is enough to rule it out of consideration. I shall take it, that is to say, that our task is to account, if possible, for arithmetic as standardly practised by us. Only if all our attempts fail should we contemplate an account which requires a revision of that practice.

0.4 Psychologism

So numbers, we say, cannot be physical. Could they be something mental — ideas? We saw in the last section that if numbers were physical it would not straightforwardly follow that arithmetical truths are physical laws; notice now that the claim that numbers are mental is similarly distinct from the claim that arithmetical truths are psychological laws. But if our aim is to justify arithmetic as standardly practised, the view that numbers are mental must in any case be rejected.

If number were an idea, then arithmetic would be psychology. But arithmetic is no more psychology than, say, astronomy is. ... If the number two were an idea, then it would have straight away to be private to me only. Another man's idea is, *ex vi termini*, another idea. We should then have it might be many millions of twos on our hands. ... Yet, in spite of all this, it would still be doubtful whether there existed infinitely many numbers, as we ordinarily suppose. 10^{10}, perhaps, might be only an empty symbol, and there might exist no idea at all, in any being whatever, to answer to the name.[20]

Frege here presents two objections to psychologism about numbers. First, it makes arithmetic private. When I say that $2 + 2 = 4$, the numbers I am referring to are as personal to me as my pains. So when you say that $2 + 2 = 4$, you mean something different by it, since the numbers you are referring to are private to you in turn. Although problematic, this consequence of psychologism about numbers is not quite as absurd as Frege apparently took it to be. If each of us says 'I am in pain', we mean different things by our utterances, but there is an obvious sense in which what your utterance means to you is the same as what mine means to me. Moreover, we can communicate about our respective pains well enough. So it seems wrong to say that psychologism makes arithmetic incommunicable. It does, admittedly, index every arithmetical proposition to a thinker and, since memories fade, to a

[20] *Gl.*, § 27.

time as well, but although this is undoubtedly 'weird and wonderful' as Frege says,[21] it is not quite clear that it is absurd.

Frege's second objection is the converse of the first. Just as some ubiquitous numbers have too many instances, others have none. Since only finitely many numbers ever have or ever will be thought of, psychologism leads to a version of strict finitism. It is not, however, quite the version we considered earlier in connection with empiricism. In that version if a number exists all lesser numbers exist, whereas in this version whether a number exists will depend much more on the length of our expression for it than on its size: on the psychologistic account the number $10^{10^{10}}$ does indeed exist since I am thinking of it now, but not all the numbers less than it exist since it is plainly impossible that each of them should have been thought of by someone. Nevertheless it remains the case that the psychologistic account of numbers provides no support for arithmetic as standardly conceived.[22] For that reason we shall not consider it any further here since, as I have said, our aim is to see whether we can justify the whole of arithmetic and not just some bastardized fragment.

0.5 Pure formalism

The fact that quantifier-free elementary arithmetic reduces to the mechanical application of a finite number of rules allows us to decouple it from its meaning: there is an obvious sense in which doing this sort of simple arithmetic does not require *thought* at all. It is natural, therefore, to wonder whether we can obtain an account of arithmetic that focuses entirely on the signs and abandons any attempt to argue that arithmetical propositions express thoughts about a subject matter distinct from the signs occurring in them. I shall call this view *formalism*.

The most extreme version — what I shall call *pure formalism* — abandons the idea that arithmetical sentences express thoughts at all. On this view, indeed, it is inappropriate to describe the strings of signs that occur in arithmetic *as* sentences: they are better conceived as positions in a game. The most celebrated proponent of this view (although only because he was pilloried for it by Frege) was Thomae:

For the formalist, arithmetic is a game with signs, which are called empty. That means they have no other content (in the calculating game) than they are assigned by their behaviour with respect to certain rules of combination (rules of the game). The chess player makes similar use of his pieces; he

---

[21]Ibid., § 27.   [22]Cf. Nelson, *Predicative Arithmetic.*

assigns them certain properties determining their behaviour in the game, and the pieces are only the external signs of this behaviour.[23]

Pure formalism is not, of course, forced on us by the simple act of formalizing a piece of mathematics, but it is in a sense dependent on it, since if the rules of the language game have not been made precise, it is hard to see how we could hold that the game is all there is to language. (The example of games with vague rules is not appropriate here: if we are to play such a game, we must have a means of deciding the vague cases, and that means will generally involve us in recognizing that the game has some point; if, on the other hand, we decide the vague cases in a wholly random way, e.g. by tossing a coin, then that is in fact a rule, a non-deterministic rule admittedly, but a rule nonetheless and as precise as any other.)

Whatever its apparent plausibility, however, pure formalism can be dismissed straight away. The reason is that to hold pure formalism strictly — to think, in other words, that the string '$7 + 5 = 12$' is just a position in a game — one would have to accept that logic as *ordinarily* understood has no place whatever in the practice of arithmetic. There might well be among the rules of the game formulations bearing a verbal similarity with familiar rules of logic, such as *modus ponens* or the rule of existential generalization, but the formalist account would leave this similarity wholly unexplained: the rules of the game cannot be properly called logical since they are simply rules for manipulating symbols and have no connection with sentences expressing *thoughts*; what we do when we calculate therefore cannot on this account be described as *reasoning* at all.

The mistake of pure formalism, then, is to treat equations, which ought to be bearers of meaning, as mere positions in a game. If equations are meaningless, they are incapable of being applied. Indeed Thomae himself admitted that

there is an important difference between arithmetic and chess. The rules of chess are arbitrary; the system of rules for arithmetic is such that by means of simple axioms the numbers can be referred to perceptual manifolds and can thus make important contribution to our knowledge of nature.[24]

But by making this concession Thomae nullified the force of his claim that arithmetic may be thought of as a game: a map showing the disposition of troops during a war no doubt bears a superficial similarity to a war-game, but to explain the map *as* a game would be wholly to ignore its point. If, as Thomae seems now to grant, it is essential to

---

[23] *Elementare Theorie der analytischen Functionen*, 3.   [24] Ibid.

arithmetic that its rules are *not* arbitrary, his point collapses into no
more than the observation we began with, that arithmetical identities
may be checked by applying a series of mechanical rules.

An alternative which might at first seem to hold out a better hope of
explaining arithmetic's applicability is to treat *number terms* as positions and to formulate the game as a series of substitution rules allowing
number terms to be substituted for one another. The statement that
$7 + 5 = 12$ will therefore be a report that there is a game playable
according to the rules in which the first position is '$7 + 5$' and the
last position is '12'. Equations thus interpreted are genuine propositions about which we can reason logically. Even on this interpretation,
though, we are severely restricted in the reasoning we are permitted on
purely logical grounds. It might seem, for instance, that we can deduce
from the equations '$7 + 5 = 12$' and '$12 = 4 \times 3$' that the equation
'$7 + 5 = 4 \times 3$' holds, since if there is a game taking us from '$7+5$' to
'12' and another taking us from '12' to '4×3' there must be one taking
us from '$7 + 5$' to '4×3'. But this conclusion is not in fact licensed by
logic alone: it depends on a feature of the rules of arithmetic, namely
that the concatenation of two arithmetical games is also an arithmetical
game. There are plainly many other sorts of game which do not share
this feature: chess is an obvious example.

We shall still have to explain why it should matter in arithmetic
that games with certain starting and finishing positions are possible
when it does not matter in chess (where what counts is winning and
losing). We are therefore at this point no nearer to an explanation of
the applicability of arithmetic. Notice too that we are now not playing
the game but reasoning about what games are possible. The question
with which we began, as to how arithmetical knowledge is possible,
has been transformed into another, as to how metatheoretic knowledge
about games is possible, which seems just as hard to answer. We have
in fact had to abandon formalism in order to invest our arithmetical
equations with meaning. Arithmetic as we are now interpreting it is not
itself a game but the metatheory of a certain sort of game: it therefore
has a subject matter quite distinct from the signs used to express it,
just as the metatheory of chess has a subject matter distinct from the
wooden chess pieces used to play it.

0.6 Trivial formalism

If pure formalism does not work, a strategy with more superficial appeal
is to claim that arithmetic is true by definition. This was held by

Leibniz, who demonstrated that $2 + 2 = 4$ as follows:

That *two and two are four* is not quite an immediate truth. Assume that *four* signifies three and one. Then we can demonstrate it, and here is how.
    Definitions.   *Two* is one and one.
                 Three is two and one.
                 Four is three and one.
    Axiom. If equals be substituted for equals, the equality remains.
    Demonstration.
                    2 and 2 is 2 and 1 and 1 (def. 1)
                    2 and 1 and 1 is 3 and 1 (def. 2)
                    3 and 1 is 4 (def. 3)
                    Therefore (by the Axiom)
                    2 and 2 is 4.
                    Which is what was to be demonstrated.[25]

Before we discuss Leibniz's 'demonstration' let us first rewrite it in symbolic notation. His definitions are:

$$2 = 1 + 1 \qquad (1)$$
$$3 = 2 + 1 \qquad (2)$$
$$4 = 3 + 1 \qquad (3)$$

The demonstration then runs:

$$2 + 2 = 2 + 1 + 1 \quad \text{by definition 1}$$
$$= 3 + 1 \qquad\qquad \text{by definition 2}$$
$$= 4 \qquad\qquad\quad \text{by definition 3.}$$

That $2 + 2 = 4$ is not quite, Leibniz says, 'an immediate truth': it is not in Locke's sense trifling, i.e. a *direct* consequence of a definition, as it is that $4 = 3 + 1$, for example. It does, however, follow from the definitions by a series of steps appealing only, Leibniz thought, to a general logical law (Leibniz's 'axiom'). There can be little doubting this general law. So Leibniz's 'demonstration' would indeed, if it were correct, show that $2 + 2 = 4$.

But it is not. The fallacy lies in the fact that '$2 + 1 + 1$' is ambiguous between '$(2 + 1) + 1$' and '$2 + (1 + 1)$'. When brackets are inserted to disambiguate the expression, we see that there is a suppressed premiss which is an instance of the general law

$$x + (y + 1) = (x + y) + 1.$$

[25] *New Essays*, bk. IV, ch. vii, § 10.

The corrected proof runs as follows:

$$
\begin{aligned}
2 + 2 &= 2 + (1 + 1) && \text{by definition 1} \\
&= (2 + 1) + 1 && \text{by the general law} \\
&= 3 + 1 && \text{by definition 2} \\
&= 4 && \text{by definition 3.}
\end{aligned}
$$

By pointing out the gap in Leibniz's 'proof' we do not thereby show that arithmetic could not be true by definition. To do that we should have to demonstrate quite generally that no such proof is possible. The hope that arithmetic would turn out to be true by definition therefore did not die when Leibniz's error was recognized.

The programme of deriving arithmetical truths logically from explicit definitions is a purely technical one, and to that extent the view stands or falls on whether the programme can be successfully completed. But even if it can, that will not on its own explain the applicability of arithmetic. To see why not, we need to reflect on the reason for regarding the view as a species of formalism at all.

The point is that any non-circular series of definitions must leave some terms undefined. In the particular proposal of Leibniz that we have just considered it is '1' that is undefined: for there to be any prospect of applying the proposition outside arithmetic '1' would in turn have to be defined in terms that explained its non-arithmetical use. To define 'bachelor' as meaning unmarried man is useful because 'unmarried' and 'man' already have meanings. If I define 'shug' to mean thwock and 'rannock' to mean bartling, on the other hand, it may perhaps follow that every rannock shug is a bartling thwock, but that is not a fact that could possibly be of any use to me until some of the words have been defined in terms I can understand. So the idea that arithmetic is true by definition is not on its own any advance on pure formalism.

Not on its own. But still one might be tempted to resist classifying it as a species of formalism, for although the view is consistent with formalism, it is also consistent with other accounts, such as the empiricist and psychologistic ones we considered earlier. Not to classify it as formalist would nevertheless be a mistake, because although it allows the possibility that the names occurring in arithmetical sentences may have non-linguistic meanings it nevertheless insists that the thoughts the sentences express are not about those meanings but about the linguistic conventions which the explicit definitions commit us to. Precisely because the non-linguistic meanings we assign to the numerals do not figure in our account of arithmetical truths, those truths cannot tell us anything informative about those non-linguistic entities.

0.7 Reflexive formalism

We seem driven, then, to conclude that if the applicability of arithmetical sentences is to be explicable, not only must they express thoughts but those thoughts must be about the objects named in them: trivial formalism failed because according to it arithmetical thoughts are linguistic even if numbers are not.

But what if numbers are themselves linguistic? Can we simply treat the numerals as names of themselves? If we do this, arithmetical sentences will express genuine thoughts, but those thoughts will be about nothing other than the signs themselves. The view is therefore still, according to the definition we gave earlier, a version of formalism. Let us call it *reflexive formalism.*

When we claim that a number is just the same as the sign used to express it, we cannot, of course, mean to identify it with the physical token made up of chalk or ink, since if we did there would be too many numbers: each utterance of the numeral '2' would count as a different number. And the opposite problem — that of ensuring that there are not too few numbers — shows that we must be prepared to count signs as numerals even if no tokens of them have been or ever could be written down. At once this shows that reflexive formalism is no great help if what motivates us is the worry about how to refer to abstract objects, since numerals now seem just as abstract and just as epistemologically problematic as numbers traditionally understood.

We must not identify a number with just any name for it, of course, since '7 + 5' is not the same *name* as '12'. What we must do is to privilege one way of representing numbers and treat only *these* notations as names of themselves. If we treat the familiar base 10 notation as canonical, for example, the number twelve will be identical with the numeral '12', and all the other notations, such as '7 + 5' and '3 × 4', will name not themselves but this numeral.

Why, then, does 7 + 5 = 12? We are still left with the task of laying down rules for addition of numerals that have this equation as a consequence. This is not hard: we simply codify the mechanical instructions for addition that are taught to school children. But now we are back at just the difficulty we had with pure formalism, since our account would work *whatever* mechanical rules we chose. We might hope, of course, that the difficulty is only temporary and demonstrates not that our account is wrong but that it is incomplete: we need to add to it an explanation of the use of numbers in counting, and we shall then — the hope is — be in a position to justify our definition of addition. But it is by no means clear that this is so. By saying that the numerals are just signs with no other meaning we seem to have barred the route back from any subsequent application to properties of the signs themselves.

We might, moreover, be gripped by an even more basic concern. Can we *ever* use an object as a name of itself? In *Gulliver's Travels* the people of Lagado are encouraged to adopt just this practice despite its evident inconvenience:

If a Man's Business be very great, and of various Kinds, he must be obliged in Proportion to carry a greater Bundle of Things upon his Back, unless he can afford one or two strong Servants to attend him. I have often beheld two of those Sages almost sinking under the Weight of their Packs, like Pedlars among us; who, when they met in the Streets, would lay down their Loads, open their Sacks, and hold Conversation for an Hour together; then put up their Implements, help each other to resume their Burthens, and take their Leave. But, for short Conversations, a Man may carry Implements in his Pockets and under his Arms, enough to supply him.[26]

Onomatopoeia is perhaps a less outlandish example of items referring to themselves, but what it shares with the practice of the Lagadoians is that it involves importing the non-linguistic into the linguistic, whereas the reflexive formalist has to do the reverse: in onomatopoeia we imitate sounds of which we have a conception distinct from the rôle we give them when we adopt them as names, and can therefore make statements that are of independent interest; but in reflexive formalism the numbers are *given* to us linguistically, and therefore await an explanation of their applicability in counting.

This argument does not in itself show that numerals cannot name themselves. But a further difficulty for the view arises from the fact that alternative numbering systems are possible. I have mentioned so far the familiar notation to the base 10, but any other base would do, and the representation of numerals as rows of strokes is especially convenient because it makes the definition of addition coincide with that of concatenation. If numbers *are* numerals, then base 10 numbers are different from stroke numbers.

Even if we argued that stroke numbers had primacy because addition is easier to explain for them, we could not argue for the primacy of '|||' over (say) '@@@' as a notation for three, so we would be forced to say that '|' is the same sign as '@'. This is not merely contrary to

[26]Bk. III, ch. vi.

ordinary usage: it seems now that *anything* capable of being repeated and concatenated could be used as the 'stroke'. But now what force is left in the claim that it is a sign? And if the number *one* is really any sign whatever, how do we know how to use it? More importantly, it becomes hard to explain how we could ever *not* use it: indeed, it seems that if any sign can be taken to be a number, *all* language is now part of arithmetic.

0.8 Arithmetic and reason

From this introductory survey we can already draw a number of tentative conclusions. The sentences of arithmetic cannot be regarded merely as moves in a game because that would not explain their applicability. If they are regarded instead as genuine propositions, we must be capable of knowing at least some of them, and that knowledge does not depend ultimately on experience. But what then are these propositions about? We have dismissed the notion that they are either directly about the physical world or about mental entities since in either case we could not thereby justify arithmetic except as practised by a few extinct tribes. What else is left? It seems hard to maintain that arithmetic is about nothing at all, since it is difficult to prevent this view from collapsing into the trivial formalism which we have already rejected. But the only alternative seems to be that it is about a realm of entities that are neither physical and causally efficacious nor mental and private — that are, in short, abstract. It then begins to seem mysterious how we could know anything at all about such a realm. Moreover, we are no closer to accounting for the applicability of arithmetic, for it is not immediately clear why the properties of abstract objects should be relevant to counting physical or mental ones.

Each of us has experiences, both of what we take to be an external world and of our own inner mental life. These experiences do not occur in us merely as an unstructured stream: we have thoughts involving them, and those thoughts can by the act of thinking become the objects of further experiences. Experience, though, is essentially private: my experience is intrinsically mine and I cannot share it with you, however hard I try. But although we have no experiences in common, our shared humanity somehow permits us to communicate them to each other: I do not thereby have your experiences, but I do come to know something about them. This is achieved through the medium of language, not just written language but others too — speech, gesture, music, flags.

One has only to reflect on it to realize that this link between experience, language, thought, and the world, which is at the very centre of what it is to be human, is truly remarkable. It is indeed, as Schlick remarked,

astonishing that by hearing certain sounds issuing from the mouth of a person, or by looking at a few black marks on a piece of paper I can become aware of the fact that a volcano on a distant island has had an eruption ... The marks on the piece of paper and the eruption of the volcano are two entirely distinct and different facts, there is apparently no similarity between them, and yet knowledge of the one conveys to me knowledge of the other.[27]

The challenge of accounting for the applicability of arithmetic to the world evidently participates in this wider puzzle of explaining the link between experience, language, thought and the world. It is therefore natural to try to base an answer to the question what grounds the truths of arithmetic on one of these four elements. In this book we shall consider answers of all these types.

The first answer is that arithmetic is based not on experience itself — for that would make it empirical — but on a feature of the way we humans experience the world. What this feature is supposed to be is different for different philosophers. Kant took it to be the spatio-temporal structure of experience; Hilbert took it more narrowly to be the structure of finite arrangements of objects. But for both of them we are justified in applying arithmetic to the world just because we have based it on a feature of the way the world inevitably appears to us.

The second answer is that 'language itself ... supplies the necessary intuition'.[28] We use language to describe the world and arithmetic is merely part of that structure. This answer is due to Wittgenstein, who treated arithmetic as an inevitable by-product of our use of language to describe the world, but Carnap also gave an account that made arithmetic depend on language as a whole.

The third answer, due to Frege, is that what grounds arithmetic is a feature not of the way we experience the world but of the way we think. We use language to communicate our thoughts to others, so thoughts cannot be private mental entities but must be communally available. The subject matter of arithmetic is, or is at any rate derived from, these communally available thoughts themselves. Arithmetic is thus applicable to everything thinkable because its structure is already that of thought. And if logic is the study of the laws of thought, this view will make arithmetic part of logic.

---

[27] *Philosophical Papers*, II, 286. [28] *TLP*, 6.233.

The fourth answer is due to Russell. He too thought that arithmetic is reducible to logic, but he did not take its subject matter to be a communally available realm of thoughts: he conceived of the world as having a logical aspect which is the subject matter of logic, just as it has a physical aspect which is the subject matter of physics. He took the analogy between the world's logical and physical aspects far enough to assimilate the epistemology of the former to that of the latter: in logic we try to devise theories that account for the data just as we do in physics.

What proponents of all four solutions to the problem of arithmetical content have to do is to explain how arithmetical propositions can depend on such a source for their truth without their truth thereby being rendered contingent on inessential features of that source. Frege, in a famous quotation from which the title of this book is taken, remarked that

[i]n arithmetic we are not concerned with objects which we come to know as something alien from without through the medium of the senses, but with objects given directly to our reason and, as its nearest kin, utterly transparent to it.[29]

The transparency to reason which Frege mentions is a striking feature familiar to anyone who has grasped arithmetic at all, and it is what gives the philosophy of arithmetic its special character. All the accounts we shall be considering in this book go some way towards explaining it. I do not think any of them is wholly right, nor that any is wholly wrong, but the best way to see what is right about them is surely to understand what is wrong.

[29] *Gl.*, § 105.

1

Kant

Our problem, I have said, is to reconcile the necessity of arithmetic with its applicability. This is an instance of the more general problem of explaining the applicability of the propositions of pure reason to experience. For Kant it becomes urgent only in relation to propositions which, although in some sense the products of pure reason, nevertheless have a subject matter: the danger is that we conceive of this subject matter as consisting of objects existing in a realm wholly isolated from the world of experience, and it is then apt to seem puzzling how features of this abstract realm could possibly be relevant to reasoning about the empirical one. The key to the way out of this difficulty that Kant recommended is for us to contrive that

those *concepts* and *principles* which we adopt a priori be used for viewing objects from two different points of view — on the one hand, in connection with experience, as objects of the senses and of the understanding, and on the other hand, for the isolated reason that strives to transcend all limits of experience, as objects which are thought merely.[1]

Kant's explanation of this twofold use of a priori concepts appeals to a non-logical faculty called sensibility which supplies us with intuitions. His view is therefore starkly opposed to the varieties of logicism that much of this book will be concerned with since logic is commonly supposed to need no intuitions for its grasp. Kant's influence on all the other authors I shall be discussing is nevertheless unquestionable: Frege, for instance, described him as 'a genius to whom we must all look up with grateful awe'; and Gödel said of a list of philosophers including Wittgenstein that 'only Kant was imp[ortant]' to him. These instances do not merely demonstrate how influential Kant's works were in the late nineteenth century among educated people generally (especially in German-speaking countries), but are due also to the fact that although Kant was not the first philosopher to address our central problem of reconciling the necessity of mathematics with its applicability, he was the first to attempt a sophisticated solution of it.

---

[1] *KrV*, B xviii–xix.

1.1 Intuitions and concepts

All our knowledge, Kant said,[2] begins with experience. But knowledge is not atomic: each piece of knowledge is not an indivisible whole unrelated to any other. In forming our judgements we make use of components which we combine in various ways. In order that the knowledge we have should be about the objects we experience, some of these components must be capable of relating to those objects. Kant's conception of the structure of our thinking is based on a fundamental distinction between those components that relate to objects indirectly and those that do so directly. He called the former *concepts*, and his word for the latter is *Anschauung*: this is standardly translated as intuition, presumably because Kant occasionally used the Latin word 'intuitus' with the same meaning, but the German word's primary meaning is *view*. In any event what Kant's use of *Anschauung* does not have is any strong connection with the usual meaning of the English word 'intuition'. It should therefore be treated here as a technical term: an intuition is a representation that 'relates immediately to the object and is single'; a concept, on the other hand, 'refers to it mediately by means of a feature which several things may have in common'.[3]

An immediate representation (or intuition) must be of exactly one object: its very immediacy prevents it from referring to several objects, or to none. A mediate representation (or concept), on the other hand, may have many objects, one object, or none. Which of these is the case does not — not invariably, at any rate — depend on the concept itself: it is not part of the concept 'author of *Principia Mathematica*', for instance, that it relates to exactly two objects. The way Kant expressed the point was to say that it is the *use* of a concept that is singular or general, not the concept itself.[4]

According to Kant the immediacy of intuitions, which guarantees them their objects, makes them incapable of expressing thoughts. Intuitions provide us with experience of the world, but they do not in themselves give us the resources to think anything about the world. For that we need to be able to connect the intuition with a concept. Now it is hard to find in Kant's writings any arguments for this doctrine. Why, then, did he hold it? Perhaps it is tolerably clear that one intuition on its own cannot constitute a thought, but it is not obvious that several in combination could not. To a modern eye it would be natural to transform Kant's doctrine into one about language. We might suppose that an intuition is what I grasp when I understand a

[2]Ibid., B1. [3]Ibid., A320 = B377. [4]*Logic*, §1, n. 2.

logically proper name, and that a concept corresponds similarly to a predicate. Kant's claim would then amount to the observation that a string of names cannot be a sentence. This is true about English or German, but it is not clear that it must be true about any human language whatever: as we shall see later, Wittgenstein took the languages he considered in the *Tractatus* to constitute a sort of exception to it. Kant did not in any case express the matter in these linguistic terms, but the fact that strings of names are not sentences, even if it is a parochial fact about the languages he was familiar with, may well have been influential in leading him to his doctrine.

Let us for the moment merely accept that for Kant the combination of intuitions alone cannot produce thoughts. He did not hold the same view about concepts: they can be combined to produce thoughts. Nevertheless, the point of thinking is to express judgements about the world, and concepts cannot do this, however they are combined, unless it is possible to relate them to intuitions. So what is expressed by a mere play of concepts will not yield genuine knowledge on its own. If a concept is to have any use, we must possess a means of judging whether or not it applies to any object, and Kant treated this rule for judging as a further element, called a *schema*, over and above the concept itself.

We demand in every concept, first, the logical form of a concept (of thought) in general, and secondly, the possibility of giving it an object to which it may be applied. In the absence of such object, it has no meaning and is completely lacking in content, though it may still contain the logical function which is required for making a concept out of any data that may be presented. Now the object cannot be given to a concept otherwise than in intuition; for though a pure intuition can indeed precede the object a priori, even this intuition can acquire its object, and therefore objective validity, only through the empirical intuition of which it is the mere form. Therefore all concepts, and with them all principles, even such as are possible a priori, relate to empirical intuitions, that is, to the data for a possible experience. Apart from this relation they have no objective validity, and in respect of their representations are a mere play of imagination or of understanding. Take, for instance, the concepts of mathematics, considering them first of all in their pure intuitions. Space has three dimensions; between two points there can be only one straight line, etc. Although all these principles, and the representation of the object with which this science occupies itself, are generated in the mind completely a priori, they would mean nothing, were we not always able to present their meaning in appearances, that is, in empirical objects. We therefore demand that a bare concept be made sensible, that is, that an object corresponding to it be presented in intuition. Otherwise the concept would, as we say, be without sense, that is, without meaning.[5]

[5] *KrV*, A239 = B298.

The statements of pure mathematics thus get their meaning from the fact that they are applicable. But this is not for Kant a special feature of pure mathematics: *any* concept must, if it is to be meaningful, be capable of being applied, i.e. it must be capable of having — or not having — 'an object corresponding to it ... presented in intuition'.

So concepts not grounded in intuition are useless because we do not know how to apply them, whereas 'through mere intuition nothing at all is thought':[6] only in combination do intuitions and concepts deliver genuine knowledge.

Intuition and concepts constitute ... the elements of all our knowledge, so that neither concepts without an intuition in some way corresponding to them, nor intuition without concepts, can yield knowledge. ... Thoughts without content are empty, intuitions without concepts are blind.'[7]

As we shall see, Kant conceived of intuitions and concepts as arising through distinct faculties of the human mind, intuitions in the sensibility, concepts in the understanding. It was therefore central to his project of explaining how genuine knowledge is possible to give an account of the relationship between these faculties. In a passage strikingly prefiguring Wittgenstein's rule-following argument Kant describes concepts as being rules for judging which are useless unless we have criteria for telling when to apply them; we cannot on pain of circularity conceive of these criteria as being themselves rules of the same kind.

[S]ince general logic abstracts from all content of knowledge, the sole task that remains to it is to give an analytical exposition of the form of knowledge [as expressed] in concepts, in judgments, and in inferences, and so to obtain formal rules for all employment of understanding. If it sought to give general instructions how we are to subsume under these rules, that is, to distinguish whether something does or does not come under them, that could only be by means of another rule. This in turn, for the very reason that it is a rule, again demands guidance from judgment. And thus it appears that, though understanding is capable of being instructed, and of being equipped with rules, judgment is a peculiar talent which can be practised only, and cannot be taught. ... Deficiency in judgment is just what is ordinarily called stupidity, and for such a failing there is no remedy.[8]

What drives this insistence that concepts should be grounded in intuition if they are to be meaningful is not a concern about empty concepts such as 'round square': our ability to judge whether something is or is not a round square is not in doubt; although we cannot intuit one, we can intuit instances of roundness and squareness separately, and understand quite well what it is to conjoin these two concepts. Kant's

---

[6]Ibid., A253 = B309. [7]Ibid., A50–1 = B74–5. [8]Ibid., A132-3 = B171-2.

concern is rather that concepts should not be regarded as meaningful if we have no means of deciding what falls under them, even though we may be able to form thoughts involving them: we might agree, for instance, that every good thwock is a thwock, without having the least idea what a thwock is. What Kant calls 'general logic' consists precisely in forms of reasoning such as this which do not depend for their validity on the relation of a concept to its object.

1.2 Geometrical propositions

It seems natural to draw a distinction between what is involved in grasping the meaning of a proposition and what is involved in knowing whether or not it is true. In accordance with this distinction we shall try to settle what Kant understood to be the meaning of an arithmetical proposition before we discuss his account of how we come to know it. But Kant says less in the *Critique* about arithmetic than he does about geometry, and what he does say about the former is most easily understood by comparing it with what he says about the latter. So we shall adopt the pattern throughout this chapter of considering the geometrical case first, even though it is not directly relevant to the subject matter of this book.

For Kant, as for all his contemporaries, geometry meant primarily Euclid's *Elements* together with commentaries and textbooks derived therefrom. The propositions contained in the *Elements* are of two sorts. Those of the first sort, such as 'In isosceles triangles the angles at the base are equal to one another',[9] may be represented logically as having the form 'All Fs are Gs': they express a relation of containment between two concepts. (In this case, of course, F is the property of being an isosceles triangle and G is the property of having two equal angles.) Propositions of the second sort, such as 'On a given finite straight line to construct an equilateral triangle',[10] are often called 'problems' rather than 'propositions' in commentaries on Euclid. The Greek verb here translated as 'to construct' is an aorist infinitive middle: it expresses an instruction to the reader to perform the construction on the particular straight line in question for himself. This phrasing signals a logical form slightly more complex than that of the first sort of proposition: we could represent our new proposition as 'For each thing that is F we can construct an R of it'; in symbols, $(x)(Fx \supset R(x, fx))$, where f is the construction in question.

---

[9] *Elements*, bk. 1, prop. 5.   [10] Ibid., bk. 1, prop. 1.

Now it is not hard to see how Kant would have seen intuition as essential to understanding propositions of the second sort: to conceive of constructing a triangle on a line segment, we have to have a line segment given to us in intuition on which to perform the construction. But in the first case too Kant thought intuition was essential: as we saw in the last section, the meaningfulness of the concept *triangle* depends on our ability to have an intuition of a triangle and to recognize it as such.

The ability to intuit a triangle is not especially problematic: the concept of a triangle is applicable to intuition because it is derived from intuition. Moreover, the origin of geometrical concepts in intuition limits their applicability as well as grounding it: it makes no sense whatever to ask of something non-spatial whether or not it is a triangle. But the triangles that the propositions of pure geometry are about are not empirical triangles: if we took a geometrical proposition to be about an empirical triangle (even an arbitrary one), 'no universally valid proposition could ever arise out of it — still less an apodeictic proposition — for experience can never yield such.'[11] It follows, then, that for the propositions of geometry to be applicable we must be capable of having intuitions that are in some sense spatial but yet not empirical. This is much more problematic; we shall have to come back later to how Kant thought it was possible.

1.3 Arithmetical propositions

There were for Kant two significant differences between the theorems of geometry and numerical equations such as $7 + 5 = 12$. The first is that geometry deals, at least in the standard cases with which Kant was principally concerned, in generalities, whereas a numerical equation is only singular. So far as we are here attending merely to the synthesis of the homogeneous (of units), that synthesis can take place only in one way, although the employment of these numbers is general. If I assert that through three lines, two of which taken together are greater than the third, a triangle can be described, I have expressed merely the function of productive imagination whereby the lines can be drawn greater or smaller, and so can be made to meet at any and every possible angle. The number 7, on the other hand, is possible only in one way. So also is the number 12, as thus generated through the synthesis of 7 with 5.[12]

A geometrical proposition, as we have seen, typically expresses a relation between concepts, but it would be meaningless if it were not

----

[11] *KrV*, A48 = B65.　[12] Ibid., A165 = B206.

possible to exhibit an intuition of an object in relation to which the concepts in question could be judged as applying or not. A numerical equation also expresses a relation between concepts, and obtains its meaning from the possibility of realizing these concepts. The difference is that in the numerical case there is only one way of carrying out the realization.

Kant goes into no detail as to what he means by this, but I take it that he intends to appeal to a contrast between intrinsic and extrinsic properties of an object. The concept 'triangle' can be realized variously by triangles that differ not merely in how they are situated in space (their extrinsic properties) but in what their angles are (their intrinsic properties). The concept 'seven', on the other hand, is realized by an object consisting of seven units: this object is to be thought of as having no other intrinsic properties, even though it could be realized in various spatio-temporal configurations, which would then differ in their extrinsic properties because they would bear different relations to other spatio-temporal objects.

Numbers must be given to us by means of intuitions if numerical equations are to mean anything. Intuitions, according to the *Critique*, are immediate singular representations of objects. But it seems quite implausible that we should be capable of an *immediate* grasp of a large number such as 100,000. So large numbers cannot be given to us directly as intuitions. Frege famously used this as an objection to the account,[13] but in fact what Kant required is not that we should be able to intuit 100,000 directly, but only that we should be able to understand this number in a way that is *grounded* in intuition, for instance by combining our intuitions of the numbers 10 and 5 with our grasp of the arithmetical operation of exponentiation to obtain a representation of the number 10^5; such a representation is intuitive because it depends on intuitions, even though it is not itself immediate. This may be at least part of what Kant meant when he said that

Our counting (as is easily seen in the case of large numbers) is a synthesis according to concepts, because it is executed according to a common ground of unity, as, for instance, the Decade.[14]

(C. D. Broad once aptly commented, however, that 'this, like many of Kant's remarks, might mean anything, though it probably does not mean nothing.'[15])

The second difference between geometry and arithmetic is more fundamental. Geometrical concepts such as *triangle* are derived from the

[13]See *Gl.*, §§ 5,12.   [14]*KrV*, A78 = B104.   [15]'Kant's mathematical and philosophical reasoning'.

form of our intuitions. Numerical concepts such as *five* or *seven*, on the other hand, seem to be for Kant 'pure concepts of the understanding': they are a priori and do not depend on intuition. The way Kant delineated the pure concepts of the understanding was to list twelve such concepts which he regarded as primary, called *categories* or *predicaments*: he presented them in four groups of three, of quantity, of quality, of relation, and of modality. Other pure concepts, which he called *predicables*, are derivable from the primary ones. The group that is relevant to arithmetic is that of quantity, whose members are unity, plurality, and totality. By unity and plurality I take it that he means sameness and difference. So a being that possesses a grasp of the categories of quantity is one that can compare its intuitions with one another and categorize them as the same or different. If we try once more to express Kant's thought in an unhistorically linguistic manner, we may say that the categories of quantity amount to the same as the grasp of a language containing signs of equality and inequality. Now Kant seems to have held that the finite numerical concepts are among the pure concepts of the understanding that belong to the category of quantity; in other words, he thought that they are obtainable from unity, plurality, and totality. Kant never quite says this explicitly, however. He specifically notes[16] that *infinite* numbers are not straightforwardly obtainable by combining the concepts of plurality and unity but require a 'special act of the understanding'; he stops short of saying that on the other hand finite numbers *are* obtainable simply by combining unity and plurality. But it seems reasonable to infer that they are. If this is right, it follows that finite numerical concepts are independent of the special features of the manner in which objects are given to us: a creature without spatial intuition could have no concept of a triangle, but would, if it had an understanding like ours, have the concept of the number seven.

1.4 The Transcendental Deduction

It is at this point, though, that there arises what Kant saw as one of the central problems of the *Critique*, namely to explain how concepts that do not arise from intuition can nevertheless be applicable to it. We have seen how Kant distinguished between 'the function of understanding expressed in' a concept and 'the universal condition under which alone [it] can be applied to any object',[17] which last he called its schema. In the case of the concept of quantity he called the schema

---

[16] *KrV*, B111. [17] Ibid., A140 = B179.

number,[18] but the terminology is relatively unimportant. What matters is that the schema is the rule for applying the concept to intuition: it is, in short, the means by which we count. But if the concept to be applied is wholly independent of intuition and could be present in a being without the forms of intuition that we humans have, it is apt to seem puzzling how such a schema — counting — could be possible at all. The argument which Kant supplies to dissolve this puzzle is the Transcendental Deduction.

It is here that the asymmetry between geometry and arithmetic becomes striking. There is for Kant no corresponding puzzle in the case of geometry because it is evident that its range of applicability coincides with the range over which its concepts make sense:

Geometry ... proceeds with security in knowledge that is completely a priori, and has no need to beseech philosophy for any certificate of the pure and legitimate descent of its fundamental concept of space. But the concept is employed in this science only in its reference to the outer sensible world — of the intuition of which space is the pure form — where all geometrical knowledge, grounded as it is in a priori intuition, possesses immediate evidence. The objects, so far as their form is concerned, are given, through the very knowledge of them, a priori in intuition. In the case of the pure concepts of understanding, it is quite otherwise; it is with them that the unavoidable demand for a transcendental deduction, not only of themselves, but also of the concept of space, first originates. For since they speak of objects through predicates not of intuition and sensibility but of pure a priori thought, they relate to objects universally, that is, apart from all conditions of sensibility. Also, not being grounded in experience, they cannot, in a priori intuition, exhibit any object such as might, prior to all experience, serve as ground for their synthesis.[19]

The difficulty is thus to explain how the categories, which are not grounded in sensibility, can nevertheless be applicable to it. One might be tempted to take this as obvious, since we do make statements in which concepts such as causality and difference are meaningfully applied to objects. But Kant cautions us against taking this to be as obvious as it seems. The danger is that we may confuse a pure concept with its empirical surrogate, so that what seems to be an application of a category to experience is in fact a straightforwardly empirical judgement. The example Kant gives is that of confusing the category of causation with its empirical *ersatz* of constant association. He does not say what the corresponding confusion would be in the case that interests us here, namely that of the categories of quantity, but one might speculate that it would be the confusion between the pure concept of

---

[18]Ibid., A142 = B182.   [19]Ibid., A87–8 = B120.

equality and the empirical concept of having the same (empirical) properties. What we need to guard against is thus the possibility that what appears to be an application of the former concept (equality) might in fact be an application of the latter (coincidence of properties). Because of this possibility we cannot straightforwardly argue from the evident fact that we can count to the conclusion that the category of quantity is applicable to experience.

The difficulty we are now considering is one that is engendered by Kant's separation of the faculty of sensibility from that of understanding. How can the latter influence the former? If we resist the error of dissolving the difficulty by mistaking a pure concept for its empirical surrogate, we must equally ensure that we do not fall into the corresponding error of mistaking an intuition for its object and hence confusing the subjective with the objective. When I say that a body is heavy, I do not merely assert that if I support it, I feel an impression of weight.

Thus to say 'The body is heavy' is not merely to state that the two representations have always been conjoined in my perception, however often that perception be repeated; what we are asserting is that they are combined *in the object*, no matter what the state of the subject may be.[20]

This distinction between subjective and objective judgements hinges on the distinction between intuitions and objects, which in turn depends on our conception of objects as being capable of being intuited in different ways: if we did not have a grasp of what it is for two different intuitions to arise from the very same object, we could not be said to be experiencing an external world at all. It is just because we understand what it is for an object to have different aspects that we are able to conceive of our experience as being experience *of* something else.

So there are two conditions necessary for objective judgements to be possible: I must be capable of having different intuitions; and I must be able to unite different intuitions in such a way as to constitute my grasp of an object. That the first of these is possible is for Kant little more than a grammatical triviality. My intuitions are mine: I think them. If I did not think them, they would be nothing for me. On the other hand, the possibility of the second condition, the combination of intuitions that enables my judgements to be objective,

does not ... lie in the objects, and cannot be borrowed from them, and so, through perception, first taken up into the understanding. On the contrary, it is an affair of the understanding alone, which itself is nothing but the faculty

---

[20]Ibid., B142.

of combining a priori, and of bringing the manifold of given representations under the unity of apperception.[21]

So if knowledge is to be possible there must be in the understanding concepts capable of combining intuitions so as to constitute knowledge of objects. But that is just what is meant by the categories. Therefore we can conclude that intuitions are subject to the categories.

1.5 Analytic and synthetic

The propositions of arithmetic make use of concepts — the categories — which do not derive from sensibility. One might then suppose that their truth is similarly independent of it, but Kant denied this. Although the understanding — the faculty of concepts — is spontaneous in its ability to create new concepts, its lack of any subject matter limits what it can achieve on its own. Without any grounding in intuition the only propositions that can be known are those Kant called *analytic*.

It is far from straightforward to say what 'analytic' means: one article on the subject distinguishes 'nine traditional definitions of analyticity'[22] and there are others the article does not mention. The term itself is Kant's, but the idea of distinguishing a class of propositions whose truth is in some way trivial goes back at least to Locke, who gave the name 'trifling propositions' to those 'universal propositions that, though they be certainly true, yet they add no light to our understanding, bring no increase to our knowledge'. Locke distinguished two sorts of trifling proposition. The first sort, 'purely identical propositions' such as 'What is, is',[23] seem to correspond to what Kant in his *Logic* called 'tautologies', propositions whose triviality is wholly explicit on their face. The triviality of such propositions seems totally unproblematic — so much so that Kant did not trouble to mention them at all when he defined analyticity in the *Critique*. Locke's second sort of trifling proposition consists of those, such as 'A palfrey is an ambling horse', in which 'a part of the complex idea is predicated of the name of the whole'.[24] These seem at first sight to coincide with those Kant explicitly labelled as analytic in the *Critique*, namely those which add 'nothing through the predicate to the concept of the subject, but merely [break] it up into those constituent concepts that have been thought in it, although confusedly.'[25] This is not quite right, however. Locke held that trifling propositions 'are purely about the signification of words, and contain

[21]Ibid., B134–5.   [22]Gasking, 'The analytic-synthetic controversy', 108.   [23]*Essay*, bk. IV, ch. viii, §5.   [24]Ibid.   [25]*KrV*, A7 = B11.

nothing in them but the use and application of these signs',[26] whereas
Kant took analyticity to be primarily a property of judgements rather
than of the sentences used to express them. The example Kant used
to make this point was one of Locke's own. Locke thought it trifling
that gold is yellow.[27] Is it? If 'analytic' meant 'true by definition', this
would obviously depend on the definition of 'gold'. Locke supposed that
the colour of gold was part of its definition, but if we define gold to be
the element whose atomic number is 79, it becomes (presumably) an
empirical fact, and therefore non-trifling, that gold is yellow. Kant, by
contrast, focused on the judgement rather than its verbal expression.
'[I]n the concept of *gold* one man may think, in addition to its weight,
colour, malleability, also its property of resisting rust, while another will
perhaps know nothing of this property.'[28] If he had treated analyticity
as an attribute of *sentences*, Kant would no doubt have deduced from
this, as others have done more recently, that analyticity is an unstable
notion, but since for Kant analyticity was an attribute of *judgements*,
he drew the alternative moral that genuine definitions are impossible
in ordinary language. 'There remain ... no concepts which allow of
definition, except only those which contain an arbitrary synthesis that
admits of a priori construction.'[29] It may be hard to determine which
judgement is being expressed by a particular sentence, but if it *can* be
determined there is no further vagueness about the question whether
the judgement is analytic.

1.6 The principle of analytic judgements

In this book, though, we are concerned only with mathematics. So for us
the contrast between Locke's trifling propositions and Kant's analytic
ones is not significant in connection with the point about vagueness:
according to Kant this sort of vagueness does not arise in mathematics,
which is the only science that does admit definitions in the strict sense.
The importance of the contrast is rather to do with the rôle of logic. If,
as Locke held, trifling propositions are 'purely about the signification of
words', even the simplest reasoning about such propositions is in need
of justification. If 'All *A*s are *B*s' and 'All *B*s are *C*s' are expressions of
linguistic conventions, why should it follow that 'All *A*s are *C*s' is one
too? There is nothing in Locke to answer this question, or indeed to
suggest that he took the class of trifling propositions to be closed under
any sort of logical reasoning at all.

[26] *Essay*, bk. 4, ch. 8, § 13.   [27] Ibid., bk. IV, ch. viii, § 5.   [28] *KrV*, A728 = B756.
[29] Ibid., A729 = B757.

Kant, on the other hand, attempted an alternative delineation of the class of analytic propositions by means of just such a notion, namely the law of contradiction. He intended this principle to operate both positively and negatively: positively, to show how analytic judgements are possible; negatively, to enable us to set limits to the class of analytic judgements more precise than can be deduced from the psychologistic definition of analyticity already given.

By adopting the law of contradiction as a criterion of analyticity Kant included within the scope of the analytic a part, but not the whole, of traditional logic. The part which is to count as analytic he called *general* logic. He did not, of course, conceive of any of logic as a formal system in the way that has been familiar since Frege. So there is an inevitable distortion in asking what portion of modern formal logic would count as general according to Kant's criterion. It is moreover hard for anyone who reads, for instance, his essay on 'The false subtlety of the four syllogistic figures' to regard Kant as a gifted logician by modern standards. The following attempt to determine the scope of the Kantian analytic is therefore at best a reconstruction.

To those schooled in many modern axiom or natural deduction systems of formal logic the idea that any significant part of logic could flow from the law of contradiction *alone* is apt to seem puzzling, since it is typically conceived of as merely one law among many without any privileged status. Yet the idea that a significant part of logic does flow from it is not by any means peculiar to Kant: it was stated by Aristotle and repeated often by logicians throughout the period since. To understand the point from a modern perspective it is best to focus on tableau systems of logic, since they are motivated by the same idea. A tableau proof breaks down the sentences in the sequent to be proved into their constituent parts in an attempt to find parts which violate the law of contradiction: if any of the parts that occur in a branch contradict one another, that branch is said to be closed. Tableau systems thus distinguish between the rule for branch closure (the principle of contradiction) on the one hand and the rules for branch construction on the other.

The distinction is not purely formal, however: the rules for branch construction — at least in the case of the tableau rules for the propositional connectives ($\sim$, $\vee$, $.$, $\supset$, $\equiv$, etc.) — merely exhibit more fully the structure (and hence one aspect of the meaning) of the sentences in the sequent in question, whereas the law of contradiction provides the criterion for establishing, once the structures have been exhibited, that the sequent is thereby shown to be proved. The whole of the propositional calculus is thus part of general logic, and hence analytic on

Kant's account.

I said earlier that what Kant says about the analytic goes beyond what Locke says about trifling propositions. This is the point at which this difference becomes explicit. There is nothing in Locke that determines whether he would have regarded the truths of the propositional calculus as trifling. Moreover, the point is one of some significance since it is just here that Kant's account sustains the notion that a precisely expressed proposition can be analytic without its being so on its face. The reason is that there is a fundamental difference between the process of exhibition of meaning that occurs when we observe that it is part of the concept *triangle* to be three-sided, and the process that occurs when we split a disjunction into its two components in the construction of a tableau. The difference lies in the degree of generality which is inherent in the latter process but not in the former. Formally speaking, the tableau rule for splitting up a disjunction is expressed schematically, whereas a rule for unpacking the meaning of 'triangle' can be expressed directly. The importance of this is that without the presence of schematic rules logic would be wholly unable to make any progress at all: we might be able to progress by means of a particular rule from A to B, and by means of another from B to C, but we should not be licensed thereby without applying a schematic rule to progress from A to C.

Kant's conception of general logic thus encompassed an understanding of the notion of what it is to apply a general rule. We must not, however, leap to the conclusion that his conception also encompassed the notion of generality as it is normally understood in the predicate calculus. For the understanding of this something further is required than the mere notion of applying a rule: we need in addition the notion of a range of possible application of the rule; we need, that is to say, a conception of a certain range of things and a method for judging to which of these things the rule is applicable.

In short, we need the notion of an *object*. It is just this that in Kant's view is unavailable in general logic:

General logic ... abstracts from all content of knowledge, that is, from all relation of knowledge to the object, and considers only the logical form in the relation of any knowledge to other knowledge.[30]

This does not rule out the whole of predicate calculus, but it does rule out a large part of it. What remains is Aristotle's logic of the syllogism, which is the calculus of relations of containment between concepts nowadays sometimes taught by means of the nineteenth-century

---

[30]Ibid., A55 = B79.

tool of Venn diagrams. This calculus is of no greater logical complexity than the propositional calculus, and according to Kant no more object-involving than it.

General logic includes, then, both the propositional calculus and the syllogistic calculus of monadic predicates. It is very far from including everything we nowadays think of logic, but more interestingly it does not even include everything that Kant himself thought of as logic. For example, general logic is incapable of recognizing 'Socrates is a man' as being of a different form from 'All Greeks are men'. Aristotelian logic, let us recall, allows such syllogisms as:

All Greeks are men.
All men are mortal.
_____
All Greeks are mortal.

The most often quoted example of a syllogism, however, is slightly different:

Socrates is a man.
All men are mortal.
_____
Socrates is mortal.

Despite its ubiquity as an example, this is not in fact an Aristotelian syllogism, because Aristotle's system was a logic of containment of concepts and therefore had no way of coping directly with syllogisms involving proper names such as 'Socrates'. Aristotle himself mentioned syllogisms of this sort only outside the context of his logical system. They were, however, frequently discussed by the medievals, who adopted the device of subsuming them under Aristotle's account by representing the syllogism above as (in effect):

All Socratizers are men.
All men are mortal.
_____
All Socratizers are mortal.

It is the distinction between this argument about Socratizers and the previous one about Greeks that syllogistic logic is blind to.[31]

To summarize. 'What is is' is as trivial as anything gets. It is what Kant called a tautology. Locke's account goes beyond such trivialities to allow as trifling those propositions which are immediate consequences of definitions. Kant's conception of the analytic goes further still by allowing within its scope what we should nowadays describe as the consequences of implicit definitions of logical constants. What Kant's conception rules out is any dependence in analytic reasoning on a substantial notion of objects as more than mere place-holders in arguments. A direct consequence of this limitation is that just as Locke

[31]Ibid., A71 = B96.

had held trifling propositions to be what he called verbal and not instructive, so Kant's analytic propositions, despite their wider range, remained merely what he called explicative and not ampliative. In other words, the application of general logic does not enable reasoning to go beyond the class of propositions already characterized as analytic, namely those which add 'nothing through the predicate to the concept of the subject'.[32]

General logic is thus according to Kant 'a dry but a short science'.[33] We cannot possibly by its means alone extend our knowledge because in order to do so our reason would have to be supplied with material with which to construct the extension, and that is precisely what is not available in general logic. Analytic judgements do not provide genuine knowledge and are lacking in content; synthetic (i.e. non-analytic) judgements, by contrast, are capable of supplying genuine knowledge and must have content. Kant regarded this content as consisting of *objects*, which thus play a permissive role in Kant's system as things capable of grounding ampliative reasoning. Now it is a recurring feature of many parts of philosophy that what is permissive constrains also. This is true here: objects, thus understood, constrain the combinations of concepts that we may coherently think. The concepts *red* and *green*, for example, do not contradict one another, but we cannot conceive of a single object having both these colours simultaneously.

From a modern perspective one might be tempted to think that what made general logic non-ampliative for Kant was that it is decidable, but in fact decidability is only a necessary and not a sufficient condition for a procedure to be non-ampliative. To see that decidability is necessary we need only reflect that without it we should have to accept the possibility that we could have a concept which has constituents we not only have not yet recognized but have in principle no method for recognizing. That decidability is not sufficient, on the other hand, will become apparent shortly, when we examine Kant's reasons for holding that $\mathbf{EA}_0$, which is decidable, nevertheless validates forms of ampliative reasoning.

1.7 Geometry is not analytic

Before we turn to arithmetic, though, we shall consider the more straightforward case of geometry, which Kant also took to contain synthetic judgements. One of the examples which Kant discusses is the proposition that the sum of the angles of a triangle is always two right

[32]Ibid., A7 = B11. [33]*Logic*, trans. Richardson, 124.

angles. This proposition may be expressed as 'All triangles are figures whose angles sum to two right angles' and is therefore, like many
in Euclid, of the form 'All *F*s are *G*s'. Kant certainly did not think
that all judgements of this form, even in geometry, are synthetic: the
proposition that all right-angled triangles are triangles is an obvious
counterexample. If the propositions of Euclid are synthetic, then, this
cannot be because of their logical form alone. Nor does Kant's view
result from a concern to avoid the fallacies (famously committed by
Aristotle) which result from arguing about an *F* if there are no *F*s,
since Euclid's argument would be valid even if there were in fact no
triangles.

Kant's reason for thinking it synthetic that the angles of any triangle
sum to two right angles is rather to be explained by means of a contrast he liked to make between the mathematical and the philosophical
method. 'Philosophy is simply what reason knows by means of concepts,'[34] whereas mathematics 'achieves nothing by concepts alone but
hastens at once to intuition.'[35] So if anyone attempts to prove the Euclidean proposition by means of the philosophical method, i.e. without
any appeal to intuition,

[h]e has nothing but the concept of a figure enclosed by three straight lines,
and possessing three angles. However long he meditates on this concept, he
will never produce anything new. He can analyse and clarify the concept of
a straight line or of an angle or of the number three, but he can never arrive
at any properties not already contained in these concepts.[36]

The sum of the angles of a triangle is not, it is claimed, deducible
from the concept *triangle* alone. How, though, do we know that this is
so? We cannot infer it directly from the distinction between intrinsic
and extrinsic properties that we exploited earlier, since the sum of its
angles is presumably an intrinsic property of a triangle just as much as
the number of its sides is.

The modern reader will at this point invoke hyperbolic geometry,
in which the angles of a triangle sum to less than two right angles.
If the word 'triangle' means the same in hyperbolic as in Euclidean
geometry, it cannot be part of the concept *triangle* what the sum of the
angles is; this must rather depend on properties of the space in which
the triangles in question are situated. But although Gauss studied the
subject around 1800, nothing was published on non-Euclidean geometry
until 1827, long after Kant's death. So it is very unlikely that Kant
had anything like this thought in mind. (It has recently been popular
to suggest that Kant could have learnt about non-Euclidean geometry

[34] *KrV*, A732 = B760.   [35] Ibid., A715 = B743.   [36] Ibid., A716 = B744.

from the mathematician Karl Lambert, with whom he corresponded, but Lambert's work on the subject — which, like that of Gauss, was not published in his lifetime — consists largely of attempts to prove that space is Euclidean by attempting to derive a contradiction from the contrary hypothesis: Lambert makes only the very briefest allusion to the idea that non-Euclidean geometry might be consistent.)

But even if Kant *had* known about non-Euclidean geometry, it is not clear that he could have employed it to show that geometry is not analytic. Whether the structure we impose on space is Euclidean or non-Euclidean, on Kant's account it is that way a priori. So if our understanding of the concept *triangle* is, as noted earlier, limited to things in space, it is presumably thereby limited to things in whichever sort of space — Euclidean or non-Euclidean — we impose a priori on our intuitions.

Kant's difficulty here is a consequence of his attempt to derive the conclusion that geometry is not analytic from the psychological criterion of analyticity. It is asking a lot to expect me to distinguish on the basis of introspection between facts about a concept that are there to be seen if I did but think the right way, and facts which require some new intuition for their proof. How can I be sure that the reason I cannot prove a geometrical theorem by meditating on the concept *triangle* alone is the lack of an appropriate intuition and not mere stupidity on my part?

The alternative would have been for Kant to appeal to the characterization of analyticity in logical terms introduced in the last section and provide a demonstration that a proof of the Euclidean proposition by syllogistic reasoning alone is impossible. But logic had not by Kant's time attained a state of development which put such demonstrations of impossibility within reach.

1.8 Arithmetic is not analytic

Kant's claim that the theorems of geometry are synthetic has been widely accepted, especially since the emergence of non-Euclidean geometry. His corresponding claim for arithmetic is much more controversial: indeed this whole book is in a way a history of attempts to refute it. Kant denied that even simple numerical equations are analytic, but in the first edition of the *Critique* all he said to justify this claim was the following:

The assertion that 7 + 5 is equal to 12 is not an analytic proposition. For neither in the representation of 7, nor in that of 5, nor in the representation of the combination of both, do I think the number 12. (That I must do so in the *addition* of the two numbers is not to the point, since in the analytic proposition the question is only whether I actually think the predicate in the representation of the subject.)[37]

Perhaps Kant realized that more needed to be said. In a passage in the *Prolegomena*, which also appears in the second edition of the *Critique*, Kant even went as far as to grant the superficial appeal of the thesis he was denying. 'We might indeed at first suppose', he says, 'that the proposition $7 + 5 = 12$ is a merely analytic proposition, and follows by the principle of contradiction from the concept of a sum of 7 and 5.'[38] Kant then proceeds to sketch a positive account of how we know that $7 + 5 = 12$ and attempts to show that since this positive account depends on intuition, i.e. on the substantial notion of objecthood which purely explicative reasoning does not require, the proposition must be synthetic. What Kant needs at this point, then, is an argument that the dependence on intuition here is ineliminable. All he gives, though, is a restatement of the argument we have already quoted:

[T]he concept of the sum of 7 and 5 contains nothing save the union of the two numbers into one, and in this no thought is being taken as to what that single number may be which combines both. The concept of 12 is by no means already thought in merely thinking this union of 7 and 5; and I may analyse my concept of such a possible sum as long as I please, still I shall never find the 12 in it. ... That 5 should be added to 7, I have indeed already thought in the concept of a sum = 7+5, but not that this sum is equivalent to the number 12.[39]

Kant thus based his denial of the analyticity of numerical equations on his psychological criterion that a judgement is analytic if it 'adds nothing through the predicate to the concept of the subject, but merely breaks it up into those constituent concepts that have been thought in it, although confusedly.'[40] As a general test for analyticity this is, as we have noted, far from satisfactory: one man may think of resistance to rust as part of the concept *gold* 'while another will perhaps know nothing of this property'. The criterion had rather more plausibility in the mathematical case, though, since mathematical concepts, unlike others, permit of precise definition. So once we have grasped a mathematical concept we cannot then be surprised by some new aspect of its meaning that we were not previously aware of. In order to show that $7 + 5 = 12$ '[w]e have to go outside these concepts, and call in the aid of the intuition which corresponds to one of them';[41] in arithmetic conceptual thought unsupported by intuition cannot advance us beyond

[37]Ibid., A164 = B205.   [38]Ibid., B15; *Proleg.*, § 2.   [39]*KrV*, B15-16.   [40]Ibid., A7 = B11.   [41]Ibid., B15.

what is explicitly contained in the definitions. If $7 + 5 = 12$ were an analytic judgement, 'I would have to think exactly the same thing by' either side of the equation.[42]

The flaw in this argument is that the scope of the analytic is not limited to what is *wholly* trivial: logic, even general logic, is capable of grounding arguments taking us to consequences which are not *immediately* apparent to anyone who grasps the premisses. It follows that an introspective report that when I think of $7 + 5$ I do not thereby find myself thinking of 12 is not conclusive proof that 12 was not already there to be thought if I had but noticed it. Even if the consequence relation of general logic is, as Kant held, non-ampliative by virtue of its lack of material with which to progress to genuinely new conclusions, it is not quite degenerate. There is therefore no reason to suppose that our thought is closed under its application (i.e. that when I think something I must thereby be able to think all its non-ampliative consequences). For this reason Kant's refutation of the claim that arithmetic is analytic can hardly be said to be conclusive.

1.9 The principle of synthetic judgements

It remains, however, that it was central to Kant's project to deny that arithmetic is analytic. To see why it was so important we need to turn to Kant's positive account of synthetic judgements. Kant distinguished various functions which the mind performs. He called them *faculties*: I have already mentioned *sensibility*, which supplies us with intuitions, and *understanding*, which supplies concepts; intuitions and concepts are combined in *judgement*; and deductions are drawn from them by *reason*. The constraint which our finiteness places on us — indeed what Kant meant by our finiteness — is that *all* our intuitions come to us via sensibility. Now as we have stated the matter so far, this appears to be a mere matter of definition rather than a substantive claim, and this is an appearance Kant seems to confirm when he asserts that

the capacity (receptivity) for receiving representations through the mode in which we are affected by objects is entitled *sensibility*. Objects are *given* to us by means of sensibility, and it alone yields us *intuitions*.[43]

But the appearance here is misleading. Kant conceived of sensibility as an essentially passive faculty ('receptivity') in contrast with the understanding, which is active. The fact that all our intuitions come to us via sensibility is thus according to him a genuine constraint on us,

---

[42] *Phil. Corr.*, 130. [43] *KrV*, A19 = B33.

constitutive of our finiteness, since this amounts to the claim that we cannot create intuitions out of nothing. The contents of our thoughts are formed from matter which is made available to us but which we do not invent. This is not, of course, to say that hallucinations are impossible, but rather that the content (if any) of a hallucination must be formed from contents genuinely supplied to us by sensibility.

That Kant conceived of the passivity of the faculty supplying us with intuitions as a genuine constraint emerges from his explicit recognition of a non-sensible kind of intuition which he called *intellectual*. I have said that what Kant meant by a finite intelligence is any being with a consciousness dependent wholly on sensibility for the supply of intuitions to serve as the subject matter of its thought. Now God could not be finite since it is no part of our conception of God that He should be limited in this way. So if God is possible, intellectual intuitions are possible for Him. It is thus on Kant's view possible for there to be a being that is not finite, but it is a largely unargued premiss of Kant's system — one that was denied by post-Kantian philosophers in the romantic tradition such as Schelling — that we humans are nevertheless finite in this sense.

Because sensibility is passive and cannot create something out of nothing, what we obtain from it must depend on a thing or things external to it, that is to say on an external world. The intuitions we receive via sensibility which represent this world to us are called *empirical* intuitions. It might seem at first as if the fact that all our intuitions are sensible implied that they must all be empirical, but this would be a mistake. The error lies in our tendency to suppose that the structure we perceive in experience must itself be an object of experience. If it were — if there were, in other words, a structure relating our empirical intuitions which was in itself something we could experience — there would have to be a further structure relating the empirical intuitions to the relational structure, and we should have to be able to experience *that* structure in turn.

This is an example of a familiar sort of circle, and Kant thought he could avoid it by making the *Copernican turn*; by concluding, that is to say, that the structure of experience is not itself part of experience but is something supplied by us through which we filter the raw data that come to us from the world. Moreover, this structure is something which we can intuit directly. Our sensibility thus supplies us not only with empirical but with *pure* intuitions, i.e. intuitions deriving not from experience itself but from its structure.

The route we have just described to the conclusion that the structure of experience is supplied by us is a direct one. Because it grounds the notion that we can have pure (i.e. non-empirical) intuitions, it thus explains, in outline, how synthetic a priori knowledge is possible. But Kant was also attracted (especially in the *Prolegomena*) to an argument to broadly the same conclusion by means of what he called the *regressive* method. This argument takes as its premiss our knowledge of pure mathematics and draws the conclusion that pure intuition is possible.

We have already seen how it is possible for there to be judgements, namely analytic judgements, that are applicable to empirical intuitions even though our grasp of their truth depends only on the relationship between the concepts involved and not on intuition. But according to Kant the substantive theorems of mathematics cannot be grasped in this way. There is no great mystery either, in Kant's view, about a posteriori judgements: they are applicable to empirical intuitions because they are derivable directly from them. Such judgements may be universal — the judgement that all ravens are black might be an example — but their generality is then only accidental and, as Wittgenstein said much later, 'the generality which we need in mathematics is not the *accidental* one.'[44] So the truths of pure mathematics are synthetic a priori. If we know any such truths, it can only be because we have intuitions that are not empirical. 'Experience teaches us what is, but does not teach us that it could not be other than it is.'[45]

Notice, though, that this regressive argument is both weaker and less general than the direct one: weaker because it establishes only that pure intuitions are possible without giving the least clue what form they take; less general because it applies only to beings which are capable of synthetic a priori knowledge. Kant took it to be indubitable that we humans are indeed capable of such knowledge, but if the argument is to apply to *all* finite beings, we shall need an independent reason, such as the direct argument supplies, to think that they must necessarily be capable of synthetic a priori knowledge, provided only that they are capable of experience.

According to Kant, then, the experiences which a being with a finite intelligence receives will be subject to a structure supplied by the mind which is distinct from the experiences themselves, even if the being could not be aware of the structure without having the experiences. In the case of us humans the structure in question is that of space and time: Kant provides (in the Transcendental Aesthetic) a lengthy account of how we know that this is so, but he does not explain why it is so: he takes it to be a brute fact about us, and says indeed[46] that no explanation for it is possible.

---

[44] *TLP*, 6.031. [45] *KrV*, A734 = B762. [46] Ibid., B145–6.

As we shall see, Kant made his account in the *Critique* of our knowledge of mathematics depend on features of the spatio-temporal form that human experience inevitably has, features that it is the purpose of the Transcendental Aesthetic to single out. Not only the distinction between the matter of experience and its form but the identification of space and time as forms of experience are to be found already in Kant's *Inaugural Dissertation* of a decade earlier, but there he makes a brief allusion to 'all sciences whose principles are given intuitively, either by a sensual intuition (experience) or at least by an intuition which is sensitive but pure (concepts of space, time and number),'[47] which seems to suggest that he thought number might itself be a third form of intuition. Now there is a superficial attraction in the notion that arithmetical intuition is *sui generis* and not derived from space and time. After all, we have already seen that Kant was at pains to point out the non-sensible origins of the *concepts* of arithmetic, distinguishing them in this respect from those of geometry. It might seem natural, therefore, to suppose that our knowledge of arithmetical truths is correspondingly independent of space and time. But if we attempt to derive this conclusion simply by positing — *contra* the Transcendental Aesthetic — a third source of pure intuitions in addition to space and time, we are left unable to explain the applicability of these truths. For if our knowledge of arithmetical propositions depends on the properties of a further dimension of experience independent of the spatio-temporal ones, there seems to be no good reason why these propositions should be applicable to objects located in space and time at all.

Kant was evidently sensitive to this issue of applicability even in the *Dissertation*, since he stresses there that the concept of number, 'though itself indeed intellectual, yet demands for its actualization in the concrete the auxiliary notions of time and space.'[48] What he did not have until the *Critique* was his account of what makes this 'actualization in the concrete' possible. From then on it was essential for him to reject (if he had ever really held) the view that arithmetic involves a form of intuition that is not spatio-temporal.

1.10 Geometry as synthetic

If geometry is synthetic, as Kant held, our knowledge of it must depend on intuition. I have said already that the geometry with which Kant and his contemporaries were familiar was that of Euclid's *Elements*;

---

[47] *Inaug. Diss.*, § 23.   [48] Ibid., § 12.

and Kant's positive account takes its pattern from features of Euclid's treatment. Euclid first laid down the meanings of certain primitive terms such as 'point' and 'line'. He then listed five postulates:

1. *To draw a straight line from any point to any point.*

2. *To produce a finite straight line continuously in a straight line.*

3. *To describe a circle with any centre and distance.*

4. *That all right angles are equal to one another.*

5. *That, if a straight line falling on two straight lines makes the interior angles on the same side less than two right angles, the two straight lines, if produced indefinitely, meet on that side on which are the angles less than two right angles.*[49]

From these postulates Euclid proved a great many propositions not only of what would nowadays be called geometry but also, it is worth noting, of arithmetic. We shall focus for the moment on the one which we mentioned briefly before, the proposition that the sum of the angles of any triangle is two right angles. Euclid's proof of this proposition is as follows:

Proposition. *In any triangle* ... *the three interior angles are equal to two right angles.*[50]

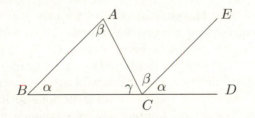

Proof. Let ABC be a triangle, and let one side of it BC be produced to D;
   I say that the three interior angles of the triangle ABC, BCA, CAB are equal to two right angles.
   For let CE be drawn through the point C parallel to the straight line AB.
   Then since AB is parallel to CE and AC has fallen upon them, the alternate angles BAC, ACE are equal to one another.
   Again, since AB is parallel to CE, and the straight line BD has fallen upon them, the exterior angle ECD is equal to the interior and opposite angle ABC.
   But the angle ACE was also proved equal to the angle BAC;
   therefore the whole angle ACD is equal to the two interior and opposite angles BAC, ABC.

[49] *Elements*, Intro.   [50] Ibid., bk. 1, prop. 32.

Let the angle ACB be added to each;

therefore the angles ACD, ACB are equal to the three angles ABC, BCA, CAB.

But the angles ACD, ACB are equal to two right angles;

therefore the angles ABC, BCA, CAB are also equal to two right angles.

Q.E.D.

We saw earlier that Kant thought someone who has merely the concept of a triangle does not thereby have the resources to ground this proof; whereas if he is permitted the use of intuition

[h]e at once begins by constructing a triangle. Since he knows that the sum of two right angles is exactly equal to the sum of all the adjacent angles which can be constructed from a single point on a straight line, he prolongs one side of his triangle and obtains two adjacent angles, which together are equal to two right angles. He then divides the external angle by drawing a line parallel to the opposite side of the triangle, and observes that he has thus obtained an external adjacent angle which is equal to an internal angle — and so on. In this fashion, through a chain of inferences guided throughout by intuition, he arrives at a fully evident and universally valid solution of the problem.[51]

Very roughly, Kant's account is this. For the proof to be valid we have to be able to construct the triangle ABC. But it cannot be the triangle in the picture that is in question, because a conclusion we draw about it cannot have the general validity we take Euclid's proposition to have. Indeed, for that reason the triangle which we conceive of the proof as referring to cannot be empirical at all. We must therefore be capable of what Kant calls 'constructing' it in intuition, i.e. producing on demand an intuition of a triangle. Pure geometry thus consists of propositions proved by means of constructions in intuition. When we construct a geometrical figure such as a triangle in intuition, our construction is not empirical but is nevertheless subject to the form of spatial intuition which we supply. Any empirical triangle with which I come into epistemic contact will necessarily be subject to that same form of intuition. Since all we used about the pure triangle in proving propositions about it was that it was a triangle in space, those propositions must be applicable to the empirical triangle. The applicability of pure geometry to the world of appearances is thus for Kant an a priori matter.

Put more generally, the situation is as follows. One common method of proving a sentence of the form 'All Fs are Gs' is to suppose Fa and deduce Ga. In symbols,

[51]*KrV*, A716-7 = B744-5.

$$\require{cancel}$$

$$
\begin{array}{c}
\cancel{F}a \\
\vdots \\
\underline{Ga} \\
(x)(Fx \supset Gx)
\end{array}
\qquad (1)
$$

If in the course of arguing for Ga we never make use of any property of a other than that Fa, then 'a' in the argument is merely a place-holder whose use is strictly speaking unnecessary, and the eventual conclusion, that all Fs are Gs, is analytic. If, on the other hand, we do use such a property — in the case we considered earlier, the property that a is a figure in Euclidean space — then 'a' is functioning not merely as a place-holder but as a name of an object, and for us to be assured of the validity of the argument we must have an intuition of that object.

There is, however, a difficulty with this account which was pointed out by Frege. In the proof we were considering earlier we aimed to show that if something is a triangle then the sum of its angles is two right angles. We did so by supposing that something is a triangle and showing that the sum of its angles is two right angles. In the symbolism we have adopted, therefore, 'Fa' stands for 'Something is a triangle' and 'Ga' stands for 'The sum of its angles is two right angles'. These are not propositions expressing thoughts on their own: we do not know what to make of the question 'Is the sum of its angles two right angles?' outside the context of the proof. They are instead what Frege called *pseudo-propositions* and have meaning only in the context of the argument in which they are deployed.

The hypothetical mode of argument represented schematically by (1) is, of course, routinely used in logic. If Frege's criticism is correct, however, the method is strictly speaking wrong since the individual steps in the argument from Fa to Ga do not express thoughts on their own and are therefore incapable of being asserted.

The standard defence to this criticism is to note that proofs of the form in question can always be rewritten, albeit much less perspicuously, as direct arguments which do not use the procedure of introducing an hypothesis and subsequently discharging it. In the realm of pure logic this defence is reasonable enough. It will not serve Kant's purpose, however. In the course of the argument from Fa to Ga we make use of properties of a which are not intrinsic to it but follow from the location of a in Euclidean space. If we try to rewrite the argument as a series of universally quantified propositions, we shall no longer be talking about anything located in space, and shall therefore have no justification for introducing the required extrinsic properties into the argument. The proof will therefore collapse.

It is hard, though, to see what other account can be given of this kind of argument. If the argument is to work, we need '*a*' to be a genuine name and not a variable, but it seems that it will have to name a most mysterious object. Plainly we cannot take '*a*' to denote any *particular* object which is *F*, since the object we took might by chance be *G* even if not all *F*s are *G*s. Only two broad alternatives seem to be left: one is to suppose that '*a*' denotes an *arbitrary F*; the other is that it denotes the *ideal F*. Let us consider these possibilities in turn.

The first choice is to say that '*a*' names an arbitrary triangle. We seem now to be back in the account which Frege ridiculed. If we are to accept that the arbitrary triangle exists, we must insist that it is not another triangle over and above all particular triangles. We must agree instead that '*a*' denotes a particular triangle but that it is radically indeterminate which one it is.

Logic since Frege has viewed arbitrary objects with almost universal disapproval;[52] the way of achieving a similar effect which it has sanctioned is to conduct the argument with a schematic letter 'α' instead of a name '*a*'. Replacing '*a*' with 'α' is, of course, in itself a matter of mere typography: its significance is that 'α' is treated as a symbol not of the language but of the metalanguage. Our argument is therefore now only a schema which can be converted into a valid argument in the language of the theory by substituting any genuine name '*a*' for the schematic letter 'α'.

Fregean hygiene has its price, however. In the previous account we had to intuit the triangle *a* in space in order to deduce the properties it has in virtue of its location in space. Now we must apparently perform the more elaborate manœuvre of conditional intuition: we must deduce the properties that would be possessed by the triangle denoted by any name which could be substituted for 'α'.

Without doubt our account is now radically unKantian: the distinction between a schematic letter and the name of an arbitrary object, even though it may plausibly be said to be present in Aristotle, would surely have been lost on Kant, who did not have the conception of a formal language on which the distinction relies. However that may be, matters in any case become even worse when we consider how to couch the rule of inference (1). If '*a*', '*b*', '*c*', etc. are the various names for

---

[52] An exception is Fine, *Reasoning With Arbitrary Objects*.

which 'α' is a place-holder, the rule is now

$$\frac{\begin{array}{ccc} \not{F}a & \not{F}b & \not{F}c & \cdots \\ \vdots & \vdots & \vdots \\ Ga & Gb & Gc & \cdots \end{array}}{(x)(Fx \supset Gx)}$$

(2)

This is an infinitary rule since it may have infinitely many premisses. The detour via schematic letters is thus a red herring: as long as we work with schematic letters, we are not dealing with anything subject to the constraints of spatial structure that we need to appeal to if we are to prove the geometrical theorem; but if we descend from the metalanguage in order to correct this difficulty, we find ourselves reasoning about not one triangle but an infinite number, since what unites these infinitely many cases into one — the schematic letter — is simply not available to us in the object language.

The second broad alternative, we have said, is to treat 'a' as referring not to an arbitrary actual triangle but to the Triangle, conceived of now as an ideal object abstracted from the actual. Talk of such abstractions makes us think at once of Plato's Forms, but if it is to do the work Kant requires of it the Triangle cannot be, as Plato said it was, outside of space and time.[53] It must be located in space in order for it to have the properties which validate the geometrical proof. That this should be so follows in any case from part of Kant's doctrine that we have already discussed (§ 1.9): we are finite intelligences, whose only source of intuitions is sensibility; everything we intuit must therefore be intuited as located within the spatio-temporal structure which sensibility supplies.

We are thus confronted with two different accounts of the objects mentioned in geometrical proofs: on the first they are empirical but arbitrary; on the second they are ideal and yet still located in space and time. Notice straightaway that neither account is any good when applied to the geometrical proposition itself: the accounts are to be assessed as attempts to explain not the proposition itself but our proof of it. Berkeley, when he considered this question, was resolute in his defence of the first account.[54] Kant, on the other hand, seems to have had some sympathies with the second account, but did in the end come down in favour of something closer to the first:

To construct a concept means to exhibit a priori the intuition which corresponds to the concept. For the construction of a concept we therefore need a *non-empirical* intuition. The latter must, as intuition, be a *single* object,

---

[53] Cf. *KrV*, A314 = B371 n. [54] *Principles*, Intro., § 16.

and yet nonetheless as the construction of a concept (a universal representation), it must in its representation express universal validity for all possible intuitions which fall under the same concept. Thus I construct a triangle by representing the object which corresponds to this concept either by imagination alone, in pure intuition, or in accordance therewith also on paper, in empirical intuition — in both cases completely a priori, without having borrowed the pattern from any experience. The single figure which we draw is empirical, and yet it serves to express the concept, without impairing its universality. For in this empirical intuition we consider only the act whereby we construct the concept, and abstract from the many determinations (for instance, the magnitude of the sides and of the angles), which are quite indifferent, as not altering the concept 'triangle'.[55]

There is, Kant is saying, a way of viewing the triangle we construct which abstracts from its particular features so as to make it in a sense arbitrary. This way of viewing the triangle 'serves to express the concept, without impairing its universality'. The triangle we construct is indeed objectively a particular triangle with particular sides and particular angles, but if we construct it merely as an instance of the concept 'triangle', our *representation* of it will 'express universal validity for all possible intuitions which fall under the same concept'.

One thing that remains for us to explain, though, is why Kant says[56] that we are guided by intuition *throughout* the chain of inferences in a geometrical proof. We need to intuit *a*, and we need intuition to ground the postulates, but thereafter, it might seem, we proceed purely according to logic in a way which does not require any support from intuition. We can see why this is not so if we consider the proof of the very first proposition in Euclid, which is the example we came across earlier of a geometrical proposition of the sort that are phrased as problems to be solved rather than as propositions to be proved.

Proposition. *On a given finite straight line to construct an equilateral triangle.*[57]

Proof. Let *AB* be the given finite straight line.

Thus it is required to construct an equilateral triangle on the straight line *AB*

With centre *A* and distance *AB* let the circle *BCD* be described [postulate 3]: again, with centre *B* and distance *BA* let the circle *ACE* be described: and from the point *C* in which the circles cut one another, to the points *A*, *B* let the straight lines *CA*, *CB* be joined [postulate 1].

Now, since the point *A* is the centre of the circle *CDB*, *AC* is equal to *AB*.

[55] *KrV*, A713-4 = B741-2. [56] Ibid., A717 = B745. [57] *Elements*, bk. 1, prop. 1.

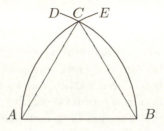

Again, since the point B is the centre of the circle CAE, BC is equal to BA.

But CA was also proved equal to AB; therefore each of the straight lines CA, CB is equal to AB.

And things which are equal to the same thing are also equal to one another: therefore CA is also equal to CB.

Therefore the three straight lines CA, AB, BC are equal to one another.

Therefore the triangle ABC is equilateral, and it has been constructed on the finite straight line AB.

Q.E.D.

The point about this proposition that is significant here is that there is nothing in Euclid's postulates to guarantee that the two circles AE and BD referred to in the proof do intersect. Euclid seems to treat it as obvious from the diagram that they do (as indeed it is), but in order for us to see this we must construct the circles in question, whether on paper or in our imagination. The diagram is therefore essential to the proof. Kant was thus right to say that in a Euclidean proof we are guided throughout by intuition: the proof depends not only on the possibility of the construction it describes but on properties which become apparent to us once we have carried out the construction — properties it has by virtue of its location in Euclidean space.

Kant's account of geometry may thus be summarized as follows. The proposition of pure geometry which we wish to prove is about not actual triangles but pure ones. In order to prove the proposition, we represent the pure triangle by means of an empirical triangle either on paper or in imagination. If we take care, in reasoning about this triangle, to make use only of its general properties — those it has simply by virtue of being a triangle — and to ignore the accidental features of the particular representation we have chosen, we can be confident that the conclusions we draw will be valid not merely for the empirical triangle before us but for the pure triangles the original proposition was about. It follows that the geometrical proposition is not merely true but a priori.

1.11 *Arithmetic as synthetic*

Kant tried hard to make his account of proofs in arithmetic parallel
the account of geometry we have just outlined. The first step in the
geometrical proof we considered earlier was to construct a triangle to
form the subject matter of the proof, on which various operations could
then be performed. What enabled it to establish a general proposition
about pure triangles was that we took care to use in our reasoning
only general properties which our constructed triangle had by virtue of
being situated in space. For this reason Kant was not very interested in
whether the triangle we actually used was empirical (e.g. on paper) or
imaginary rather than pure: in either case the proof would establish the
geometrical proposition as a priori. Kant displayed just the same lack
of interest in the nature of the objects which form the subject matter
of arithmetical proofs.

> The concept of 12 is by no means already thought in merely thinking this
> union of 7 and 5; and I may analyse my concept of such a possible sum as
> long as I please, still I shall never find the 12 in it. We have to go outside
> these concepts, and call in the aid of the intuition which corresponds to one
> of them, our five fingers, for instance, ... adding to the concept of 7, unit by
> unit, the five given in intuition. ... Arithmetical propositions are therefore
> always synthetic.[58]

The apparent subject matter of the proof may well be empirical ('our
five fingers, for instance'), but the proof is nevertheless able to establish its conclusion with apodictic certainty because the operations we
perform in the course of the proof are ones which do not depend for
their correctness on particular features of the subject matter we have
chosen.

   Although the proof does not depend on our having chosen our fingers
rather than our toes as exemplars of the number five, Kant does insist
that whatever exemplar we choose must be subject to the structure of
sensibility. In the case of our geometrical proof, of course, there is no
doubt that it is the spatial structure of sensibility alone that is relevant.
What about the arithmetical case?

   In his *Inaugural Dissertation* Kant said that the intellectual concept
of number 'demands for its concrete actualization the auxiliary notions
of time and space (in the successive addition and in the juxtaposition
of a plurality)',[59] implying that the spatial and temporal structure of
sensibility are both implicated in the process of counting. But by the
time of the *Critique* Kant treated time alone as supplying us with the

---

[58] *KrV*, B15–16. [59] *Inaug. Diss.*, § 12.

structure within which numbers are to be constructed. Indeed, many of his interpreters have had him advancing a neat parallelism: arithmetic depends on time just as geometry depends on space. The first of these interpreters was Johann Schultz, whose *Erläuterungen* we know Kant read and approved of:

Since geometry has space as its object, and arithmetic has numbers as its object, and counting comes about only by means of time, it becomes clear how geometry and arithmetic, i.e. pure mathematics, are possible: namely because a pure intuition, as the material of synthetic a priori propositions, lies at the basis of all mathematical concepts.[60]

Even if the parallelism was never for Kant quite this neat, Schultz's interpretation is lent support by a passage in the *Prolegomena* where Kant says that 'arithmetic *produces* its concepts of number through successive addition of units in time'.[61] This suggests that time plays a role in grounding proofs in arithmetic comparable to the role of space in geometry. But why? There is no doubt that counting (at least for larger numbers) takes time; but so does reasoning in general logic, and Kant was clear (at any rate when he wrote the *Critique*) that this does not show general reasoning to be *dependent* on time.[62] The examples Kant gives of intuitions which can be used to ground counting — 'the fingers, ... the beads of the abacus, ... strokes and points which can be placed before the eyes'[63] — suggest a dependence on space much more strongly than a dependence on time.

But the reason it was important for Kant that arithmetic should depend on the structure of sensibility was that this was what grounded its applicability. A geometrical proof performed on a triangle constructed in intuition justifies the application of the proposition proved to empirical triangles because they are subject to the very same spatial structure that regulates what is possible in the proof. In just the same way, Kant thought, the fact that the proof of a numerical equation is regulated by the structure of sensibility is what guarantees the application of the equation to counting empirical objects intuited as subject to that same structure.

The advantage, then, of supposing that it is the temporal structure of sensibility alone that is involved in legitimating the construction of numbers in intuition is that this ensures the applicability of arithmetic to non-spatial intuitions such as thoughts. It will nevertheless remain the case that 'we cannot subject any object other than an object of a possible *sensible* intuition to quantitative, numerical assessment.'[64]

[60]*Erläuterungen*, 24.   [61]*Proleg.*, § 10.   [62]See *KrV*, A152–3 = B191–3.   [63]Ibid., A240 = B299.   [64]Letter to Schultz, 25 Nov. 1788, in *Phil. Corr.*, 131.

Arithmetic is applicable to what we intuit because it depends on features of the structure that sensibility imposes on all our intuitions. Judged by the criteria we set ourselves at the outset, this account is as attractive as any that had yet been offered. In particular, the explanation it offers of the applicability of arithmetic is pleasingly direct: the dependence of arithmetic on sensibility explains its applicability to experience since human experience is subject to the structure our sensibility imposes. And this dependence explains its necessity too since we cannot think of any object except by means of an intuition that is subject to that same structure. But insofar as arithmetic depends on sensibility, it is thereby on Kant's account an activity distinctive of humanity — or at any rate of beings that share our forms of intuition. The necessity Kant found in arithmetic was therefore in Plato's terms human, not divine.

1.12 Arithmetic and sensibility

There is a terminological distinction which is helpful at this point. Euclid distinguishes between the assumptions he calls 'postulates', whose subject matter is specific to geometry, and those he calls 'common notions', which have quite general applicability. But we noted earlier how Euclid discriminated among the propositions he proved according to their form: existential propositions are called *problems*; universal ones are called *theorems*. By the seventeenth century it was common for mathematicians to distinguish in the same manner among the assumptions of a mathematical theory:

> According to some, the difference between axioms and postulates is analogous to that between theorems and problems; the former expressing truths which are self-evident and from which other propositions may be deduced; the latter, operations which may be easily performed, and by the help of which more difficult constructions may be effected.[65]

There is no trace of this distinction in the *Critique*, where Euclid's common notions are regarded as analytic and the synthetic principles of geometry are indiscriminately labelled as 'axioms', but shortly afterwards we find Schultz applying the distinction consistently in his second commentary on the *Critique*, the *Prüfung*.

Once we have the distinction in place we may say that the need for axioms as well as postulates is what shows that geometrical proofs are

---

[65]Wallis, *Opera*, II, 667–8.

grounded *throughout* in intuition. The postulates tell us what geometrical constructions are possible; however, some of the properties a Euclidean figure has do not flow from the mere possibility of the figure but depend in some further respect (encoded in the axioms) on the fact that the figure is located in space. Space contributes to geometrical constructions, in other words, something beyond their possibility alone.

Now the construction of the numbers involved in a numerical equation plays a rôle in grounding its truth, and hence its applicability, comparable to the rôle the diagram plays in a geometrical proof: the construction of a number in intuition exhibits its possibility just as the construction of a triangle does. Yet it is striking that Kant suggests nothing in his discussion of arithmetic comparable to his claim that geometrical proofs are guided throughout by intuition. He appeals to time (and perhaps to space) in order to ground the possibility of numbers, but he does not suggest that these forms have any further rôle in determining which numerical equations are true.

If this omission of a continuing rôle for intuition in regulating the progress of arithmetical proof is no mere accident but represents Kant's considered view, it could be expressed using the terminological distinction between axioms and postulates which we have been discussing by saying that whereas geometry has both axioms and postulates, arithmetic has only postulates. And this is indeed just what Kant said once he had read a draft of Schultz's book and therefore been introduced to the distinction in question:

Certainly arithmetic has no axioms, since its object is actually not any *quantum*, that is, any quantitative object of intuition, but rather *quantity as such*, that is, it considers the concept of a thing in general by means of quantitative determination. On the other hand, arithmetic has *postulates*, that is, immediately certain practical judgments. For if I regard $3 + 4$ as the setting of a problem, namely, to find a third number (7) such that the one number will be seen as the *complementum ad totum* of the other, the solution is found by the simplest operation, requiring no special prescription, namely, by the successive addition that the number 4 proposes simply as a continuation of the counting up to 3.[66]

If Kant is right in this, the options for a non-standard arithmetic are somewhat more restricted than for a non-Euclidean geometry. We humans represent the world within a structure that makes allowance for an infinity of possible locations, but there might be a being of a different sort, without our spatio-temporal way of structuring experience, whose sensibility represented to it only some finite number N of possible locations: such a being would have no way of constructing more

---

[66]Letter to Schultz, 25 Nov. 1788, in *Phil. Corr.*, 129–30.

than N objects in intuition and would therefore be unable to represent the possibility of any more objects to itself: its arithmetic would therefore be the system $\mathbf{EA}(N)$ that we have already encountered (§ 0.1) in connection with the arithmetic of South American tribes.

Now the Guaranies and the Aranda were not beings of the radically different kind currently under consideration: it would be ridiculous to infer from their lack of number words that they did not represent the world of experience as having more than five possible locations in it. The point is that these peoples are on Kant's account *capable* of acquiring a grasp of the whole of arithmetic, but as a matter of fact have not done so. A being with only five positions in its map of the world, on the other hand, would be in principle incapable of knowing that $7 + 5 = 12$.

The system $\mathbf{EA}(N)$ is a severely limited form of arithmetic, but it is not (for us humans) an incorrect one: the Guaranies do not deny, but merely fail to comprehend, the equation $7 + 5 = 12$. If it is right to suppose that we need appeal to the structure of experience only to license the constructions of the numbers and not to derive their properties once they have been constructed, it follows that a being which denied that $7 + 5 = 12$ would have to have not just a different sensibility from ours but a different understanding; the pure concepts by which it constituted its notion of an object would be different.

2

Grundlagen

It follows from Kant's account of the pure concepts of the understanding not only that such concepts are applicable to sensible intuitions, but also that these are all they are applicable to:

> When all is said and done, we cannot subject any object other than an object of a possible *sensible* intuition to quantitative, numerical assessment, and it thus remains a principle without exception that mathematics can be applied only to *sensibilia*. The magnitude of God's perfection, of duration, and so on, could only be expressed by means of the *totality* of reality; it could not possibly be represented by means of numbers.[1]

If our ability to count depends on the structure of space and time, this may explain its applicability to the things we intuit in space and time, but it will also by the same token limit its applicability to just those things: we shall, in short, be left without the ability to count anything that is not made up of spatio-temporal elements. This evidently did not bother Kant — indeed he took it as a point in favour of his explanation that it makes us unable to count God — but it has seemed implausible to many subsequent authors. The most notable of these was Frege, who published *Die Grundlagen der Arithmetik* (in English, 'The Foundations of Arithmetic'), a book arguing against Kant's conclusion, in 1884.

For Kant the denial that arithmetic has a content derived from intuition is tantamount to saying that it is merely explicative and cannot genuinely extend our knowledge. But not for Frege. What, then, did he take to be the source of its content? What he conjectured was that we need look no further for it than logic itself. He modestly claimed that this was 'not the first time that such a view has been put forward',[2] but in fact the conjecture was quite new: Frege was the first to put forward the thesis, now known as *logicism*, that logic is capable of grounding mathematical truths without thereby rendering them wholly trivial.

But it is hardly surprising that no one before Frege advanced this thesis: the notion that we can extend our knowledge just by thinking had

---

[1] *Phil. Corr.*, 131. [2] *Gl.*, §17.

only recently begun to seem at all plausible. This was a by-product of a transformation that took place during the nineteenth century not just in arithmetic but throughout pure mathematics. What characterized this transformation above all was an increase in rigour. Ever since Berkeley's scathing attack[3] of 1734 it had been plain that the triumphs of the differential and integral calculus rested on insecure foundations. Theorems were proved by appeal to notions (such as that of infinitesimal magnitude) for which no proper explanation had been given. Examples such as Bolzano's continuous nowhere differentiable function and Peano's space-filling curve showed, allegedly, that geometrical intuition is not always reliable.

Various mathematicians contributed to the reform. Bolzano proved the intermediate value theorem in 1817. Cauchy banished the non-rigorous manipulation of divergent series. Most prominent of all was Karl Weierstrass, who began to teach at the University of Berlin in 1856 and for the next thirty years gave courses of lectures on the calculus which progressively replaced the appeal to geometrical intuition and infinitesimals with logical reasoning that took the theory of real numbers as its base. These improvements in rigour, with which Frege was doubtless familiar, created the climate that made his work possible.

2.1 Axiomatization

Increasing rigour spawned increasing axiomatization. In geometry this was nothing new, of course: Euclid's *Elements* are the *locus classicus* for the axiomatic presentation of a mathematical theory. But Euclid's axiomatization was incomplete: as we saw in § 1.7, many of his proofs cannot be justified by appeal to the axioms alone but make essential appeal to properties of the diagram that accompanies them. Geometry was not axiomatized completely until 1899, when David Hilbert gave a list of twenty-one propositions, treating as primitive the concepts 'point', 'line', and 'plane' and the relation 'between', from which all the theorems in Euclid follow by logic alone without any further appeal to intuition. Thus, for example, in the construction of an equilateral triangle which we considered in § 1.10 the fact that the two circles AE and BD intersect follows from one of Hilbert's twenty-one propositions without the need for any further appeal at that point to properties of the diagram that accompanies the proof.

---

[3] *The Analyst.*

Whether Hilbert's work showed Kant to have been wrong to describe proof in geometry as 'a chain of inferences guided *throughout* by intuition'[4] depends on whether quantified logic is itself independent of intuition, but even if we granted this, it would not in itself do anything to disturb Kant's more fundamental contention that our geometrical knowledge is grounded in intuition and hence synthetic: if we wished to do that, we should have to argue in addition that the truth of Hilbert's *axioms* is independent of intuition.

The same point applies equally to arithmetic, of course: the mere existence of an axiom system is not in itself enough to refute Kant's claim that arithmetic is synthetic. Indeed there is a sense in which his account is already axiomatic: each numerical equation and inequation is to be regarded in effect as a postulate in its own right. But if we regard arithmetic in this way, it differs from geometry because its postulates are now particular and not general. Frege saw three difficulties with this.

First, because the postulates — the individual equations and inequations — are not general, there have to be infinitely many of them. How, then, do we grasp them? They cannot all be immediately evident to us since we are finite beings and cannot grasp an infinity of distinct facts. Frege thought it 'incongruous and paradoxical' for arithmetic to depend on infinitely many assumptions, since it 'conflicts with one of the requirements of reason, which must be able to embrace all first principles in one survey'.[5] If arithmetic is transparent to reason, as Frege maintained, the infinitely many individual equations cannot be at the very base of it: they must follow from a finite number of more fundamental principles, which we *are* capable of surveying. It is far from clear that this is a good objection to Kant, however. For one thing he was aware of the point.[6] And in any case the rule according to which addition is performed might indeed be finitely graspable, even though each numerical equation required a calculation according to the rule in order to determine its correctness. If so, it is not obvious that it would be wrong to describe the equations as postulates.

Frege presented his second objection to Kant as if it were quite distinct from the first, but it is really little more than a variant of it. The objection arise from the observation that the truth of an equation involving large numbers, such as

$$135664 + 37863 = 173527,$$

is not immediately evident but requires proof. So if *immediate* evidence

---

[4] *KrV*, A717=B745, my emphasis. [5] *Gl.*, § 5. [6] See *KrV*, A165=B205.

were ever to be a ground of arithmetical truth, it would only be in cases involving small numbers. But then our account of the ground of truth would differ according to the sizes of the numbers involved. That would be awkward since

it would scarcely be possible to draw any sharp boundary between them. If the numerical formulae were provable from, say, 10 on, we should ask with justice 'Why not from 5 on? or from 2 on? or from 1 on?'[7]

Like the earlier objection of which it is a variant this seems a little unfair to Kant. As we have seen, he held that the truth of any numerical equation, whether involving large numbers or small, becomes apparent to us only when we perform the necessary construction in intuition. Frege seems simply to have assumed without argument that in that case 'the correctness of our formula, if it were unprovable, would have to be evident right away',[8] but it is hard to see how this could be what Kant meant by calling postulates 'immediately certain practical judgements'.[9]

Frege's third objection is aimed not at Kant's account of numerical equations itself but at the difficulty involved in extending it. If arithmetic has particular numerical equations at its base, how is it possible to advance from these to generalizations about numbers?

One geometrical point, considered by itself, cannot be distinguished in any way from any other; the same applies to lines and planes. Only when several points, or lines or planes, are included together in a single intuition, do we distinguish them. In geometry, therefore, it is quite intelligible that general propositions should be derived from intuition; the points or lines or planes which we intuit are not really particular at all, which is what enables them to stand as representatives of the whole of their kind. But with the numbers it is different; each number has its own peculiarities. To what extent a given particular number can represent all the others, and at what point is own special character comes into play, cannot be laid down generally in advance.[10]

Frege's point is that if, for instance, each of the equations

$$5 + 7 = 7 + 5, \ 3 + 1 = 1 + 3, \text{ etc.}$$

is justified by a particular construction, a fresh explanation is required of how we can see all of them *as* instances of the commutative law for addition. Precisely *because* the postulates of arithmetic are particular and not general, they have nothing in common that would enable us to see them as instances of more general rules.

All these objections, whatever their merits, have as their target the particularity of Kant's justifications for numerical equations. So we

[7] *Gl.*, §5. [8] Ibid. [9] Letter to Schultz, 25 Nov. 1788, in *Phil. Corr.*, 131. [10] *Gl.*, §13.

could avoid them altogether if we succeeded in finding a method of deducing individual equations logically from a finite number of assumptions. This task was begun by Johann Schultz in his *Prüfung*, a commentary on the *Critique* published in 1789. Schultz states as a postulate the possibility of adding any two numbers together, and then gives two axioms, namely the associative and commutative laws for addition,

$$x + (y + z) = (x + y) + z$$
$$x + y = y + x$$

He then demonstrates how to prove individual equations in something like Leibniz's way, but avoiding Leibniz's fallacy by appeal to the axioms.

Schultz's work was an important first step towards the axiomatization of arithmetic, but it is nevertheless incomplete: although his axioms were general, he did not deal with how to derive from them conclusions which are themselves general, and he did not discuss multiplication at all. A much more detailed account was supplied by Hermann Grassmann in his *Lehrbuch der Arithmetik* of 1861, a textbook intended for use in Prussian secondary schools. Grassmann chose to present an account of the integers, not the natural numbers, but it is not hard to perform the conversion from one to the other. He assumed the recursion equations for addition and multiplication:

$$x + 0 = x;$$
$$x + (y + 1) = (x + y) + 1.$$
$$x . 0 = 0;$$
$$x . (y + 1) = (x . y) + x.$$

He then gave detailed derivations from the recursion equations of the properties of addition and multiplication (including the associative and commutative laws for additions that Schultz had taken as axioms). Grassmann's axioms were still incomplete, however: he did not — even implicitly — assume anything which would allow us to prove any *in*equalities, as we can see by observing that his axioms are trivially satisfied in a one-element set. They were incomplete in another respect too: Grassmann did not identify the principle of mathematical induction as an assumption. However, the central rôle of this principle is apparent if one studies Grassmann's proofs: he repeatedly proves general arithmetical laws by its means. This technique did not originate with him: the first examples of proofs by mathematical induction date from the seventeenth century, and by the middle of the nineteenth the method was a commonplace. So it is striking that Grassmann did not explicitly enunciate the central principle on which his treatment depended.

2.2 Arithmetic independent of sensibility

Grassmann's work fell short of providing a complete presentation of arithmetic as an axiomatic system, but it at least held out the prospect that such a presentation was possible. If so, it might, depending on its form, meet the objections Frege raised to Kant's treatment based on an infinite number of particular numerical equations. But the existence of an axiomatization, whatever its form, would not in itself settle whether arithmetic is dependent on sensibility as Kant maintained: it would show that the truths of arithmetic are deducible logically from a certain number of assumptions, but this would only transfer the question of their status to that of the assumptions. This is well illustrated by the case of Schultz, who despite giving an axiomatic treatment of arithmetic argued explicitly that the axioms and postulates depend on time: if that were correct, Kant's conclusion as to the nature of arithmetic would stand, even though our route to its truths would not be quite what he supposed.

But Frege's purpose in the *Grundlagen* was not just to object to details of Kant's account but to refute the claim on which it rests, that arithmetic depends on the spatio-temporal structure of experience. Now the most decisive way to refute such a claim would of course be to supply a positive account of arithmetical truth making no appeal to intuition; and a large part of the *Grundlagen* is taken up with outlining such an account. But Frege also made two direct objections to Kant's view that arithmetic depends on intuition.

The first objection is that we cannot have intuitions of large numbers since intuitions according to Kant are immediate whereas our grasp of a large number is not. There is obviously a close connection between this and one of the objections we considered earlier to taking numerical equations as postulates: postulates must be immediately evident truths, but our knowledge of an equation involving large numbers is mediated by the calculation required to check it.

Frege's argument may indeed show that we do not have intuitions of large numbers: it seems fairly clear that my grasp of a large number such as $10^{10^{10}}$ is not immediate, as it would have to be if it were an intuition. But Frege was wrong to think it followed that our grasp of large numbers is independent of intuition. After all, just the same argument can be used in the case of geometry, which Frege continued to think depends on our intuition of space. For if we cannot have an intuition of a large number N, we presumably cannot have an intuition of the regular N-gon either, and yet we can certainly know various geometrical theorems about that figure, such as that the sum of its interior angles is $(N - 2)\pi$. What Frege seems not to have allowed is that a Kantian account could *base* arithmetic on intuition without requiring my grasp of any particular number to be itself an intuition.

Frege's second objection to the dependence of arithmetic on intuition is more successful precisely because it makes the contrast with geometry that is lacking in his first objection. His point is in essence one that we have already noted when we addressed the question whether Kant wished to appeal to sensibility to ground the properties of numbers or only to ground their existence. We observed then that there seem to be more constraints on what is possible in arithmetic than in geometry.

For purposes of conceptual thought we can always assume the contrary of some one or other of the geometrical axioms, without involving ourselves in any self-contradictions when we proceed to our deductions, despite the conflict between our assumptions and our intuition. The fact that this is possible shows that the axioms of geometry are independent of one another and of the primitive laws of logic, and consequently are synthetic. Can the same be said of the fundamental propositions of the science of number? Here, we have only to try denying any one of them, and complete confusion ensues. Even to think at all seems no longer possible.[11]

This is a powerful thought which it is hard to gainsay. We can have some success in imagining worlds with radically different spatial geometries from ours, but if we try to imagine a world in which $2 + 2 = 5$ then, as Frege says, 'complete confusion ensues'. This of course reflects the constraint we placed on our enquiry at the start that it should respect our sense that arithmetic as it is standardly practised is necessary. Notice too that although Frege knew nothing of non-standard models of arithmetic, it is hard to see how his point — that arithmetic is independent of sensibility — could be threatened by their existence: what is meant by calling a model non-standard is that it shares all the properties of the standard model that can be stated in the formal language under consideration but differs from it in some other respect. So conceiving of a non-standard model does not involve denying any of the 'fundamental propositions of the science of number' unless those propositions cannot be stated in the language.

[11]Ibid., § 14.

2.3 *The* Begriffsschrift

Frege's conclusion, then, was that arithmetic is in a sense more general, since more widely applicable, than geometry.

Empirical propositions hold good of what is physically or psychologically actual, the truths of geometry govern all that is spatially intuitable, whether actual or product of our fancy. The wildest visions of delirium, the boldest inventions of legend and poetry, where animals speak and stars stand still, where men are turned to stone and trees turn into men, where the drowning haul themselves up out of swamps by their own topknots — all these remain, so long as they remain intuitable, still subject to the axioms of geometry. ... The truths of arithmetic govern all that is numerable. This is the widest domain of all; for to it belongs not only the actual, not only the intuitable, but everything thinkable.[12]

It is evident what path Frege's thought is taking here: he is suggesting that the scope of arithmetic is just the same as that of logic. 'Should not the laws of numbers, then, be connected very intimately with the laws of thought?'[13] If we could show that arithmetic is part of logic, its applicability to 'everything thinkable' would be thereby explained.

The truths of arithmetic would then be related to those of logic in much the same way as the theorems of geometry to the axioms. Each one would contain concentrated within it a whole series of deductions for future use and the use of it would be that we need no longer make the deductions one by one, but can express simultaneously the result of the whole series. If this be so, then indeed the prodigious development of arithmetical studies, with their multitudinous applications, will suffice to put an end to the widespread contempt for analytic judgements and to the legend of the sterility of logic.[14]

It may have been Frege who finally killed off the 'legend of the sterility of logic', but in truth it had been dying for some time: the mathematical achievements of the nineteenth century, with which we began this chapter, showed vividly that more can be achieved with logic alone than Kant ever imagined. What is undoubtedly due to Frege, though, is the credit for being the first to analyse the reason: it was the power of quantified logic with multiple generality to reveal hidden complexities in our concepts that enabled mathematicians such as Weierstrass to prove logically so much that had previously been justified by direct appeal to intuitions.

Here formalization, which was part of the general trend towards rigour, was undoubtedly important. Two motives, one practical and one theoretical, were at work. The invention of clever and suggestive

---

[12]Ibid.   [13]Ibid.   [14]Ibid., §17.

symbolization (for which Peano and Whitehead had a particular talent) could make arguments clearer and mathematical discovery easier. And formalization was an aid to rigour because once all the stages of an argument were formalized as symbolic manipulations according to rules, the question of whether the argument is valid reduced to that of the correctness of the symbolic rules. Of especial significance in this regard, given the central role of logic in our enquiry, is the formalization of quantified logic.

The formalization of syllogistic logic was begun by Aristotle himself when he introduced two of its central ideas: using letters to express generality; and listing a series of inference rules adequate to derive all the correct inferences of the system. Nascent in Aristotle, too, is the notion of a formal language distinct from natural language whose syntax could be described with complete precision. But it was Leibniz who noted the analogy between arithmetic and the manipulations of language, and saw in principle how to reduce the latter to the former.

The explicit presentation of Aristotelian logic as a formal system in the modern sense emerged when Boole and Schröder transformed this analogy between arithmetic and language to a wider analogy between algebra and logic. The decisive step, though, was undoubtedly the formalization of quantified logic. This was carried out by Frege, who in 1879 published *Begriffsschrift* (Conceptual Notation), a monograph containing a description of a formalized logical symbolism in which, for instance, the expressions we nowadays distinguish as

$$(x)(\exists y)f(x,y) \quad \text{and} \quad (\exists y)(x)f(x,y)$$

are written as

$$-\!\!\!\!a\!-\!\!\!\!\top\!\!\!\!-b\!-\!\!\!\!\top\!\!f(a,b) \quad \text{and} \quad \top\!\!\!\!-b\!-\!\!\!\!\top\!\!\!\!-a\!-\!\!f(a,b)$$

There are two aspects to the formalization of logic: the formalization of the means of expression (formation rules) and the formalization of deduction (transformation rules). It is worth distinguishing them. Although it is hard to imagine how the rules of deduction could be fully formalized before the expressions to which the rules are to be applied were formally describable, the converse is quite possible: one can formalize the formation rules without formalizing the transformation rules. For our purposes here it is fully formalized systems — systems with formal formation rules *and* formal transformation rules — that are of interest; if only the formalization of the notation were in question, Frege's achievement would not have been especially significant. This is not because of the fact that in practical terms it was a total failure —

no one else ever used it — but rather because the invention of quantifier notation did not enable Frege to express what had previously been inexpressible: the thoughts involved can quite easily be expressed in more or less idiomatic English (or German). What is important is rather the extent to which formalization made plain the sorts of logical reasoning that cannot be reduced to Aristotelian syllogisms. It became apparent to Frege that polyadic logic is ampliative in Kant's sense. We are not merely, as in the Aristotelian case,

taking out of the box again what we have just put into it. The conclusions we draw ... extend our knowledge. ... The truth is that they are contained in the definitions, but as plants are contained in their seeds, not as beams are contained in a house.[15]

Now the distinctive feature of reasoning that is ampliative rather than merely explicative is that it depends on objects as its subject matter. If polyadic logic is ampliative, it must therefore depend on objects in a way that syllogistic logic does not. The feature which makes this dependence manifest is the variable. Variables are what enable logic to handle the two features that give it its distinctive complexity (and therefore its power), polyadic predicates and nested quantification. Thus, for example, the distinct concepts of murder and suicide can both be extracted from the sentence 'Cassius killed Cassius' by using variables to differentiate between 'x killed y' and 'x killed x'.[16] Aristotelian reasoning, on the other hand, is confined to what we nowadays call pure monadic logic, i.e. logic involving only sentences with monadic predicates and no constants. Any such sentence can be rewritten straightforwardly to eliminate nested quantifications, at which point the use of variables to differentiate between argument places becomes unnecessary. Indeed when Aristotelian reasoning is represented by means of Boolean algebra it is customary to omit the variables entirely. Thus the Kantian analytic is a logic of inclusion of concepts thought of quite independent of any possibility of their application to objects.

The point to stress, then, is that it is not the shift from concepts to relations that is significant in Frege's logic but the introduction of variables. An unquantified logic of relations was developed by the Megarians, and even if Kant was unaware of this logic he would not have denied the existence of a relationship, however regrettable, between a murderer and his victim. The difficulty was rather that without the device of variables there could be for Kant (and others of his day) no logical connection between murder and suicide.

[15] Ibid., § 88.   [16] Cf. Dummett, *Frege: Philosophy of Language*, 31.

2.4 Frege's conception of analyticity

If we succeed in showing that arithmetic is part of logic, that does not in itself contradict Kant's claim that arithmetic is genuinely ampliative, since logic — not syllogistic logic but the polyadic quantified logic of the *Begriffsschrift*— is capable of extending our knowledge. Up to this point, then, there is nothing in Frege's positive account that Kant need disagree with. But it was Frege's intention to establish, contrary to Kant, that arithmetic is independent of intuition. To do that he had to make the further claim that polyadic logic, despite being ampliative, is nevertheless analytic, by which he meant independent of intuition.

Although Frege was here in explicit disagreement with Kant, he tried to minimize the extent of his disagreement: the tenor of Frege's remarks is that it was only Kant's ignorance of polyadic logic that prevented him from realizing that analytic reasoning can be ampliative.[17] As we have seen, Kant called anything deducible from tautologies by logic analytic, and anything else synthetic. Since Frege did not propose to change the *wording* of this definition, he could claim that he did not 'mean to assign a new sense to these terms, but only to state accurately what earlier writers, Kant in particular, have meant by them.'[18] But by understanding the word 'logic' in the definition to mean the polyadic logic of the *Begriffsschrift* instead of the monadic logic of Aristotle, Frege did vastly enlarge the scope of the term. Frege thus hoped to show

how pure thought (regardless of any content given through the senses or even given a priori through an intuition) is able, all by itself, to produce from the content which arises from its own nature judgements which at first glance seem to be possible only on the grounds of some intuition.[19]

The keystone, then, is Frege's claim that even polyadic logic does not depend on intuition. Given the centrality of this claim to his project, it is perhaps unfortunate that Frege did not argue for it in much detail. At this point, indeed, he offered no more by way of explanation than a vague analogy. 'We can', he said, 'compare this to condensation by which we succeed in changing air, which appears to be nothing to the childlike mind, into a visible drop-forming fluid.'[20]

Frege did, however, correctly see that his view of logic as independent of intuition had at its root a difference between his understanding of the word 'object' and Kant's.[21] For Kant, as we have seen, our contact with an object is always via intuitions of it. It is essential to our grasp of what an object is that it is possible for distinct intuitions to be of the

---

[17]See *Gl.*, §88. [18]Ibid., §3. [19]*Bs.*, §23. [20]Ibid. [21]See *Gl.*, §89.

same object. In Frege's hands this intuitive criterion of objecthood is transformed into a logical one. 'If we are to use the symbol a to signify an object, we must have a criterion for deciding in all cases whether b is the same as a, even if it is not always in our power to apply this criterion.'[22] What matters here, though, is not this transformation of a psychological criterion into a logical one, but the question whether our representations require anything further in order to be representations of the same object. According to Kant we can understand how it is possible for two intuitions to represent the same object only because we have a grasp of a structure — the spatio-temporal structure supplied by sensibility — within which we locate the intuitions: he did indeed believe that we cannot think of an object independent of thinking something about it, but he did not believe that we can obtain a conception of an object merely by the act of thinking on its own. On Frege's conception, on the other hand, the thought is indeed in this sense prior to the object.

At this point, then, Frege's account becomes radically unKantian, for it allows the new possibility that the structure of thought can provide us with objects independent of sensibility. At first sight it might seem that Kant could have no response that does not make logic depend implausibly on the structure of sensibility for its validity. Is this correct?

We should at once concede to Kant — what is surely true — that we could not communicate with a being whose sensibility had a radically different structure from ours: it would not, to use Wittgenstein's phrase, share our form of life. But the issue at stake here is not whether we can communicate with it, about logic or about anything else, but what judgements it is capable of making. We conceive of quantified logic as dealing in a wholly general fashion with how objects behave, not with how they behave when embedded in the spatio-temporal structure that human sensibility is wont to supply.

It seems as if a possible relief from this difficulty is afforded by taking the structure of sensibility as schematic in the Kantian account of quantified logic, which will then be true for finite intelligences of any sort by virtue of the structure of their sensibility. We shall, of course, still need a Transcendental Deduction to guarantee that for intelligences of any sort the pure concepts of the understanding are applicable to the objects which sensibility represents to *them*. But this does not force us to maintain implausibly that logic depends in some way on time.

The relief is largely illusory, however. If we treat the structure of sensibility as schematic, that merely obscures the fact that what grounds logical reasoning is different for beings with different structures. *Our*

[22] Ibid., §62.

logical reasoning is still tied to *our* sensibility and therefore has no validity outside its limits. It can be of no use to us (because strictly we are not in a position to know) that other beings reason similarly in relation to their sensibilities, because the similarity in question is one that could only be apparent from a perspective outside sensibility altogether. As Kant remarks, 'we cannot form the least conception of any other possible understanding ... that may possess an underlying mode of sensible intuition which is different in kind from that in space and time.'[23]

The Fregean response will presumably be to say that although we can, when arguing within the realm of Aristotelian syllogistic, ignore the argument places in the concepts involved, it is nevertheless essential to these concepts that they should *have* argument places. The notion of a concept makes no sense independent of the possibility of uniting the concept with an object to form a judgement. If concepts are like rules, judgements are like applications of rules; it is coherent — the thought runs — to imagine grasping a rule without being able to tell when to apply it, but it is not coherent to imagine grasping a rule while yet being altogether unaware that what the rule is for is to be applied.

I have described this as a Fregean response, but it would be more accurate to call it Frege's conception recast in Kantian terms. For Frege the observation that the notion of a concept presupposes that of an object did not require argument since it was a complete triviality. The reason was that his account proceeded in the opposite direction from Kant's (and Aristotle's):

Instead of putting a judgement together out of an individual as subject and an already previously formed concept as predicate, we do the opposite and arrive at a concept by splitting up the content of possible judgement. Of course, if the expression of the content of possible judgement is to be analysable in this way, it must already be itself articulated. We may infer from this that at least the properties and relations which are not further analysable must have their own simple designations. But it doesn't follow from this that the ideas of these properties and relations are formed apart from objects: on the contrary they arise simultaneously with the first judgement in which they are ascribed to things.[24]

When Frege's thought is expressed in this way, his divergence from Kant emerges clearly. For Frege what is objective is now simply anything which can be united with a concept to form a judgement:

What are things independent of the reason? To answer that would be as much as to judge without judging, or to wash the fur without wetting it.[25]

[23] *KrV*, B139. [24] *Posthumous Writings*, 17. [25] *Gl.*, § 26.

The world is shot through with the structure of thought: it is, in Frege's striking metaphor, already soaking wet. The conception presented here of the world we reason about as necessarily subject to the structure of thought is of course thoroughly Kantian, but Frege has now abandoned Kant's idea that, insofar as the mind supplies objects to form the content of reasoning, it can do so only as subject to the structure of sensibility.

We have arrived now at what was fundamentally new in Frege's logicism. Kant had conceived of the objects we make judgements about as necessarily subject to the structure sensibility imposes, and had therefore conceived of us as constrained in reasoning about these objects to construct them in intuition in order to warrant to ourselves their possibility relative to this structure. According to Frege we are subject to no such constraint: there is no further criterion that needs to be satisfied by a term in order for it to denote an object than that it should function linguistically in the correct manner, since objects are not required to be subject to any circumambient structure.

Frege enshrined this doctrine that there are no more constraints on objecthood than those of logic in what is now known as the *context principle*. In the Introduction to the *Grundlagen* he mentions three principles that are to guide his enquiry and the context principle is one of them. It enjoins us 'never to ask for the meaning of a word in isolation but only in the context of a proposition.' This principle is stated not only here in the Introduction but twice in the main text and again in the conclusion.[26] Frege stresses that 'only by adhering to this can we ... avoid a physical view of number without slipping into a psychological view of it.'[27] The purpose of the context principle is thus at this stage essentially a negative one, to rule out as irrelevant the complaint that our stipulations have not supplied us with a mental idea to go with them:

Only in a proposition have the words really a meaning. It may be that mental pictures float before us all the while, but these need not correspond to the logical elements in the judgement. It is enough if the proposition taken as a whole has a sense; it is this that confers on its parts also their content.[28]

But the context principle has a positive application too: if we introduce into our language what is intended to be a proper name and succeed in giving a sense to all the identity statements formulable using it, we have thereby ensured that it is indeed a genuine proper name and refers to what Frege calls a 'self-subsistent object'.

[26]Ibid., §§60, 62, 106. [27]Ibid., §106. [28]Ibid., §60.

2.5 Numerically definite quantifiers

So much for generalities. What remains is to provide an account of the natural numbers that enables us to treat arithmetical truths as logical. One strategy that seems on the face of it to have much to recommend it is that of defining not the numbers themselves but the numerically definite quantifiers. The proposal is that we define

$$(\exists^0 x)Fx =_{\mathrm{Df}} \sim(\exists x)Fx \tag{1}$$

$$(\exists^{n+1} x)Fx =_{\mathrm{Df}} (\exists y)(Fy \,.\, (\exists^n x)(Fx \,.\, x \neq y)), \tag{2}$$

reading '$(\exists^n x)Fx$' as 'The number n belongs to the concept F'. If we then follow Leibniz in defining

$$1 = 0 + 1, \quad 2 = 1 + 1, \quad 3 = 2 + 1, \quad 4 = 3 + 1,$$

we can prove logically that, for example,

$$((\exists^2 x)Fx \,.\, (\exists^2 x)Gx \,.\, (\exists^0 x)(Fx\,.\,Gx)) \supset (\exists^4 x)(Fx \vee Gx),$$

which we could reasonably enough take to be the meaning of '$2 + 2 = 4$'. In this way, indeed, all of the *positive* part $\mathbf{EA}_0^+$ of quantifier-free elementary arithmetic (the equalities but not the inequalities) could with a little logical ingenuity be made to follow.

What is noteworthy straight away about this proposal is that it does not amount to an explicit definition of the numerals: it gives a sense to a numeral 'n' not on its own but only in the context of phrases such as 'The number n belongs to the concept F'. But this is not in itself any reason for Frege to reject the proposal. We have seen already that Frege treated the context principle as fundamental to his project, and it might seem nicely suited to the task of licensing just such contextual stipulations as this.

Even so, Frege did not adopt the proposal to introduce numerals in the context of numerically definite quantifiers. His reason was that

we can never — to take a crude example — decide by means of our definitions whether any concept has the number JULIUS CAESAR belonging to it, or whether that same familiar conqueror of Gaul is a number or not.[29]

This difficulty is nowadays known, because of Frege's 'crude example', as the *Julius Caesar problem*. Notice, though, that it is not an objection to the numerically definite quantifiers themselves, but only to their use as a route to obtaining numbers as objects. Equations (1) and (2)

[29] Ibid., § 56.

are perfectly respectable definitions, and may indeed be regarded as contextual stipulations contributing to the senses of components of their *definienda*, but they do not justify regarding the numerals as proper names. If some terms

are to be understood as standing for self-subsistent objects ... that is enough to give us a class of propositions which must have a sense, namely those which express our recognition of [one of them] as the same again. If we are to use the symbol a to signify an object, we must have a criterion for deciding in all cases whether b is the same as a, even if it is not always in our power to apply this criterion.[30]

In order that a term should be understood it is by the context principle sufficient that the sentences in which it can occur have been given a sense. But if what the term is to be understood as referring to is a self-subsistent object, it is necessary that among the sentences which have been given a sense are all the identity statements relating the term to any other antecedently understood name. What the example of Julius Caesar is intended to illustrate is that the definitions of the numerically definite quantifiers have not given any sense to 'mixed' identities with a numeral on one side and a term of another sort (such as 'Julius Caesar') on the other: the definitions therefore do not suffice to ensure that the numerals refer to 'self-subsistent objects'.

It is only an illusion that we have defined 0 and 1; in reality we have only fixed the sense of the phrases

'the number 0 belongs to'

'the number 1 belongs to'

but we have no authority to pick out the 0 and 1 here as self-subsistent objects that can be recognized as the same again.[31]

But what reason do we have to think that numbers *are* 'self-subsistent objects'? This claim is central to Frege's account. It is therefore astonishing how weak his argument for it is:

Precisely because it forms only an element in what is asserted, the individual number shows itself for what it is, a self-subsistent object. I have already drawn attention to the fact that we speak of 'the number 1', where the definite article serves to class it as an object. In arithmetic this self-subsistence comes out at every turn, as for example in the identity $1 + 1 = 2$.[32]

Number words have in ordinary language both an adjectival and a substantival use.[33] It is quite correct to say, as Frege does elsewhere, that the adjectival use can be explained in terms of the substantival one;

---

[30]Ibid., §62. [31]Ibid., §56. [32]Ibid., §57. [33]Cf. Dummett, *Frege: Philosophy of mathematics*, ch. 9.

that, 'for example, the proposition "Jupiter has four moons" can be converted into "the number of Jupiter's moons is four".'[34] Frege intended the Julius Caesar problem to be a bar to the converse — to explaining the substantival use in terms of the adjectival one — but it succeeds in this only if the grammar of the substantival use is not misleading, i.e. if number terms used substantivally do indeed refer to objects. Frege had just recommended us to regard the grammar of the *adjectival* use as misleading. It is therefore remarkable that he did not consider the corresponding possibility that it is the substantival use which misleads, especially since it was one of his three fundamental principles 'never to lose sight of the distinction between concept and object'.[35]

One way of seeing more clearly what is involved in defining numbers by means of numerically definite quantifiers is to split the procedure into two parts. The first part involves writing '$\mathbf{n}(F)$' instead of '$(\exists^n x)Fx$', so that (1) and (2) become

$$\mathbf{0}(F) =_{\mathrm{Df}} \sim(\exists x)Fx;$$
$$s(\mathbf{n})(F) =_{\mathrm{Df}} (\exists y)(Fy \, . \, \mathbf{n}(\lambda x(Fx \, . \, x \neq y)).$$

(Here '$\lambda x \ldots x \ldots$' is a notation for the concept under which fall just those x such that $\ldots x \ldots$.) These are now not *implicit* definitions of the objects 0, 1, etc., but *explicit* definitions of the concepts $\mathbf{0}$, $\mathbf{1}$, etc. They give criteria for deciding whether any first-level concept F falls under these second-level concepts.

The second part of the procedure is to associate with each numerical concept $\mathbf{n}$ obtained in this way an object n. The only constraint the account places on our choice of n is that the objects associated with numerical concepts should be the same if and only if the concepts are coextensive.

If we were unpersuaded by Frege's argument from the surface grammar of our talk about numbers to the conclusion that numbers are objects, we might indeed consider the possibility that numbers *are* second-level concepts, i.e. that the second stage of the procedure can simply be dropped. The question whether Julius Caesar is a number now cannot even be posed because it is ungrammatical.

We are not quite out of the woods yet, though. If numbers are second-level concepts, we cannot ask whether a particular object is a number, but we can ask whether a particular second-level concept is one. If nationalities are first-level concepts under which people may fall, we are

[34] *Gl.*, § 57. [35] Ibid., intro.

entitled to ask, for instance, whether the second-level concept of European nationality is a number. Our definition of numbers as numerically definite quantifiers does not answer this question directly because it does not tell us what we mean in general by **n**. It provides us only with explicit definitions of the concepts **0**, **1**, **2**, and so on. We can therefore answer negatively each in turn of the questions

Is **0** the concept of European nationality?

Is **1** the concept of European nationality?

And so on.

But to convert these into an understanding of a variable **n** ranging over all of them, and hence to conclude that our concept is not a natural number, we need to explain what 'and so on' means here.

There is a technical device which answers this difficulty. We can define explicitly what it is for **m** to be a number, namely that **m** should belong to the ancestral of **0** with respect to s. In symbols, **m** is a number if

$$(X)((X(\mathbf{0}) . (\mathbf{n})(X(\mathbf{n}) \supset X(s(\mathbf{n})))) \supset X(\mathbf{m})),$$

where the variable X ranges over third-level concepts. Frege was familiar with this manœuvre. He had defined the general notion of the ancestral of a relation in *Begriffsschrift*, and he made use elsewhere in *Grundlagen* of what is in essence the device we have outlined.

This trick answers the immediate difficulty: by its means we could derive logically a few properties of the numbers, thought of as second-level concepts. But in order to make any significant progress with the proposal we should need to supply a criterion of identity for the second-level concepts involved. And this is just what Frege did not have when he wrote the *Grundlagen*: there the word *Begriff* fluctuates in usage between what we should now distinguish as objective concepts and their senses; he did not yet have a theory on which concepts could have identity conditions or anything analogous to them. Eventually Frege did adopt such a theory: we shall consider it in § 4.4, at which point we shall be in a position to return to this proposal of treating numbers as second-level concepts and assess its chances of success more fully.

2.6 The numerical equivalence

The attempt to introduce numbers by means of numerically definite quantifiers was in any case a failure if, as Frege thought, numbers are self-subsistent objects. There is a sense, though, in which the attempt was nonetheless on what he took to be the right track, because it made use of the technique of contextual stipulation. Explicit definitions cannot give us anything new: they merely provide us, in the *definiendum*, with a new way of describing something which was already available to us via the *definiens*. By contrast Frege thought that contextual stipulations could give us access to objects not independently available to us, while still making no appeal to intuition. He therefore went on to consider an alternative contextual stipulation, namely that the number of Fs should be said to be equal to the number of Gs if and only if the Fs and the Gs are equinumerous. To express this in symbols we introduce a term-forming operator N, so that '$NxFx$' is to denote the number of Fs. The proposal is then that this should be defined contextually by the stipulation

$$NxFx = NxGx \equiv F \sim G, \tag{3}$$

where '$F \sim G$', which is read as 'F is equinumerous with G', is defined to mean

$$(\exists R)((x)(Fx \supset (\exists!y)(Gy . xRy)) . (y)(Gy \supset (\exists!x)(Fx . xRy))). \tag{4}$$

(In words: there is a relation which relates each F to exactly one G and by which each G is related to exactly one F.)

The equivalence (3), by which it is proposed that numbers should be contextually defined, has gone under various names in the literature. Boolos calls it 'Hume's principle', taking his lead from Frege himself,[36] who quotes Hume: 'When two numbers are so combined as that the one has always an unit answering to every unit of the other, we pronounce them equal.'[37] Dummett, on the other hand, is strongly opposed to calling it this, since he thinks that 'it credits Hume with an idea he probably did not have and certainly did not state',[38] namely that equinumerosity should be defined by the existence of a one-to-one correspondence as in (4) above. Dummett remarks that this definition is itself open to question, and that if another way of defining equinumerosity were to be found, much of what follows from adopting (3) would remain intact. Although this is true, it will not be of much relevance here since I shall not be considering the objections which have been advanced (notably by Husserl and Waismann) to (4) as a correct definition of equinumerosity: I shall simply assume without argument that it *is* a correct

---

[36] Ibid., § 63. [37] *Treatise*, bk. 1, part iii, § 1. [38] 'Neo-Fregeans: In bad company?'

definition. I shall nevertheless defer to Dummett's terminological sensibilities and call the equivalence (3), read as mentioning the concept of equinumerosity thus defined, the *numerical equivalence*.

Frege states this equivalence in § 63 of *Grundlagen*. In § 74 *et seq.* he gives a series of definitions, closely mirroring the account of numbers as concepts which we briefly considered at the end of § 2.5, which can be summarized symbolically as follows:

$$0 =_{\mathrm{Df}} \mathrm{N}x(x \neq x)$$
$$1 =_{\mathrm{Df}} \mathrm{N}x(x = 0)$$
$$m \, S \, n \equiv_{\mathrm{Df}} (\exists F)(\exists x)(Fx \,.\, \mathrm{N}yFy = n \,.\, \mathrm{N}y(Fy \,.\, y \neq x) = m)$$
$$x < y \equiv_{\mathrm{Df}} (F)((a)(x \, S \, a \supset Fa) \,.\, (d)(a)(Fd \,.\, d \, S \, a \supset Fa) \supset Fy)$$
$$x \leq y \equiv_{\mathrm{Df}} (x < y \lor x = y)$$
$$\mathrm{nat}(x) \equiv_{\mathrm{Df}} 0 \leq x$$

Frege then notes a few arithmetical laws that can be deduced logically from these definitions:

$$0 \, S \, 1 \tag{5}$$
$$(F)(\mathrm{N}xFx = 1 \equiv \exists!xFx) \tag{6}$$
$$(x)(y)(z)(x \, S \, z \,.\, y \, S \, z \supset x = y) \tag{7}$$
$$(x)(y)(z)(x \, S \, y \,.\, x \, S \, z \supset y = z) \tag{8}$$
$$(x)((\mathrm{nat}(x) \,.\, x \neq 0) \supset (\exists y) \, y \, S \, x) \tag{9}$$

Moreover, although he does not point this out explicitly, his definition of number is precisely designed to ensure that the principle of mathematical induction is trivially valid:

$$(F)(F0 \,.\, (x)(Fx \,.\, x \, S \, y \supset Fy) \supset (x)(\mathrm{nat}(x) \supset Fx)).$$

Finally Frege devotes some space to sketching a proof of the following law:

$$(n)(\mathrm{nat}(n) \supset n \, S \, \mathrm{N}x(x \leq n)).$$

This last result provides us with a particularly graphic demonstration of the power of the numerical equivalence in second-order logic, since it follows from it that every natural number has a successor, and hence, because of (7), that there are infinitely many natural numbers.

Frege held that the source of the concept of number is the notion of cardinality. In keeping with this view he did not, among the arithmetical laws he singled out for mention, distinguish those that do not mention number terms. If he had done so, they would have been recognizably a variant of what are now called Peano's axioms. What Frege sketched in this part of *Grundlagen* is thus a proof of what Boolos has proposed calling *Frege's theorem*, i.e. the proposition that the natural numbers, if introduced into second-order logic by means of the numerical equivalence, satisfy Peano's axioms.

What is most striking about this part of *Grundlagen*, though, is not what it contains but what it omits. Once we have Peano's axioms, it is of course possible to define the functions of addition and multiplication and to prove their basic arithmetical properties. Yet Frege neither sketches a proof of this nor even states that it can be done. The significance of this is apt to escape the modern reader, who is likely to be familiar at least with the possibility of this development, if not with its details. Frege could scarcely have taken this knowledge for granted in his contemporary audience, though, since the first demonstration (Dedekind's) did not appear in print until 1888. The nearest thing to what Frege required that had yet appeared was the detailed deduction in Grassmann's *Lehrbuch* of the laws of arithmetic from a rather short list of basic assumptions. Frege was undoubtedly familiar with this work — he criticized it in the *Grundlagen*— but if we simply append Grassmann's work to Frege's there is a lacuna at the join. What is missing is a justification of the recursive definitions of addition and multiplication. Grassmann simply took these definitions as given: this is precisely what Frege criticized him for. But the treatment of the definition of functions by recursion is in fact the least obvious part of the deduction of arithmetic from Peano's axioms: as we shall see in the next chapter, it is one of the most impressive achievements of Dedekind's later work. So perhaps the reason for Frege's sudden silence at this point is that he had by then seen the difficulty but not yet worked out the solution.

2.7 Frege's explicit definition

Despite its remarkable power Frege did not adopt the contextual definition of numbers by means of the numerical equivalence. This should by now not surprise us. In § 2.5 we saw that he rejected the contextual definition of numbers by means of numerically definite quantifiers because that definition failed to settle whether Julius Caesar is a natural number. The contextual definition now under consideration evidently suffers from precisely the same defect. The numerical equivalence lays down a condition for the truth of what is apparently an identity sentence, 'NxFx = NxGx'. What it does not do is to settle the meaning more generally of sentences of the form 'NxFx = q' where 'q' is a singular term, except for the one case where q is given in the form of 'NxGx'.

The similarity between the two proposals for introducing numbers that we have been considering — by means of numerically definite quantifiers, and via the numerical equivalence — is in fact even closer than appears at first sight. This will emerge clearly if we express them in a slightly different way. Let us use the term *equinumerosity concept* for any second-level concept such that all the first-level concepts falling under it are equinumerous. The second proposal, which took numbers to be objects subject to the contextual condition encapsulated in the numerical equivalence, amounted to the requirement that we associate with each equinumerosity concept an object in such a way that concepts are associated with distinct objects unless they are coextensive. The first proposal, on the other hand, gave the contextual condition in terms of numerically definite quantifiers. It amounted to defining explicitly a sequence **0**, **1**, **2**, ... of so-called numerical concepts and then picking for each such concept **n** a corresponding object n: once again the only constraint was that numerical concepts that are not coextensive had to have distinct objects attached to them. The connection between the proposals is apparent when we notice that **0**, **1**, **2**, etc. are all, in the terminology we have just adopted, equinumerosity concepts. So the second procedure is simply a generalization of the first. (It is strictly more general because it can be used to give an account of infinite cardinal numbers while the first cannot.)

With both the contextual definitions shown by the Julius Caesar problem to be insufficient to license us to regard numbers as objects, Frege had to fall back after all on an explicit definition. What he required, let us recall, was a way of associating with each equinumerosity concept an object in such a way that distinct concepts give rise to distinct objects. Frege took it that there was available a general method of doing this not just for equinumerosity concepts but for all concepts whatever: the method is to associate with each concept the class of all objects falling under it, which Frege called the *extension* of the concept. If, as is nowadays usual, we write '$\{x : Fx\}$' for the extension of the concept F, we may express the assumption Frege made about extensions — that concepts which are not coextensive have distinct extensions — as follows:

$$\{x : Fx\} = \{x : Gx\} \equiv (x)(Fx \equiv Gx).$$

Let us call this the *extensional equivalence* by analogy with the term
'numerical equivalence' introduced earlier. Frege then defined the number of Fs to be the extension of the concept 'equinumerous with the
concept F'. In symbols, this amounts to the following explicit definition:

$$N x F x =_{\mathrm{Df}} \{ X : X \sim F \}.$$

It is then straightforward to deduce from the extensional equivalence
that

$$N x F x = N x G x \equiv F \sim G.$$

The numerical equivalence thus emerges as a consequence of the explicit definition. But now that we have the equivalence, no longer as
a stipulation but as a theorem, the deduction of Peano's axioms can
proceed as described in § 2.6.

Frege's explicit definition solves the Julius Cæsar problem, but in
doing so it encounters what is in a sense its obverse. The Julius Cæsar
problem was the worry that the numerical equivalence did not determine
which objects the natural numbers are, and hence did not suffice to
secure a reference for numerical terms. In order to overcome it Frege
picked some objects to serve as references for these terms. The ones
he picked have, he believed, the advantage of being logical objects, so
their properties are derivable by purely logical means. In particular,
it is straightforward to prove that the numerical equivalence holds of
them. Our new difficulty is that, as Frege conceded, there are many
other explicit definitions from which the numerical equivalence could
be derived:

This way of getting over the difficulty cannot be expected to meet with universal approval, and many will prefer other methods of removing the doubt
in question [i.e. the Julius Caesar problem]. I attach no decisive importance
even to bringing in the extensions of concepts at all.[39]

There is no doubt that Frege's definition is an especially simple one, but
it nevertheless has the whiff of expediency about it. Moreover, it forces
us to admit truths involving the natural numbers which stem not from
the numerical equivalence but from particular features of the definition
Frege chose. The number of Galilean moons of Jupiter — to use one of
Frege's own examples — is four. So does the concept *Galilean moon of
Jupiter* belongs to the number four? On Frege's definition it does. On
many others he could have chosen, it does not. Which is right?

[39] *Gl.*, § 107.

A way of apparently avoiding this difficulty that was open to Frege was to ensure that he used the explicit definition solely to derive the numerical equivalence and then make no further mention of it. But when he came to the detailed work of deriving arithmetical laws in his later book, *Grundgesetze der Arithmetik*, he did not in fact adopt this suggestion; instead he made use of extensions of concepts in a number of places. All these uses of extensions are easily (and uniformly) eliminable,[40] but even if we do eliminate them, we are only avoiding the difficulty and not solving it. By choosing not to mention consequences of our explicit definition such as that the concept *Galilean moon of Jupiter* belongs to the number four, we do not stop them *being* consequences of it.

2.8 The context principle again

While the numerical equivalence was under consideration as a route to the introduction of natural numbers, it may have seemed as if the rôle of the context principle was solely to license such contextual introductions. Now that the Julius Caesar problem has intervened to rule this route out, that rôle for the context principle becomes redundant. One might almost suppose that the Julius Caesar problem is a late intrusion into an already finished manuscript, and that the significance Frege claimed for the context principle was a mistaken survival from the earlier draft.

That this view is wrong is made clear by the summary Frege gives at the end of the book of the procedure he has followed. He there stresses that adherence to the context principle is essential if we are to 'avoid a physical view of number without slipping into a psychological view of it'.[41] What the context principle tells us is that if we understand how a word contributes to the meaning of sentences in which it occurs, there is nothing further about its meaning that has been left unsaid. As Wittgenstein later expressed it in the *Tractatus*, 'If everything in the symbolism works as though a sign had meaning, then it has meaning.'[42]

Now the context principle is stated as a general principle about the way we understand language. Its application is by no means restricted to the introduction of new singular terms. In that case, however, we face a particular difficulty: we are constrained by the fact that we already have an understanding of identity as a binary predicate which can stand between any two singular terms. In order for us to be able to treat a range of new expressions as singular terms, and therefore as

[40]See Heck, 'The development of arithmetic in Frege's *Grundgesetze*'.   [41]*Gl.*, § 106.
[42]*TLP*, 3.328.

introducing a way of referring to objects, we have to lay down a sense for *all* identity statements involving not only them but also any other singular terms previously introduced. This, again, is the Julius Caesar problem.

The numerical equivalence is of course a partial solution to this problem in the case of number terms since it constitutes a contextual stipulation of the sense of identity statements involving such terms alone. If we could treat arithmetic in isolation as a language on its own, this would be sufficient: there would be no other singular terms already available in the language, and the context principle would entitle us to regard the numerical equivalence not merely as a contextual stipulation but as a contextual definition. But if we treat arithmetic as a language on its own, we thereby fail to explain its applicability. When we embed arithmetic in a larger language with other singular terms, the licence given to us by the context principle becomes a conditional one: the numerical equivalence will count as a contextual stipulation of the sense of numerical identities only if we can complete it by settling in some way or other the senses of the other identities involving number terms.

2.9 The analyticity of the numerical equivalence

Frege's central claim in the *Grundlagen* was that

in arithmetic we are not concerned with objects which we come to know as something alien from without through the medium of the senses, but with objects given directly to our reason and, as its nearest kin, utterly transparent to it.[43]

He intended to substantiate this claim by deriving the basic laws of arithmetic logically from the numerical equivalence. He gave only a sketch of this derivation, however, and did not even mention the crucial step of justifying the recursive definitions of addition and multiplication. So there remained to Frege at the technical level the task, carried out fully in his *Grundgesetze* ten years later, of filling in the gaps. But even if, as Frege thought, the whole of logic is analytic in a suitably extended sense, a logical derivation of a range of propositions from an axiom shows nothing about their analyticity unless the axiom in turn is analytic. Frege's further claim to have shown that arithmetic is analytic therefore turns on the status of the numerical equivalence.

[43] *Gl.*, § 105.

What is clear from the technical part of Frege's work is that the numerical equivalence yields an immensely rich content. What needs to be explained is how this content can arise from purely analytic principles. Frege considered two such explanations, one direct and one indirect. The direct explanation was that the numerical equivalence is in itself the means of introducing natural numbers and is justified because its left-hand side merely expresses the same content as the right-hand side but in a different way. Frege abandoned this strategy because the numerical equivalence does not settle whether Julius Caesar was a number, adopting instead the indirect strategy of defining numbers explicitly as classes and deriving the numerical equivalence as a theorem.

This indirect strategy is not in itself an explanation of the source of content in arithmetic, however, but a postponement of it. We have already noted the remarkable power of the numerical equivalence in conjunction with second-order logic to generate Peano's axioms. If we were puzzled how an analytic principle involving numbers could yield such a rich content, Frege's definition merely transfers the puzzlement to the corresponding principle for extensions. What Frege achieved was therefore only to transform the original question, 'How are numbers given to us?', into another, 'How are extensions of concepts given to us?', which remains to be answered.

In the quest for content the detour via extensions of concepts is in any case somewhat irrelevant since we know from Frege's theorem that the content of arithmetic can be extracted logically from, and must therefore in some sense already be contained in, the numerical equivalence. Frege's objection to the numerical equivalence was solely that it is insufficient, not that it is incorrect. So even if Frege's claim that the numerical equivalence is analytic depends on the details of his explicit definition and hence on a claim of analyticity for the corresponding equivalence for extensions, it will still be the case that the content of arithmetic according to Frege is encapsulated in his remark that the content of the two sides of the numerical equivalence is identical.

In later writings Frege distinguished, as he had not done in the *Grundlagen*, between the two notions of sense and reference. When he had done so, it became possible for him to rephrase the claim in terms of sense: it is the *sense* of the right-hand side of the equivalence that is recarved in a different way on the left-hand side. But it remains the case that Frege's claim to have grounded arithmetic in logic, broadly understood, is conditional on some such claim: if, for instance, our grasp of the extensional equivalence depended on intuition, Frege's account would in its essentials collapse into Kant's.

3

Dedekind

While Frege was writing the *Grundlagen* in Jena, Richard Dedekind was independently writing a monograph on the same subject a hundred miles away in Brunswick. Dedekind's project was at root the same as Frege's: he was explicit, as Frege was, that 'arithmetic is part of logic', by which he meant to imply that he considered 'the number-concept entirely independent of the notions or intuitions of space and time'.[1] Moreover, he did not limit himself to justifying the necessity of arithmetic; he shared Frege's view of the importance of explaining its applicability, as the title of his monograph — *Was sind und was sollen die Zahlen?* ('What are numbers and what are they for?') — makes clear.

There are considerable similarities between the two treatments, then, but there are also marked differences, not just in the technical details of their developments of arithmetic within logic, but in the way they tackled the dual problems of establishing the existence and uniqueness of the number sequence. In particular, although Dedekind's characterization of the natural numbers faced a version of the Julius Caesar problem just as Frege's did, Dedekind solved it in a very different way and thus avoided the problem of extraneous properties with which we ended the last chapter.

3.1 Dedekind's recursion theorem

I have already mentioned the progress made by Schultz and Grassmann towards the complete axiomatization of arithmetic. The decisive step is often taken to be Peano's publication in 1889 of a list of axioms satisfied by the relation of successorhood on the natural numbers, but Peano acknowledged in the preface to his work the influence of Dedekind's monograph, which had been published the previous year. Dedekind did not present his account axiomatically, but it is easy to extract an axiomatic treatment from it and there is little reason to doubt that this is

[1] *Zahlen*, preface.

how Peano proceeded. Although it is therefore Dedekind who deserves the principal credit, I shall nevertheless continue to follow precedent by calling them Peano's axioms:

$$(x)(y)(z)(xSy \, . \, xSz \supset y = z)$$
$$(x)(y)(z)(xSz \, . \, ySz \supset x = y)$$
$$(\exists y)(x)\sim xSy$$
$$(x)(\exists y)xSy$$
$$(\exists x)(F)((Fx \, . \, (y)(z)(Fy \, . \, ySz \supset Fz) \supset (y)Fy)$$

(I have stated the theory using just one non-logical constant S standing for the successor relation: this is not quite what Peano did, but it will be convenient to have the axioms in this form since it allows us to introduce the term *Peano relation* to refer to any interpretation of S which satisfies the axioms with the first-order variables in them interpreted as ranging over the domain of the relation and the second-order variables as ranging over its subsets.)

There is, however, a significant difficulty with Peano's treatment of addition and multiplication. After stating axioms for the successor relation Peano set out the recursion equations for addition and multiplication (see § 2.1). He then simply appended Grassmann's derivations of the arithmetical laws from those equations. If he had treated addition and multiplication as further primitives of the system and the recursion equations as axioms, the procedure would have been formally correct (although inelegant). But in fact Peano took the recursive equations to be *definitions*. He evidently thought that these equations in themselves define the addition and multiplication functions uniquely. He failed to realize the necessity for a proof that there are indeed functions satisfying them. There is therefore a lacuna in Peano's account at just this point.

Peano's error is rendered all the more egregious by the fact that Dedekind had already supplied the requisite proof. What Dedekind proved in general was the following theorem:[2]

Dedekind's recursion theorem. *If a is an element of a set A and g is a function from A to itself, there is exactly one function f from the natural numbers to A such that*

$$f(0) = a; \tag{1}$$
$$f(n + 1) = g(f(n)) \text{ for every natural number } n. \tag{2}$$

[2]Ibid., no. 126.

It is a mark of the significance of Dedekind's achievement that Peano was not the only mathematician of stature to miss the need for it: Landau, for example, omitted the proof from the first draft of his account of arithmetic in 1930 and was saved from error in the published version only by the intervention of a colleague.[3] What misled Landau was no doubt the following short but fallacious argument for Dedekind's result. Equation (1) enables us to define $f(0)$ uniquely. And if $f(n)$ is defined uniquely, equation (2) enables us to define $f(n + 1)$ uniquely. Hence by induction the two equations together define $f(n)$ uniquely for every natural number n. The fallacy in this argument lies in the potential ambiguity of saying that $f(n)$ is 'defined uniquely' in advance of a proof that the function f exists. Dedekind realized that it is necessary to prove the result in two stages. We show first (by induction) that for each m there is a partial function f_m defined for all arguments $\leq m$ such that

$$f_m(0) = a; \tag{3}$$
$$f_m(n + 1) = g(f_m(n)) \text{ for all } n < m. \tag{4}$$

If we set $f(n) = f_n(n)$ for each n, it is then easy to show that f satisfies (1) and (2).

One straightforward consequence which Dedekind drew from his recursion theorem is worth singling out for attention since it is at least as significant as the theorem itself.

Dedekind's categoricity theorem. *Any two Peano relations are isomorphic.*

The reason this corollary of the recursion theorem is important is that it shows Dedekind's work to be a complete solution to a particular technical problem: to say that the successor function on the natural numbers is a Peano relation is to give a complete characterization of its structure.

3.2 Frege and Dedekind

The account of the natural numbers in *Was sind und was sollen die Zahlen?* is technically superior to that in the *Grundlagen*: Dedekind proved the validity of the method of defining functions by means of recursive equations and derived from this a demonstration that his characterization of the natural numbers is categorical; no trace of either

---

[3] *Grundlagen der Analysis*, pp. ix–x.

result is to be found in Frege until his later *Grundgesetze*, and by the time he wrote that work he had access to Dedekind's monograph. But it is worth noting that once these omissions from Frege's account are made good, there is a clear sense in which the two treatments are equivalent. One half of this equivalence is a result we have already noted under the name of Frege's theorem, namely that if N is a cardinality operator satisfying the numerical equivalence and if we define the successor relation as Frege recommends in the *Grundlagen*, then the finite cardinals can be proved in second-order logic to satisfy Peano's axioms. If Frege's theorem may reasonably be said to be implicit in *Grundlagen*, the converse result is quite explicit in *Was sind und was sollen die Zahlen?*. Suppose that S is a Peano relation and let Z_n be the strict ancestral of n with respect to S. We can prove using second order logic that

$$Z_m \sim Z_n \equiv m = n.$$

Call a concept *finite* if there exists n in the domain of S such that $F \sim Z_n$. It follows at once that for each finite concept F there is exactly one n such that $F \sim Z_n$. If we write '$\mathrm{N}xFx$' for this unique n, then whenever F and G are finite,

$$\mathrm{N}xFx = \mathrm{N}xGx \equiv F \sim G.$$

We retrieve, in other words, the numerical equivalence for finite concepts.[4]

This equivalence between the two treatments allows us to compare the philosophical attitudes of Frege and Dedekind directly. Neither of them thought, as Peano seems to have done, that laying down the fundamental principles (the numerical equivalence in Frege's case, Peano's axioms in Dedekind's) was in itself sufficient to ground arithmetic. Both thought that for this it was necessary in addition to justify the natural numbers as a series of objects, and that this necessity made both the difficulties that have been troubling us so persistently — the existence of a number series, and its uniqueness — genuine problems that any account of the matter had to solve.

As we shall see, their solutions to the uniqueness problem diverged sharply: Frege solved it by arbitrary stipulation, a method Dedekind attacked because it gave numbers spurious properties they did not really have; Dedekind solved it by abstraction, a method Frege delighted in ridiculing whenever the opportunity arose. But their solutions to the existence problem were perhaps more similar than they knew, since

---

[4]See Heck, 'Finitude and Hume's principle'.

both made use of their respective versions of the class concept: Frege used classes (extensions) to obtain his explicit definition of the number operator; Dedekind used classes (systems) to demonstrate the existence of what he called a 'simply infinite system'. As we try to understand the constraints circumscribing Dedekind's account of the matter, it will be as well to have this comparison with Frege's treatment always in mind.

3.3 Axiomatic structuralism

Dedekind gave a definitive solution to the problem of giving a logical characterization of the successor function, but this does not in itself provide an answer to the philosophical questions concerning the natural numbers that we are investigating here. As we have already noted, Dedekind did not present his account of arithmetic in axiomatic form — we shall come to how he did present it later — but even if we extract an axiomatic treatment from it, as Peano did, we are no further forward in arithmetic than we were in geometry. In both cases the axiomatization simply localizes the problem (assuming for the moment that we can justify our logic) to the axioms: what reason do we have to believe *them*? On this problem Peano himself had almost nothing to say, but the method of axiomatization is so popular among mathematicians that it will be important for us to be clear about what it involves.

What is plain, I hope, is that we cannot simply write down the axioms, stipulate that they are to be regarded as 'true', and proceed to draw consequences from them according to formal rules, since that would be to lapse into the pure formalism we have already rejected. But the axioms we are dealing with are not just structureless strings of signs: many of the signs that occur in them (most notably the logical constants) already have familiar meanings, and the other signs belong to recognizable grammatical categories. We can thus read the axioms as sentences, even though they contain words we do not yet understand:

'Twas brillig, and the slithy toves
Did gyre and gimble in the wabe;
All mimsy were the borogoves,
And the mome raths outgrabe.[5]

It is tempting, therefore, to suppose that the undefined terms are indeed meaningful and obtain their meaning from the rôle they play in the axioms: the axioms of geometry are to be seen as implicitly defining

---

[5]Carroll, *Through the looking glass*, ch. 1.

the terms 'point', 'line', etc., for instance; and Peano's axioms implicitly define the sign 'S' for the successor function. In formal terms this amounts to introducing the non-logical symbols which occur in the axioms as new primitive terms and treating the axioms as true by stipulation. This method is nowadays common in books on abstract pure mathematics. Authors typically include informal explanations intended to motivate the axioms, but it is made clear that these explanations are only there to help the reader and play no part in the formal argument, which commences with the dogmatic exposition of axioms containing the primitive terms of the theory and proceeds by the logical deduction of consequences of these axioms, treated now as if they are bearers of meaning. The justification for this procedure is taken to be a matter of pure logic.

We shall call the idea that mathematical terms can be introduced by means of implicit definitions on a purely logical basis *axiomatic structuralism*. It is much easier to see what it involves if we first of all transform the account according to a procedure first enunciated by Frege. According to his recommendation, we should regard Peano's axioms not as an implicit definition of the sign 'S' which occurs in them but as an explicit definition of what it is to be a Peano relation. What corresponds to the adoption of Peano's axioms as true is now a stipulation of the form 'Let S be a Peano relation'. On this new way of presenting matters the axioms themselves merely contribute to an explicit definition, which is entirely unproblematic. Attention therefore focuses entirely on the procedure by which we introduce a new expression 'S' into our language and stipulate that it should be a Peano relation. But this is now recognizably an instance of the familiar practice of introducing a new name and giving it a meaning.

The case in which that practice is straightforward is the one in which there is exactly one thing having the stipulated properties: if I choose to call the present Archbishop of Canterbury Dwayne, I may be eccentric but I do not violate any logical laws, and as long as I advertise my stipulation I risk not misunderstanding (since I know no one else called Dwayne) but only ridicule. There is, however, exactly one Archbishop of Canterbury. If the stipulations by which I try to give meaning to a name pick out too many things or none, matters are not so straightforward. In order to solve these two difficulties the axiomatic structuralist appeals to a particular conception of the properties an object has if it is introduced by means of a purely logical stipulation of the general form 'Let a be such that Fa': we shall call a a *stipulated* object in such circumstances. Let us consider this conception as it relates to each of the difficulties in turn.

3.4 Existence

If I use the name 'Dwayne' to refer to the Archbishop of Canterbury, I am eccentric but commit no logical blunder. If I use it for the integer whose square is 2, on the other hand, I am generally held to have made an error since there is no such integer. The reason is that we adopt the convention when we engage in logical argument that the proper names we use have reference. There is no necessity about this, of course — we could quite easily (and in natural language occasionally do) adopt the opposite convention — but given the convention the logical error follows.

Just the same error is involved if we lay down an inconsistent system of axioms. Almost everyone who has written about axiomatic structuralism has realized this and laid formal consistency down as a necessary condition for the axioms to be treated as meaningful. Many have thought that this condition is sufficient as well as necessary, but very few have been able to say why.

The *locus classicus* for the view is the writings of David Hilbert around the turn of the century in which he defended the conception of the axiomatic method contained in his *Grundlagen der Geometrie*:

> If it can be proved that the attributes assigned to the concept can never lead to a contradiction by the application of a finite number of logical inferences, I say that the mathematical existence of the concept ... is thereby proved.[6]

In this Hilbert was strongly opposed by Frege, for whom it was essential to the epistemological order that the only way to demonstrate the existence of a model for a list of axioms is to give them an interpretation on which they are true. It was therefore not enough for him that the numerical equivalence should be consistent; it had also to be true. So even if he had not been led by the Julius Caesar problem to drop the idea of introducing number terms by means of the numerical equivalence, Frege would certainly not have adopted an axiomatic structuralist account of it. This is the reason for the importance he attached to showing that the numerical equivalence suffices of itself to confer meaning on identities involving number terms: 'we carve up the content in a different way ... , and this yields us a new concept,' he wrote.[7]

But was Frege right to oppose the idea that consistency implies existence? What is clear straightaway is that this cannot be true across the board. There is, I assume, no logical inconsistency in the notion

---

[6]'Mathematische Probleme', 4. [7]*Gl.*, § 64.

that Scotland might win the World Cup one day, but if consistency implied existence I could achieve that end simply by making the consistent stipulation that Craig is to be a member of a winning Scottish World Cup team. The example Frege used in his correspondence with Hilbert to make this point is instructive: there is presumably no inconsistency in supposing the existence of an omnipotent, omniscient creator, but I cannot prove that such a being does exist merely by deciding to call it God.[8] The reason this example is instructive is that it is not quite as preposterous as the attempt to make Scotland win the World Cup without troubling to play any games. There is an intellectually respectable argument to the effect that theology has special features not present in rugby which have the consequence that in the theological case consistency does imply existence. It is a natural thought that the same applies to mathematics: in mathematics what is consistent is actual. But if we were to say either one of these things, we should have to argue for it, and our argument would presumably have to appeal to particular features that the concepts involved — mathematical concepts in the mathematical case, the concept of God in the theological one — do not share with sublunary concepts such as that of a winning rugby player. Perhaps this is why Hilbert said only that the *mathematical* existence of the concept is established by the consistency of the axioms. But for this distinction to be of any use we should have to have an account, which Hilbert does not at this stage supply, of what is meant by mathematical (as opposed to ordinary) existence.

Bertrand Russell once famously remarked that the advantages of postulating mathematical objects such as numbers are those of theft over honest toil.[9] The task of the axiomatic structuralist must be to find a principled difference between the cases which explains why postulating the natural numbers is not like postulating a winning rugby team. That difference will presumably hinge on the idea that on the axiomatic structuralist conception there is no more to the natural numbers than is laid down in the axioms. We cannot postulate rugby players — even logically consistent ones — because rugby players are people, and what there is in the domain of people is constrained by many factors other than logic, talent at rugby being only one such. Numbers, points in the Euclidean plane and the objects of other axiomatic theories are different: they are, the axiomatic structuralist will claim, subject to no constraints except those of pure logic. We have no prior conception of a domain of objects into which these mathematical entities must fit. It would perhaps be inappropriate to talk of their being created, but

---

[8]See letter to Hilbert, 6 Jan. 1900, in *PMC*, 47. [9]*IMP*, 71.

they nevertheless owe their identity to the axioms by means of which they are defined. This, the axiomatic structuralist maintains, is what is involved in taking seriously the idea that the meaning of the primitive terms of the theory consists in their rôle in its axioms.

So if we are to adopt this procedure we must take Frege's side rather than Kant's on the question of the connection between polyadic logic and sensibility. If, as Kant thought, the only objects to which we can apply the categories are subject to the spatio-temporal structure supplied by sensibility, then what there is is necessarily constrained not by logic alone but by what that structure permits. For logic to be, as the axiomatic structuralist claims, the sole arbiter of what there is, there must be no prior conception of a domain of objects to which logic is applicable. This is the difference between rugby players and numbers: the former, being people, must fit into a domain which is already circumscribed; numbers, being abstract, need not.

Even so, it is not yet clear that the gap between the cases is sufficiently wide to remove all doubt about the coherence of the structuralist position. One way of putting what is wrong with Craig is to observe that by adding his name to our vocabulary we make something the case within the pre-existing language that was not already so, namely that Scotland would win the World Cup. But in just the same way by positing the natural numbers the axiomatic structuralist seems to make it the case that there is a Peano relation, thus magically turning possibility into actuality at a stroke.

Nor can we straightforwardly avoid this awkward conclusion by decreeing that what we posit, being abstract, is not to be understood as lying in the range of the quantifiers we use to range over the empirical domain. The problem that disposed of pure formalism was its inability to explain the applicability of arithmetic. If axiomatic structuralism is to avoid the same fate, the numbers we posit under its licence must fall within the range of the same quantifiers as the objects we want to count by their means, since otherwise we shall indeed, as Russell once remarked, be like 'a watchmaker who is so absorbed in making his watches look pretty that he has forgotten their purpose of telling the time, and has therefore omitted to insert any works.'[10]

A determined axiomatic structuralist might not be fazed by this objection, however. It might be said that by positing numbers we do not magically make anything the case; we merely make manifest what was true all along. What is possible in mathematics not only is actual but always was. But just as rugby players can be logically consistent

---

[10] *Principles*, 2nd edn., p. vi.

on their own but logically impossible as a group (e.g. Craig and his equally and simultaneously successful antipodean counterpart, Bruce), so there are pairs of theological or mathematical concepts such that each is consistent but both together are not. In the theological case, for instance, one might well think that there are conceptions of God and the Devil which are consistent on their own but mutually incompatible. In the mathematical case the standard example is due to Boolos.[11] We have already noted that the numerical equivalence — the abstraction principle derived from the equivalence relation of equinumerosity — is a consistent addition to second-order logic which has the consequence that there are infinitely many objects. Let us now say that two concepts F and G are *equiparous* just in case the number of things which are F and not G or G and not F is finite and even. Then equiparity is an equivalence relation and the parity equivalence — the abstraction principle derived from it — is a consistent addition to second-order logic which logically entails that there are only finitely many objects. Plainly, then, the numerical and parity equivalences, although consistent individually, are not consistent with one another.

So positing cannot be quite as innocent as it seemed at first sight. Notice, too, that even if we succeeded in establishing that in mathematics consistency is enough to imply existence, we should still need to be given a reason to believe that mathematics is consistent. In the case of geometry Hilbert achieved this by the construction of a model, but we cannot hope to apply this method across the board since the assurance of consistency it provides is only relative: it demonstrates only the conditional result that geometry is consistent if the theory in which the model is constructed is consistent. If axiomatic structuralism is to apply quite generally as an account of the whole of mathematics, there must be a base theory whose consistency can be established absolutely without appeal to any further theory. Hilbert chose arithmetic as his base theory. At this point the process of formalization of arithmetic and logic, which we alluded to at the beginning of the last chapter, plays a crucial rôle: because Peano Arithmetic is a formal theory, the question whether it is consistent is a well-posed mathematical problem, which Hilbert hoped to solve by purely syntactic means. In 1904 he sketched such a proof for a weak theory of arithmetic not including the induction scheme and announced that he also had a proof of consistency for the full theory. But there is a fundamental objection to his approach, first raised by Poincaré. Even in the case of very weak systems of arithmetic without induction such as the one he proved consistent in 1904,

[11] *Logic, Logic, and Logic*, 214–15.

Hilbert's method was to use induction on the length of proofs in the system in question. If the system to be proved consistent contains a principle of induction, this procedure seems straightforwardly circular. As we shall see in Chapter 9, it was almost twenty years before Hilbert published anything that began to answer Poincaré's objection.

3.5 Uniqueness

Frege likened Hilbert's axiomatization of geometry to a system of equations in several unknowns: even if we know that the system has a solution there is a further question as to whether the solutions are uniquely determined.

If they were uniquely determined, it would be better to give the solutions, i.e. to explain each of the expressions 'point', 'line', 'between' individually through something that was already known. Given your definitions, I do not know how to decide the question whether my pocket watch is a point. The very first axiom deals with two points; thus if I wanted to know whether it held for my watch, I should first have to know of some other object that it was a point. But even if I knew this, e.g., of my penholder, I still could not decide whether my watch and my penholder determined a line, because I would not know what a line was.[12]

We faced the same difficulty earlier when we discussed what is involved in saying at the beginning of a geometrical proof 'Let ABC be a triangle'. That prescription did not fix the identity of ABC uniquely, and as a result it seemed that sentences involving 'ABC' would not express genuine propositions. In the same way the prescription 'Let S be a Peano relation' does not fix the identity of S. The difference between the cases is only that before what 'ABC' referred to was a triangle, i.e. an object, but now what 'S' refers to is a Peano relation, i.e. a certain sort of first level relation.

The embarrassment is heightened by the fact that *any* countably infinite set is the domain of some Peano relation. Since on the account we are considering 'natural number' will be taken as synonymous with 'member of the domain of S', no object whatever is prevented by the prescription from being a natural number. Axiomatic prescriptions do not settle whether my pocket watch is a point any more than they settle — to revert to Frege's more famous example — whether Julius Caesar is a natural number. So we have the same choices to consider for Peano relations as we had in § 1.10 for triangles. Let us consider some of them.

[12]Letter to Hilbert, 6th Jan. 1900, in Frege, *PMC*, 45.

Treating S as an *arbitrary* Peano relation stands or falls with the coherence of arbitrary objects in general. Making 'S' a schematic letter is hardly an improvement since it appeals to a distinction between object language and metalanguage which does not exist in practice. Even if we grant this distinction, however, it makes statements involving numbers into metalinguistic schemas awaiting determination. In order for these schemas to be applied within the object language, we must determine a value for the schematic letter, and at that point the difficulty returns with its previous force intact.

When we were considering triangles, we dismissed at once the strategy of simply choosing some particular a such that Fa. The reason was that if we deduced anything about a we should have no way of telling whether this was true just because a had the property F or because of some other properties of the particular a that we chose. In the numerical case, though, we can meet this objection to the strategy by means of Dedekind's categoricity theorem, which states that any two Peano relations are isomorphic to one another. Since all arithmetical properties are defined solely in terms of the Peano relation, it follows that all Peano relations have the same arithmetical properties. Definitions of the set of natural numbers which conform to this paradigm abound in modern textbooks on set theory: some follow Zermelo by defining the set of natural numbers to be the closure of the empty set under the operation $x \mapsto \{x\}$; but it is nowadays more popular to use the operation $x \mapsto x \cup \{x\}$ instead, since that produces the convenient by-product that each natural number n has n elements.

The principal difficulty with this strategy of choosing a particular Peano relation to be by stipulation the successor relation on the natural numbers is that it invites us to regard arithmetical properties as in some way internal and the others as external. This distinction between internal (arithmetical) and external (non-arithmetical) properties can be made quite precise, but it does not solve the problem: if we have defined the numbers in some particular way, then all their properties are genuinely theirs; calling some of them external does not change this. This difficulty is nowadays attributed to Benacerraf[13] but was adumbrated by Dedekind in 1888, when he wrote that if one defines a cardinal number to be a class of equinumerous classes in Frege's way,

one will say many things about the class (for example that it is a set of infinitely many elements ...) which one would certainly be most unwilling to attach to the number (as a burden).[14]

---

[13]'What numbers could not be'. [14]Letter to Weber, 24 Jan. 1888, in *Werke*, III, 490.

To put the point quite generally, if we introduce a name 'a' by means of an explicit definition and then prove that Fa, this theorem cannot then be given any privileged status as stating a property of a that is in some way salient. The object a has the properties it has by virtue of its definition, and we cannot subsequently limit them by fiat.

The axiomatic structuralist's response to the difficulty is to appeal to the idea sketched earlier that the objects of an axiomatic theory owe their identity solely to the axioms of the theory. This is what is involved, it is argued, in taking seriously the idea of mathematical objects as purely logical that we encountered in the last section. The indeterminacy that plagued the idea of an arbitrary triangle does not arise, it is claimed, once we recognize that there is no more to a stipulated object than the stipulation says there is.

The proposal arises most naturally, then, in the case where the stipulated object is a mathematical structure of some kind. In that case the internal properties will be those expressible in the language of the type of structure in question. The proposal is then that the introduction of a name to refer to such a structure is legitimate provided that the description we give of the structure is sufficient to determine all its internal properties. This will be the case if the description takes the form of a complete axiomatization. Dedekind's categoricity theorem demonstrates that the stipulation that S should be a Peano relation constitutes just such a description.

The internal properties of S are thus completely determined by the stipulation that it is a Peano relation. What of its external properties? The axiomatic structuralist appeals here to a disanalogy between this case and the geometrical one. It seems natural to say that although calling something a triangle does not settle its internal properties completely, calling something a unit circle does; but a unit circle must be located in space, and we are entitled to ask what external relationship it bears to other spatial objects. For the Peano relation S introduced by stipulation such questions do not arise. Since it is not located within any structure, it has no external properties except those forced on it by logic itself.

Notice straightaway that what we have just said about S is according to the structuralist a consequence of the way it is introduced, not of the mere fact that it is a Peano relation. If space contains infinitely many points, for example, there will be Peano relations whose domains are subsets of space, and these will have non-logical external properties in abundance; it is because it is given by means of a purely logical definition that S is supposed to be no more than its definition says it is.

Notice, too, that although stipulated objects have no non-logical properties, they may bear external logical relations to non-logical objects. Indeed they must do so if they are to be applicable in reasoning about the world. The Julius Caesar problem does not arise if we set up an entirely new language and treat our axioms as giving meaning to its terms, but the price to be paid is that we have thereby to give up the idea that our account can ground the application of the formal system to reasoning in a wider language. If, on the other hand, we intend arithmetic to be part of our wider language, the set $\{0, 1\}$ must bear the logical relation of equinumerosity to the set of apples in the bowl in order for it to be the case that there are two apples there. But if numbers can bear logical relations to pieces of fruit, they can bear them to Roman emperors. On the account we are considering it is therefore meaningful to ask whether Caesar was a number, and the answer is that he was not, because it does not follow logically from the stipulation by which S was introduced that he was, and S has no other properties than those.

One might by now have a sense of unease about the turn this account has taken. The relationship a number bears to Julius Caesar ought to depend on the number's identity. Yet our argument that Julius Caesar was not a number trades on the fact that our definition of S counted as a stipulation rather than on the property that the definition attributed to S. We can give this unease more concrete form if we consider a case where we have a logical property F which we know on logical grounds to have instances in abundance. Suppose first that we introduce three new names 'a', 'b', and 'c' into the language with the following stipulations:

Let a be such that Fa;

Let b be such that Fb;

Let c be such that Fc and $b \neq c$.

Should we conclude that $a = b$? Plainly we should, since a and b were introduced by identical stipulations. But suppose now that we introduce the names by the following stipulations:

Let a be such that Fa;

Let b and c be such that Fb and Fc and $b \neq c$.

Now we have no more reason to conclude that $a = b$ than that $a = c$. We have therefore to conclude that $a \neq b$. So introducing b and c together has had a different effect from introducing them *seriatim*. This consequence of the structuralist's position does not in itself amount to a refutation of it, but it indicates the difficulties that it leads to.

3.6 Implicationism

Before we consider in detail Dedekind's resolution of the twin problems of existence and uniqueness we need to dispose of another view that has been frequently, but mistakenly, attributed to him.[15] The stipulation that S should be a Peano relation leads, as we have seen, to serious difficulties. One way out of these difficulties is to treat 'S' as a variable, not a constant. The proposal is thus to reinterpret arithmetical propositions as conditionals: when I assert an arithmetical proposition, I should be understood as doing no more than making a claim about what follows from Peano's axioms. This seems nicely to avoid the issues of existence and uniqueness that have been troubling us.

This doctrine was at one time advocated by Russell, whose book, *The Principles of Mathematics*, begins:

Pure mathematics is the class of all propositions of the form 'p implies q', where p and q are propositions containing one or more variables, the same in the two propositions, and neither p nor q contains any constants except logical constants.[16]

The doctrine has had other distinguished adherents: Menger[17] called it *implicationism*; Putnam,[18] who later abandoned it, less euphoniously called it *if-thenism*. Here we shall conform to Menger's terminology. (More recently Parsons has given the name *eliminative structuralism* to the general proposal to eliminate reference to mathematical objects, of which this doctrine is the most obvious instance.)[19]

The use of the axiomatic method is widespread and by no means restricted to arithmetic and geometry. For most uses of the method Russell's account is surely correct. Thus when we prove from the axioms of topology that any intersection of closed sets is closed, we should be read as asserting a conditional 'p implies q', where p is the assertion that a structure satisfies the axioms of topology and q is the statement that any intersection of sets closed in the structure is also closed in the structure. We can bring out the dependence on a variable more clearly if we write the proposition $(x)(Fx \supset Gx)$, where Fx means that x is a topological space and Gx means that any intersection of sets closed in x is closed in x.

But the strength of topology lies precisely in its generality. The axioms of topology (and of a host of other axiomatic theories in mathematics) are deliberately chosen in such a way that many different structures

---

[15] e.g. Parsons, *Mathematics in Philosophy*, 20; Wright, *Frege's Conception of Numbers as Objects*, 117. [16] *Principles*, §1. [17] 'On Intuitionism'. [18] 'The thesis that mathematics is logic'. [19] 'The structuralist view of mathematical objects'.

satisfy them. The word 'closed' is given a meaning in topology relative to the structure of the space under consideration. There is therefore no temptation to think that it means anything on its own outside the context of the theory.

When it is applied to pure geometry, implicationism fares less well. 'The angles of any triangle sum to two right angles' is according to the implicationist a pseudo-proposition, whose correct rendering is the conditional that in any Euclidean geometry the angles of any triangle sum to two right angles. In symbols, then, we render it once more as $(x)(Fx \supset Gx)$, where on this occasion Fx means that x is a model of Euclidean geometry and Gx means that the angles of any triangle in x sum to two right angles. The applicability of the theorem of pure Euclidean geometry that we have just quoted is explained by the observed fact that empirical space is, to a good approximation, a model of the axioms of Euclidean geometry and the consequent of the conditional must therefore be true when instantiated as a claim about empirical space.

Now in the paraphrase just given the word 'triangle' does not occur free: it is merely a place-holder for a further (restricted) variable inside the scope of x, and thus has no meaning on its own. We are therefore forced to indulge in elaborate rewriting if we are to explain uses of the word 'triangle' in applications.

The difficulty becomes particularly acute when we consider the possibility that empirical space is non-Euclidean. The word 'triangle' as it occurs in the theorems of Euclidean geometry is, as we have just noted, a variable with no meaning on its own. The word 'triangle' as it occurs in the theorems of non-Euclidean geometry is similarly a variable. The two words have only a verbal similarity to connect them. We therefore cannot apply either word to empirical space in advance of coming to a view as to whether space is Euclidean or not. How, then, are we to explain the fact that what we have to decide if we are to settle whether space is Euclidean is whether the angles of all triangles sum to two right angles? How does the word 'triangle' function *here*?

This difficulty is perhaps not insuperable, but it does show that the implicationist translation does not easily cope with the application of individual terms of an axiomatic theory within ordinary language. It is, in other words, an indication of a more general worry: we seem to understand the word 'triangle' (and the words 'point', 'line', etc.) as having a meaning not limited to the scope of one particular set of axioms. But this more general worry applies with even greater force in the arithmetical case. To see why, we need to consider in a little more detail how the implicationist translation works for arithmetic.

The implicationist regards $2 + 2 = 4$, for example, as a pseudo-proposition whose correct interpretation is

If S is a Peano relation then $2_S +_S 2_S = 4_S$

(where 2_S is the appropriate element of the domain of S, $+_S$ is the operation of addition on that domain, etc.). The difficulty now is that we have to find a meaning for 'I have two apples'. If we interpret it as

If S is a Peano relation then I have 2_S apples

it will be vacuously true, however many apples I have, if there are no Peano relations. It is just as bad to interpret it as

There is at least one Peano relation and if S is a Peano relation then I have 2_S apples,

because this is false if there are no Peano relations.

It is a presupposition of my use of the sentence 'My aunt is at the shops' that I have an aunt, even if this is not part of what the sentence asserts. In the same way it seems that we must, on the account we are considering, regard it as a presupposition of all our use of number words that there is at least one Peano relation. But the account provides no clue as to how this presupposition might be established. Indeed it was precisely the attraction of implicationism that it allowed us to conditionalize the reference to a Peano relation. This presupposition, however, is unconditional and therefore cannot be subsumed under the implicationist account. If we are implicationists about the theory itself, we need a further, genuinely contentful, account to show that the theory is instantiated.

3.7 Systems

Speaking for a moment with the (relatively) vulgar, we may say that the successor function on the natural numbers is a Peano relation. The difficulty with implicationism that we have been facing lies in our attempts to reinterpret this statement in such a way that the successor function is not thereby required to exist. Let us now abandon these attempts and turn instead to showing that it does exist. As a first step we need to establish that there is at least one Peano relation. How? Axiomatic structuralists generally hold that it is enough if we can show the assumption to be consistent, but we have seen that there are substantial difficulties with this view. Nor can we simply import a belief in the existence of a Peano relation unless that belief can be justified on the basis of the account of arithmetic currently being considered. The most obvious way of proving that there is a Peano relation is to construct a model. But how are we to do this? In Dedekind's answer to this question the notion of what he called a *system* plays a rôle akin to that of the extension of a concept in Frege's. Dedekind does not in fact go into much detail as to what a system is, but rather takes it for granted (much as Frege in the *Grundlagen* took that of the extension of a concept), saying merely that a system S 'is completely determined when with respect to everything it is determined whether it is an element of S or not',[20] but that 'in what manner this determination is brought about, and whether we know a way of deciding upon it, is a matter of indifference for all that follows'.[21] Dedekind's general aim in appealing to a form of aggregation was the same as Frege's, namely to show that the concept of number is 'entirely independent of the notion or intuitions of space and time':[22] although Frege gave no account of extensions in *Grundlagen*, he was explicit that they are logical objects and that truths about them are analytic and hence graspable by 'purely logical means'; Dedekind similarly described his project as 'purely logical'.

Despite these similarities of rôle there were, however, two points of difference between Frege's notion of aggregation and Dedekind's. The first may be expressed in terms of a distinction between what are nowadays called *sets* and *fusions*. The difference between them is that a fusion is conceived of as being nothing over and above its members — it is simply them considered as a single object rather than a plurality — whereas a set is thought of as distinct from that plurality. Sets are therefore intrinsically hierarchical in a way that fusions are not. A fusion of a single thing is just the same as that thing, whereas its singleton (the set with that thing as its only member) is distinct from it. Although he is not explicit on the matter, Dedekind's usage often suggests that by 'system' he meant fusion: he says, for example, that 'every element s of a system S ... can be itself regarded as a system',[23] which fits fusions much better than it does sets. If, as Frege alleged, Dedekind was a little confused about the distinction between sets and fusions, it would not be surprising: Dedekind acknowledged in the preface to his book the influence of Schröder's *Lehrbuch*, which exhibits the very confusion that is at issue.[24] Indeed it was in a review of a later work of Schröder's that Frege clearly enunciated for the first time the distinction between the two conceptions. A fusion, he said, 'con-

[20] *Zahlen*, no. 2.   [21] Ibid., no. 2, note.   [22] Ibid., preface.   [23] Ibid., no. 3.   [24] See *Lehrbuch*, ch. 1, no. 20.

sists of objects; it is an aggregate, a collective unity, of them; if so, it must vanish when these objects vanish. If we burn down all the trees of a wood we thereby burn down the wood.'[25] Thus there can be no empty fusion. On this point Dedekind equivocated, and was elsewhere ridiculed by Frege for doing so.[26]

The second point of difference is that Dedekind was prepared to use language that is apparently more psychologistic than Frege's. Systems, he said, are our creations: they consist of things which 'for some reason can be considered from a common point of view, can be associated in the mind'.[27] He attributed the formation of a system from given determinate elements to a creative ability (*Schöpferkraft*) of the mind.[28] What is at work here is another distinction between sorts of aggregation, this time between the *logical* conception of aggregates as derived from a predicate and the *collective* conception of them as formed from their elements.

3.8 Dedekind on existence

What Dedekind offers in order to prove the existence of Peano relations is a beautifully simple application of what he called chains but are nowadays called closures. A system A is said to be *closed* with respect to a relation R if whenever x belongs to A and xRy it follows that y belongs to A. The *closure* of a with respect to R is by definition the intersection of all the systems which contain a and are closed with respect to R. With this terminology a Peano relation is simply a one-to-one function whose domain is the closure with respect to it of some element not in its range. Dedekind called a system *simply infinite* if it is the domain of a Peano relation and *infinite* if it is equinumerous with a proper subsystem of itself. With this terminology Dedekind's theorem asserts that every infinite system has a simply infinite subsystem. The proof is as follows. If A is infinite, there is a one-to-one function f from A to a proper subsystem of A and so there must be an element a of A which is not in the range of f. The closure of a with respect to f is then a simply infinite set and the restriction of f to this set is a Peano relation. This proves the result.

Dedekind had proved, then, that every infinite system has a simply infinite subsystem. In order to conclude unconditionally that there exists a simply infinite system he needed to show additionally that there exists at least one infinite system. As soon as we make the attempt we

[25]'Kritische Beleuchtung...', 436–7. [26]*Gg.*, I, 2. [27]*Zahlen*, no. 2. [28]Ibid., 3rd edn., preface.

find ourselves once more embedded in the problem of content. Can logic create content on its own? If not, any construction of an infinite system must appeal to some infinite domain of objects whose availability to us is independently grounded. But it is presumably hopeless to try to do this empirically since even if the empirical world is infinite we have acquaintance only with a finite part of it.

In the light of his understanding of systems as creations of our minds, it is not surprising that Dedekind's proof of the existence of an infinite system has the same apparently psychologistic slant. His example of an infinite system is 'the totality S of all things which can be objects of my thought'. To show that S is infinite we note first that 'if s signifies an element of S, then the thought s' that s can be an object of my thought is itself an element of S.' The mapping that takes s to s' is evidently one-to-one. It follows that S is infinite once we observe that 'there are elements in S (e.g. my own ego) which are different from all such thoughts s'.'[29]

In a footnote Dedekind remarks on the similarity between his argument and one due to Bolzano, who argued that any proposition A must be distinct from the proposition that A is true since A is a proper part of the latter but not of the former. In fact, though, Dedekind's argument has no more similarity with Bolzano's than it does with a host of others that can be arbitrarily constructed. A notable example is one to be found in the *Critique* to show that space is infinite. Kant's argument shows only that space has infinitely many regions within it: it does not follow from this that there are infinitely many intuitions since Kant did not think we have intuitions of regions of space. He does indeed refer to 'the limitlessness of the progression of intuition'[30] as a condition of the infinitude of space, but he appears to argue elsewhere[31] that this is only a limitlessness of possibility: if space is infinite, then since we can intuit objects in any position in space it follows that infinitely many intuitions are possible. But this is not yet enough for our purposes: if infinitely many things are possible, it does not follow immediately even that there is a possibility in which all of them are realized; and even if there is such a possibility, we need a further argument for the conclusion that this possibility is actual.

So according to Kant sensibility supplies us with a structure within which a potential infinity of pure intuitions may be constructed, but not one in which we may construct a pure intuition of an actually infinite system. And whether or not we agree with the details of Kant's discussion of the paradoxes of the infinite, a position that derives the

[29] Ibid., no. 66.   [30] *KrV*, A25.   [31] Ibid., A427 ff = B455 ff.

possibility of the infinite from the structure of space and time will in any case be unacceptable to anyone who wishes, as Dedekind did, to show that arithmetic is independent of that structure.

Dedekind's proof has found few adherents. An exception was Russell, who quoted a version of it with approval in the *Principles*.[32] Even he apostatized fifteen years later,[33] however, objecting that

[i]f the argument is to be upheld, the 'ideas' intended [i.e. Dedekind's possible thoughts] must be Platonic ideas laid up in heaven, for certainly they are not on earth. But then it at once becomes doubtful whether there are such ideas. If we are to know that there are, it must be on the basis of some logical theory, proving that it is necessary to a thing that there should be an idea of it. We certainly cannot obtain this result empirically, or apply it, as Dedekind does, to 'meine Gedankenwelt' — the world of my thoughts.[34]

Russell is quite right, of course, to observe that the existence of the ideas appealed to in the proof (Dedekind's 'things that can be objects of my thought') cannot be an empirical matter, but Dedekind would certainly not have accepted that in that case it must be a consequence of 'some logical theory' as Russell contends.

The standard modern objection to Dedekind's proof amounts to little more than the trivial observation that if logic is wholly general and hence applies in all domains, including finite ones, the existence of an infinite system cannot be a logical truth. But the way Dedekind posed the question he took his proof to be answering is significant. 'Does [a simply infinite system] exist at all in the realm of our ideas?'[35] The infinite system whose existence Dedekind had demonstrated was to be conceived of as occurring within the realm of our thoughts. Logic as we nowadays understand it cannot provide such a structure, but Dedekind took it that reason can.

The doctrine that by appealing to the range of possible thoughts available to it reason can, independent of space and time, supply us with objects to form the subject matter of further reasoning is of course radically unKantian since it requires us to be capable of intuiting thoughts, but what we have said so far leaves open two distinct ways of interpreting the divergence from Kant.

On the first interpretation we conceive of the thoughts we intuit as lying within a realm which is itself capable of being intuited. Dedekind's proof of the existence of an infinite system is then to be taken as a construction in intuition analogous to the spatio-temporal examples we discussed in Chapter 1. The infinite system cannot owe its existence to the construction, since intuition remains on this interpretation wholly

[32]§ 339. [33]*IMP*, 137 ff. [34]Ibid. 139. [35]Letter to Keferstein in van Heijenoort, 101.

passive: the function of the construction is to represent to us the properties of a structure of which we already have an intuitive grasp. This interpretation, although of course inimical to the Kant of the *Critique*, is evidently suggestive of the hint in his *Inaugural Dissertation* that arithmetic might supply a third form of intuition (see § 1.9).

The second interpretation is even more radically opposed to the doctrine of the *Critique* since it abandons the passivity of intuition and ascribes to our intellects the power to represent directly entities of our own creation. This interpretation is unKantian not merely because it credits us with a capacity Kant took to belong only to God but because according to it we are capable of intuiting objects not lying within any structure of which we have an a priori grasp.

Nothing I have said so far determines which of these two interpretations best fits Dedekind's own views, and indeed I have quoted remarks of his — about 'the realm of our ideas' on the one hand, and 'a creative ability of the mind' on the other — in favour of both interpretations. The choice is only settled, I believe, when we turn to Dedekind's way of solving the uniqueness problem.

3.9 Dedekind on uniqueness

If there is one simply infinite system, then there are many. So we cannot simply define the natural numbers to be a simply infinite system and leave it at that: we need to say *which* simply infinite system is meant. We have already canvassed various solutions to this difficulty and not found one that is altogether satisfactory. Dedekind's solution was abstraction:

If in the consideration of a simply infinite system we entirely neglect the special character of the elements, simply retaining their distinguishability and taking into account only the relation to one another in which they are placed by the successor function, then these elements are called *natural numbers* ... With reference to this freeing of the elements from every other content (abstraction) we are justified in calling numbers a free creation of the human mind.[36]

In this passage Dedekind gestures towards two competing metaphors, of forgetfulness and of creation, which correspond to different ways of regarding abstraction. We saw Kant attracted to both these ways when we considered the corresponding question for triangles. The metaphor of forgetfulness suggests that we can by inattention to its special features make one triangle (or simply infinite system) go proxy for them

[36] *Zahlen*, no. 73.

all. The metaphor of creation suggests that once we have at least one triangle (or simply infinite system) we can create a new one with the special feature that it has no special features: no more is true of it than is true of every triangle (or simply infinite system).

The first metaphor, that of forgetfulness, is one that Frege delighted in ridiculing at every opportunity. 'If, abstracting from the difference between my house and my neighbour's, I were to regard both houses as mine, the defect of my abstraction would soon be made clear.'[37] The difficulty with what we might call *forgetful* abstraction is that once we have a conception of a domain of objects, this carries with it the idea that each element of the domain has its own identity; we can then make nothing of the notion that there might be an element which was not a particular element.

We considered this problem at length in § 1.10. There we found Kant contending that a single triangle which we construct can 'express the concept' of a triangle 'without impairing its universality' because we consider 'only the act whereby we construct the concept'. Although the triangle itself is indeed particular, our representation of it can be general provided that we construct it ourselves. Now that was, in effect, Kant's account of the method of condition proof. It is only the representation that is general, not the object itself, and the generality is effective only within the scope of the proof: for there we can ensure that we refer to the object only by means of the representation we obtained when we constructed it; whereas outside the scope of the proof we cannot limit by fiat how we represent it since objects in general are capable of being intuited in different ways and from different perspectives.

We must therefore reject forgetful abstraction in the realm of thoughts just as we rejected arbitrary triangles in the realm of space and time. It is the second metaphor, that of creation, that we should regard as dominant in Dedekind's conception. Assuming always that we can prove the existence of at least one simply infinite system, we create a new one without any arbitrary properties, which Dedekind called the 'abstract type'[38] of the simply infinite systems from which it is abstracted. I shall call this position *creative structuralism*: we obtain the system of natural numbers from a simply infinite system that is already given, not merely by forgetting which simply infinite system it is but by creating a new system from it. What Dedekind did by invoking creative abstraction was thus to side decisively with the second interpretation outlined earlier according to which numbers are creations of the intellect not lying within any more general structure that we can

---

[37] *Gg.*, II, 107. [38] In van Heijenoort, 101.

grasp. Nor did he make any attempt to hide the mysteriousness of this creative faculty. We are, he said in a letter to Weber, 'of divine descent [*göttlischen Geschlechtes*] and without doubt possess creative power not merely in material things but especially in intellectual ones.'[39] By saying that we are of divine descent Dedekind here alludes to a passage from the Acts of the Apostles,[40] but there is an evident echo too of Kant's notion of intellectual intuition. But if Dedekind's solution to the uniqueness problem forced him to ascribe to us an ability to create new abstractions which Kant had held to be possible only for God, that only presented him with another, more substantial problem. By severing the connection with sensibility Dedekind cut himself off from Kant's account of the applicability of arithmetic to the world; but by appealing to our creative power he went beyond what is narrowly logical — beyond, that is to say, the part of logic that it seems natural to regard as analytic even on Frege's extended conception. He had now to explain how the products of our creative intellects are relevant to our grasp of what we receive by means of passive sensibility. Kant's Transcendental Deduction was intended to show only that what sensibility intuits must conform to the pure concepts of the understanding. Now we need a further argument to show that it must also conform to the structure of our intellectual creations.

[39] *Werke*, III, 490.   [40] Acts 17: 29.

4

Frege's account of classes

In the *Grundlagen* Frege sketched a proof of the basic properties of natural numbers from the numerical equivalence and showed how that equivalence could be proved if numbers were explicitly defined as extensions of certain second-level concepts. Two tasks were left to complete: to provide in the formal system of his concept script a derivation of the basic properties of numbers from the explicit definition in terms of extensions; and to show how extensions are given to us as logical objects independent of intuition. Frege did not delineate either task with any great clarity in the *Grundlagen*: on the need to derive Grassmann's recursion equations he was wholly silent; and on the question how extensions are given to us logically he merely observed (in a footnote) that 'I assume it is known what the extension of a concept is.'[1] But in *Grundgesetze der Arithmetik* he set about completing both tasks. The first involved little that was essentially new: Frege had sketched what amounts to a proof of Peano's axioms in the *Grundlagen* and by the time he came to write *Grundgesetze* he had available to him Dedekind's derivation from them of the existence of functions satisfying Grassmann's recursion equations for addition and multiplication. The reason that it was necessary to convert both of these into detailed proofs in the formal system was just to confirm that they made no illicit appeal to intuition for their justification. We shall therefore concentrate here on the second task, that of accounting for the existence and uniqueness, independent of intuition, of extensions of concepts, i.e. objects satisfying what I have called the *extensional equivalence*:

$$\{x : Fx\} = \{x : Gx\} \equiv (x)(Fx \equiv Gx).$$

4.1 The Julius Caesar problem yet again

The extensional equivalence is visibly similar in form to the numerical equivalence. It is therefore natural to ask why Frege did not reject it for the same reason, namely that it does not determine uniquely the

[1] *Gl.*, §68.

identity of the objects referred to by the terms whose introduction it is intended to license. Our discussion of Frege's answer to this question is complicated by its entanglement with a claim which Frege ought not to have made, namely that every declarative sentence is a name of one of the two objects Truth and Falsity, which are called *truth-values*. This claim can be split up into two parts: first, that the references of sentences are of the same logical type as the references of proper names; and second, that the references of sentences are truth-values. Both claims are mistaken, but only the first is relevant to the Julius Caesar problem.

To see why it is wrong, notice that if we regard sentences as a special case of proper names (and hence treat their references as objects), we must also regard concept-words as a special case of function-symbols (and hence treat concepts as functions). Let us now[2] define a function f by

$$f(\xi) = \begin{cases} \top & \text{if } \xi \text{ is a person born after Bernard Shaw died;} \\ 0 & \text{otherwise.} \end{cases}$$

That such a function f should exist is not the worry: what causes the difficulty is that we can grasp its sense, and therefore the sense of 'f(John Lennon)', without knowing whether that sense is a thought or not. It seems plain that thoughts are not the sort of things that we can grasp without being aware that they *are* thoughts. Hence Frege was wrong to deny that there is a difference of logical type between what sentences refer to and objects.

But since Frege did deny this, he was led correspondingly to deny that there is a difference of logical type between concepts and functions. Just as a sentence is for Frege by the time of *Grundgesetze* a name of a truth-value, so a concept is a function all of whose values are truth-values. The fundamental distinction he had drawn in the *Grundlagen* between objects and concepts is now replaced by one between objects and functions, but it is at root the same distinction: objects are saturated; functions are unsaturated. Frege's conception can be summarized by means of a diagram:[3]

Value	Argument	Function
Sentence	Proper name	Concept word
↓	↓	↓
Thought	Sense of proper name	Sense of concept word
↓	↓	↓
Truth-value	Object	Concept

[2]Cf. Sullivan, 'The sense of a name of a truth value'. [3]Cf. Frege, *PMC*, 63.

Since concepts are for Frege merely some among functions, the notion
of the extension of a concept must be generalized too. He assumed
that every function has associated with it a logical object called its
value-range. (The German is *Wertverlauf*: the translations 'graph'
and 'course-of-values' are also used.) In the case where the function in
question is a concept, its value-range is what Frege had previously called
its extension. The axiom which Frege adopted as governing value-ranges
is a straightforward generalization of the extensional equivalence, and is
known as Basic Law V. In Frege's idiosyncratic notation it is written

$$\vdash(\acute\epsilon f(\epsilon) = \acute\alpha g(\alpha)) = (\neg\mathfrak{a}\!-\!f(\mathfrak{a}) = g(\mathfrak{a})),$$

but if we write it in modern notation as

$$\{x : f(x)\} = \{x : g(x)\} \equiv (x)(f(x) = g(x)),$$

it becomes recognizably the generalization to functions of the extensional equivalence for concepts. The extra generality Frege obtained by
adopting this principle is in the present context inessential, and nothing
will be lost in what follows if as a consequence of rejecting his treatment
of sentences as proper names we restrict our attention to the special case
of Basic Law V which we have called the extensional equivalence.

That said, we can return to the question with which we began this
section. Why did Frege not reject the extensional equivalence for the
same reason that he had earlier rejected the numerical equivalence,
namely that it 'says nothing as to whether the proposition "$\{x : \phi(x)\} =
q$" should be affirmed or denied, except for the one case where q is given
in the form of "$\{x : \psi(x)\}$" '?[4] Frege's solution to this difficulty — the
Julius Caesar problem for extensions — is one which we mentioned
in passing in connection with numbers, namely to restrict ourselves to
a language in which no name for Julius Caesar exists and hence no
question as to his being an extension can even be formulated. This
solution to the problem is, of course, implausible in the context of the
Grundlagen, which has no formal language and hence no distinction
between the language under discussion and language in general. It is
much more plausible in the case of *Grundgesetze*, which deals with a
precisely formulated language in which reference to Julius Caesar is
impossible. In the formal language of *Grundgesetze* it is true almost
without exception that the objects it is possible to refer to are already
given as value ranges and hence have their identity conditions settled
by Basic Law V. The only exceptions to this — the only names in

---

[4] *Gl.*, § 66, modified.

the formal language which are not value-range terms — are sentences: Frege's incorrect doctrine that sentences are names therefore required him to solve not the Julius Caesar problem but the corresponding one for the references of sentences. He did so by fiat, laying it down that if 'ψ' is a sentence, then $\{\psi\} = \psi$.

Since Frege was wrong to treat sentences as names, he had no need to deal with the question whether what they denote are value ranges: the effect of saying that sentences are not names is to rule that question out as meaningless. What we cannot dismiss in this way is Frege's solution to the Julius Caesar problem more generally, namely to restrict his attention to a formal language in which the problem cannot be posed.

We have already noted, though, what is wrong with this solution: a formal language in which Julius Caesar cannot be spoken of is one in which he cannot be counted, and in such a language the applicability of arithmetic remains unexplained. At some stage in the development we shall have to extend the formal language by adding some empirical vocabulary, and we shall then have to address the Julius Caesar problem just as before. Nothing will have been gained by the delay.

One way of settling the matter is to apply again the trick that Frege used on sentences: when we introduce a new name 'α' whose intended reference is not a value-range, we stipulate that $\alpha = \{\alpha\}$, thus turning α into a value-range by fiat. This is hardly the most satisfactory solution, since instead of making 'Julius Caesar is a value-range' either false or meaningless as we should expect, it makes it true. But this is nothing really new. We saw earlier how Frege's solution of the Julius Caesar problem for numbers led to unexpected truths about numbers. What we have here is simply another instance of the same phenomenon: where identity conditions are underdetermined, we complete them by relatively arbitrary stipulations.

Frege himself considered this strategy in *Grundgesetze* and rejected it. He was right to do so, since we are not in fact free to make the suggested stipulation. The reason we could do so in the case of sentences was that that nothing we had laid down so far made it the case that sentences already referred to value-ranges. (We could be sure of this because the two truth-values were taken as antecedently known and hence not already equal to value-ranges.) But in the case of names more generally, it will not always be apparent whether they name value-ranges or not. A name 'α' that we introduce might already refer to a value-range different from $\{\alpha\}$: if so, the stipulation that $\alpha = \{\alpha\}$ is inconsistent. But the fact that 'α' refers to a value-range might not be obvious from the way in which it was introduced, in which case we would not know whether we were free to make the stipulation.

4.2 The context principle in Grundgesetze

One of the difficulties in the way of regarding either the numerical equivalence or the extensional equivalence as analytic is that the two sides of the biconditional in each case appear to have different onto-logical commitments: the left-hand side commits us to the existence of numbers or extensions; the right-hand side does not. I want now to consider whether some such distinction as that between sense and reference might allow us to describe how this comes about.

Frege published nothing between 1886 and 1890, and the first volume of *Grundgesetze* did not appear until 1893. One reason for the delay was the changes he made in his conception which forced him, he said, 'to discard an almost completed manuscript'.[5] Principal among these changes was the introduction of the distinction between the sense of a linguistic item and its reference. This is not a particularly subtle distinction, and was indeed drawn by the Stoics — Sextus Empiricus remarked that we can understand the sense of a name when the barbar-ians do not, even though they may hear the name uttered and see its reference — but it is nonetheless wholly absent from *Grundlagen*, where Frege operates with the undifferentiated notion of content (*Inhalt*).

One reason Frege gives for introducing the distinction between sense and reference is that 'only in this way can indirect discourse be cor-rectly understood'.[6] But despite its importance in Frege's thought, the notion of sense is therefore not central to *Grundgesetze* since the formal language Frege develops there is entirely extensional in character and cannot be used to construct the contexts of indirect discourse which the notion of sense is needed to explain. Later in his life Frege saw the senses of expressions as abstract entities which occupy a third realm of mind-independent entities but which are nevertheless what we com-municate when we use language successfully. The account of senses in *Grundgesetze*, on the other hand, while it does not contradict this pic-ture, does not commit us to it either, since it treats sense merely as the mode of presentation of reference.

When Frege says in the *Grundlagen* that in introducing new terms by abstraction 'we carve up the content in a way different from the original way',[7] it is now apparent that we should read 'content' as meaning something like what we are now calling sense. Confirmation that this is Frege's intention is provided when he says of a similar example that the left-hand side 'expresses the same sense, but in a different way'.[8] So what the disparity between the apparent ontological commitments

---

[5] *Gg.*, p. ix.   [6] Ibid., p. x.   [7] *Gl.*, § 64.   [8] *Funktion und Begriff*, 10.

of the two sides of the equivalence suggests is that the way in which the reference of an expression depends on the references of its parts need not be the same as the way its sense depends on the sense of its parts: it must be possible to carve up a sense in different ways.

We saw earlier that in *Grundlagen* Frege took it to be the context principle that allows us to see the numerical equivalence as a route to securing the reference of numerical terms. But as it is stated in the *Grundlagen* the context principle is ambiguous:

It is enough if the proposition taken as a whole has a sense; it is this that confers on its parts also their content.[9]

The reason for the ambiguity, of course, is simply that Frege did not at that time make any principled distinction in his use of the words for sense (*Sinn*) and content (*Inhalt*). When we translate the context principle to the surrounding semantic theory of *Grundgesetze*, it seems to bifurcate:[10] the context principle for sense is the claim that there is no more to the sense of a word than its contribution to the thoughts of which it is a constituent; the context principle for reference is the claim that we cannot specify the references of subsentential expressions directly but only lay down the references of whole sentences. The bifurcation is only apparent, however. Since the sense of an expression is the mode of presentation of its reference, the context principle for sense follows from that for reference.

Frege did not state the context principle for reference explicitly in *Grundgesetze*, but it is clear that it is this principle that guides Frege's attempt to secure reference for the names in his formal language. As soon as we try to formulate the principle, however, we notice how difficult it is to do so without contradicting the incorrect Fregean doctrine which we considered in the last section. If sentences are merely some among proper names, it is wholly unclear how there could be a general principle which insisted that the references of other names can be accounted for only in terms of the references of sentences.

However much this procedure may be in tension with his other doctrine, it is nevertheless the one he follows. He gives the two truth-values, which he takes to be the references of declarative sentences, a distinctive rôle as being the only objects of which we are required to have an antecedent grasp if we are to understand the formal language. He then proceeds to lay down conditions intended to settle for each sentence of the language which of the two truth-values it refers to. If we make allowance for changes in terminology, Frege's conditions are recognizably those nowadays familiar from accounts of the semantics of predicate

---

[9]*Gl.*, § 60.   [10]See Dummett, *Frege: Philosophy of Language*, ch. 14.

calculus, with one vital difference: Frege nowhere assumes that a range of objects has been stipulated in advance to provide the domain of the interpretation.

Frege realized, of course, that there are contexts, such as those of belief and *oratio obliqua*, in which the two truth-values are too indiscriminate for us to take them to be the references of sentences. He therefore admitted that in such contexts the sentence refers not to its usual reference but to its sense, although, as already noted, such examples are nowhere discussed in *Grundgesetze* because the formal language under discussion there is not one in which the indirect contexts which force such a move can ever arise.

But we cannot give meaning to the expressions of a formal language merely by stipulating which ones are to refer to Truth and which to Falsity. To see why, we have only to consider the minimal formal language in which there are only two symbols, '$\top$' and '$\bot$'. We stipulate that '$\top$' is to refer to Truth and '$\bot$' to Falsity. On Frege's criteria we have thereby given '$\top$' and '$\bot$' senses: each of them now expresses a thought. If we write $\vdash\top$, we have, according to Frege, asserted the truth. But this is absurd. We cannot assert the truth without asserting a particular truth. Our stipulation has not in fact attached any sense to the symbol '$\top$'. Since Frege's account does not rule this example out as incoherent, we must, I think, conclude that his account is wrong.

This argument is not, of course, an objection to the proposal that we take the references of sentences to be truth-values, considered in isolation, since until we know the rôle of reference in Frege's theory of meaning such a proposal is in itself unobjectionable. What the argument shows is rather that Frege's proposal is incompatible with his further claim that the thought expressed by a sentence should be taken to be a mode of presentation of the reference of the sentence. Truth-values are simple, so if thoughts are modes of presentation there must be some further constraint on the notion of a mode of presentation to ensure that thoughts are complex.

It follows from this that Frege's attempt to give sense to the expressions of his formal language merely by stipulating which are true and which false is a failure. Moreover, it cannot be straightforwardly repaired. The project could not even begin to be plausible if it were not for his supposition that what sentences refer to are truth-values, for it is this that allows him to take their references to be antecedently known. If Frege had taken their references to be more finely individuated — to be Russellian propositions, for example — it would have been impossible for him to assume, of a formal language newly constructed, that we have a prior grasp of the references of its sentences.

4.3 Russell's paradox

We must conclude that Frege did not succeed in raising his formal language above the status of the empty formalisms whose inadequacy he himself had so decisively demonstrated. That does not of itself show that the account is wholly valueless, however: it might nevertheless be regarded as a formal consistency proof showing that every sentence of the language has exactly one truth-value.

But even when we regard it in this light it is a complete failure: his system is not in fact formally consistent, and his purported proof that it is is fallacious. The letter which Russell wrote to Frege on 16th June 1902 to inform him of this is one of the most famous in the history of philosophy:

I find myself in complete agreement with you in all essentials .... There is just one point where I have encountered a difficulty. You state that a function, too, can act as the indeterminate element [i.e. the variable]. This I formerly believed, but now this view seems doubtful to me because of the following contradiction: Let w be the predicate to be a predicate which cannot be predicated of itself. Can w be predicated of itself? From each answer its opposite follows.[11]

To see how Russell's paradox arises in Frege's system, we first express Frege's definition of membership in modern notation and prove a fundamental property of it.

Definition. $x \in y \equiv_{Df} (\exists X)(Xx \, . \, y = \{z : Xz\})$.

Lemma. $a = \{x : Fx\} \supset (x)(x \in a \equiv Fx)$.

Proof. If $a = \{x : Fx\}$, then

$$x \in a \equiv x \in \{z : Fz\}$$
$$\equiv (\exists X)(Xx \, . \, \{z : Fz\} = \{z : Xz\}) \text{ by the definition}$$
$$\equiv (\exists X)(Xx \, . \, (z)(Fz \equiv Xz)) \text{ by the extensional equivalence}$$
$$\equiv Fx.$$

Q.E.D.

Russell's paradox now follows immediately.

Russell's paradox. *If* $a = \{x : x \notin x\}$ *then we obtain a contradiction.*

Proof. $(x)(x \in a \equiv x \notin x)$ by the lemma. In particular $a \in a \equiv a \notin a$. Contradiction.   Q.E.D.

[11] *Selected Letters*, I, 246.

Frege himself was aware that Basic Law V might be regarded as problematic:

A dispute [over the acceptability of the axioms] can only arise, so far as I can see, because of my fundamental law of 'value-ranges', which perhaps has not yet been specifically expressed by logicians, though it is in their minds when, e.g., they speak of extensions of concepts.[12]

The discovery of Russell's paradox showed him that he was right to be hesitant about value-ranges. As he later put it in a letter to Russell:

I myself was long reluctant to recognize value-ranges and hence classes; but I saw no other possibility of placing arithmetic on a logical foundation. But the question is, How do we apprehend logical objects? And I have found no other answer to it than this, We apprehend them as extensions of concepts, or more generally, as value-ranges of functions. I have always been aware that there are difficulties connected with this, and your discovery of the contradiction has added to them; but what other way is there?[13]

Now it is an obvious thought, since Russell's proof is so short, that by analysing its steps we might find an emendation of Frege's formal system that renders the proof invalid. However, if the emendation does not stem from a diagnosis of the reason for the paradox, it is likely to be unsuccessful: as Russell himself quickly realized, his paradox is merely the simplest of a great variety of paradoxes which can be derived in Frege's system; blocking one is no guarantee of blocking them all.

Frege himself suggested just such an *ad hoc* emendation in an appendix which he added to volume II of *Grundgesetze* just before it was published. He proposed to replace the contradictory Basic Law V with the following:

$$\{x : f(x)\} = \{x : g(x)\} \equiv$$
$$(y)(f(y) = g(y) \lor y = \{x : f(x)\} \lor y = \{x : g(x)\}).$$

In words: two concepts or other functions have the same value-range if and only if they always have the same value for any argument that is not the value-range of either of them.[14] This emendation succeeds in blocking Russell's proof, but it fails more generally; in Frege's amended system it is possible to prove that there is at most one object;[15] since on Frege's account the two truth-values are objects, it follows that Truth and Falsity are the same. The amended system is therefore contradictory just like the original one.

---

[12] *Gg.*, preface. [13] 28 July 1902, in Frege, *PMC*, 140–1. [14] *Gg.*, II, 262. [15] Quine, 'On Frege's way out'.

Frege himself evidently came to realize this in 1906 while he was preparing a critique of an article on the paradoxes by Schoenflies. 'Russell's contradiction cannot be eliminated in Schoenflies' way,' he noted. 'Remedy from extensions of second-level concepts impossible. Set theory in ruins.'[16] He later wrote that his

efforts to throw light on the questions surrounding the word 'number' and the words and signs for individual numbers seem to have ended in complete failure.[17]

What had gone wrong? By the time he wrote *Grundgesetze* Frege had the semantic theory for concepts (and value-ranges in general) that he had previously lacked: he held now that concepts under which the same objects fall are identical. In symbols,

$$F = G \equiv_{\text{Df}} (x)(Fx \equiv Gx).$$

If we now put

$$e(F) =_{\text{Df}} \{x : Fx\},$$

the extensional equivalence becomes

$$e(F) = e(G) \equiv F = G.$$

The point of writing it like this is to show that it can be thought of as stating that the function e which takes any first-level concept to its extension is a one-to-one correspondence. Suppose for a moment that there are n objects in total, where n is some finite number. There must then be 2^n first-level concepts, since each object can either fall under a first-level concept or not. (A similar argument shows that there are 2^{2^n} second-level concepts, $2^{2^{2^n}}$ third-level concepts, etc.) But it is a familiar fact of arithmetic that $n < 2^n$. So there cannot be the one-to-one correspondence between first-level concepts and their extensions that the extensional equivalence requires. Frege no doubt knew this well enough. But so far there is no contradiction: we can take the argument just given as a *reductio* of the assumption that there are n objects for any finite n, and conclude — as Frege did by another method — that there must be infinitely many objects. What Frege did not realize was that there is an analogous difficulty if there are infinitely many objects. The general result, which is known as 'Cantor's theorem', is that there cannot be a one-to-one function from first-level concepts to objects: there are, briefly, strictly more of the former than of the latter. Russell's paradox results from applying Cantor's theorem in the case where the purported function from first-level concepts to objects is e.

[16] *Posthumous Writings*, 176.   [17] Ibid. 265.

4.4 Numbers as concepts

We discussed in §2.5 how the numerical concepts **0**, **1**, **2**, etc. can be defined as second-level concepts. We could not take this proposal any further then because we had no criterion of identity for concepts and hence no way of representing numerical equations. Now that we have introduced Frege's criterion of identity, according to which concepts are identical if and only if they are coextensive, it is time to reopen discussion of the proposal. The idea, let us recall, is that we split Frege's account of arithmetic into two parts: the first, in which we associate with each first-level concept *F* the second-level concept *equinumerous with the concept F*, is consistent. It is the second part, in which Frege attempted to associate with every second-level concept a distinct object, that is inconsistent.

Frege eventually realized this himself. In a letter to Richard Hönigswald in 1925 he took it as the moral of the paradoxes that 'we must set up a warning sign visible from afar: let no one imagine that he can transform a concept into an object.'[18] He therefore contemplated simply abandoning the attempt to associate objects with the concepts **0**, **1**, **2**, etc.

These second-level concepts form a series and there is a rule in accordance with which, if one of these concepts is given, we can specify the next. But still we do not have in them the numbers of arithmetic; we do not have objects, but concepts. How can we get from these concepts to the numbers of arithmetic in a way that cannot be faulted? Or are there simply no numbers in arithmetic? Could the numerals help to form signs for these second-level concepts, and yet not be signs in their own right?[19]

This is just the proposal we canvassed in §2.5 before adjourning the discussion for lack of a criterion of identity. Even now that we have such a criterion, the proposal still has its difficulties, though. One is the problem of numbers of numbers. Numbers, as Frege saw, attach to concepts. Jupiter has four Galilean moons, so four is the number that attaches to the concept *Galilean moon of Jupiter*. On the proposal we are now considering, **4** is thus a second-level concept, since it can meaningfully be predicated of the first-level concept *Galilean moon of Jupiter*. So *prime number less than ten* is a third-level concept under which the second-level concepts **2**, **3**, **5**, and **7** fall. The number of prime numbers less than ten is thus a fourth-level concept. It therefore cannot be four since four is, we agreed, a second-level concept. We therefore seem unable to say — what is surely true — that the number of primes less than 10 equals the number of Galilean moons of Jupiter.

[18] *PMC*, 55. [19] *Posthumous Writings*, 256–7.

Another difficulty is that we have still only generated the positive part of arithmetic; we need also to be able to justify inequalities such as $n \neq s(n)$. But on the extensional treatment just adopted this inequality will be true only if the second-level concepts n and $s(n)$ are not coextensive, i.e. if there is a first-level concept falling under only one of them. But this will not be true unless there are at least n objects, and the account gives us no logical reason to suppose that this is so.

The third problem caused by the abandonment of extensions is that of the concept *horse*. On Frege's conception any expression which functions linguistically as a singular term in true sentences refers to an object. It follows conversely that no concept can be referred to by a singular term. Since 'the concept *horse*' is a singular term, it therefore does not refer to what it appears to refer to. Frege identified this difficulty in an article of 1892 and he referred to it again frequently in his later writings, but he was inclined to dismiss it as 'an awkwardness of language'.[20] If he *had* taken it seriously, he would have realized that what it exhibits is no mere awkwardness of language but a genuine incoherence in his account. An alternative to Frege's view is to regard concepts as saturated but to suppose that there is an unsaturated element, the copula, which links together objects and concepts to form their values. This alternative does not, of course, solve the difficulty completely, but it restricts it to the single case of the copula, so that the phrase 'the copula' cannot refer to what we want it to refer to. We therefore simply have to accept that there is a central element in our theory which is simply inexpressible.

There is a further problem, though. On Frege's account the difference between objects and concepts is total: objects are saturated, concepts are not. We are of course here expressing matters at the level of analogy: we understand quite well what it is for a phrase to be unsaturated, much less well what this means for an entity. Nevertheless, the analogy gives us a way of picturing the sort of difference that is intended. The stratification of concepts into levels is explained on this account by the difference in the natures of their unsaturated gaps. On the new account this analogy is not available to us. We now have a large class of *entities*, split up into objects, first-level concepts, second-level concepts, and so on. But what is now the difference between an object and a concept, or between a first-level concept and a second-level one? Our theory must, as Wittgenstein later said of another theory, 'explain why it is impossible to judge nonsense'. There is nothing in Frege's thought at this point that would help us to do this.

[20]'Über Begriff und Gegenstand', 196.

4.5   The status of the numerical equivalence

Frege thought that he could give sense to the sentences of his formal language by laying down which are to refer to Truth and which to Falsity. The sense of subsentential expressions would then emerge as the contribution they made to the senses of sentences. His downfall came because he supposed that the compositional conception of senses that this procedure implies was consistent with the notion that the two sides of Basic Law V always have the same sense. Russell's paradox demonstrates conclusively that it is not. But Russell's paradox has a wider significance even than this, for it shows that there is something seriously amiss with Frege's notion of a logical object and hence with the context principle which he used to underpin it.

We should be wary, therefore, of using the paradox as an excuse to return to the strategy of basing arithmetic directly on the numerical equivalence. Even if we could solve the Julius Caesar problem that caused Frege to reject it, we should still be faced with the task of justifying the numerical equivalence as analytic. Now that we know that the extensional equivalence, which is strikingly similar in form to the numerical equivalence, is not even true and hence certainly not analytic, that task is apt to seem somewhat harder. If there is to be a notion of sense on which the two sides of the numerical equivalence have the same sense, as there must if Frege's route to its analyticity is to be vindicated, it cannot also make the two sides of the extensional equivalence have the same sense. It must, in other words, be a notion of sense which carries with it a way of distinguishing good abstraction principles like the numerical equivalence from bad ones like the extensional equivalence. Perhaps there is such a notion,[21] but if so, then it cannot also play the explanatory rôle of being what it is that we grasp when we understand a sentence, since whether an abstraction principle is good is not an epistemically transparent question.

The comparison between Frege's treatment and Dedekind's is illuminating in this context. The two accounts are, as we saw in § 3.2, in a precise sense technically equivalent. Once that equivalence is taken into account Frege's solution to the existence problem is rather similar to Dedekind's. For Frege the content of arithmetic arises from the recarvability of the sense of the equinumerosity relation — from a feature, in other words, of the thoughts that are available to us — whereas for Dedekind it is established by means of a proof appealing to 'the totality of all things that can be objects of my thought'. Frege himself remarked

---

[21] Cf. Hale, 'Grundlagen § 64'.

that Dedekind's use of the word 'thought' in his proof coincided with his own.[22] Both of them, that is to say, conceived of thoughts as objective, publicly available entities.

But Dedekind's solution to the existence problem left it open, which of two accounts of our access to these entities, one passive and one creative, he adopted. Only his solution to the existence problem required him to settle for the creative account. Since Frege had nothing corresponding, it is unsurprising that he did not feel compelled to go the same way, but retained a conception of the third realm as having a structure objectively available to us. This account had the advantage that it gave him a ready explanation of the universal applicability of arithmetic: it applies to everything since its structure is that of thought; and nothing is independent of thought, 'for what are things independent of reason?'[23]

What lies behind Russell's paradox, however, is an objection to Frege's notion of a third realm unconnected with his solution to the uniqueness problem. Frege saw the metaphor of recarving as providing a way of seeing how the denizens of an objective totality of thoughts could by reconceptualization yield up objects which had not previously been apparent to us. The moral of the paradox is that this process is potentially explosive: the new objects allow us to form new thoughts, which in turn yield up further objects. It is far from clear that we can coherently lay claim to an intuitive grasp of a totality of thoughts that is closed under such a process.

[22] *Posthumous Writings*, 136.   [23] *Gl.*, § 26.

5

Russell's account of classes

Russell discovered the paradox in the course of writing *The Principles of Mathematics*. When this book appeared in 1903, it contained a discussion of the paradox but no more than a sketch of a solution. He then began to work, together with his former teacher Whitehead, on a second volume, in which the formal development of mathematics from logic was to be presented. When it eventually appeared almost ten years later, this second volume had metamorphosed into a separate three-volume work called *Principia Mathematica* which bears somewhat the same relation to the *Principles* that *Grundgesetze* bears to the *Grundlagen*: just as Frege intended *Grundgesetze* to be a detailed demonstration of the thesis he had enunciated in the *Grundlagen* that arithmetic is part of logic, so Whitehead and Russell intended in *Principia* to provide the complete logical derivation promised in the *Principles* of the foundations, not just of arithmetic, but of the whole of pure mathematics.

5.1 Propositions

The programme Russell was engaged in was thus in a sense a direct continuation of Frege's: his task was to repair the error in Frege's system and hence establish the logicist thesis. But in Frege's case the opposition to Kant which this thesis implies was local in scope: only arithmetic was included, and Frege continued to adhere to a broadly Kantian account of geometry. For Russell, on the other hand, logicism was part of a much broader attack on idealism. Not only did he wish to expel Kantian intuition from geometry as well as arithmetic; he wanted more generally to show that we are genuinely capable of thinking and talking about the world, rather than a mind-dependent surrogate.

Russell took the first step in this anti-idealist project in conversations with Moore in 1898. What they did was to adopt a conception of propositions as complexes capable of having real objects as constituents. In regarding propositions as complexes, which we are capable of judging true or false but whose existence is independent of us, they thus agreed with Frege, who used the term 'thought' for just such entities. But for Frege it is not the objects themselves that are constituents of the thought but modes of presentation of these objects ('senses'). Neither Russell nor Moore was aware of Frege's views when they formulated their conception of propositions, but it is plain that they would not have found it conducive to the anti-idealist project they were undertaking. For if we take the objects of our judgements to be Fregean thoughts in which the objects that make up the world do not figure, we owe an explanation of how we succeed in judging anything about the world at all. When Frege asserted in a letter to Russell that 'Mont Blanc with all its snowfields is not itself a component part of the thought that Mont Blanc is more than 4000 metres high',[1] Russell responded:

I believe that in spite of all its snowfields Mont Blanc itself is a component part of what is actually asserted in the proposition 'Mont Blanc is more than 4000 metres high'. We do not assert the thought, for this is a private psychological matter: we assert the object of the thought, and this is, to my mind, a certain complex (an objective proposition, one might say) in which Mont Blanc is itself a component part. If we do not admit this, then we get the conclusion that we know nothing at all about Mont Blanc. This is why for me the *meaning* of a proposition is not the true, but a certain complex which (in the given case) is true. In the case of a simple proper name like 'Socrates', I cannot distinguish between sense and meaning; I see only the idea, which is psychological, and the object. Or better: I do not admit the sense at all, but only the idea and the meaning.[2]

Russell thus regarded Fregean senses as a Kantian veil behind which, on Frege's account, would lie a world wholly opaque to language.

But there is a difficulty with Russell's view too. Frege expressed it in an unsent draft of a letter to Jourdain written in 1914 (in which the example under discussion is now not Mont Blanc with all its snowfields but Mount Etna with all its lava flows):

Now that part of the thought which corresponds to the name 'Etna' cannot be Mount Etna itself; it cannot be the meaning of this name. For each individual piece of frozen, solidified lava which is part of Mount Etna would then also be part of the thought that Etna is higher than Vesuvius. But it seems to me absurd that pieces of lava, even pieces of which I had no knowledge, should be parts of my thought.[3]

There are two objections here: one is that on Frege's conception a thought could not have something concrete as a part; the other is that in order to grasp a thought we must have a grasp of all its parts. The first would not have fazed Russell since it would not have seemed strange

---

[1] 13 Nov. 1904, in Frege, *PMC*, 163. [2] 12 Dec. 1904, ibid. 169. [3] Ibid. 79.

to him that an abstract complex could have concrete parts, but the second objection is more troublesome. If it is valid, it seems that the only response available to Russell is to agree that, despite superficial appearance to the contrary, 'Mount Etna' and 'Mont Blanc' are not logically proper names. But it is not just mountains that we can think about without having complete knowledge of them: Frege's criticism will apply with equal force to anything capable of having unexpected aspects. Russell was eventually forced by this criticism to conclude that hardly any of the phrases that occur in ordinary language are logically proper names since I cannot be in the right epistemic relationship with something to enable me to denote it with a logically proper name unless I am immediately acquainted with it.

What Russell's exchange with Frege concerning Mont Blanc demonstrates vividly is that Russell conceived of objects literally as constituents of propositions. But Russell did not at this time see the structure of propositions as different from the structure of the sentences that express them: among the constituents of a proposition will be the entities referred to by phrases occurring in the sentence which expresses it. If the phrases in question are logically proper names ('names in the narrow sense', as Russell then called them),[4] the proposition will also be about these same objects. As we have seen, however, not all such phrases can be proper names in this sense; Russell called those which are not logically proper names *denoting phrases* and the propositional constituents corresponding to them *denoting concepts* (or sometimes *denoting complexes*).

A concept *denotes* when, if it occurs in a proposition, the proposition is not *about* the concept but about a term connected in a certain peculiar way with the concept. ... If I say 'I met a man', the proposition is not about *a man*: this is a concept which does not walk the streets, but lives in the shadowy limbo of the logic-books. What I met was a thing, not a concept, an actual man with a tailor and a bank-account or a public-house and a drunken wife.[5]

('Term' is Russell's general word for any sort of entity.)

On this conception the relationship between a denoting concept and its denotation (if any) is a logical, not a linguistic, one.

There is a sense in which we denote, when we point or describe, or employ words as symbols for concepts; this, however, is not the sense I wish to discuss. But the fact that description is possible — that we are able, by the employment of concepts, to designate a thing which is not a concept — is due to a logical relation between some concepts and some terms, in virtue of which such concepts inherently and logically *denote* such terms. It is this sense of denoting that is here in question.[6]

---

[4] *Papers*, IV, 315. [5] *Principles*, § 56. [6] Ibid.

5.2 The old theory of denoting

It was of course central to Russell's project for him to find a solution to the paradox. He soon decided that Frege's proposed emendation of Basic Law V (§ 4.3), which he had in an appendix to the *Principles* said was 'very likely ... the true solution',[7] not only did violence to our understanding of what a class is but was in any event inconsistent. It became apparent to him that any correct solution would involve denying that every propositional function determines a class, and in May 1903 he hit upon the idea of implementing this proposal in the most radical way possible — by eliminating class terms entirely and conceiving of talk about class membership as just talk about predication in another guise. Thus if we use Russell's later notation '$\hat{y}\phi y$' to denote the class of all ϕs, the idea is that '$x \in \hat{y}\phi y$' is to be thought of as just a variant of 'ϕx'. This was hardly an original move: it was evidently how Peano thought of classes and was indeed the motivation for his introduction of '$\in$' as the symbol for the 'is' of predication (as an abbreviation for '$\epsilon\sigma\tau\iota$'). Nevertheless, it briefly seemed to Russell that the elimination of classes had resolved the paradoxes. 'Four days ago,' he wrote in his journal on 23 May 1903, 'I solved the Contradiction. The relief of this is unspeakable.'[8] He wrote immediately to Frege with the news that 'classes are entirely superfluous'.[9] Whitehead was equally pleased, and sent Russell a telegram proclaiming, 'Heartiest congratulations Aristoteles secundus.'[10]

Their joy was short-lived; they had not solved the paradoxes. A theory which straightforwardly replaces propositions about classes with propositions about propositional function will simply replace Russell's paradox about classes with a corresponding paradox about propositional functions. If we are permitted to define a propositional function by

$$f(\phi). =_{\mathrm{Df}}. \sim\!\phi(\phi),$$

then obviously $f(f) \equiv \sim\!f(f)$, which is a contradiction. All that Russell's elimination of classes had achieved was to enable propositional functions to be treated like Fregean concepts by defining for them a notion of extensional identity. Russell's mistake was to allow propositional functions to appear in entity positions in propositions.

Nevertheless, although Russell's idea of eliminating classes was a wrong turning, it was not a blind alley. His mistake was not that he eliminated classes, but that he straightforwardly replaced them with

[7]Ibid., § 496. [8]*Papers*, IV, p. xx. [9]Frege, *PMC*, 158. [10]*Papers*, IV, p. xx.

propositional functions. Already in the *Principles* Russell had taken denoting to be the key to understanding our ability to make use of the class of all numbers, because

the concept *all numbers*, though not itself infinitely complex, yet denotes an infinitely complex object. This is the inmost secret of our power to deal with infinity. An infinitely complex concept, though there may be such, can certainly not be manipulated by the human intelligence; but infinite collections, owing to the notion of denoting, can be manipulated without introducing any concepts of infinite complexity. Throughout the discussions of infinity ... , this remark should be borne in mind: if it is forgotten, there is an air of magic which causes the results obtained to seem doubtful.[11]

So it was natural that the paradoxes should have led Russell to re-examine his theory of denoting to see whether it did indeed dispel the air of magic which surrounds our talk of the infinite in mathematics and, more urgently, whether it provided the resources to solve the paradoxes. Since it was by now evident to Russell that the solution would involve accepting that some phrases which apparently denote classes do not in fact do so, he took an especial interest in cases (such as 'the present King of France') where the denoting concept does not denote anything. Thus he wrote to his wife on 14 April 1904:

Alfred [Whitehead] and I had a happy hour yesterday, when we thought the present King of France had solved the Contradiction; but it turned out finally that the royal intellect was not quite up to that standard.[12]

The reason Russell paid attention to the case of the present King of France was not, however, that he had only just realized the possibility of concepts which do not denote anything. Russell stated explicitly in the *Principles* that 'a concept may denote although it does not denote anything. This occurs when there are propositions in which the said concept occurs, and which are not about the said concept, but all such propositions are false.'[13] In a paper which he wrote later, but still well before he rejected the theory of denoting in the *Principles*, Russell was even more explicit. The concept of nectar or ambrosia, he says,

is an entity, but it does not denote anything. To take a simpler case: 'The present King of England' is a complex concept denoting an individual; 'the present King of France' is a similar complex concept denoting nothing. The phrase intends to point out an individual, but fails to do so: it does not point out an unreal individual, but no individual at all. The same explanation applies to mythical personages, Apollo, Priam, etc. These words have a *meaning*, which can be found by looking them up in a classical dictionary; but they have not a *denotation*: there is no entity, real or imaginary, which they point out.[14]

[11] § 72. [12] *Selected Letters*, I, 277. [13] § 73. [14] *Papers*, IV, 487.

What led Russell to reject his early theory of denoting when he came
to re-examine it was therefore not simply that it fails to deal with the
case of a denoting concept which does not denote anything. The difficulty is rather that even if a denoting concept does denote something,
Russell was unable to explain the 'peculiar way'[15] in which the concept
is connected with its denotation. It was considering this that led to
what Russell described as an 'inextricable tangle'.[16]

Suppose that 'C' is a denoting phrase and $\langle C \rangle$ is the denoting concept
corresponding to it, i.e. what Russell was by now calling its meaning.
(Russell talks of 'C' instead of $\langle C \rangle$ in his discussion of the matter, but
the use of quotation marks to mention things is now too well established
for Russell's usage not to be confusing to the modern reader.)   Let
us suppose for the moment that the phrase 'C' does in fact have a
denotation. There must then be, Russell thought, a logical relationship
between the meaning $\langle C \rangle$ and the denotation C.   The 'inextricable
tangle' arises when we try to say what that relationship is. It seems
at first as if we can express it by saying that $\langle C \rangle$ denotes C. But
the notation '$\langle C \rangle$' is misleading: it does not depend functionally on
C. 'There is no backward road from denotations to meanings, because
every object can be denoted by an infinite number of different denoting
phrases.'[17] So $\langle C \rangle$ is not a function of C, and it is therefore misleading
to write it in this form. But if we use a new symbol for it, say 'D', then
we have to express the relationship we want by saying that D denotes
C. This is no longer in any way explanatory of the general relationship
which we wanted to describe, but has to be expressed afresh for each
denoting concept D. In short, our account leaves the relation of $\langle C \rangle$ to
C 'wholly mysterious'.[18]

Various other ways of referring to $\langle C \rangle$ might be attempted, but each
has its difficulties. 'The meaning of C', for example, designates not
$\langle C \rangle$ but the meaning (if any) of C. What causes confusion here, and
makes us inclined to misunderstand the phrase, is that in most cases
C will not be the sort of thing that can have a meaning.   So at this
stage, to make the point more vivid, Russell considers an example in
which C does have a meaning, namely where 'C' is the denoting phrase
'The first line of Gray's Elegy'. The meaning of the first line of Gray's
Elegy is then the same as the meaning of 'The curfew tolls the knell of
parting day', and it is clear that this is not the same as $\langle$The first line
of Gray's Elegy$\rangle$, i.e. as the meaning of 'The first line of Gray's Elegy'.

The most natural way for us to designate $\langle C \rangle$, of course, is as the
meaning of 'C', but 'the meaning of "C"' is not a function of C any

---

[15] *Principles*, § 56.   [16] *Papers*, IV, 422.   [17] Ibid.   [18] Ibid.

more than $\langle C \rangle$ is: it is rather a function of the *phrase* '*C*', so if we try to express what we want by saying that the meaning of '*C*' denotes C, we are making the relationship between meaning and denotation 'linguistic through the phrase'. But this it cannot be: the meaning and the denotation are both entities in the world whose existence is independent of language, and the relationship between them must therefore also be independent of language.

We could consider further attempts to express the relationship we want, but there is no point. A moment's reflection shows that the difficulty we are facing is quite general. We cannot denote the meaning by a proper name, since any proposition in which the meaning occurs is not about it but about its denotation. Thus the meaning 'cannot be got at except by means of denoting phrases'. But any denoting phrase we construct to denote $\langle C \rangle$ will not depend functionally on C. So if our aim is to express the relationship between $\langle C \rangle$ and C we will first of all have to express the relationship between the denoting concept which denotes $\langle C \rangle$ and $\langle C \rangle$ itself. This, of course, is just a further (and logically more complex) case of the same general question.

Russell did not, I have said, conceive of propositions as occupying a mysterious realm cloaked by a veil of language: our inability to express the relationship between $\langle C \rangle$ and C was for him evidence that there is no proposition expressing that relationship, in which case there just is no such relationship, and the old theory of denoting, which required us to suppose that there is, is wrong.[19]

5.3 The new theory of denoting

Russell's solution to the Gray's Elegy problem was to rewrite any sentence containing a denoting phrase so as to eliminate the occurrence of the phrase. If this can be done, he thought, we no longer have any reason to suppose that the proposition which the sentence expresses contains a denoting concept; so the difficulty of explaining the relationship between denoting concepts and what they denote disappears.

The mistake of the previous theory of denoting had been to assume that if a denoting phrase occurs in a sentence then there must be a corresponding denoting concept as a constituent of the proposition. What the new theory showed was that there can be phrases occurring in sentences in what appeared to be entity-positions but where the

---

[19]See Makin, 'Making sense of "On denoting" ', to which this discussion of the Gray's Elegy argument is heavily indebted.

proposition expressed by the sentence does not have a constituent corresponding to the phrase: such phrases Russell later[20] called *incomplete symbols*. Thus for the first time in Russell's work we see the structure of the proposition prized apart from the structure of the sentence.

The way in which Russell expressed his new doctrine in 'On denoting' — 'that denoting phrases never have any meaning in themselves, but that every proposition in whose verbal expression they occur has a meaning'[21] — is strikingly reminiscent of Frege's enunciation of the context principle. However, the rôle of the doctrine in Russell's philosophy is quite different. Although the new theory of denoting required Russell to pay more attention than before to the distinction between a proposition and its linguistic expression, it did not induce in him anything corresponding to Frege's 'linguistic turn': it was not until about 1918 that Russell came to see the study of language and its relation to thought as important. The significance of Russell's context principle is rather that it does not secure reference for an incomplete symbol, even if we give an account, by means of elimination rules, of the truth conditions for all sentences in which the symbol might occur. The reason why it does not secure reference is that there is no requirement for the elimination rules to be in harmony with the logical rules of the system. The natural way to translate 'The present king of France is not bald' is as expressing the proposition that

There is exactly one present king of France and no present king of France is bald.

(which is false), whereas 'The present king of France is bald' translates into

There is exactly one present king of France and all present kings of France are bald.

(which is also false). So the first sentence is not the negation of the second and hence we cannot, on pain of incoherence, regard the elimination rules as allowing us to regard 'the king of France' as a genuine singular term.

Russell's doctrine in the *Principles* had been that if we know a proposition we must be acquainted with its constituents. He applied this doctrine to logical constituents as well as empirical ones.

The discussion of indefinables — which forms the chief part of philosophical logic — is the endeavour to see clearly, and to make others see clearly, the entities concerned, in order that the mind may have that kind of acquaintance with them which it has with redness or the taste of a pineapple.[22]

[20] *PM*, Intro., ch. 3.   [21] *Papers*, IV, 416.   [22] *Principles*, p. v.

One of the virtues of the new theory of denoting was that it allowed Russell to restrict the range of entities he had to suppose acquaintance with. But it did not remove entirely the necessity to appeal to acquaintance with logical entities. This is because there is one sort of denoting concept that his theory did not eliminate — the *variable*. All that can be claimed for the theory is that it reduces the general problem of explaining the connection between denoting concepts and their denotations to the particular case where the concept is a variable. This is made clear by Russell's reply to a query Moore raised when he read 'On denoting' for the first time:

You say '*all* the constituents of propositions we apprehend are entities with which we have immediate acquaintance'. Have we, then, immediate acquaintance with the variable? and what sort of entity is it?[23]

Russell replied:

I only profess to reduce the problem of denoting to the problem of the variable. This latter is horribly difficult, and there seem equally strong objections to all the views I have been able to think of.[24]

We nowadays think of the word 'variable' as referring to symbols of a certain sort. Russell, on the other hand, generally used it to refer to the entities such symbols are to be taken as meaning. The difficulty is then to see what sort of entity a variable could be. It could not be complex, since then it would be a denoting concept of the sort which the 1905 theory had shown to be impossible. But if it is simple, it must be unrestricted — apply, in other words, to anything whatsoever. This is because any restriction on the range of such a variable must be expressible in a proposition, but in this proposition a variable with a wider range of significance must occur:

The older symbolic logicians had a doctrine of the *universe of discourse*, setting, as it were, bounds of decency, outside which no well-conducted variable would wander. Thus when they asserted that (say) ϕx was always true, they only meant that it was always true so long as x was within the universe. Let us call the universe i. Then they really meant: ' "x is an i" implies ϕx'. But was this to hold only when x is an i? If so, we should have to say ' "x is an i" implies that "x is an i" implies ϕx'. And so on *ad infinitum*. Thus a statement, such as ϕx, which is true under an hypothesis, can only be stated to be true under that hypothesis if the statement that the hypothesis implies ϕx can be made without any limitation on x. Any limitation on x is part of the whole which is really asserted; and as soon as the limitation is explicitly stated, the resulting implicational proposition remains true when the limitation is false. Thus a variable must be capable of all values. This argument may be fallacious, but I have never seen any attempt to refute it.[25]

[23]Russell, *Papers*, IV, p. xxxv. [24]Ibid. [25]*Essays in Analysis*, 205.

There is a further difficulty with Russell's idea of the variable as a simple non-linguistic entity. Russell calls it *the* variable, thus suggesting that it is unique. And indeed if there were two different variables there would, on Russell's conception, have to be a proposition expressing the difference between them, but such a proposition would be susceptible to an argument of the same sort as that just considered against the restricted variable. But if the variable is unique, how are we to explain the meaning of '$(x)(\exists y) . Rxy$', for example? The letters 'x' and 'y' in this sentence must both mean the variable, but the way they mean it must be different if we are to distinguish the meaning of this sentence from the meaning of '$(x)(\exists y) . Ryx$'. But as soon as we consider the propositions expressing the different ways in which the various letters mean the variable, we are back in something like our previous difficulty.

Russell was therefore right to think that the problem of the variable is 'horribly difficult'. Indeed the difficulty with it that we have just been considering is one Russell recognized in the *Principles*. However, his response to it there — that 'a variable is not any term simply, but any term as entering into a propositional function'[26] — can hardly be said to amount to an answer. As we shall see, much of the difficulty in Russell's attempts to construct a satisfactory logical theory lay in his need to reconcile the theory with his incoherent conception of the variable as a simple entity and hence both unrestricted and unique.

5.4 The substitutional theory

At about the time he wrote 'On denoting' Russell was considering[27] three general strategies for avoiding the paradoxes. He called them the *zigzag* theory, the *limitation-of-size* theory, and the *no-class* or *substitutional* theory. The zigzag theory held that propositional functions determine classes unless they are 'complicated and recondite'; the limitation-of-size theory held that they do so unless they are too big; and the no-class theory that they never do. Each of these strategies led to considerable technical difficulties, and it is clear that such practical concerns were at this stage as important to Russell as any philosophical arguments in settling which strategy to follow. What led him to reject the first two strategies was not only that 'On denoting' gave the no-class strategy a philosophical context that lent it plausibility but above all that it seemed to him — for a time — to *work*.

[26]§ 93.   [27]See *Essays in Analysis*, 144–56.

Russell had tried a no-class strategy in 1903, but at that time he simply replaced classes with propositional functions everywhere they appeared: the elimination of classes did not affect the compositional structure of the proposition at all. The reason Russell described 'On denoting' as 'the source of all my subsequent progress'[28] was that it showed him a way of eliminating denoting phrases in such a way as to change this structure fundamentally. The sentence 'The present king of France is bald' can have a perfectly definite meaning even though 'the present king of France' does not stand for anything on its own. What Russell took to be the correct analysis of this sentence — 'One and only one man at present governs France, and everyone who governs France is bald' — contains no part corresponding to the king of France, who thus emerges as what Russell called a 'false abstraction'.[29] In the theory of classes Russell now proposed, classes are also false abstractions in this sense.

Russell sometimes expressed himself by the negative claim that 'there are really no such things as classes.'[30]   At first sight this might be thought to go too far: treating classes as false abstractions in itself amounts only to refraining from the positive claim that there are such things as classes, and does not compel us to deny it. After all, 'the present king of England' must by parity of form be regarded as a false abstraction too, as Russell himself noted (in an article written when Edward VII was on the throne and the sensibilities of Scots were not thought important). The difficulty with this, though, is that even if the theory itself merely remains silent on whether classes exist, and does not preclude the possibility that *that* question might be amenable to consideration by other means, it is difficult to see what those other means might be: if we take seriously the idea that talk about classes has been methodically explained away, we are left strictly speaking without the resources to make sense of the notion that classes might nevertheless still exist behind our logical backs, as it were.

Treating classes as linguistic fictions was not new. Frege had considered and rejected the strategy of regarding class-names as incomplete symbols (or 'sham proper names', as he called them) in the appendix to *Grundgesetze*. (It is worth noting that his objection to this strategy was just what Russell later regarded as one of its virtues, namely that incomplete symbols do not function logically in the same way as proper names.) And as we mentioned earlier, Russell tried a no-class theory in 1903. What scotched it then was that he simply took propositional functions as entities instead, thus reintroducing the paradoxes

[28]Letter to Jourdain in Grattan-Guinness, 79.   [29]*Essays in Analysis*, 165–6. [30]Ibid. 166.

in another guise.

The further step which Russell took in the wake of 'On denoting' was to treat propositional functions as false abstractions as well: propositions in which they apparently occur were to be rewritten in such a way that they were eliminated, after the fashion of the elimination of definite descriptions. The variable was still taken as a primitive idea as it had been in 'On denoting', but now there was a further primitive idea of *substitution*. If the variable was for Russell not a sign but the entity it stands for, it follows that substitution must be understood not as the (unproblematic) process of replacing one sign with another within a string, but as a corresponding relationship between the entities these strings are supposed to express. Russell made no attempt to give an account of this relationship; it is 'more or less in the nature of a technical device, to be replaced by a more convenient device if one should be discovered.'[31] This is rather lame: substitution must on Russell's view be a purely logical notion, and yet if any relationship is 'linguistic through the phrase' it is surely this one.

The details of the substitutional theory are as follows. If a, p, and x are entities, we write '$(p|a)x$' to denote the result of substituting x for a everywhere it occurs in p. In the case that will concern us most, p is a proposition, a is an object, and x is a variable, but Russell takes the notion of substitution to apply more generally. The symbol '$p|a$' is called a *matrix of the first type*; it is wholly devoid of meaning on its own and only becomes significant in the context of an appropriate proposition. In the same way we can write '$(p|a, b)(x, y)$' for the result of simultaneously substituting x and y for a and b in p. The incomplete symbol '$p|a, b$' is called a *matrix of the second type*. And so on. Matrices are intended to take the place of propositional functions. Two matrices α and β of the first type are said to be equal if $(x)(\alpha(x) \equiv \beta(x))$. Similarly two matrices ϕ and ψ of the second type are said to be equal if $(\alpha)(\phi(\alpha) \equiv \psi(\alpha))$.

Theories that reduce one sort of entity to another have an evident appeal to anyone inclined, as Russell undoubtedly was, to wield Ockham's razor. The primary virtue of the substitutional theory for him was not its ontological parsimony, however, but its generation of a type-theoretic hierarchy. Since matrices are false abstractions, they do not genuinely occur in propositions. We have first of all to eliminate the matrix expressions in order to obtain paraphrasing sentences from which they have been eliminated: it is *these* sentences which allow us to see the structure of the propositions being expressed. But it turns out that among the phrases containing incomplete symbols which seem at

[31] Ibid. 200.

first glance to be sentences there are some which do not permit of the required eliminations: these are precisely the ones which violate type restrictions. We shall see later that one of the greatest difficulties with the theory of types is that by stating it we violate it, since we need to explain what it is for two objects to have the same type but cannot do so: if it is meaningful to say that *a* and *b* are of the same type, it must be meaningful to say that they are not, but this is precisely what the theory of types requires us to reject as meaningless. Russell's substitutional theory, on the other hand, holds out the hope that the type restrictions may not have to be stated at all: they may simply drop out of the account we give of the rules for eliminating incomplete symbols.

5.5 Russell's propositional paradox

The substitutional theory had considerable virtues, then, but it was extremely short-lived, even by Russell's hectic standards of theory revision. Russell read his paper on it to the London Mathematical Society in May 1906. By 14th June he was writing to Jourdain that although he felt 'more and more certain' that the no-class theory was right, 'in order, however, to solve the Epimenides, it is necessary to extend it to general propositions'.[32] So Russell decided not to publish the paper but to set about 'purging it of metaphysical elements'.[33]

The difficulty lay in what Russell had all along recognized to be the 'only serious danger' of the substitutional theory, namely that 'some contradiction should be found to result from the assumption that *propositions* are entities.'[34] What Russell came to see was that on the understanding he then had of the notions involved a paradox does indeed result from the assumption that propositions are entities; and that propositions are therefore 'the metaphysical elements' to be purged from the system.

The paradox Russell discovered was in fact of the same type as the paradox of the non-self class assertion (sometimes called the 'Russell–Myhill paradox'), which he had considered already in the *Principles*. We call a proposition a *class assertion* if it asserts all the propositions which have some property ϕ, and a *self class assertion* if it has the property ϕ itself. If now ψ is the property of being a non-self class assertion (i.e. a class assertion which is not a self class assertion) and p is the assertion of all non-self class assertions, then p is plainly a class assertion since it asserts all the propositions with the property ψ: but

[32]In Grattan-Guinness, 89. [33]Letter to Jourdain, 22 Oct. 1906, ibid. 93. [34]*Essays in Analysis*, 188.

if it is a self class assertion, by definition it has ψ itself and is therefore a non-self class assertion; and if it is a non-self class assertion, it has ψ and is therefore a self class assertion. Contradiction.

The paradox can easily be formalized. Define a function $f(\hat{\phi})$ by

$$f(\phi). =_{\text{Df}}. (p). \phi(p) \supset p,$$

so that $f(\phi)$ is the assertion of all propositions with the property ϕ. Note first that since $f(\phi)$ on Russell's conception has ϕ as a constituent,

$$f(\phi) = f(\psi) . \supset. \phi = \psi. \tag{1}$$

Now let ψ be the property of propositions given by

$$\psi(p) :=_{\text{Df}}: (\exists \phi). p = f(\phi) . \sim\phi(p)$$

and let $q =_{\text{Df}} \psi(f(\psi))$. If $\sim q$, then

$$(\phi). f(\phi) = f(\psi) . \supset. \phi(f(\psi))$$

and in particular $\psi(f(\psi))$, i.e. q. But if q, then

$$(\exists \phi). f(\phi) = f(\psi) . \sim\phi(f(\psi))$$

and so $\sim\psi(f(\psi))$ by (1), i.e. $\sim q$. Contradiction.

When the proof is presented in this form, it becomes clear that the exact form of $f(\hat{\phi})$ is unimportant. It takes a function from propositions to propositions as argument; it takes a proposition as value; and its value depends on its argument, in the sense that $f(\phi)$ has ϕ as a constituent. This is all we need in order to obtain a contradiction since on the Russellian conception (1) now follows. (Of course, presenting the proof in this way also demonstrates the connection with Cantor's theorem: what we have shown is that there are more functions from propositions to propositions than there are propositions.)

It is not immediately obvious that the paradox survives the introduction of the substitutional theory, since on this theory both ϕ and $f(\hat{\phi})$ are incomplete symbols, to which Russell's account of propositions cannot be applied. It turns out, in fact, that it does survive: here are the details. What we need in order to obtain a contradiction is a function $f(\hat{r}, \hat{s})$ with the property that

$$f(p, q) = f(r, s) :\supset: (r|s)f(p, q). \equiv. (p|q)f(p, q). \tag{2}$$

For suppose that we can construct such a function. Now let

$$p = (\exists r, s). q = f(r, s). \sim(r|s)(q).$$

If $\sim(p|q)f(p,q)$, then

$$f(p,q) = f(r,s) \supset_{r,s} (r|s)f(p,q),$$

and so $(p|q)f(p,q)$, which is absurd. If, on the other hand, $(p|q)f(p,q)$, then

$$(\exists r,s).\, f(p,q) = f(r,s).\sim(r|s)f(p,q),$$

and so $\sim(p|q)(f(p,q))$ by (2), which is also absurd. Contradiction.

It remains to construct a function $f(\hat{r},\hat{s})$ with the stipulated property (2). But on Russell's conception r and s are constituents of $r \supset s$. So if we let $f(r,s).=_{\text{Df}}.r \supset s$, then

$$f(r,s) = f(p,q) .\supset. r = p . s = q,$$

and (2) follows at once.

This paradox shows that the substitutional theory cannot consistently be held without rejecting Russell's conception of propositions. There is no need for us to speculate on whether it was this paradox that led Russell himself to abandon the substitutional theory: in a letter to Ralph Hawtrey he describes 'the paradox that killed the substitutional theory'[35] and gives a proof that differs from ours (other than notationally) only in using a different function $f(\hat{r},\hat{s})$; Russell defines

$$f(r,s).=_{\text{Df}}.t = (r|s)(b)$$

and notes that for this function (2) holds because if $t = (r|s)(b)$ is the same proposition as $t = (p|q)(b)$, then $(r|s)(b)$ is the same proposition as $(p|q)(b)$, whence

$$(x).\, (r|s)(x) \equiv (p|q)(x),$$

and hence in particular

$$(r|s)f(p,q) \equiv (p|q)f(p,q).$$

There is a puzzle here, though. Russell expounded his propositional paradox in the *Principles* in 1903. Why did he in 1906, however briefly, adopt a theory which is incapable of dealing with this paradox? The answer to this question may lie in the emendation to his formal system that Frege appended to *Grundgesetze* in an attempt to save it from paradox. When Russell corresponded with Frege about the propositional paradox, his last mention of it was that 'now these difficulties

[35] 22 Jan. 1909, RA3 Rec. Acq. 394.

have been overcome by means of the theorem in your appendix'.[36] The theorem Russell was alluding to states that

$$(\exists \phi, \psi).\, f(\phi) = f(\psi)\,.\, \sim\!\phi(f(\phi))\,.\, \psi(f(\psi)).$$

If Russell had analysed the reason for the apparent resolution of his propositional paradox by this result, he would surely have realized that Frege's result is itself in direct opposition to Russell's conception of propositions. Not doing so, though, Russell thought instead that the theorem dissolved the paradox. If he later discovered that the formal system in which this theorem was proved is in any case contradictory, and the theorem therefore worthless, he may not immediately have realized that the propositional paradox was thus reinstated as a crux on which to test any new theory.

5.6 Frege's hierarchy of senses

Before we discuss the account that succeeded Russell's substitutional theory, there is one question about the paradoxes of propositions which remains to be answered: why are they not a difficulty for Frege? I have already remarked that Frege had available to him an extensional hierarchy of concepts based on a conception of sentences as names of truth-values: although this conception is flawed, the hierarchy itself is perfectly consistent. But if instead we regard sentences as names of their senses (i.e. of the thoughts which they express), then one might suppose that the argument establishing a paradox will apply, showing that Frege's conception of the sense of sentences as forming an unstratified domain must be inconsistent.

This is not correct, however. On the Fregean conception of sense it is simply incoherent to conceive of a name as *always* referring to its sense rather than its reference. The sense of a name is a mode of presentation of the purported reference of the name: this is not comprehensible unless the name is capable, at least in principle, of purporting to refer to its reference. Put differently, the primary use of a name is to refer to its reference. We may, with Russell, dispute whether the reference of a sentence is correctly identified as its truth-value; what we cannot do, on Frege's account, is to deny that the sense of a sentence is to be seen as a route to the reference. We are then led to Frege's doctrine that when a name 'α' occurs in an indirect context, it refers to the sense of 'α' (which we shall call an 'indirect meaning of the first degree'), not to α itself. If 'α' is a sentence, then in 'I believe that α', for example,

---

[36] 24 May 1903, in Frege, *PMC*, 160.

α is referring to the thought expressed by α, not to its truth-value. If it occurs doubly embedded in indirect contexts (e.g. 'You believe that I believe that α'), Frege held that it must refer to something doubly indirect called an 'indirect meaning of the second degree' (*'ungerade Bedeutung zweiten Grades'*).[37] We thereby obtain a stratification of Fregean senses into degrees of indirectness. Frege does not identify any further the indirect reference of the second degree of α: for the moment we shall take it to be the sense of 'the sense of "α" '. To see how this stratification avoids Russell's propositional paradox, we need only label the occurrences of 'ϕ' and 'ψ' in the argument according to the degree of indirectness of their reference (with the genuine reference of the name regarded as being of degree zero). The supposition of the first part of the argument is that $\sim\psi_0(f(\psi_2))$. It follows then that

$$(\phi). \ f(\phi_1) = f(\psi_2) \ . \supset . \ \phi_0(f(\psi_2)),$$

from which we cannot conclude a contradiction because of the difference of degree between ϕ_1 and ψ_2.

Michael Dummett has suggested that the proposal we have just made — to regard the indirect sense of 'α' as being the same as the ordinary sense of 'the sense of "α" ' — is 'rather implausible'.[38] He proposes instead to amend Frege's theory by denying that there is any such thing as the indirect sense of a word. There is therefore in his view

no reason to think that an expression occurring in double *oratio obliqua* has a sense or a reference different from that which it has in single *oratio obliqua*: its referent in double *oratio obliqua* will be the sense which it has in single *oratio obliqua*, which is the same as the sense it has in ordinary contexts, which is the same as its referent in single *oratio obliqua*.[39]

Unfortunately, Dummett's proposal appears to fall foul of the propositional paradox, since the only way to resist it on a Fregean conception of sense is to distinguish between indirect meanings of the first and second degrees.

Nevertheless, there is a genuine worry underlying Dummett's proposal, and it applies quite generally to the Fregean distinction between sense and reference. If the sense of a name is the mode of presentation of its reference, then it seems right to say that we cannot understand how the name comes to have the reference it has without understanding its sense. However, if we equate understanding how the name 'α' has the sense that it has with understanding how the name 'the sense of "α" ' has the reference that *it* has, then we are led to a vicious regress: we cannot understand how 'the sense of "α" ' refers without understanding

[37]Letter to Russell, 28 Dec. 1902, ibid. 154.   [38]*Frege: Philosophy of Language*, 267.   [39]Ibid. 268–9.

its sense, and this will require us to understand how 'the sense of "the sense of 'α'" ' refers. And so on.

If we are to resist this regress, we must deny that understanding how the name 'α' has its sense involves understanding how 'the sense of "α" ' refers. The direction of explanation here in fact points the opposite way. Whatever account we give of the sense of 'α', we should not expect it to go *via* an account of the reference of 'the sense of "α" '. And when we come to explain the sense of 'the sense of "α" ', we find little to say about the matter. The reason, though, is just that there is very little to say. The sense of 'the sense of "α" ' is given by the fact that it refers to the sense of 'α', and that is all there is to it.

This disquotational account may at first seem somewhat unsatisfying: it is, after all, perfectly correct that to say in general that the sense of 'α' is given by the fact that 'α' refers to α is to give a very thin account of the notion of sense. There is indeed typically more to say about the link between sense and reference than this. In particular, the thin disquotational account says nothing about the fact that different senses can be modes of presentation of the same object — that there can be, in other words, no backward road from reference to sense. When the object in question is itself a sense, however, matters are different: in this case there is a backward road from reference to sense, supplied by a feature which senses do not share with objects in general, namely that there is a privileged route to each of them.

5.7 Mathematical logic as based on the theory of types

If we abandon Russell's earlier account of propositions and accept that they must be stratified into types, it is not yet clear how this stratification is to be achieved. Russell's first suggestion was that propositions be stratified according to the number of quantifiers they contain. He hoped that this method of stratification would allow him to retain the universality of the variable. The only genuine propositions were to be those not involving quantifiers, and propositional variables would range only over these.

It remains, though, to supply the reduction rules which will allow us to regard as incomplete symbols not merely descriptive phrases, class terms, and terms for relations in extension, but all general statements as well. Russell claimed that this project 'would require much mathematics, and is impossible in the present article'.[40] In fact, it is impossible *simpliciter*. Quantification cannot just be eliminated, as the limitative

---

[40] *Essays in Analysis*, 206.

results of the 1930s — in particular, the insolubility of the *Entschei-dungsproblem* (the decision problem for first-order logic) — made clear. Although this conclusive argument for its impossibility was not available to him, Russell came readily enough to realize that his project was too ambitious. When he next presented a theory of logic, in a paper called 'Mathematical logic as based on the theory of types' which he wrote in 1907, the method of stratification of propositions had changed. The guiding principle from now on was what became known as the *vicious circle principle*: 'Whatever involves all of a collection must not be one of the collection.'[41]

In the new account propositions are stratified according not to the number of quantifiers in them but to their range of significance. Propositions in which no quantifiers occur are called *elementary* and these together with those quantifying only over individuals are called *first-order*. Propositions containing quantifiers ranging over first-order propositions are called *second-order* propositions. And so on. In this account quantification is permitted only over individuals or over propositions of a certain order, never over *all* propositions. It is this restriction which blocks the derivation of the propositional paradoxes considered earlier: the proposition $(p). \phi(p) \supset p$, for instance, contains a quantifier which must be interpreted as ranging not over all propositions but only over those of a particular order n; the proposition itself is therefore of order $n + 1$ and cannot be applied to itself, thus blocking the paradox.

But what is the explanation for this restriction on the ranges of quantification? Russell continued in the 1908 paper to believe in an unrestricted notion of the variable for the reason we discussed before. The restrictions are due not to the nature of the variable but to limits on the significance of the propositional functions in which the variable occurs: no propositional function is significant for every proposition as argument. But on the account we are now considering propositional functions are still to be explained as incomplete symbols exactly in accordance with the substitutional theory of 1906. So the reason why a propositional function is significant only for some arguments will be, as it was in 1906, that only for these arguments can propositions in which the propositional function apparently occurs be successfully rewritten so that the propositional function is eliminated. Thus the claim Russell was trying to substantiate — that no propositional function is significant for every proposition as argument — can be seen, in the light of this rewriting procedure, to be a claim about the extent to which quantification over propositions is significant. But now we have come round in a circle, for it was this that the claim in question was originally

---

[41] *Logic and Knowledge*, 63.

intended to explain.

The only way one might imagine breaking into this explanatory circle would be by a variant of the strategy we just rejected, namely that of treating all except elementary propositions as incomplete symbols. If we attempt this, however, we quickly find ourselves making use in our explanation of quantification over propositional functions, which on the present account are still to be regarded only as incomplete symbols and not entities. We are thus led to consider an alternative explanatory strategy, namely that of treating propositional functions as genuine entities to be quantified over and regarding propositions derivatively as incomplete symbols.

In the published paper Russell adhered officially to the earlier view according to which any quantification over propositional functions is to be explained in terms of a twofold quantification over propositions and individuals, but remarked that it is 'technically inconvenient'.[42] In his unpublished writings, on the other hand, Russell was meanwhile struggling unsuccessfully to find a reason for choosing one course or the other. His dilemma is nicely summarized in a letter Whitehead wrote to Russell at about this time:

The nastiness which you wanted to avoid is the Frege bugbear of prop[osition]al functions becoming unmeaning when certain terms are substituted. According to the doctrine of types we have got to put up with this. — Thus certain things (such as functions) which can be named and talked about won't do as arguments in some prop[osition]al functions. The result is that we have to use the restricted variable. The doctrine of substitution was on stronger ground here; for it did without the function entities, and simply brought in $p|a$ as a typographical device for pretending that we were talking of one entity when we were really talking of two. Hence if you want the unrestricted variable, the doctrine of substitution is the true solution. — But then this doctrine won't work, will it?[43]

In September 1907, shortly after writing 'Mathematical logic as based on the theory of types', Russell began the immense labour of writing out *Principia Mathematica*. A year later he would give the paper only the weak endorsement that 'there is nothing in it of whose falsehood I feel *convinced*'.[44] Much of *Principia* was independent of the details of the hierarchy of types and could be written out before a final decision had been taken on what formal system to adopt, but this could not be postponed indefinitely: in the end, although he did not actually outlaw quantification over propositions, Russell focused in his account on quantification over propositional functions. What remained constant from now on was that Russell conceived of the hierarchy of propositional

[42]Ibid. 77.   [43]Undated letter, RA1 710.057398.   [44]Letter to R. G. Hawtrey, 5 Sept. 1908, RA3 Rec. Acq. 394.

functions as *ramified*, i.e. as falling into types distinguished by two distinct principles, according to their level and according to their order.

5.8 Elementary propositions

Russell took as his starting point in describing the hierarchy those propositions in which quantifiers do not occur. He called these propositions *elementary*. The range of elementary propositions is evidently closed with respect to the truth-functions: if p and q are elementary, so are $\sim p$, $p \vee q$, $p.q$, $p \supset q$, etc.

Let us call propositions with no propositions as proper parts *atomic*; anyone familiar with modern treatments of logic is likely to assume, then, that the elementary propositions are simply the truth-functional combinations of atomic propositions, but in the system of *Principia* this would be unwarranted. Indeed the text of *Principia* makes no mention of the notion of atomic propositions at all. This is deliberate.

'A believes p' is a function of p which will vary its truth-value for different arguments having the same truth-value: A may believe one true proposition without believing another, and may believe one false proposition without believing another. Such functions are not excluded from our consideration, and are included in the scope of any general propositions we may make about functions.[45]

In other words, Russell wanted to include within the scope of logic such propositions as 'A believes p', which is not atomic because it has p as a proper part, but appears to be elementary since it contains no quantifiers. Nor would it help if he had instead defined propositions to be atomic if they contain no logical constants, and then constructed the elementary propositions from these by means of the propositional connectives, since this procedure could not generate 'A believes $p \vee q$', which appears to be elementary if p and q are.

The point at issue here is not so much whether 'A believes p' is indeed elementary. (It is plainly not a truth-function of p, but to be sure that it is elementary we should have to rule out the possibility that its correct analysis is as a function not of p but of the components of p.) What matters is that Whitehead and Russell — especially Whitehead — wanted to make their account of logic free of suppositions about the correct analysis of non-logical statements. Whitehead wanted 'the explanation to be as non-committal as possible and to point out its adaptability to widely divergent lines of thought.'[46] The way they adopted of making the account 'as non-committal as possible' was simply to say

---

[45] *PM*, I, 8. [46] Letter to Russell, 16 June 1907, RA1 710.057402.

nothing about what the elementary propositions are. This is apt to induce a sense of puzzlement in the modern reader, who looks in vain for a precise specification of the formal language of *Principia*, but any such specification would inevitably contravene Whitehead's injunction against committing logic to a particular account of the world.

This makes the account they give of propositional logic especially puzzling because it does not separate the logical from the non-logical. The starting point of the explanation of logic in *Principia* is the class of elementary propositions, which already contain the logical constants $\sim$ and $\supset$. The caesura seems therefore to lie, according to this account, not between the logical and the non-logical but between propositional logic and predicate logic, since the former is inextricably entangled with the non-logical propositions at the outset and only the latter can be regarded as a distinct domain of enquiry. The lack of separation between logic and the world that the account implies by no means contradicts Russell's conception of logic. I have already remarked that it was from 1898 onwards central to Russell's rebuttal of idealism for propositions to be complexes capable of having objects as parts. Only thus, he thought, could they be genuinely *about* the world. The subject matter of logic is therefore not a Fregean third realm of thoughts but an aspect of the world. He later came to think, under the influence of Wittgenstein, that the logical aspect of the world can be distinguished from the physical one and does not interact with it as the theory of *Principia* permits, but while he held to his earlier view he was committed to allowing the primitive logical constants to be entities of the sort he called universals with which we are capable of immediate acquaintance:

We have immediate knowledge of an indefinite number of propositions about universals: this is an ultimate fact, as ultimate as sensation is. Pure mathematics — which is usually called 'logic' in its elementary parts — is the sum of everything that we can know, whether directly or by demonstration, about certain universals.[47]

*5.9 The hierarchy of propositional functions in * $*12$

The first type of variable to be introduced in the description of the hierarchy is one that ranges over individuals. If an elementary proposition contains an individual, we can replace it with an individual variable to obtain what Russell calls a first-order elementary propositional function. For example, if $f_0(a, b)$ and $g_0(a)$ are elementary propositions,

$$f_0(\widehat{x}, b), \ f_0(a, \widehat{y}), \ f_0(\widehat{x}, \widehat{y}), \ g_0\widehat{x}, \ \text{etc.}$$

[47] *Essays in Analysis*, 290.

are all first-order elementary functions. (Russell used the circumflex to distinguish a propositional function such as $g_0\widehat{x}$ from its value g_0x for the argument x: the distinction is nowadays more commonly achieved by the lambda notation, which uses '$\lambda x g_0 x$' to denote the same thing.)

Next we have variables ranging over first-order elementary functions. Russell wrote these with an exclamation mark. So for example $\phi!a$ is a variable ranging over elementary propositions in which a occurs. Just as at the first stage we took as given a range of elementary propositions about individuals, so now we can form functions of first-order elementary functions, still without using any quantifiers. The obvious way of doing this is by means of truth-functional connectives. Once more the modern reader may be tempted into a misunderstanding, namely that of thinking that this is the only way of doing it, but that would be to overlook examples such as the function 'A believes $\phi!a$', whose dependence on ϕ is not truth-functional.

The process can be repeated again and again. We can write, for instance, $f!(\phi!a)$ for a variable ranging over second-order elementary functions, i.e. elementary functions in which the first-order elementary function $\phi!a$ occurs. In this way a hierarchy of elementary functions is created, none of them containing any quantifiers.

Russell calls propositional functions *matrices* if they do not contain any quantifiers. Thus every elementary function is a matrix (since if it contained a quantifier, its values could not be elementary propositions). But because the only variables in the system we have described apart from the individual variables range over matrices, which are in turn free of quantifiers, it follows conversely that in this hierarchy every matrix is an elementary function.

Only at this point do we introduce the universal and existential quantifiers, which we take to be able to bind any of the variables in the matrix hierarchy just described. If we bind some of the variables in a matrix of the nth order by quantifiers, we obtain what Russell calls a propositional function of the nth order; if we bind *all* of the variables in it, what we obtain is a proposition of the nth order. We have thus constructed a hierarchy of elementary functions of the first, second, etc. orders.

5.10 The hierarchy of propositional functions in the Introduction

Russell finished writing out the main text of *Principia* in October 1909. At about that time he wrote an article responding to Poincaré's criticisms of the project he and Whitehead were engaged on. In this article, which appeared in French as 'La théorie des types logiques' although he wrote it originally in English, Russell described a hierarchy of functions that differs from that in *12 of *Principia* by giving different ranges of significance to the function variables.

In our account of *12 we described the hierarchy of matrices in its entirety first, and only then mentioned the possibility of quantifying over the real variables in a matrix to obtain other propositional functions. If our concern is only with avoiding paradox, there is plainly no necessity for us to describe matters in this order. Once we have at our disposal the first-order matrices (i.e. those containing only individual variables) we can at once form all the first-order functions. There is then nothing to prevent us from introducing variables ranging not only over the first-order matrices as in *12 but over all first-order functions whatever. This is what is done in 'La théorie des types logiques'. We can then form second-order matrices using such variables. In their *expression* these matrices will look just like the matrices of *12, of course, but their meaning will be different because the variables occurring in them are understood as having a wider range. In particular, it is no longer true in this hierarchy, as it was in that of *12, that every matrix is an elementary function: $\phi!\hat{x}$, for example, is a second-order matrix one of whose values is $(y)f_0(\hat{x}, y)$, which is plainly not elementary.

The procedure for defining the hierarchy of propositional functions continues successively from level to level. Once we have all the second-order matrices, we form second-order propositional functions and propositions from them by quantifying over the real variables occurring in them. But at this stage we have our first encounter with the notion of predicativity: a function is said to be *predicative* if it contains a real variable of order at least as high as the order of the highest apparent variable in it. This definition was not needed when we were describing the first stage in the hierarchy because *all* first-order propositional functions are predicative. But the second-order function $(\exists\phi). \phi!(g_0\hat{x})$ has a first-order apparent variable but only an individual real variable and is therefore not predicative. When we come to form third-order matrices, i.e. matrices containing variables ranging over second-order functions, we therefore have a choice. Nothing Russell has said so far prevents him from introducing a variable ψ_2 to range over *all* second-order functions, since it would not violate the vicious circle principle, but he does not do so. Instead he introduces a more limited variable to range only over the predicative ones. Thus $(\exists x). \phi!(g_0 x)$ is among the values of the third-order matrix $\psi!(\phi!(g_0 x))$, but $(\exists\phi). \phi!(g_0 x)$ is not. More generally, every function variable in the new hierarchy is taken to be restricted to range over predicative functions of some particular level.

To illustrate the hierarchy more fully let us suppose once more that $f_0(a, b)$ and $g_0(a)$ are elementary propositions. Then

$$f_0(\hat{x}, b), \quad f_0(a, \hat{y}), \quad f_0(\hat{x}, \hat{y}), \quad g_0\hat{x}, \quad \text{etc.}$$

will all be matrices. Among the first order propositions obtainable from these matrices by quantification will be

$$(x). f_0(x, b), \quad (\exists y)(x). f_0(x, y), \quad (\exists x). g_0 x, \quad \text{etc.}$$

Once we have constructed all the first-order functions and propositions, we can construct second-order matrices, i.e. matrices containing only individual and first-order variables. The latter are to be understood as encompassing all first-order functions within their scope. We can then obtain a second-order function (proposition) by quantifying over some (all) of the variables in a second-order matrix. Russell used the device of an exclamation mark to indicate that a variable is predicative. So, as all first-order functions are predicative, the variable $\phi!\hat{x}$ ranges over all first-order functions of one individual variable. With this notation we can construct, to continue the example from above, second-order matrices

$$\phi!(f_0(\hat{x}, \hat{y})), \quad \phi!(g_0\hat{x}), \quad \text{etc.}$$

The matrix $\phi!(g_0\hat{x})$ has values

$$(\exists x). g_0 x, \quad g_0 a, \quad (x). f_0(x, b) : \vee : g_0 a, \quad \text{etc.}$$

We can obtain from it by quantification the second-order functions

$$(\exists \phi). \phi!(g_0 x), \quad (\exists x). \phi!(g_0 x), \quad \text{etc.,}$$

and the second-order propositions

$$(\phi). \phi!(g_0 a), \quad (x)(\exists \phi). \phi!(g_0 x) \quad \text{etc.}$$

The fact that the hierarchy Russell described in 'La théorie des types logiques' is different from that of *12 of *Principia* is not particularly remarkable in itself. What makes the difference between the two hierarchies striking, however, is that the 1910 article reappeared, slightly edited but with the description of the hierarchy intact, as chapters II and III of the Introduction to *Principia*. The result is that the hierarchy described the text of *Principia* is not the same as that in the Introduction. Much else that is important in the account (for instance, the axiom of reducibility, which we shall discuss shortly) therefore has two distinct interpretations depending on whether the variables are read as elementary or predicative. In the remainder of this chapter we shall accordingly adopt the convention that references to the type of 'predicative' functions may be taken equally to be references to elementary functions, depending on which interpretation is being considered.

This ambiguity highlights the fact that Russell laid no great stress on the particular way in which the variables are restricted. In *12 he says merely that 'the variables occurring in the present work, from this point onwards, will all be either individuals or matrices of some order in the above hierarchy.'[48] He thus intended no general ban on variables of wider range. As the predicative variables of the Introduction do not contravene the vicious circle principle, they are evidently admissible. Nevertheless, having said all this the difference between the two hierarchies remains quite bizarre and can only be explained as an oversight on Russell's part.

5.11 Typical ambiguity

Russell had now to abandon finally his belief in the unrestricted nature of the variable and to replace it with a whole series of variables differentiated as to type. Propositional functions fall into a hierarchy of types. For each type we can introduce a variable ranging over all the functions in that type. But the key to avoiding the paradoxes is that there can be no such thing as an unrestricted variable ranging over all types. How then do we describe the hierarchy? Any attempt to do so will involve generalizing across types, which is just what we cannot do.

Russell's way out was to say that what appear to be propositions generalizing across types in *Principia* are *typically ambiguous*: the variables they contain are indeed restricted to types, but it is not yet specified *which* types they are restricted to. When we assert a typically ambiguous proposition, we are to be taken as asserting any determination of it that makes it meaningful.

What Russell calls typically ambiguous propositions are thus not strictly speaking propositions at all. Nowadays we should call them metalinguistic schemas, but this way of conceiving of them was not open to Russell as he did not make the distinction this requires between the formal language of the system and the metalanguage in which it is described. 'Logic', he believed, 'is concerned with the real world just as truly as zoology, though with its more abstract and general features.'[49]

<hr />

[48] *PM*, I, 172. [49] *IMP*, 169.

The symbolic language is therefore to be thought of not as distinct from ordinary language but as an extension of it.

Without a metalanguage the difficulty about how to regard typically ambiguous propositions is substantial. Even in January 1911, when the main text of *Principia* was long complete, Whitehead and Russell were still arguing about the content of a note on the subject to insert in volume II. The view they arrived at was that we should think of the ambiguous proposition as being asserted and proved for some specific determination of its variables. We then ' "see" that symbolically the same proof holds in any other assigned type'.[50] Whitehead expressed it as follows:

The real difference between us (I think) is that you leave a typical ambiguity or an apparent variable (any or some) type *under* the ⊢ sign — while I deny that we can do so consistently with our P[rimitive] I[dea]s, P[rimitive] p[roposition]s and type theory —

According to me until all ambiguities are definitely settled there is simply a sequence of meaningless shapes.

We have also rules for the assigning of meaning to the symbols so as to produce a prop[osition]. There are really a succession of sets of rules one set for each type as it is defined. All the sets have a formal identity of procedure in relation to the various symbols.

To say that a prop[osition] holds for any type is to say, — If after any acts of definition of types, the corresponding sets of formal rules of interpretation be applied to a sequence of symbols, we can then rightly assert the proposition or propositional function which is then obtained. Thus the P[rimitive] I[dea] 'act of definition of a type' is used — but not in the S[ymbolic] T[heory]. In the S[ymbolic] T[heory] we *prove* for the one or two types we do define, and outside the S[ymbolic] T[heory] we *say* that whoever works away at defining more types will find the corresponding prop[osition]s still true.[51]

So in order to express the view Whitehead found himself having to draw a distinction between what can be said in the symbolic theory and what can be said outside it. But if we allow this distinction we are left unable to give an appropriate explanation of the similarity between the propositions of various types that are determinations of a single typically ambiguous expression: if, as Russell believed, the similarity is logical, it must be explicable in a way that does not make it 'linguistic through the phrase', as on this account it seems to be. Moreover, if we regard the primitive propositions of *Principia* as meaningless signs not expressing thoughts until we determine the types of their variables, we are left without a perspective from which to explain why we write down these strings of signs rather than any others: as soon as we determine

---

[50] *PM*, II, xii.   [51] Letter to Russell, 29 Jan. 1911, RA1 710.057457.

the types so as to express a thought we lose the generality which it was the object of the whole exercise to create.

5.12 Cumulative types

In *Principia* Russell took it as a primitive proposition that 'if "ϕx" is significant, then if x is of the same type as a, "ϕa" is significant, and vice versa.'[52] Now it is a straightforward consequence of this assumption that sameness of type is an equivalence relation. Hence 'two types which have a common member coincide and ... two different types are mutually exclusive.'[53] This was not forced on Russell by the need to avoid paradox: the dangers of impredicativity lurk when a variable at one level is taken to include entities of a higher level within its compass; the vicious circle principle gives us no reason to be concerned about the case of a variable ranging over entities of lower levels. So if avoidance of paradox is the only constraint, there is an alternative to Russell's assumption of a hierarchy of disjoint types: he could have assumed instead that types are cumulative, so that if $(x)\phi x$ is of order n, the variable x is taken to range over all entities of order less than n, rather than just those of order $n - 1$. Just such a cumulative hierarchy was recommended to Russell in 1908 by Ralph Hawtrey, a friend of his who had been reading parts of *Principia* in draft. Hawtrey realized that the difference between the two hierarchies is more than cosmetic: the cumulative hierarchy 'enables you to obtain types of infinite order — all the way up the ordinals in fact.'[54] This is because once we have a variable of order n for each finite n we can form a new variable ranging over everything of finite order. Let us say that functions involving this variable are of order ω. We can then form a variable ranging over all such functions and say that functions involving it are of order $\omega + 1$. And so on, 'all the way up the ordinals'.

Modern mathematical practice has undoubtedly sided with Hawtrey against Russell: in Zermelo–Fraenkel set theory the sets are conceived of as arranged in a cumulative hierarchy proceeding into the transfinite just as Hawtrey recommended. Is there anything to be said for Russell's more restrictive convention that overlapping types must coincide? He himself offered Hawtrey no more by way of explanation than 'a sort of symbolic instinct, which I rely upon more than I can explicitly justify'.[55]

The response is telling since it exposes an unclarity in Russell's conception. Logic was still for him the study not of language but of an

---

[52]Ibid., *9.14. [53]Ibid., I, 161. [54]RA1 710.050866. [55]22 June 1908, RA3 Rec. Acq. 394.

aspect of objective reality. Indeed he had recently rejected his earlier
account of denoting because it made a certain relationship linguistic
when it ought to be logical. In that case why was his 'symbolic instinct' relevant? Even if it is true that *grammatical* types which have
a common member coincide (and I do not share Russell's instinct that
it is), what reason do we have to suppose that *logical* types have this
property? To arrive at that conclusion we would need a further argument to show that the form of reality — even its non-physical aspect
— is deducible from the form of language.

5.13 *The hierarchy of classes*

What we have been describing in the last few sections are intensional
hierarchies, whether of propositions or of propositional functions: the
extensional hierarchy of classes has not played a role in their description.
We turn to the latter hierarchy now. As we have seen, as early as 1903
Russell had the idea of eliminating classes and replacing them with
propositional functions. This is not in itself an original thought: it is
part of any view of classes as derived from intensions that '$x \in \hat{y}\phi y$'
should be thought of as synonymous with 'ϕx'. But what was wrong
with the 1903 account was that the paraphrase did nothing to encourage
the idea that the complexity of the proposition could be different from
what the grammar of the sentence expressing it suggested. Russell now
had to provide a general method for eliminating classes from contexts
such as '$f\{\hat{x}\phi x\}$' without merely replacing the class by a propositional
function.

'On denoting' had supplied a paradigm for dealing with singular
terms by treating them as incomplete symbols without commitment
to the existence of objects, simple or complex, which they denote. But
so far this is merely programmatic advice and gives us little clue as to
what the rewriting rules should be in any particular case. When he still
had unrestricted variables, Russell could put

$$f\{\hat{x}\phi x\} : \equiv_{\mathrm{Df}} : (\exists\psi) : \phi x. \equiv_x. \psi x : f\{\psi\hat{z}\}, \qquad (3)$$

which defines $f\{\hat{x}\phi x\}$ to mean that f is true of some propositional
function extensionally equivalent to ϕ. Once Russell abandoned the
substitutional theory and with it unrestricted quantification over propositional functions, he could no longer do this, because 'ψ' is an unrestricted variable here. He could, however, put

$$f\{\hat{x}\phi x\} :\equiv_{\mathrm{Df}}: (\exists\psi) : \phi x. \equiv_x. \psi!x : f\{\psi!\hat{z}\}, \qquad (4)$$

which defines $f\{\widehat{x}\phi x\}$ to mean that f is true of some predicative function extensionally equivalent to ϕ.

Russell came upon this treatment of classes as incomplete symbols in 1907 while writing 'Mathematical logic as based on the theory of types'. Whitehead's response when he read the manuscript was enthusiastic:

Your transition from intension to extension by means of

$$f\{\widehat{x}\phi x\} : \equiv_{\mathrm{Df}} : (\exists\psi) : \phi x. \equiv_x. \psi!x : f\{\psi!\widehat{z}\}, \qquad \text{Df.}$$

is beyond all praise. It must be right. That peculiar difficulty which has worried us from the beginning is now settled for ever. ... The theory is simple and avoids contradictions, and introduces no difficulty in technical development. I could easily acquiesce in it in the same way in which liberal Catholics acquiesce in Papal decisions.[56]

Now Russell took the effect of (4) to be that it made the existence of the class of ϕs equivalent to the existence of a predicative function extensionally equivalent to $\phi\widehat{x}$. His reason was as follows:

Given any propositional function ψx, of whatever order, this is assumed to be equivalent, for all values of x, to a statement of the form 'x belongs to the class α.' Now assuming that there is such an entity as the class α, this statement is of the first order, since it involves no allusion to a variable function.[57]

The idea is that if $\widehat{x}\psi x$ exists and is called 'α', $\psi\widehat{x}$ is extensionally equivalent to the elementary function $\widehat{x} \in \alpha$. This argument is not quite as transparent as it first seems, however. The expression 'α' which Russell introduces to refer to the class $\widehat{x}\psi x$ cannot, if the argument is to be valid, be thought of merely as an *abbreviation* for the expression '$\widehat{x}\psi x$' since if it were, '$x \in \alpha$' would just be 'ψx' and would therefore contain the same quantifiers: no reduction in the order of the propositional function would have been achieved. For the argument to work as intended 'α' must presumably be a proper name. But introducing a new proper name changes the language. We have been given no reason to think that in the *original* language there is an elementary function equivalent to $\psi\widehat{x}$. Moreover, for it to be legitimate to introduce a proper name what it denotes must be an individual. But Russell admits that the contradiction about the classes which are not members of themselves shows that 'if there are classes they must be something radically different from individuals.'[58] So Russell's argument seems to be in danger of flirting with the very danger — of treating classes as individuals — which the whole theory was designed to avoid.

[56]RA1 710.057402. [57]*PM*, I, 173. [58]Ibid., I, 173.

A slightly different argument is available, however. The sentence '$\hat{x}\phi x$ exists' can informally be thought of as equivalent to 'Something can be truly predicated of $\hat{x}\phi x$'. So let us take as f in (4) some function that is true of anything whatever of the appropriate type. The left-hand side of the definition then says (given this informal understanding) that $\hat{x}\phi x$ exists, whereas the right-hand side is equivalent to $(\exists\psi).\phi x \equiv_x \psi!x$, i.e. to the existence of an elementary function extensionally equivalent to $\phi\hat{x}$. We thus retrieve the conclusion we wanted, namely that Russell's definition (4) makes the existence of a class $\hat{x}\phi x$ equivalent to the existence of an elementary (or predicative) function extensionally equivalent to $\phi\hat{x}$.

When we come to defining identity there is a difficulty similar to that which arose in connection with predication of classes. We cannot just define

$$x = y. \equiv_{\text{Df}}. (\phi). \phi x \equiv \phi y,$$

since this involves an illegitimate quantification over all propositional functions. So Russell instead defines

$$x = y. \equiv_{\text{Df}}. (\phi). \phi!x \equiv \phi!y, \tag{5}$$

i.e. objects are equal if they agree in all their elementary (or predicative) properties. Given the link between functions and classes just described, this amounts to saying that for objects to be distinct there must be a class that one of them belongs to and the other does not. The disadvantage of this definition is that we cannot by appeal to it alone justify Leibniz's law that

$$x = y. \supset. \phi x \equiv \phi y$$

for an arbitrary propositional function $\phi\hat{z}$. The definition leaves open, in other words, the possibility that there could be things declared to be equal because they have all their elementary properties in common but distinguishable by means of higher-order properties. We shall return shortly to Russell's means of resolving this difficulty.

After treating class terms as incomplete symbols in the way I have outlined, Russell then gives a corresponding account of relation terms, obtained from propositional functions of two variables in the same way that class terms are obtained from propositional functions of one variable. The inelegance this involves, whereby theorems proved for classes have to be proved once more for relations, could be avoided if the notion of an ordered pair were to be taken as a primitive idea in the system (for then a relation between two terms could be regarded as a function of their ordered pair); and even this is unnecessary if we adopt a manœuvre devised later by Wiener[59] whereby ordered pairs can be defined within the theory of types.

5.14 Numbers

Once we have the theory of classes and relations in *Principia*, the definition of the cardinal numbers can proceed in a way that is superficially similar to Frege's. The number 2, for example, is defined to be the class of all two element classes. But this definition is ambiguous as to type. If we wished to remove the ambiguity, we should have to indicate the type by a subscript and say that the number 2_α is the class of all those classes containing two elements of type α. So the numerical inequality $5 < 6$, for instance, is not really a single proposition at all but a typically ambiguous schema standing for any of the propositions $5_\alpha < 6_\alpha$.

On the face of it this device gets round the problem Frege had over counting things of different types. If we write (0) for the type of individuals, (1) for the type of classes of individuals, etc., then in Frege's system the number of Galilean moons of Jupiter is $4_{(0)}$ and the number of (level 0) prime numbers less than $10_{(0)}$ is $4_{(2)}$. The difficulty we encountered was that the expression

A The number of Galilean moons of Jupiter equals the number of primes less than 10

was meaningless. In *Principia*, on the other hand, the phrase 'the number of Galilean moons of Jupiter' is typically ambiguous. Its determination could be $4_{(n)}$ for any n, depending on context. Just the same applies to the number of prime numbers less than 10. So on this account the expression **A** is not itself a sentence but is typically ambiguous. Each determination of this schema that is meaningful is true. (Russell called an expression 'stably true' in such circumstances.) But it is dubious whether this really does solve Frege's problem. As Whitehead said, 'until all ambiguities are definitely settled there is simply a sequence of meaningless shapes', and if the sentence **A** really is ambiguous, it seems mysterious how the ambiguities in it can ever be resolved so as to let it express anything.

Matters are further complicated by the fact that the instances of a schema such as $5 < 6$ need not all have the same truth-value. If, for

---

[59]'A simplification of the logic of relations'.

instance, the total number of individuals is 4, then $5_{(0)} = 6_{(0)}$ since both are the empty class; but there must be at least 16 classes of individuals, 2^{16} classes of classes of individuals, etc., and so $5_{(n)} < 6_{(n)}$ for $n \geq 1$. This case is typical of the general situation: the familiar propositions of elementary arithmetic are all true eventually, i.e. at all sufficiently high levels, but they need not be true at *all* levels unless we adopt an axiom of infinity — see below. Whitehead and Russell met this difficulty by adopting the convention that when we assert a numerical identity we should be interpreted as meaning the level to be sufficiently high. This device makes typically ambiguous versions of all the truths of $\mathbf{EA_0}$ come out true. So, for instance, every instantiation of the inequality $n < n+1$ by a particular formal number n is true provided that the type of n is taken sufficiently high. What the device does not do, though, is to justify us in asserting that $n < n + 1$ for every natural number n: to be able to do that we should need there to be a single type in which all the natural numbers are distinct, i.e. in which the number of things is not finite. The claim that this is so Russell called the *axiom of infinity*. He did not claim in *Principia* that it is a logical truth but stated it as a premiss whenever it was required: so if the proof of a proposition p involves infinity, the theorem that appears in *Principia* will be not 'p' but 'Infin ax $\supset p$'.

Shortly after finishing *Principia* Russell said explicitly that the axiom of infinity for the type of individuals 'is purely empirical' since 'it is a priori possible' for the number of individuals in the universe to be any cardinal whatever. But because 'the finitist hypothesis is much more difficult and less simple than the other' from an empirical point of view and 'not at all preferable a priori', he concluded that

for the reasons which usually decide scientific hypotheses, it is better to assume that the number of individuals is infinite, while keeping in mind, however, that this assumption could be false, even though the sensible evidence is such that one could never know that it is false.[60]

On this account the axiom of infinity for individuals thus occupies a very curious position: like Newtonian mechanics it is a scientific hypothesis about the world which might be useful without being true, but unlike Newtonian mechanics it is incapable of empirical refutation.

Notice, moreover, that the axiom of infinity is not strictly speaking a proposition at all since it is once more typically ambiguous: for each type α there is a proposition asserting that the number of things of type α is infinite, but these propositions have no logical product as they are all of different types. What Russell says about the axiom of infinity

[60] *Papers*, VI, 52.

for individuals therefore might not apply to other types: even if there are as a matter of empirical fact only finitely many individuals in the world, there might be some type of functions the number of which is not finite; and it might, moreover, be a priori that this is so. For suppose that there are n individuals. It is then true that there are 2^n classes of individuals, 2^{2^n} classes of classes of individuals, etc., so that each of these types is finite. But there is nothing in Russell's account to prevent there being, for instance, infinitely many different properties that the n individuals may have; and there might indeed be infinitely many *logical* properties. So in those circumstances the axiom of infinity for properties of individuals would be a priori true even though the axiom of infinity for individuals was empirically false.

What is more, in that situation an arithmetical theorem proved using the axiom of infinity would still not be of any real use since it would be typically ambiguous: in one determination of types it would be true a priori but not applicable to the world of individuals; in another it would be applicable to the world but we should have no reason to suppose it true.

5.15 The axiom of reducibility

If we are to develop mathematics within Russell's theory of types, we need to be able to prove, for various propositional functions $\phi\hat{x}$, the existence of the class $\hat{x}\phi x$ of all ϕs; but nothing we have said so far guarantees that this should exist for an arbitrary $\phi\hat{x}$. Now we established in §5.13 that $\hat{x}\phi x$ exists just when the propositional function $\phi\hat{x}$ is extensionally equivalent to an elementary or predicative function, i.e. when

$$(\exists\psi).\, \phi x \equiv_x \psi!x. \tag{6}$$

So what corresponds in the theory to the informal principle that every propositional function determines a class is that (6) holds for arbitrary $\phi\hat{x}$. Russell found that in order to obtain a system strong enough for mathematics he had to lay down this (typically ambiguous) assertion as an axiom. Moreover, because his account of relations is separate from and parallel to his account of classes, he also had to assume the corresponding schema for propositional functions with two variables, namely that

$$(\exists\psi).\, \phi(x, y) \equiv_{x,y} \psi!(x, y) \tag{7}$$

for any propositional function $\phi(\hat{x}, \hat{y})$. There is no need to assume further axioms for functions of three or more variables because they can all be easily expressed in terms of functions of two variables. (Any function of the form $f(\hat{x}, \hat{y}, \hat{z})$ can be expressed as $g(\hat{x}, h(\hat{y}, \hat{z}))$ for appropriate g and h, for instance.) Indeed if Russell had made use of the trick mentioned earlier for defining ordered pairs, he could even have dispensed with the axiom for functions of two variables. Russell gave the names *axiom of classes* and *axiom of relations* respectively to the assumptions that classes exist and that relations do, but he much more commonly used the term *axiom of reducibility* to refer to both principles indifferently.

The most prominent virtue of the axiom of reducibility is that it allows us to deduce Leibniz's law from the definition of identity mentioned earlier: if there is a property that x has but y does not, it follows from the axiom of reducibility that there is a predicative property that x has but y does not, which by (5) means that $x \neq y$. Without reducibility Russell would have had no choice but to treat identity as primitive.

The usefulness of the axiom of reducibility is not limited to validating the definition of identity, though. Without it we are constrained by the theory of types to use only predicative reasoning. Three fundamental mathematical principles whose proofs seem to require impredicative methods are salient: the principle of mathematical induction for higher-order properties; the completeness principle, on which real analysis is based; and the principle that every initial segment of the ordinals is well ordered (which can be seen as a transfinite generalization of the principle of mathematical induction).

The first of these principles is the only one directly relevant to arithmetic. To see how the axiom of reducibility enters into its proof, recall that the fundamental idea in the definition of the natural numbers is that of the *ancestral R_** of a relation R. If it were not for the theory of types, we would define 'xR_*y' to mean 'y has every hereditary property possessed by x', but this is illegitimate because 'every hereditary property' involves a quantification over properties of all orders. The best we can do is to define 'xR_*y' as

$$zRw . \supset_{z,w}. \phi!z \supset \phi!w :\supset_\phi: \phi!x \supset \phi!y,$$

i.e. 'y has every *predicative* hereditary property possessed by x.' In the presence of the axiom of reducibility it follows directly that

$$xR_*y :\supset: zRw . \supset_{z,w}. \phi z \supset \phi w . \supset. \phi x \supset \phi y, \tag{8}$$

where $\phi\hat{z}$ is a propositional function of arbitrary type, i.e. if xR_*y then any hereditary property possessed by x is also possessed by y. The natural numbers are defined to be the objects which stand in the ancestral of the successor relation to zero, and when applied to this case (8) is just the principle of mathematical induction. Moreover, this dependence on the axiom of reducibility is ineliminable: Myhill[61] has shown that in the formal system of *Principia* with the axiom of infinity but without the axiom of reducibility the natural numbers cannot be defined. The axiom of reducibility is what enables us to define the natural numbers within the ramified theory: without it we would have had no alternative but to treat 'natural number' as a primitive idea and state (8) as an axiom.

5.16 Propositional functions and reducibility

What the axiom of reducibility achieves (apart from validating the definition of identity) is thus to justify the use of impredicative methods when dealing with classes. The careful distinctions within the intensional hierarchy of propositional functions on the basis of order as well as level are obliterated when we make the transition to the extensional hierarchy of classes. This gives rise to the following worries. If the simple hierarchy of propositional functions without the stratification by orders already avoids the paradoxes and is in any case obliterated by the axiom of reducibility, the ramified hierarchy seems like an idle wheel that drops out as unnecessary. If, on the other hand, there is a paradox involving propositional functions that is blocked only by the ramified hierarchy, it seems that the axiom of reducibility may by removing the distinctions used to block the paradox reintroduce it.

Both worries are misconceived: they trade on a failure to appreciate Russell's understanding of a proposition as anything that can coherently be judged and a propositional function as anything that can be obtained from a proposition by replacing a simple component of it by a variable of the appropriate type. In particular, Russell thought that there are some propositions that do not depend extensionally on their parts. If Russell had been willing to endorse the *axiom of extensionality*

$$\phi x \equiv_x \psi x . \supset . f(\phi \widehat{x}) \equiv f(\psi \widehat{x}), \tag{9}$$

i.e. that extensionally equivalent propositional functions are indistinguishable, the axiom of reducibility would have had the effect of licensing the replacement of each propositional function everywhere it occurs by a predicative function; there would then indeed have been nothing

[61] 'The undefinability of the set of natural numbers in the ramified *Principia*'.

to be gained by the detour via the ramified hierarchy. Since he did not endorse it, however, he left open the possibility that there might be non-extensional functions that distinguish between propositional functions and their predicative equivalents. It is true that in *Principia* no means are provided for constructing non-extensional functions, but Russell thought that if there *are* such functions then logic could not exclude them, even if our principal concern is mathematics, where, as he explicitly remarked,[62] such functions do not arise.

This deals with the first worry; let us now turn to the second. We have seen that Russell drew a distinction among paradoxes between those involving classes, relations or propositional functions, first, and those involving propositions, second. His general strategy was to treat symbols apparently referring to paradoxical entities as incomplete, to be eliminated on analysis. By applying this strategy to propositions he would thus have eliminated the paradoxes of the second kind entirely. So if the paradoxes of the first kind were, as he thought, all solved by the simple theory of types, then the extra elaboration involved in the ramified theories would be unnecessary. But they are not. Although the distinction between propositions and propositional functions was fundamental to Russell's ontology, it is not the one which underlies the difference between the simple and ramified theories of types, for there are paradoxes of Russell's first kind which are not solved by the simple theory.

If we suspect that the axiom of reducibility reintroduces a paradox which the ramification of the intensional hierarchy eliminated, it is natural to consider a paradox of this sort as the most likely candidate. One of the simplest such is Weyl's heterological paradox. If we say that an adjective is 'heterological' when it does not apply to itself, paradox results from asking whether 'heterological' is itself heterological. If it is, then it does not apply to itself and hence is not heterological; if it is not, then it does not apply to itself and hence is heterological.

This paradox is formalized in the simple theory by writing 'Het x' for

$$(\exists\phi)(x \text{ means } \phi\hat{z}. \sim\phi x).$$

Now

$$\text{'Het' means Het } \hat{z},$$

and so

$$\text{Het('Het')} \equiv (\exists\phi)(\text{'Het' means } \phi\hat{z}. \sim\phi(\text{'Het'}))$$
$$\equiv \sim\text{Het('Het')},$$

[62] *PM*, Intro., 8.

since 'Het' cannot mean two different things. In the ramified theory, on the other hand, the quantification in the definition of Het $\hat{x}$ must be limited to a particular order. We can thus define 'Het$_1 x$' to mean

$$(\exists!\phi)(x \text{ means } \phi!\hat{z}. \sim\phi!x). \tag{10}$$

The derivation of

$$\text{Het}_1(\text{'Het}_1\text{'}) \equiv \sim\text{Het}_1(\text{'Het}_1\text{'})$$

is blocked because the propositional function Het$_1\hat{z}$ is not among the possible values of the predicative variable $\phi!\hat{z}$ in (10).

The argument purporting to show[63] that the axiom of reducibility reinstates the paradox which the ramification of the hierarchy eliminates proceeds as follows. By that axiom there is a predicative function — let us call it 'Het!$\hat{z}$' — formally equivalent to Het$_1\hat{z}$, i.e. $(z).\text{Het}!z \equiv \text{Het}_1 z$. In particular, therefore,

$$\begin{aligned} \text{Het}!(\text{'Het}!\text{'}) &\equiv \text{Het}_1 z \\ &\equiv (\exists!\phi)(\text{'Het}!\text{' means } \phi\hat{z}. \sim\phi(\text{'Het}!\text{'})) \\ &\equiv \sim\text{Het}!(\text{'Het}!\text{'}). \end{aligned}$$

We thus seem to have derived a contradiction once more.

But this is to commit just the fallacy we fell into when trying to expound Russell's argument for the link between classes and predicative functions. The mistake lies in assuming that we are entitled to give a name to the predicative function whose existence the axiom of reducibility asserts. The procedure of giving things names is indeed a familiar one, and it is harmless in the case with which Tarski has made us most familiar, namely that of a language which does not contain any semantic apparatus. But of course the paradox we are currently examining trades on just that apparatus; more particularly, it trades on the ability to treat names as objects susceptible to predication. If we assume not only that to each propositional function corresponds a predicative function but that to each of these in turn corresponds an object (its name), then we have recreated precisely the circumstances which led to Russell's paradox in the first place.

If the axiom of reducibility is not to be contradictory, then, we must take care not to suppose that every predicative function has a name. I referred earlier to the error the modern reader of *Principia* is apt to make of supposing that Whitehead and Russell intended there to be in

[63] Copi, 'The inconsistency or redundancy of *Principia Mathematica*'.

Principia a description, which frustratingly they never quite supply, of a fixed formal language. Our current considerations are an even more vivid illustration of the same point. If there is a countable infinity of individuals, the axiom of reducibility shows that there are uncountably many classes of individuals. Each of these classes has a predicative function corresponding to it, so there are uncountably many predicative functions and hence uncountably many elementary propositions. All this shows, though, is that elementary propositions cannot on Russell's conception be conceived of as straightforwardly linguistic items; it does not show that the axiom of reducibility is contradictory.

5.17 The regressive method

But the mere consistency of the axiom of reducibility is not itself sufficient reason to adopt it. One reason Russell gave was that it 'seems to be what common-sense effects by the admission of *classes*'.[64] As we have seen, though, the link between classes and predicative functions is a more or less accidental by-product of the eliminative paraphrase in Russell's system of propositions apparently about classes. One difficulty with adopting the axiom of reducibility on the basis of this link is that by treating class terms as incomplete symbols Russell had prescinded from the attempt to explain what classes are. He was therefore left without the resources to mount any sort of argument in favour of their existence. If there are classes,

they must be something radically different from individuals. It would seem that the sole purpose which classes serve, and one main reason which makes them linguistically convenient, is that they provide a method of reducing the order of a propositional function.[65]

But it was disingenuous of Russell to call the assumption of classes a linguistic convenience: without the assumption of classes the theory of types is quite inadequate as a foundation for mathematics.

Russell had to grant that 'what common-sense effects' is scarcely an argument for regarding the axiom of reducibility as a logical truth on its own, independent of any consideration of the rôle it played in his logical system as a whole. So from 1907 onwards[66] he advocated what he called the *regressive* method of justifying the axioms of logic.

That the axiom of reducibility is self-evident is a proposition which can hardly be maintained. But in fact self-evidence is never more than a part of the reason for accepting an axiom, and is never indispensable. The reason for

[64] *PM*, I, 173. [65] Ibid., I, 173–4. [66] *Essays in Analysis*, 272.

accepting an axiom, as for accepting any other proposition, is always largely inductive, namely that many propositions which are nearly indubitable can be deduced from it, and that no equally plausible way is known by which these propositions could be true if the axiom were false, and nothing which is probably false can be deduced from it. ... In the case of the axiom of reducibility, the inductive evidence in its favour is very strong, since the reasonings which it permits and the results to which it leads are all such as appear valid.[67]

In October 1905 Russell took logic to be analytic;[68] in 1907 he adopted the regressive method. In the interim he had realized that some such axiom as that of reducibility would be needed, but that this axiom did not possess the obviousness of the other axioms.

As the quotation makes plain, however, Russell intended the regressive method to be used to justify not just reducibility but all the axioms of logic. This sort of view, for all its initial strangeness, has been quite common among writers on the foundations of mathematics since the discovery of Russell's paradox. Zermelo, for instance, wrote that in deciding the axioms of set theory

there is at this point nothing left for us to do but to proceed in the opposite direction and, starting from set theory as it is historically given, to seek out the principles required for establishing the foundations of this mathematical discipline. In solving this problem we must, on the one hand, restrict these principles sufficiently to exclude all contradictions and, on the other, take them sufficiently wide to retain all that is valuable in this theory.[69]

It has been especially common to invoke something like the regressive method as a reason to accept strong axioms of infinity in extensions of Zermelo's theory of sets. Boolos, unable to justify the axiom schema of replacement on the basis of the iterative conception, argued that its instances should be accepted because 'they have many desirable consequences and (apparently) no undesirable ones'.[70] And Gödel wrote in a similar context that

there might exist axioms so abundant in their verifiable consequences, shedding so much light upon a whole discipline, and furnishing such powerful methods for solving given problems (and even solving them, as far as that is possible, in a constructivistic way) that quite irrespective of their intrinsic necessity they would have to be assumed at least in the same sense as any well established physical theory.[71]

The analogy with physical theories here is apt, and Russell himself urged it when he first advocated the regressive method. *Principia* is thus to be thought of as containing a theory about the logical aspect of

---

[67]Ibid. 250–1. [68]*Papers*, IV, 516. [69]In van Heijenoort, 200. [70]*Logic, Logic, and Logic*, 27. [71]*Works*, II, 182–3.

the world in the same way that relativity is a theory about its physical aspect. The data to which the theory is answerable are in the latter case facts about the movements of planets or the behaviour of clocks; in the former case they are mathematical facts such as the truths of elementary arithmetic.

It is worth stressing that by adopting the regressive method Russell did not abandon logicism. He continued to regard mathematics and logic as one. 'They differ as boy and man: logic is the youth of mathematics and mathematics is the manhood of logic.'[72] Nor did Russell abandon the idea that each logical law should be thought of as a candidate for truth or falsity on its own: he saw the method as separating the logical from the epistemological order, not as assimilating the former to the latter. He continued to believe that logic speaks of 'a world of universals and of truths which do not bear directly on such and such a particular existence'.[73] Although the ground of *our* belief in the propositions of logic is, he now thought, inductive, this did not shake his conviction that their truth has ultimately an a priori basis.

At the time of *Principia* Russell did not yet embrace semantic holism. If he had done so, he might have regarded it as an attractive feature of the regressive method that it provides us with a way of understanding alternative foundations for mathematics. Two different (and perhaps mutually inconsistent) physical theories may both explain all the physical data. In the same way the theory of sets may account for all the mathematical data as well as the theory of types; so may other more distant theories such as Quine's **NF** or category theory. If so, the choice between them, as between the competing physical theories, will lie not on which is true, since on the holistic view the truth of the theory consists in its acceptance, but on considerations to do with its relation to the relevant data.

There remains, though, a difference between the data of logic and the data of physics that causes a difficulty for the regressive method, whether or not we take the further step of assimilating the logical to the epistemological order. A physical theory can have various uses. It may be used to predict the results of future experiments. If the theory is well-confirmed, we may believe its predictions to a high degree of certainty, even to the extent of concluding that we must have made a mistake if the result of an experiment does not turn out as the theory predicts. A theory may also serve to place certain physical facts in a conceptual relationship with one another in a manner we find explanatory. What a theory cannot do, on pain of circularity, is to explain how we came to

---

[72]*IMP*, 194. [73]*Essays in Analysis*, 293.

know the experimental facts we used to confirm the theory in the first place. Russell's logical theory, once it has been tested, may by analogy be used to prove new arithmetical propositions, which we may then believe with a high degree of confidence. And it may be regarded as explaining the relationship between different mathematical facts. What it cannot do, though, is to explain how we know that $2+2 = 4$, because that is one of the data that we used to confirm the theory: if a logical principle is to be justified inductively on the basis of the truth of some set of its consequences, the fact that *they* are consequences of *it* cannot be our ground for believing them. So we need another account to ground our knowledge of the data. In his paper on the regressive method Russell asserts repeatedly that the data are obvious and suggests that 'when $2+2 = 4$ was first discovered it was probably inferred from the case of sheep and other concrete cases',[74] but he does not elaborate how this inference is to be justified.

5.18 *The* Introduction to Mathematical Philosophy

Russell was willing to admit from the outset that the axiom of reducibility is not as obvious as the other axioms of his system, but we have seen that he hoped at first to justify it by means of the regressive method. This would, he thought, allow us to regard the axiom of reducibility as a priori *if* it is true, even though we are not quite certain *that* it is true. Indeed it was precisely the point of the regressive method that it avoided the 'errors liable to arise from assimilating the logical to the epistemological order, and also, conversely, from assimilating the epistemological to the logical order'.[75]

But by 1918 Russell had abandoned this view. In the *Introduction to Mathematical Philosophy* he attempted to draw a distinction between the other axioms, which he took to be logically necessary, and the axiom of reducibility, which he now took to be, if true, an empirical truth. In thus classifying reducibility as empirical Russell showed the influence of Wittgenstein, his former pupil, who had urged this in a letter to Russell from Norway in 1913:

Imagine we lived in a world in which nothing existed except $\aleph_0$ *things* and, over and above them, ONLY a *single* relation holding between infinitely many of the things and in such a way that it did not hold between each thing and every other thing and further never held between a finite number of things. It is clear that the axiom of reducibility would certainly *not* hold good in such a world.[76]

[74]Ibid. 272. [75]*Papers*, IV, 162. [76]*Cambridge Letters*, 59.

It is hard to see what model Wittgenstein had in mind here. A clearer example was given later by Ramsey:

It is clearly possible that there should be an infinity of atomic functions, and an individual a such that whichever atomic function we take there is another individual agreeing with a in respect of all the other functions, but not in respect of the function taken. Then $(\phi).\phi!x \equiv \phi!a$ could not be equivalent to any elementary function of x.[77]

As an instance of what Ramsey means, let the domain be the natural numbers, let the distinguished element a be 0, and suppose that the infinity of atomic functions Ramsey refers to are the functions $\hat{x} = n$ for $n \geq 1$. Since every elementary function is a truth-functional combination of atomic functions, it follows that any elementary function true of 0 is true of all but finitely many other numbers; and any false of 0 is false of all but finitely many other numbers. In this model Russell's definition of identity is correct since any two natural numbers are distinguishable by means of an atomic function. But any elementary function which is true of 0 must also be true of all but finitely many other natural numbers. So the function '$(\phi).\phi!\hat{x} \equiv \phi!0$', which is true only of 0, cannot be equivalent to any elementary function. The model is thus a counterexample to the strong form of the axiom of reducibility in the text of *Principia*, namely that every propositional function is equivalent to an elementary function. Moreover, because the language under consideration in this example is monadic it is easy to see that the predicative (i.e. first order) functions of an individual are all coextensive with elementary functions. Ramsey's model is therefore also, although he did not mention this explicitly, a counterexample to the weaker form of the axiom of reducibility contained in the Introduction to *Principia*, namely that every propositional function is equivalent to a predicative one. Thus it is possible to imagine a world in which the axiom of reducibility is not valid.

Russell's response to this possibility in the *Introduction to Mathematical Philosophy* is rather inadequate. He attempts to draw a contrast between the mathematical axioms (infinity and reducibility) and the strictly logical principles, on the ground that the latter, if formulated as rules of inference, cannot simply be added to the premises of the arguments that use them. But although it is true that a logical system must have *some* rules of inference, it is not true that all of what Russell wanted to regard as the unproblematically logical principles must be formulated as rules of inference; and conversely one could no doubt formulate the axioms of infinity and reducibility as rules of inference. The

[77] *FoM*, 57.

distinction between axioms and rules of inference is therefore specious in this context.

Another suggestion Russell made is that one could simply take the axiom of reducibility as a premiss of those arguments that use it. But it is worth recalling at this point just how pervasive uses of the axiom of reducibility are in *Principia*: since it is needed for proving Leibniz's Law, it is implicated in almost every mathematical theorem in the book. What Russell was now advocating was thus in effect that almost the whole of mathematics should be regarded as a hypothetico-deductive system much like the standard view of Euclidean geometry. If in place of reducibility we assumed another principle, we should obtain a different version of mathematics. Which of these versions is applicable to the world would depend on whether the axiom of reducibility is an empirical truth or not, just as the applicability of Euclidean geometry depends on whether the parallel axiom is empirically true.

Notice too that like infinity reducibility is not a single axiom but a schema, so the best we could do would be to list among the premisses of each theorem those instances of the schema that are used in its proof. This not only complicates the proposal but casts doubt on its cogency, since if we take the theory of types seriously there is not really anything but a verbal similarity (which at the level of logic is on Russell's conception no similarity at all) to unite the various instances.

On Russell's earlier view of the axiom of reducibility as logical this did not represent an especial problem. There was, as we have seen, a difficulty with his regressive account of logical knowledge, but this difficulty is not made more serious by reducibility being a schema. And the doubt which the strictures of type theory cast on our ability even to *state* a schema coherently is merely an instance of the more general puzzle about how we grasp type theory as a whole.

But now that Russell regarded the axiom of reducibility as an empirical truth if true at all, the need to find something its instances have in common becomes pressing, since otherwise empirical confirmation of one instance will have no relevance to assessing the truth or falsity of any other. Confirmation of a finite number of them gives us no reason whatever to assert the typically ambiguous schema. An argument from regularity is no use here without an account of why regularities in verbal expression should be evidence of regularities in the world.

And what in any case is to count as empirical confirmation of the axiom of reducibility? More to the point, what would count as an empirical refutation? Mathematicians now seem to be in the uncomfortable position of depending at every step they take on an empirical hypothesis whose truth or falsity they have no way of knowing.

Russell's difficulty over how to regard the axiom of reducibility was a symptom of a more general problem: he lacked a criterion for telling whether such a principle is a logical truth or not. 'It is clear', he wrote in 1918, 'that the definition of "logic" or "mathematics" must be sought by trying to give a new definition of the old notion of "analytic" propositions.'[78] Russell called the new notion *tautology* but could not see how to define it. He merely added in a footnote:

The importance of 'tautology' for a definition of mathematics was pointed out to me by my former pupil Ludwig Wittgenstein, who was working on the problem. I do not know whether he has solved it, or even whether he is alive or dead.[79]

Wittgenstein was in fact alive and had indeed solved the problem. His account of the notion of tautology is contained in the *Tractatus*, to which we now turn.

[78]*IMP*, 204.   [79]Ibid. 205 n.

6

The Tractatus

Ludwig Wittgenstein studied with Russell in Cambridge from 1911 to 1913. After a period in Norway he wrote the *Tractatus* while on active service in the Austrian army during the First World War: he probably composed the first draft, which is known as the *Prototractatus*, between September 1915 and July 1918, the final version thereafter.[1] Large parts of the book are devoted to explaining and correcting errors in the conception of logic to be found in *Principia*. Wittgenstein did not, as is sometimes suggested, reject the very idea of a hierarchy of types, but he did reject the notion that mathematics (and in particular arithmetic) could be based, as in *Principia*, on *classes*. For this reason although the account of arithmetic given in the *Tractatus* is in a sense logicist, it is very different from Russell's.

6.1 *Sign and symbol*

The *Tractatus* places the study of language at the centre of its inquiry because by understanding the structure and limits of our language we thereby obtain a conception of the structure and limits of our world. Within this account propositions occupy a privileged position as the bearers of sense. Wittgenstein endorses a version of Frege's context principle, in words which echo Frege's explicitly — 'Only the proposition has sense; only in the context of a proposition has a name meaning'[2] — but his understanding of the notion of proposition is mediated by a distinction not exploited by Frege, between sign and symbol. A *sign* is an element of syntax: if the language in question is of the usual, written sort all the signs are letters or strings of letters; but in other languages gestures, sounds, and diagrams can also be signs. A *symbol* (or *expression*) is what a sign becomes when it is read as a linguistic item in a particular way.

[1]McGuinness, 'Wittgenstein's pre-*Tractatus* manuscripts'. [2]*TLP*, 3.3.

The sign is the part of the symbol perceptible by the senses.

Two different symbols can therefore have the sign (the written sign or the sound sign) in common — they then signify in different ways.[3]

The distinction between sign and symbol is not that between token and type. A sign is already a type, of which all its physical occurrences are tokens: as Wittgenstein succinctly put it, ' "A" is the same sign as "A".'[4] Similarly, all the occurrences of the word 'of' on this page are tokens of the same sign. A symbol can also be thought of as a type, but one determined by a different, and potentially stronger, equivalence relation: two tokens are instances of the same symbol if they symbolize in the same way — if, in other words, we *read* them as the same expression. The 'bank' in 'I stood by the bank of the river' is the same sign as the 'bank' in 'I withdrew some money from the bank' but they are different symbols.

The distinction between sign and symbol is nicely placed, then, to explain instances of ambiguity in natural language. Confirmation that this is a rôle Wittgenstein intended it to fill is strikingly supplied by the *Prototractatus*, where we can see, on page 54 of the manuscript, the point at which he invented the terminology in order to make the point that 'one and the same sign (written or spoken etc.) can be common to two different symbols — in which case they will signify in different ways.'[5] But although he did not have the terminological distinction between sign and symbol until the need to make this point about ambiguity led him to invent it, he certainly had the *conceptual* distinction some time earlier: what Wittgenstein says in the *Tractatus* about recognizing the symbol in the sign[6] started out as a remark in the *Notebooks*: 'Um das Zeichen im Zeichen zu erkennen, muss man auf den Gebrauch achten.'[7] That he should have talked about 'recognizing the sign in the sign' is quite incomprehensible unless he already had the distinction firmly in place but used the same word ('Zeichen' in German but — even more confusingly — 'symbol' when he was speaking English) for both concepts.

So the distinction between sign and symbol did not first occur to Wittgenstein when he was writing page 54 of the *Prototractatus*. In fact it occupies a place in Wittgenstein's system far more central than could be explained solely by its rôle in explaining ambiguities in natural language. It is *I* who turn the dead sign into a live symbol by reading it; without me the sign could not be a symbol. Hence this is where in Wittgenstein's logical system we find the self located — in the transition from sign to symbol.

[3]Ibid. 3.32–3.321. [4]Ibid. 3.203. [5]*PTLP*, 3.2013. [6]3.326. [7]23 Oct. 1914.

For this reason the distinction is relevant even where there are no ambiguities. I said that the equivalence relation of sameness of symbol was *potentially* stronger than that of sameness of sign, but in what Wittgenstein called a *logically perfect* language they would in fact be extensionally the same: each sign would only ever be readable in one way; there would be no puns. The distinction between sign and symbol would still need to be drawn, though, for the reason just given: even if there *is* only one way of reading a sign, it still does not become a symbol until it is read.

6.2 The hierarchy of types

For Wittgenstein propositions are a particular kind of symbol; the corresponding signs he calls (unsurprisingly) *propositional signs*. A proposition is, he says, a 'propositional sign in its projective relation to the world',[8] or in other words a propositional sign parsed and read in such a way that it expresses a *sense*. 'The method of projection is the thinking of the sense of the proposition.'[9] Wittgenstein's understanding of the notion of sense will turn out to be central to his conception of the structure of the hierarchy of functions — he always called propositional functions simply 'functions' — just as Russell's notion of proposition was central to *his* conception, and we shall have to consider it in some detail later, but let us turn first to his reasons for thinking that functions stand in hierarchies at all.

What fills the rôle of the vicious circle principle in motivating Wittgenstein's account is the observation that '[n]o proposition can say anything about itself, because the propositional sign cannot be contained in itself (that is the whole "theory of types").'[10] Presumably the reason a propositional sign cannot be contained in itself is that propositional signs must be finite, but if this was his view, Wittgenstein nowhere states it explicitly. It is, of course, a reasonable enough assumption that propositional signs must be finite, not least on the epistemological ground that it is hard to see how a finite intelligence could ever read an infinite sign, but this sort of argument is alien to Wittgenstein's approach. Whatever his reasons, though, if we grant that a propositional sign cannot be contained in itself, we do not yet reach a clear view of Wittgenstein's conclusion that a proposition cannot make a statement about itself. This does of course follow for the case in which a statement is made about a proposition by mentioning it

---

[8] *TLP*, 3.12.   [9] Ibid. 3.11.   [10] Ibid. 3.332.

explicitly. But the worry is that we might be able to make a statement about it in some other way, for example by generalizing about a whole class of propositions of which the proposition in question is a member. If this possibility is to be ruled out by a feature of propositional signs — that they cannot contain themselves — the reason must be that our understanding of a propositional sign, our ability to read it as a proposition, has a structure that corresponds to the structure of the sign: in order to understand the sign, we must already understand its parts, which cannot, therefore, yet refer to the proposition. It is thus evident how Wittgenstein's claim that no proposition can make a statement about itself can be seen as a version of the vicious circle principle. Like that principle, however, it is vague in application since Wittgenstein does not make clear what it amounts to for a proposition to 'make a statement about' something.

A mention in David Pinsent's diary for 1912 of Wittgenstein's solution to 'a problem which has puzzled Russell and Frege for some years'[11] may well be a reference to Russell's paradox. Even if so, there is no need to suppose that the solution we find in the *Tractatus* is the one Wittgenstein had in 1912. (His letters to Russell from that period hint at experiments with logical theories unrecognizable to a reader of the *Tractatus*.) On the other hand, the solution in the *Tractatus* is not in its bare outlines particularly original. For Wittgenstein a propositional function is obtained from a proposition by keeping part of it constant and regarding the rest of it as an argument place into which a range of expressions could meaningfully be substituted. A propositional function is therefore a symbol which I grasp by way of a grasp of the structure of the proposition from which it is obtained. The argument for Wittgenstein's vicious circle principle for propositions therefore has an analogue in the case of functions, and it is this that he used to avoid Russell's paradox:

A function cannot be its own argument, because the functional sign already contains the prototype of its own argument and it cannot contain itself.

If, for example, we suppose that the function $F(fx)$ could be its own argument, then there would be a proposition '$F(F(fx))$', and in this the outer function F and the inner function F must have different meanings; for the inner has the form $\phi(fx)$, the outer the form $\psi(\phi(fx))$. Common to both functions is only the letter 'F', which by itself signifies nothing. ... Herewith Russell's paradox vanishes.[12]

Suppose that we apply this explanation in the particular case when $F(f\widehat{x})$ says that f does not hold of itself. Russell's paradox results from asking whether or not F is predicable of itself, whether $F(F(f\widehat{x}))$

[11] In von Wright, 37. [12] *TLP*, 3.333.

in other words. But in asking this question we use F in a different sense from the old one: one sign occurs twice but is a different symbol each time. On this analysis Russell's paradox is exposed as little more than a bad pun. The doctrine Wittgenstein is appealing to here is thus that how a sign for a function symbolizes in some way presupposes the structure of the argument place of the function.

6.3 *The doctrine of inexpressibility*

So far, so Russellian. Wittgenstein's principle that a function cannot be its own argument makes propositional functions fall into a hierarchy of levels just as Russell's vicious circle principle did. And the distinction between sign and symbol is merely a generalization of Russell's notion of typical ambiguity: what Russell called a 'typically ambiguous proposition awaiting determination' is a sort of propositional sign; by determining the types of the variables in it we read it as expressing a particular proposition.

This may indeed deal with Russell's paradox, but it is not in itself enough to render the theory secure. More needs to be said if his system is not to fall prey to the semantic paradoxes. For example, consider once more the 'heterological' paradox which we discussed in § 5.16. Russell's way of avoiding it was to stratify propositions (and hence propositional functions) into orders. No variable is permitted to range over more than one order of propositions (or propositional functions). This solves the paradox by making it impossible to define the function $\text{Het}\,\widehat{x}$ at all. The nearest we can get to it is to define a whole hierarchy of heterological functions $\text{Het}_1\widehat{x}, \text{Het}_2\widehat{x}$, etc. by writing '$\text{Het}_n x$' to mean

$$(\exists\phi_{n-1})(x \text{ means } \phi_{n-1}\widehat{z} \,.\, \sim\!\phi_{n-1}x).$$

The derivation of the contradictory

$$\text{Het}_n(\text{'Het}_n\text{'}) \equiv \sim\!\text{Het}_n(\text{'Het}_n\text{'})$$

is blocked because the propositional function $\text{Het}_n\widehat{x}$ is of order n and hence not among the possible values of the variable $\phi_{n-1}\widehat{x}$.

As we saw in the last chapter, in Russell's conception of logic the repository in which unexplained difficulties were to be dumped was from the time of 'On denoting' the variable. In that paper he solved the difficulties of denoting phrases such as definite descriptions by treating them as contextually defined expressions that disappear on analysis, but the one exception was the variable, which remained as a denoting concept that resisted analysis. In 1906 Russell briefly thought that he could solve all the paradoxes by means of a substitutional theory that treated propositional functions too as contextually defined expressions that disappear on analysis in much the same way as definite descriptions. The virtue of this theory was that it allowed him to retain an *unrestricted* conception of the variable as ranging over all entities. When he realized that the theory did not avoid all the paradoxes, he was forced to adopt the hierarchy of orders of proposition just described and to abandon finally a single unrestricted variable. It then became the central challenge for his account to explain what the relationship was between the various variables his theory now required.

Russell's conception of logic was thoroughly impersonal, however. Logic was not part of our apparatus for understanding the world but part of the world itself. In particular, Russell saw the variable not as part of our notation for describing the world, but as a logical part of the world itself. So the difficulty that the hierarchy of variables presented to him was not the fragmentation of our relationship with the world but the fragmentation of logic itself. The difficulty was that the difference between the various variables could not be a feature of their internal structure and had therefore to consist in a logical relation. Such a logical relation would have to involve an unrestricted variable, which is just what the theory said was impossible.

But now we have to face the difficulty Whitehead urged on Russell in 1911. As long as the types of the variables are undetermined, all we have is a meaningless string of signs. It is therefore nonsense to try to express a rule for its significance by referring to the meanings of the components: until their types are determined, they *have* no meaning. 'Russell's error is shown by the fact that in drawing up his symbolic rules he has to speak about the things his signs mean.'[13] Consider, for instance, the following primitive proposition, where 'in drawing up his symbolic rules' Russell 'has to speak about the things his signs mean': 'If "ϕx" is significant, then if x is of the same type as a, "ϕa" is significant, and vice versa.' To see that this is nonsense, we have only to observe that if 'x is of the same type as a' made sense, so also would 'x is not of the same type as a': but if x is indeed not of the same type as a, then 'x is of the same type as a' is nonsense, since it makes sense only when x *is* of the same type as a. What this shows is that in a language which allows for a hierarchy of types the relation between sign and symbol cannot be expressed. We are therefore forced to reject any notion of one all-embracing language within which everything, including the meaning of language itself, can be expressed. This is nowadays a

[13]Ibid. 3.331.

familiar enough observation. The liar paradox, for example, is often taken to show that the truth predicate for a language L cannot, on pain of contradiction, be taken to be expressible in L. We shall call this feature of formal languages *weak inexpressibility*.

Now there is a perspective from which this does not seem to be an insuperable problem: faced with the unsayable-in-L, we merely move to a more inclusive metalanguage L', so that what was previously unsayable-in-L is now sayable-in-L'. However commonplace the move now is, when Russell proposed it in his Introduction to the *Tractatus* it was novel. The difficulties caused by inexpressibility suggested to him

that every language has, as Mr Wittgenstein says, a structure concerning which, *in the language*, nothing can be said, but that there may be another language dealing with the structure of the first language, and having itself a new structure, and that to this hierarchy of languages there may be no limit.[14]

But Wittgenstein would have had a ready answer to Russell's suggestion, namely that what he is attempting to describe is '*the* language which I understand'.[15] It is evidently incoherent for me to imagine moving beyond *that* to a more inclusive language in order to say the unsayable, since no such perspective is available to me. Now Russell had a response to this in turn.

Mr Wittgenstein would of course reply that his whole theory is applicable unchanged to the totality of such languages [i.e. languages I understand]. The only resort would be to deny that there is any such totality.[16]

But if we adopt this last suggestion of Russell's we are left with a conception of the languages that we understand as forming an infinite hierarchy with no union. If we are finite intelligences, this is incomprehensible. On Wittgenstein's account, indeed, my relationship with the world is constituted by my grasp of language — *the* language which I understand. If, in order to express the connection between sign and symbol we need to appeal to an infinity of languages, that is tantamount to admitting that I am not one self but infinitely many. What we have now been led to is thus not merely the claim of weak inexpressibility, that every language is limited in what it can express, but what I shall call *strong inexpressibility*, the thesis that the relationship between my language and the world is inexpressible in any language, however inclusive.

It follows from this stronger doctrine that although functions fall into types, there cannot be a theory expressible in language of why they do so. When Russell read the *Tractatus*, one of his comments was:

[14]Ibid., p. xxii.   [15]Ibid., corrected edn., 5.62.   [16]Ibid., p. xxii.

3.331 The theory of types, in my view, is a theory of correct symbolism: (a) a simple symbol must not be used to express anything complex; (b) more generally, a symbol must have the same structure as its meaning.[17]

Wittgenstein's reply to this was:

That's exactly what one can't say. You cannot prescribe to a symbol what it *may* be used to express. All that a symbol CAN express, it MAY express. This is a short answer but it is true![18]

His objection, in other words, is that Russell was attempting to use the theory to prescribe the circumstances in which a symbol is meaningful. But in order for it to be a *symbol* rather than merely a sign we must already read it as being meaningful. In the notes he dictated to G. E. Moore in Norway (before he had invented the sign/symbol terminology) Wittgenstein said:

A THEORY *of types* is impossible. It tries to say something about the types, when you can only talk about the symbols. But *what* you say about the symbols is not that this symbol has that type, which would be nonsense for [the] same reason; but you say simply: *This* is the symbol, to prevent a misunderstanding.[19]

What Wittgenstein is rejecting here is not the notion that functions stand in hierarchies but the attempt to created a hierarchy by legislating the types of the symbols. Mere signs do not have types since the type is a function of how it symbolizes, i.e. of the symbol, not the sign. If, on the other hand, we can talk of symbols rather than signs, they *already* have types which we are powerless to change.

6.4 Operations and functions

But let us now return to Wittgenstein's vicious circle argument. There is a difficulty arising from its sheer generality. A propositional function 'cannot be its own argument':[20] so whatever process we use to obtain a first-level function, we must use a different process to obtain a second-level function; and so on. Let us for a moment suppose that the truth-functions can be treated on the same model. So the negation function is to be thought of as obtainable from any particular negated proposition '$\sim p$' by regarding '$\sim$' as constant and 'p' as variable. This presupposes a domain of propositions over which 'p' varies, and these propositions cannot contain '$\sim$'. So in the sign '$\sim\sim p$' the two occurrences of '$\sim$' must symbolize differently: to see this directly we need only run through the

---

[17] *Cambridge Letters*, 122. [18] Ibid. 125. [19] *Notebooks*, 109. [20] *TLP*, 5.251.

argument quoted earlier to explain why a function cannot be its own argument, with 'F' replaced by '$\sim$' throughout. So in this respect Russell's notation is not 'logically perfect'. If we wished the notation to reflect logical grammar, we could write, for example, '$\sim_2\sim_1 p$' to indicate the difference of meaning between the occurrences of '$\sim$'.

This situation is implausible, but being implausible does not in itself make it absurd. Russell had already countenanced new logical constants at each level in the type-theoretic hierarchy. The application of the vicious circle principle to the truth-functions themselves undoubtedly makes the hierarchy considerably more complex, but it is not yet clear that it makes it incoherent. Nor is the difficulty merely that the weak doctrine of inexpressibility makes it impossible for us to state within the system the rules which such a hierarchy would obey, for even in the case of a formal system with only one negation symbol the completely general statement of the rules of the system will not be by means of propositions *of* the system.

A clue to the real difficulty is contained in Wittgenstein's remark that

if logic has primitive ideas, these must be independent of one another. If a primitive idea is introduced it must be introduced in all contexts in which it occurs at all. One cannot therefore introduce it for *one* context and then again for another. For example, if denial is introduced, we must understand it in propositions of the form '$\sim p$', just as in propositions like '$\sim(p \lor q)$', '$(\exists x).\sim fx$' and others. We may not first introduce it for one class of cases and then for another, for it would then remain doubtful whether its meaning in the two cases was the same, and there would be no reason to use the same way of symbolizing in the two cases.[21]

The difficulty, then, is that if we formulate a logical system with a sequence of primitive signs $\sim_1$, $\sim_2$, $\sim_3$, etc., there is so far nothing, except the similarity in the shape of the visual representations we have chosen, to unite these signs. We have no reason to regard them all as symbolizing *negation*. Since we plainly *can* form successively from p the propositions $\sim p$, $\sim\sim p$, $\sim\sim\sim p$, etc., there follows what Wittgenstein called his *Grundgedanke*,[22] that there is not a logical constant called negation which is a constituent of the proposition $\sim p$. Negation cannot be a function, but must be an instance of another kind of process. The point is not limited to negation, though: the argument shows the impossibility of our being able to see the application of *any* propositional function as indefinitely repeatable. Every successive application must be of a fresh function, and there is no perspective available to us from

[21] Ibid. 5.451. [22] Ibid. 4.0312.

which all such functions can be seen as instances of some more general concept.

Through most of the *Notebooks* Wittgenstein seems to have accepted that propositions fall into orders, but at the end of 1916 he began to address directly the difficulty this poses:

The fact that it is possible to erect the general form of proposition means nothing but: every possible form of proposition must be FORESEEABLE.

And that means: We can never come upon a form of proposition of which we could say: it could not have been foreseen that there was such a thing as this.

For that would mean that we had had a new experience, and that it took that to make this form of proposition possible.

Thus it must be possible to erect the general form of proposition, because the possible forms of proposition must be a priori. Because the possible forms of proposition are a priori, the general form of proposition exists.

In this connection it does not matter at all whether the given fundamental operations, through which all propositions are supposed to arise, change the logical level of the propositions, or whether they remain on the same logical level.

If a sentence were ever going to be constructible it would already be constructible.[23]

Wittgenstein asserts here that it must be possible to erect the general form of proposition, but he does not say what that general form is. His difficulty is that as long as we adhere to a theory which stratified propositions into orders to avoid paradox, this general form will be inexpressible. For if there is a single operation — call it 'N', say — that generates all propositions, so that every proposition is obtainable from elementary propositions by a finite number of applications of the N operation, then quantification over all propositions is possible, which is just what we have to avoid if propositions are to remain stratified. Instead we have to assume that there is a series of operations $N_1, N_2, N_3, \ldots$ which generate the propositions of orders 1, 2, etc. successively from the elementary propositions.

Suppose that we agree to use one sign N for all the operations N_1, N_2, etc. In that case we have an example of just the sort of ambiguity Wittgenstein's distinction between signs and symbols was designed to help explain. The sign N in its various occurrences can act as infinitely many different symbols. If N_1, N_2, etc. are distinct operations with nothing in common, it follows that the way N symbolizes in each of its occurrences is different. In that case we cannot grasp all of these ways at once: each will be a new discovery and logic will not be foreseeable.

[23] *Notebooks*, 21 Nov. 1916.

To avoid this Wittgenstein supposes that they are all instances of a common form:

In the sense in which there is a hierarchy of propositions there is, of course, also a hierarchy of truths and of negations, etc.

But in the sense in which there are, in the most general sense, such things as propositions, there is only one truth and one negation.

The latter sense is obtained from the former by conceiving the proposition in general as the result of the single operation which produces all propositions from the first level. Etc.

The lowest level and the operation can stand for the whole hierarchy.[24]

But if this is not to reintroduce the paradoxes, it seems that the operation that generates the whole hierarchy of propositions must be inexpressible. This is a blatant fudge, however. Either N symbolizes in the same way each time or it does not. If it does, there is only one type of proposition and the paradoxes recur; if it does not, I am not a single finite intelligence, since I am capable of reading one sign in infinitely many different ways.

6.5 Sense

The difficulty was to explain how an operation — something you can do to a proposition to yield another proposition — can be repeatable. If propositions are stratified into orders, so that applying an operation raises the order of the proposition, the worry is that it might be a different operation that is needed for the next application. Wittgenstein was convinced that there must be a sense in which a single operation could be repeated. Some time earlier he had referred to 'an operation whose own result can be taken as its base'.[25] This notion of a single operation being repeatable was essential not only to guarantee a single general form of proposition but also in order to be able to speak about the hierarchy of propositions.

In this way, and in this way alone, is it possible to proceed from one type to another.

And we can say that all types stand in hierarchies.

And the hierarchy is only possible by being built up by means of operations.[26]

One explanation of why iteration of the mapping 'the father of ξ' does not create a vicious circle is that the domain of the mapping — people — is one of which we have a prior conception. So to see how operations

---

[24] Ibid., 7 Jan. 1917. [25] Ibid., 23 Apr. 1916. [26] Ibid., 26 Apr. 1916.

can be repeatable, as functions are not, we similarly need to find a way of conceiving of the domain of propositions which is independent of the symbols we use to express them.

The solution to this problem of finding an unstratified conception of the domain of propositions lies in Wittgenstein's notion of sense. We have already noted that Wittgenstein saw propositions as primary within language. Among them some, which he called *elementary* propositions, are as simple as possible. These should be distinguished carefully from what Russell called by the same name. Wittgenstein's elementary propositions might more naturally be called atomic since the signs which express them consist of simple names in concatenation and cannot be further decomposed. What a proposition expresses — its *sense* — is agreement or disagreement with the truth-possibilities of elementary propositions. A proposition therefore rules in or out certain ways of assigning truth or falsity to various elementary propositions. There are two extreme cases worthy of special note.

In the one case the proposition is true for all the truth-possibilities of the elementary propositions. We say that the truth-conditions are *tautological*.

In the second case the proposition is false for all the truth-possibilities: the truth-conditions are *self-contradictory*.

In the first case we call the proposition a tautology; in the second case a contradiction.[27]

Wittgenstein does not generally classify these two special cases, of agreement with all possibilities and agreement with none, as senses strictly understood. (He likens them to the number 0 in arithmetic.) So for him tautologies and contradictions do not strictly have a sense. But here we shall follow a more liberal usage and regard them as senses, albeit trivial ones.

An operation will of course typically be specified by means of a symbolic transformation, but what the notion of sense allows us to do is to delineate without using the idea of an operation an alternative domain — that of propositional senses — on which we can conceive of operations as acting. Moreover, if operations act at the level of senses, not of symbols, they must be individuated at that level too. 'Operations can vanish (e.g. denial in '$\sim\sim p$'. $\sim\sim p = p$)'.[28] The significance of this is that it makes operations repeatable, and hence gives them their central role in the logic of the *Tractatus*. The argument which we quoted in§ 6.2 to show that a function cannot be applied to itself has no parallel in the case of operations thus understood, because it depends on the notion of the *form* of a function, i.e. the way it symbolizes. Operations

[27] *TLP*, 4.46. [28] Ibid. 5.254.

do not in that sense have a form because the way in which their results (propositional senses) are characterized, as agreement and disagreement with the truth-possibilities of elementary propositions, is not one which allows their arguments to be seen as constituents of them.

6.6 *The rejection of class-theoretic foundations for mathematics*

Wittgenstein did not develop his account of the hierarchy of types any further than the bare outline we have sketched: he did not need to go into the details of the hierarchy, because he did not intend to base mathematics on a type-theoretic foundation. The reason for this is not that Wittgenstein wised to deny the coherence of the notion of a doctrine of types — on his conception functions do indeed fall into a hierarchy of levels — but rather that he thought the theory of types could not sustain a theory of classes of the kind needed for the logicist reduction of mathematics.

The problem centred on how to define identity. Russell had defined '$x = y$' to mean that x and y have all their predicative properties in common, but in Wittgenstein's system

Russell's definition of '=' won't do; because according to it one cannot say that two objects have all their properties in common. (Even if this proposition is never true, it is nevertheless *significant*.)[29]

Propositions, on Wittgenstein's account, are ways of expressing not only how the world is but how it might be. For them to express both of these things there must be part of the structure of the world which they represent as being capable of variation. That part consists of *atomic facts* (*Sachverhalte*), which we express by means of elementary propositions. But it is incoherent to suppose that *everything* is variable: if we are to conceive of some aspect of the world changing, then it must change relative to some other aspect which remains constant. This constant aspect consists of what Wittgenstein calls *objects*, which are represented in language by names. Atomic facts are independent of each other, and objects are unalterable: these are two sides of the same coin. This rules out not only Russell's definition of identity but *any* definition which makes '$a = b$' into a Wittgensteinian proposition. For if a and b are of the same type, one of the possibilities language allows for is that all the elementary propositions in which 'a' occurs have the same truth-value as the corresponding ones containing 'b'. As every Wittgensteinian proposition is a truth-function of elementary propositions, it follows

---

[29] Ibid. 5.5302.

that in such a world no proposition could distinguish between 'a' and 'b'. The identity sign is therefore 'not an essential constituent of logical notation'.[30] So some expressions which we might have been misled into treating as propositions, such as '$a = a$' or '$a = b \, . \, b = c \, . \supset . \, a = c$', 'cannot be written in a correct logical notation at all'.[31]

The difficulty all of this poses for the logicist reduction of mathematics emerges when we try to develop an account of classes. If $f\hat{x}$ is a propositional function, then by means of Russell's method of elimination we can speak of the class $\{x : fx\}$. Its members are the things, whatever they are, that are f. We can conceive (and speak) of other ways the world could be, in which other things are f and hence the members of $\{x : fx\}$ are different. Let us call this the *accidental* conception of class. But there is another notion. When we speak of the class $\{a, b\}$, we conceive of it as having a and b as members, no matter what. However the world varies, the members of $\{a, b\}$ will stay the same. Let us call this the *essential* conception. (Neither of the terms 'accidental' and 'essential' is ideal, but I have not been able to think of better ones.) It is the essential conception which is threatened by Wittgenstein's account, since in order to speak of $\{a, b\}$ in the no-class theory we need a propositional function, such as $\hat{x} = a \lor \hat{x} = b$, which holds just of a and b, however matters stand; but in Wittgenstein's system, where identity statements are not genuine propositions, it is just such functions as this that we have no means of constructing.

Yet it is the essential conception of class that we need in mathematics.

The theory of classes is altogether superfluous in mathematics.
This is connected with the fact that the generality which we need in mathematics is not the *accidental* one.[32]

If we based mathematics on the accidental conception, there could be a world in which there were infinitely many objects but they all had the same properties, and such a world would make it the case that $2 = 0$, since there would be no way of distinguishing any two things by means of a difference in their properties. This would make mathematics susceptible to the whims of the world, which it is not.

6.7 Number as the exponent of an operation

Without the theory of classes the account of mathematics given by Whitehead and Russell is simply not available. But in looking for an alternative we must bear in mind the constraint that 'the generality

[30] Ibid. 5.533.   [31] Ibid. 5.534.   [32] Ibid. 6.031.

required in mathematics is not *accidental* generality.' Wittgenstein's solution is based on the idea that arithmetic is a calculus which mirrors certain features of language. His account is intended to show how grasp of arithmetic is not a further skill over and above grasp of language. In order for the account to do this it must be based on an aspect of his logical system which exhibits the fundamental property of the number sequence, namely that of representing the concept 'and so on'. That aspect, as we have seen, is the idea of *operation*. Thus Wittgenstein wrote opposite the 6.0s in Ramsey's copy of the *Tractatus* when Ramsey went to visit him in Austria in 1923,

The fundamental idea of mathematics is the idea of *calculus* represented here by the idea of *operation*. The beginning of logic presupposes *calculation* and so number.[33]

Wittgenstein introduces his account of numbers in the *Tractatus* by reminding us that the general form of an operation is 'the most general form of transition from one proposition to another'.[34] He continues:

And thus we come to numbers: I define

$$x = \Omega^{0\prime}x \qquad \text{Def. and}$$
$$\Omega'\Omega^{\nu\prime}x = \Omega^{\nu+1\prime}x \quad \text{Def.}$$

According, then, to these symbolic rules we write the series x, $\Omega'x$, $\Omega'\Omega'x$, $\Omega'\Omega'\Omega'x, \ldots$ as: $\Omega^{0\prime}x$, $\Omega^{0+1\prime}x$, $\Omega^{0+1+1\prime}x$, $\Omega^{0+1+1+1\prime}x, \ldots$
... And I define

$$0 + 1 = 1 \quad \text{Def.}$$
$$0 + 1 + 1 = 2 \quad \text{Def.}$$
$$0 + 1 + 1 + 1 = 3 \quad \text{Def.}$$
$$\text{and so on.}$$

A number is the exponent of an operation.[35]

Numbers are thus to be seen as indexing the repeated application of an operation to a proposition.

Three oddities in Wittgenstein's way of writing the definitions are worth noting straight away. First, he writes them in the reverse of the conventional order, with the *definiendum* on the right. Second, brackets would nowadays be used instead of a superscript comma to express the result of applying an operation to a particular argument. Third, he uses the letter 'x' for an arbitrary proposition; elsewhere in the book he uses 'p' or 'q'. (The most likely explanation for this last is that it is

[33]Lewy, 'A note on the text of the *Tractatus*'. [34]*TLP*, 6.01. [35]Ibid. 6.02–6.03.

a hangover from a time when Wittgenstein conceived of operations as applying not just to propositions but to symbols generally.)[36] Correcting for these three oddities we can thus rewrite Wittgenstein's recursive definition of numbers as

$$\Omega^0(p) =_{\text{Df}} p \tag{1}$$
$$\Omega^{\nu+1}(p) =_{\text{Df}} \Omega(\Omega^\nu(p)). \tag{2}$$

6.8 The adjectival strategy

Wittgenstein's recursive definition of numbers as exponents of operations is a generalization of the definition of numerically definite quantifiers which Frege considered and rejected in *Grundlagen*. To see why, let $\phi\hat{x}$ be a propositional function, let p be the proposition that there are no ϕs, and let Ω be an operation which takes any proposition saying that there is a certain number of ϕs to the proposition saying that there is one more ϕ than that. If we do this, $\Omega^n(p)$ will have the same sense as the proposition that there are n ϕs.

It is quite hard, in fact, to describe the operation Ω at the level of sense in a way which does not make a circular appeal to the natural numbers, and Wittgenstein certainly does not trouble himself with the details, but even if it can be done the kinship of Wittgenstein's strategy with Frege's raises the question whether it is susceptible to the same objections. Frege's rejection of the definition by means of recursive definitions of the numerically definite quantifiers was, we saw in §2.5, based on a general argument against what we there called the adjectival strategy, namely that of giving an explanation of the adjectival use of numbers first and then deriving from that an account of their substantival use. Wittgenstein's recursive definitions of numbers as exponents, although they are more general than the numerically definite quantifiers, are still broadly adjectival. So one might suppose that the Julius Caesar problem will arise once more as a reason for rejecting Wittgenstein's account. There is a fallacy in this thought, however. Frege's argument is not an objection to the strategy of explaining the adjectival use of numbers in itself, but to the strategy of deriving from such an explanation an account of their substantival use. It has no force against Wittgenstein because he did not hold that numbers are objects and therefore had no reason to suppose that there is, when statements involving number words are correctly analysed, any genuinely substantival use requiring to be explained.

[36]Cf. *Notebooks*, 22 Nov. 1916.

But Frege had a second argument against the adjectival strategy which is not so easily dismissed. He stated it very briefly in the *Grundlagen*— 'Strictly speaking we do not know the sense of the expression "the number n belongs to the concept G" any more than we do that of the expression "the number $(n + 1)$ belongs to the concept F" '[37] — and spelt it out more fully in the Appendix to *Grundgesetze*, where the need to find a solution to Russell's paradox led him to consider the possibility that

there is nothing for it but to regard class names as sham proper names, which would thus not really have any meaning. They would have to be regarded as part of signs that had meaning only as wholes. Now of course one may think it advantageous for some end to form different signs that partly resemble one another, without thereby making them into complex signs. The simplicity of a sign requires only that the parts that may be distinguished within it should have no separate meaning. On this view, then even what we usually regard as a number-sign would not really be a sign at all, but only an inseparable part of a sign. A definition of the sign '2' would be impossible; instead we should have to define many signs, which would contain '2' as an inseparable part, but could not be regarded as logically compounded of '2' and another part. It would thus be illicit to replace such an inseparable part by a letter; for as regards the content of the whole sign, there would be no complexity. The generality of arithmetical propositions would thus be lost.[38]

This constitutes a more substantial difficulty for Wittgenstein's account than the Julius Caesar problem, since it cannot be defused simply by denying that numbers are objects. The thought here is that Wittgenstein has given a meaning to the symbol '$\Omega^n x$' taken as a whole but that this does not entitle us to regard the symbol 'n' occurring in this expression as having a meaning, any more than defining what 'cart' means thereby gives meaning to the word 'car'. Frege concludes from this that we are not entitled to replace numerals by variables and are therefore unable to generalize about numbers.

We have already noted that Frege's arguments for the claim that numbers are objects are surprisingly thin given the centrality of the claim to his project. But the passage just quoted continues by giving an argument whose bearing on Wittgenstein's treatment is worth noting: if numbers were not objects, Frege says, 'it would be incomprehensible how we could speak of ... a number of numbers.'[39] On Frege's conception this is a powerful objection: it is a decisive bar to Frege's resolving Russell's paradox simply by doing without extensions and making do with concepts instead. The same limitation arises for Wittgenstein. If we could use numbers to count *symbols*, we could, for

[37] *Gl.*, § 56. [38] *Gg.*, II, 255. [39] Ibid.

example, obtain the number of prime numbers less than 10 by labelling the formal series

$$\Omega^2(p),\ \Omega^3(p),\ \Omega^5(p),\ \Omega^7(p)$$

in the obvious way by the numbers 1,2,3,4. How, though, do we achieve this if we adhere to the Tractarian doctrine that an operation can only have propositions as its base?

This is not a point on which Russell's account does better than Wittgenstein's: in *Principia* numbers of individuals are second-level classes, and numbers of such numbers are fourth-level classes; only the device of typical ambiguity permits us in this system to say that there are four prime numbers less than 10. But although it is inconvenient for mathematicians, the point we are considering is not a criticism which would have troubled Wittgenstein himself.

In life it is never a mathematical proposition which we need, but we use mathematical propositions *only* in order to infer from propositions which do not belong to mathematics to others which equally do not belong to mathematics.[40]

Wittgenstein's concern was solely with explaining the application of mathematics, since he took this to be the only thing about mathematics which *could* be explained.

6.9 Equations

I have said that Wittgenstein's account of the adjectival use of numerals is not susceptible to Frege's criticism because Wittgenstein does not attempt to derive from it a general account of their substantival use sufficient to license the claim that numbers are objects. There are, however, *some* substantival uses of numerals which Wittgenstein must explain, most obviously their occurrence in equations such as '$7 + 5 = 12$'.

Although it is clear that such an explanation is needed as soon as Wittgenstein has given his account of numbers as exponents of operations in the 6.0s, Wittgenstein does not go on to it directly but delays it to the 6.2s, choosing instead to interpolate in the 6.1s a long section on logic and the nature of tautologies. The ordering is deliberate. It is intended to emphasize the parallelism Wittgenstein sees between logic and mathematics. Although equations are not tautologies (and are indeed, as we shall see, on a different logical level from tautologies),

---

[40] *TLP*, 6.211.

they share with tautologies the feature of not saying anything about the world, and hence are not properly speaking propositions at all but what Wittgenstein called *pseudo-propositions.* 'Mathematical propositions express no thoughts.'[41] Equations are therefore to be explained in a way which stresses the similarities with the account of tautologies: 'The logic of the world, which the propositions of logic show in tautologies, mathematics shows in equations.'[42]

At this point, then, having signalled that his account of mathematics is going to be restricted to equations, Wittgenstein proceeds to explain what equations mean:

If two expressions are connected by the sign of equality, this means that they can be substituted for one another. ...

And that the propositions of mathematics can be proved means nothing else than that their correctness can be seen without our having to compare what they express with the facts as regards correctness.

The identity of the meaning of two expressions cannot be *asserted.* For in order to be able to assert anything about their meaning, I must know their meaning, and if I know their meaning, I know whether they mean the same or something different.[43]

The only place numbers properly occur is as the exponents of operations. So to prove an equation we need to show that the two numerical expressions involved may be substituted for one another whenever they occur in exponent position:

The method by which mathematics arrives at its equations is the method of substitution.

For equations express the substitutability of two expressions and, starting from a number of equations, we advance to new equations by substituting different expressions in accordance with the equations.[44]

The general idea is clear enough: if 'μ' and 'ν' are numerical terms, '$\mu = \nu$' is to mean that

$$\Omega^\mu(p) = \Omega^\nu(p). \tag{3}$$

But there are several points that need to be clarified if this is to be an adequate explanation.

The first point to note is that, as I argued in § 6.5, operations are to be understood as acting at the level of sense, not that of symbols. So another way of putting (3) is to say that $\Omega^\mu(p)$ and $\Omega^\nu(p)$ express the same sense. Another way still is to say that $\Omega^\mu(p) \equiv \Omega^\nu(p)$ is a tautology. But 'that $\Omega^\mu(p) \equiv \Omega^\nu(p)$ is a tautology' is not a proposition: it cannot be expressed in the primitive language, but will merely show

[41] Ibid. 6.21.　[42] Ibid. 6.22.　[43] Ibid. 6.23–6.2322.　[44] Ibid. 6.24.

itself in the tautologousness of $\Omega^\mu(p) \equiv \Omega^\nu(p)$, which *is* a proposition. This is why Wittgenstein said that equations are pseudo-propositions:[45] they are at the wrong level to express genuine thoughts.

But we still have not said anything about the rôle of Ω and p. We cannot interpret $\mu = \nu$ as meaning that (3) holds for some *particular* operation Ω and proposition p: for if the operation chosen were negation, for example, we could then conclude from $\sim\sim p = p$ that $2 = 0$. Plainly we need to interpret $\mu = \nu$ as meaning that (3) holds for *every* operation Ω and proposition p. There is a further difficulty with this, however: we cannot achieve what we want simply by quantification, since, as just noted, 'that $\Omega^\mu(p) \equiv \Omega^\nu(p)$ is a tautology' is not a proposition, and hence cannot be quantified. So to achieve the correct interpretation we are forced to treat the occurrences of Ω and p in (3) as schematic.

So much for equations. What about inequations? The inequation $\mu \neq \nu$ cannot mean that

$$\Omega^\mu(p) \neq \Omega^\nu(p),$$

for arbitrary Ω and p. (If it did, the previously considered example that $\sim\sim p = p$ would show that we could not have $2 \neq 0$.) The right meaning for $\mu \neq \nu$ should be that there *exist* an operation Ω and a proposition p such that

$$\Omega^\mu(p) \neq \Omega^\nu(p),$$

i.e. such that

$$\Omega^\mu(p) \equiv \Omega^\nu(p) \text{ is not a tautology,}$$

but as before this is not a proposition and hence cannot be quantified. The trick of regarding the expression as a schema, which we used earlier to interpret a universal generalization, is of no help here where it is an existential generalization that is in question. So no interpretation of the inequation '$\mu \neq \nu$' is available. The awkward conclusion, not drawn explicitly by Wittgenstein but mentioned in passing by Ramsey in his critical notice of the *Tractatus*,[46] is thus that numerical equations cannot be negated.

This ought not to be too much of a surprise, however, since we have already noted that equations are according to Wittgenstein not propositions but pseudo-propositions. Just as a Russellian term shows itself not to be a logically proper name by its failure to respect all the logical

---

[45] Ibid. 6.2. [46] *FoM*, 282.

laws to which proper names are subject, so a Wittgensteinian pseudo-proposition will show itself not to be a genuine proposition by its failure to participate fully in the logical system. Nevertheless, surprise or not, this is undoubtedly a severe limitation (even in 'real life').

6.10 Numerical identities

Wittgenstein gives just one example to show how the proofs of numerical identities are carried out in his system:

Thus the proof of the proposition $2 \times 2 = 4$ runs:

$$(\Omega^\nu)^{\mu\prime}x = \Omega^{\nu\times\mu\prime}x \quad \text{Def.,}$$
$$\Omega^{2\times 2\prime}x = (\Omega^2)^{2\prime}x = (\Omega^2)^{1+1\prime}x$$
$$= \Omega^{2\prime}\Omega^{2\prime}x = \Omega^{1+1\prime}\Omega^{1+1\prime}x$$
$$= (\Omega^\prime\Omega)^\prime(\Omega^\prime\Omega)^\prime x = \Omega^\prime\Omega^\prime\Omega^\prime\Omega^\prime x$$
$$= \Omega^{1+1+1+1\prime}x = \Omega^{4\prime}x. \text{ [47]}$$

Adapted to a more conventional notation Wittgenstein's definition of multiplication is thus:

$$\Omega^{\nu\times\mu}(p) =_{\text{Df}} (\Omega^\nu)^\mu(p).$$

The corresponding definition of addition, which Wittgenstein does not give, is easy enough to supply:

$$\Omega^{\nu+\mu}(p) =_{\text{Df}} \Omega^\mu(\Omega^\nu(p)).$$

(I have reversed the natural order of 'μ' and 'ν' in the definiens here in order to be consistent with (2).)

At a purely mechanical level Wittgenstein's account is now clear; and it evidently allows us in principle to prove any true numerical equation involving addition or multiplication. We can, for example, prove that $2 + 2 = 4$ as follows:

$$\Omega^{2+2}(p) = \Omega^2(\Omega^2(p))$$
$$= \Omega(\Omega(\Omega^2(p)))$$
$$= \Omega(\Omega^{2+1}(p))$$
$$= \Omega^{(2+1)+1}(p)$$
$$= \Omega^{3+1}(p)$$
$$= \Omega^4(p).$$

[47] *TLP*, 6.241.

(In one of the typescripts of the *Tractatus* Wittgenstein gives this proof instead of the proof that $2 \times 2 = 4$ quoted above.) It is instructive to note how reminiscent this is of Leibniz's fallacious proof that 2+2=4 which I quoted in §0.6. That proof depended on an application in a particular case of the general rule

$$x + (y + 1) = (x + y) + 1.$$

In Wittgenstein's proof the corresponding step is justified by a feature of language, namely that the composition of operations is associative.

6.11 Generalization

I said earlier that prima facie there is a difficulty standing in the way of replacing numbers by variables in Wittgenstein's treatment. But in the account we have given of the meaning of the equation '$\mu = \nu$' the letters 'μ' and 'ν' are schematic, standing not merely for arbitrary numerals (such as '4' or '126') but more generally for arbitrary number terms (such as '$7 + 5$' or '$4 \times (6 + 2)$'). This allows us to give a meaning to schematic general statements about numbers. For example, the schema $\mu + 1 = 1 + \mu$ means that

$$\Omega^{\mu+1}(p) = \Omega^{1+\mu}(p),$$

with μ, Ω, and p all schematic. Nothing similar can be done with existential generalizations about numbers, however. If, for instance, we try to represent $(\exists x). \mu(x) = 0$ as meaning that

$$(\exists x)(\Omega^{\mu(x)}(p) \equiv p \text{ is a tautology}),$$

we get the wrong meaning. To get the correct meaning we should have to write

$$(\exists x)(\Omega)(p)(\Omega^{\mu(x)}(p) \equiv p \text{ is a tautology}),$$

but this is meaningless for the by now familiar reason that the expression

$$\Omega^{\mu(x)}(p) \equiv p \text{ is a tautology}$$

is not a proposition but a pseudo-proposition and hence cannot meaningfully be quantified.

We can thus coherently make universal but not existential generalizations about numbers. To be able to make them is not yet to be able to prove them, though. The proof that in general $\mu + 1 = 1 + \mu$, for instance, involves induction on μ, and nothing we have said so far licenses that. Indeed the *Tractatus* makes no explicit mention of the principle of mathematical induction at all. (The two references in the text to 'induction' seem to be to the law of induction in physics.)

At an even more basic level, notice that Wittgenstein's definition of multiplication, for example, does not give us any direct assurance that the product of two natural numbers is a natural number, i.e. that if 'μ' and 'ν' are numerals there is a numeral 'σ' such that

$$\Omega^{\mu \times \nu}(p) = \Omega^{\sigma}(p)$$

with Ω and p arbitrary. When we calculate $\mu \times \nu$ in any particular case (such as Wittgenstein's calculation of '2×2') we of course find that there is such a numeral (in this case '4'), but what *general* reason do we have for thinking that there is always one? The usual proof involves a double induction on μ and ν.

It may seem as though such appeals to induction would be a further step, requiring a new argument. On the purely formal level this is undoubtedly so, but not, I think, on a conceptual level. The reason is that in order to ask the question whether $\mu \times \nu$ is in general a number we have already to suppose that $\mu \times \nu$ has been defined. And the definition, whose coherence is not at this point in question, makes an implicit appeal to induction for its meaningfulness. This is because our understanding of the numerals 'μ' and 'ν' occurring in the definition is in turn inductive: numerals are, according to Wittgenstein's definition, symbols which can be obtained from zero inductively by adding one. We are tempted to deny this dependence because it seems that for any *particular* numerals 'μ' and 'ν' no appeal to induction is required: we merely apply the definition a finite number of times. But what this overlooks is that *each* time we apply the definition we have to understand it as the *same* multiplication function that is being calculated. And for this we do require the general grasp of the number series that is given to us by its inductive definition.

Wittgenstein's definition of number thus commits him to the validity of argument by induction on the numerals. That does not, however, explain how we ground its validity. Wittgenstein's answer to that lies in the remarks which head the section of the *Tractatus* on arithmetic and logic:

The general form of truth-function is $[\bar{p}, \bar{\xi}, N(\bar{\xi})]$.
    This is the general form of a proposition.

This says nothing else than that every proposition is the result of successive applications of the operation $N(\bar{\xi})$ to the elementary propositions.[48]

The point of making all the remarks on arithmetic subsidiary to this is that the general form of proposition is recursive: propositions are obtained from elementary propositions by iterations of the N operation. Since all operations apply to propositions, all operations are ultimately expressible in terms of the N operation. But numbers are merely a notation for expressing the repeated application of operations. So our understanding of numbers in general is also based on our understanding of the general form of proposition.

None of this, of course, amounts to an explanation of the validity of induction. What it does, though, is to base that on an appeal to something Wittgenstein takes to be fundamental, namely that grasp of language as a whole which we have when we understand the general form of proposition. Wittgenstein saw this as playing a central rôle in his theory corresponding to the rôle of intuition in Kant. Kant talks here of the 'limitlessness in the progression of intuition';[49] Wittgenstein needs the general form of proposition to do the same thing.

To the question whether we need intuition for the solution of mathematical problems it must be answered that language itself here supplies the necessary intuition.

The process of *calculation* brings about just this intuition.[50]

6.12 The axiom of infinity

Does Wittgenstein's account rule out the possibility that the numbers are not all distinct? If 'μ' and 'ν' are distinct numerals, can we conclude, in other words that $\mu \neq \nu$? In order to prove the corresponding result in their system Whitehead and Russell needed to assume an axiom of infinity asserting that there are infinitely many individuals, but the axiom of infinity cannot play the same rôle in Wittgenstein's account. The infinitude of the world (if it is indeed infinite) shows itself in the language we use to describe it and cannot be expressed by any one proposition in the language. However, there are two different ways in which the world might be infinite corresponding to the two aspects it has, that of permanence and that of possibility. For the world to be infinite in its permanent aspect there would have to be infinitely many objects, and this would be shown by there being infinitely many names in the language. For there to be infinitely many possibilities as to how

---

[48] Ibid. 6–6.001. [49] *KrV*, A25. [50] *TLP*, 6.233.

the world could be, on the other hand, there would have to be infinitely many states of affairs in the world, and this would be shown by there being infinitely many elementary propositions in the language.

Now both these — the number of names and the number of elementary propositions — are ways in which language reflects the limits of empirical reality. 'Empirical reality is limited by the totality of objects. The boundary appears again in the totality of elementary propositions.'[51] But the connection between the two sorts of limit is even closer than this suggests. The first sort of infinity obviously implies the second, since if there are infinitely many objects they must have infinitely many possible arrangements. The converse seems at first more doubtful: for one might argue that finitely many objects could occur in infinitely many atomic facts; or, at the level of syntax, that finitely many names could be used to form infinitely many elementary propositions. But this is not so: if there were different ways of putting names together to form elementary propositions, these different ways would represent a further dimension of variability which would on correct analysis be replaceable by a further name position in the form of the elementary propositions. Hence empirical reality is infinite in the first respect if and only if it is infinite in the second.

Nothing in the *Tractatus* rules out a language constructed on a base of only finitely many elementary propositions. (Indeed Georg Kreisel has reported[52] that Wittgenstein much later said he had conceived the logical system of the *Tractatus* first of all for the finite case, on the basis that if it didn't work for that case it was hardly likely to work for the infinite one.) So suppose now for a moment that there is only a finite number of elementary propositions. Then there are only finitely many propositional senses, and consequently the set of all operations, i.e. functions from propositional senses to propositional senses, is finite too. A straightforward group-theoretic argument then shows that there must be numbers M, N with $M < N$ such that for every operation Ω and every proposition p we have $\Omega^M(p) = \Omega^N(p)$. But this is just what we said was meant by $M = N$. Consequently there are no natural numbers other than $0, 1, 2, \ldots, N - 1$. By contraposition it follows that from the assumption of infinitely many numbers we can conclude that there are infinitely many elementary propositions, and hence infinitely many objects. A further consequence is that subtraction cannot be defined in Wittgenstein's system. For if it could, we would have $N - M = 0$, and so $\Omega^{N-M}(p) = p$ for every operation Ω and proposition p; in particular, if we apply this in the case where $\Omega(p) = p_0$ for all p, where p_0 is some

---

[51] Ibid. 5.5561. [52] Marion, *Wittgenstein, Finitism and the Foundations of Mathematics*, p. 34.

fixed proposition, we obtain $p = p_0$ for all p, i.e. all propositions have the same sense. Contradiction.

Although how many objects and elementary propositions there are limits reality, it does not do so in a way we can express in our language. The possibilities we can express are possibilities as to the ways the objects could be configured, not possibilities as to how many objects there are. So if the form of arithmetic is dependent on how many objects there are, that does not directly contradict Wittgenstein's injunction that 'the generality that is required in mathematics is not *accidental* generality'. The reason the dependence of arithmetic on the number of objects nevertheless seems embarrassing to Wittgenstein is that there is plainly another sense in which it *is* possible that the number of objects should be different from what it is, namely that logic allows for a different number of objects even if language as a whole does not. Language draws the limits of the world, or in other words of what it is possible. But we can divide our grasp of language into two parts, the elementary propositions and the general form of proposition, and corresponding to this division we can detect two levels of possibility that language as a whole allows for. 'Mathematics', Wittgenstein says, 'is a logical method.'[53] A consequence of this is that mathematics should not limit the world any more than logic does. If mathematics is to lie at the same level of generality as logic, it must be necessary not only with respect to the level of contingency that our language expresses, namely contingency as to which arrangements of objects into atomic facts actually occur, but also with respect to the higher level inexpressible in the language itself but represented by the general form of proposition, namely contingency as to what objects there are. So Wittgenstein does indeed seem to be in need of an argument to show that *our* language is one that represents there to be infinitely many objects.

6.13 A transcendental argument

How many things there are is one of the things that are inexpressible. This is because the possibilities our language is capable of expressing are only possibilities relative to what the language says there is: what a language with n names admits as possible is different arrangements of the n objects denoted by those names, not different objects altogether.

Now it might seem as if Wittgenstein's quantifier notation allowed a way out of this restriction. To see how, recall first that Wittgenstein avoided the need for a sign of identity in his primitive logical

[53]Ibid. 6.2.

notation by adopting the convention that different names always denote different objects. He applied this convention not only to names but also to quantified variables. We shall write $(\exists x)'$ and $(x)'$ instead of $(\exists x)$ and (x) when Wittgenstein's convention is in force. So '$(\exists x, y)' f(x, y)$', for example, is to mean what Russell expressed by '$(\exists x, y) . f(x, y) \; . \; \sim x = y$' and Russell's '$(\exists x, y) . fxy$' becomes '$(\exists x, y)' . f(x, y) . \lor . (\exists x)' . f(x, x)'$'.[54]   Russell's theory of descriptions is, Wittgenstein thought, 'quite certainly correct',[55] so the expression '$a = \imath x \, fx$' remains legitimate, but it is now to be analysed as

$$fa \; . \; \sim (\exists x, y)' . fx \; . \; fy,$$

so that the sign of identity is not ultimately needed for its expression. On the other hand, some sentences in Russell's notation involving the sign of identity cannot be expressed in Wittgenstein's, but this is a virtue, not a vice, since it simply shows that such expressions do not express genuine propositions.

And we see that apparent propositions like '$a = a$', '$a = b \, . \, b = c \, . \supset . \, a = c$', '$(x) . x = x$', '$(\exists x) . x = a$', etc. cannot be written in a correct logical notation at all.[56]

Consider now the sentence

$$(\exists x_1)'(\exists x_2)' \ldots (\exists x_n)' : fx_1 \; . \; fx_2 \ldots fx_n$$

in Wittgenstein's notation, which seems to say that there are at least n different things satisfying the propositional function $f\widehat{x}$; in particular, if $T\widehat{x}$ is a function that is true of everything of a certain type (e.g. the function $f\widehat{x} \lor \sim f\widehat{x}$), then

$$(\exists x_1)'(\exists x_2)' \ldots (\exists x_n)' : Tx_1 \; . \; Tx_2 \ldots Tx_n \qquad (4)$$

seems to say that there are at least n things of that type. What is wrong with this idea is that although on Wittgenstein's account (4) is indeed true if there are at least n things, it is not false but meaningless if there are fewer than n things. Confirmation is supplied by one of the remarks Wittgenstein wrote in the margin of Ramsey's copy of the *Tractatus* in 1923:

The prop[osition] 'there are n things such that ... ' presupposes for its significance what we try to assert by saying 'there are n things'.[57]

---

[54]See ibid. 5.531.   [55]*Cambridge Letters*, 61.   [56]*TLP*, 5.534.   [57]Lewy, 'A note on the text of the *Tractatus*', 421.

Now the same applies to the axiom of infinity: to say that there are $\aleph_0$ things is significant only if it is true. But in that case the axiom of infinity admits a transcendental proof as follows. My language — '*the* language which I understand'[58] — is fashioned with the primary purpose of saying how the world is and, correlatively, how it is not. And whether or not there are in fact infinitely many empirical objects, it seems clear that I can understand both the possibility that there are and the possibility that there are not. So the fact that I can understand both possibilities concerning how many empirical things there are shows that my language is fashioned in such a way that it can represent both possibilities. Now although Tractarian objects need not be the same as empirical things, it is hard to see how a language that only allowed for finitely many Tractarian objects could represent the possibility that there are infinitely many empirical things. For empirical things are certainly representable in my language, and the only way available in the language to represent them, if not directly as objects, is as complexes composed from objects in some uniform way. And if there are only finitely many objects, there can only be finitely many complexes of any given complexity. It follows that the axiom of infinity is significant, and hence must be true.

Ramsey wrote down something like this argument shortly after his visit to Wittgenstein:

I can say 'There are an infinite number of atoms'. This may be false, but it is possibly true and therefore significant. And for it to mean anything there must be an infinite number of things. These need not be material objects because the proposition requires analysis to discover its real form .... But roughly it involves the possibility of saying 'Here is an atom' about an infinity of 'here' 's.[59]

Ramsey never published this argument, presumably because he very soon afterwards adopted a different theory of identity according to which the axiom of infinity is either a tautology or a contradiction but always significant, and on this view the argument plainly fails. But Wittgenstein strongly disagreed with Ramsey's account of identity, so he never had Ramsey's reason not to pursue the transcendental argument for the axiom of infinity now being considered. Whether the argument would have appealed to him on its own merits is harder to judge. Later, when he returned to philosophy at the end of the 1920s, he began to explore the idea that our talk of the infinite can be analysed in such a way that it is merely part of the way we describe the finite and does not require there to be infinitely many objects: on that

[58] *TLP*, corrected edn., 5.62.   [59] *Notes*, 175.

conception the argument plainly fails, but there does not seem to be any trace of this thought in the *Tractatus*.

6.14 Another transcendental argument

In §6.5 I argued that Wittgenstein intended operations to be understood as acting at the level of sense. This leads, as we have seen, to three difficulties: it renders the notion of a number of numbers meaningless; it prevents us from giving an account of existential generalizations about numbers; and it makes even elementary arithmetic dependent on the assumption that there are infinitely many elementary propositions. Of these the first two show, it is true, that (if we adopt the narrow understanding) arithmetic remains resolutely at the lowest possible level, but it would require a further argument to establish that we need an account of existential generalization in arithmetic. The third difficulty, however, is devastating.

One response to these difficulties would be to abandon this narrow view of operations and understand them instead as acting more broadly at the level of signs. If we did this, there would no longer be any point in restricting them to propositions. Part of the motivation for Wittgenstein's narrower conception of operations was that it avoided the paradoxes. On this ground, though, the broad conception at the level of signs is equally secure: neither Wittgenstein nor anyone else could imagine that paradox lurks in the process of writing '$\sim$' in front of a string of signs to produce the sequence

$$p, \sim p, \sim\sim p, \dots .$$

The real objection to the procedure is thus not that it is contradictory, but rather that it is irrelevant. It is not signs that form my language but symbols. If we based arithmetic on the syntactic notion of operation, it would have no application because nothing significant about my language *can* follow from the fact that we can repeatedly write '$\sim$' in front of a string of signs.

The broader notion of operation that has a chance of being relevant to Wittgenstein's purposes, then, is that at the level not of signs but of symbols. An operation in this broad sense is thus a process that can be applied to a symbol of the language that always yields a symbol to which the operation can be applied again. The otherwise curious use noted earlier of 'x' as the variable rather than 'p' in Wittgenstein's account of arithmetic is perhaps explicable as a remnant of this early conception of the operation as a mapping from symbols to symbols, which he may have held for a time and then abandoned.

The proposal, then is that the numerical identity '$\mu = \nu$' is reinterpreted as meaning that $\Omega^\mu(x)$ is the same *symbol* as $\Omega^\nu(x)$. This at once gets rid of our difficulty over the dependence of arithmetic on the number of elementary propositions in the language, since however few elementary propositions there are,

$$p, \sim p, \sim \sim p, \ldots$$

is an infinite sequence of different *symbols* (although they do not, of course, all express different senses).[60] It also gets rid of our inability to speak of numbers of numbers: if numbers are merely a way of labelling formal series, we can label a formal series of numerical expressions just as easily as we can label a series of genuine propositions. Thus for example, we obtain the number of prime numbers less than 10 by labelling the formal series

$$\Omega^2(x), \ \Omega^3(x), \ \Omega^5(x), \ \Omega^7(x)$$

in the obvious way with the numbers 1, 2, 3, 4. Moreover, the extension of the allowable domain of operations from propositions to symbols in general is on Wittgenstein's account not in itself a major step, since symbols can in any case be understood only as propositional elements.[61]

The textual evidence makes it clear, I think, that Wittgenstein did not in the end adopt the broad conception of operations now under consideration. But this prompts an obvious question. Why, if the broad notion of operation at the level of symbols leads to such a pleasing account of arithmetic, did Wittgenstein apparently settle in the end for the narrower reading at the level of sense?

I have already sketched one possible answer: he came to see the broad notion as embodying a risk of circularity, since it is impossible to specify the totality of symbols which are to be legitimate bases for operations without making use of that same notion of operation. If operations are conceived of as functions from symbols to symbols, we can use operations to construct new symbols, thus giving rise to impredicativity.

It is thus possible that concern about the risk of paradoxes influenced Wittgenstein's decision to adopt the narrow conception of operations. It need not have done so, however, since the broad conception is not in fact contradictory. The boundaries of the domain of senses have already been demarcated by Wittgenstein's account of them as

[60]Cf. ibid. 179. [61]*TLP*, 3.314.

expressing agreement or disagreement with the truth possibilities of elementary propositions: this characterization would be threatened by the broad conception of operations only if they could somehow generate new elementary propositions, which they plainly cannot. So the only danger remaining is that the newly constructed signs might not be interpretable as symbols: but the requirement to avoid that danger (by ensuring that propositional signs are constructed in such a way that they *do* express senses) was present already and is not generated solely by the current proposal.

In the same note in which he mentioned the transcendental argument we discussed in the last section Ramsey briefly canvassed the broad conception of operation as a way of avoiding the axiom of infinity:

The significance of '$\sim p$' depended on its being constructed according to a rule expressive of the nature of negation according to which an infinity of forms can be constructed '$\sim p$', '$\sim\sim\sim p$', '$\sim p. \vee. \sim p$', ... Thus infinity is presupposed by our notation, and since our notation is significant there must be an actual infinity. Again the argument is not that the existence of the marks $\sim$, $\vee$ etc. proves the existence of infinity but that this is proved by the significance of the marks.[62]

'This', Ramsey remarked crisply, 'is a Kantian argument.'[63] And so it is. But therein lies the difficulty. It is a general constraint on us, independent of the current proposal, to talk in propositions, i.e. to form signs that can be read as expressing senses, but the current proposal is a stronger constraint. Our language allows an infinite sequence of propositions p, $\sim p$, $\sim\sim p$, etc. to be constructed. In order for that to be significant, it has to be an essential feature of the way these signs symbolize that there should be infinitely many of them. Yet Wittgenstein himself at one time canvassed the idea that we could symbolize the negation of p by turning the sign upside down. If this were how we symbolized it, we should have not an infinite sequence of symbols but just two, p and d. It follows that the infinitude of the sequence p, $\sim p$, $\sim\sim p$, etc. cannot be an *essential* feature of how it symbolizes and must be merely a parochial feature of the sign scheme we have chosen. We are back, in other words, at the proposal we have already rejected of treating operations as acting at the level of signs.

[62]*Notes*, 176.   [63]Ibid. 179.

7

The second edition of Principia

We saw in the last chapter that the *Tractatus* can account for only a limited part of arithmetic at best. When Russell read Wittgenstein's manuscript he was convinced straight away that this was a gap that needed to be filled. Curiously, it was not the omission of an account of real numbers that he found egregious, but that of a general account of cardinals. '*Something* true is expressed by $\text{Nc'Cl'}\alpha = 2^{\text{Nc'}\alpha}$ [i.e. in modern notation $\text{card}\,\mathfrak{P}(\alpha) = 2^{\text{card}\,\alpha}$],' he insisted.[1] Russell was therefore not willing simply to abandon the development of mathematics from the theory of types. He accepted, though, some of Wittgenstein's criticisms of the account he had given in *Principia*. So he took the opportunity presented by the publication of a second edition of *Principia* to prepare a new Introduction indicating how mathematics could be based on a new theory of types consonant with the parts of Wittgenstein's account which Russell agreed with.

7.1 *Logical atomism and empiricism*

In the second edition of *Principia* Russell committed himself to the view that the state of the world can be described by means of atomic propositions in which the logical constants do not occur. This enabled a complete separation between logic and the world, since the description of the world by means of atomic propositions is one to which logic does not contribute. In this respect the account in the second edition constrains that in the first, but does not contradict it, since Russell was simply silent there (at Whitehead's request) about the exact nature of the elementary propositions from which the hierarchy is constructed. In the second edition the elementary propositions are precisely the truth-functional combinations of finite numbers of atomic propositions. In the first edition this need not be the case because Russell wished explicitly to allow for non-extensional functions such as '*A* believes that

---

[1] Wittgenstein, *Cambridge Letters*, 122.

p', but now Russell ruled these out, accepting — albeit hesitantly — Wittgenstein's view that 'A believes that p' is indeed a truth-function (although not, of course, a truth-function of p).

Ramsey suggested in a review that Russell's detailed discussion (in an appendix to the second edition) of the question whether all functions of propositions are truth-functional is unnecessary: the assumption that they are 'could be made a mere matter of definition, by deciding that in mathematics "all functions of functions" is to include only such as fulfil the required condition.'[2] But this course would not have been acceptable to Russell since he continued to hold, as he had when he wrote the first edition, that logic is completely general: although his immediate purpose was to base mathematics on logic, the logic he based it on had to be the same logic that we use in reasoning about all other subjects. Ramsey was right to say that we are free to introduce restricted variables ranging only over extensional functions, but if we based our treatment of a piece of mathematics on such restricted quantifiers we should thereby limit its applicability.

There is another reason, though, why it was not, as Ramsey said it was, a 'gratuitous inquiry' for Russell to investigate whether all function of propositions are truth functions: it is an essential component of Russell's atomism that this should turn out to be so. If it were impossible to analyse 'A believes that p' as a truth function of atomic propositions, that would show the fact that A believes p — if it is a fact — not to be analysable in terms of the facts asserted by atomic propositions; in which case there would have to be some further aspect to the world not represented by the atomic facts.

Thus far the account bears a strong resemblance to the Tractarian atomism described in the last chapter, but at this point it begins to diverge sharply: to the extent that his account is Wittgensteinian at all, it is the Wittgenstein he taught in Cambridge before the war that Russell followed, not the Wittgenstein of the *Tractatus*. For what Wittgenstein seems to have developed only after he had left Cambridge was the neo-Kantian conception of the describable world as essentially conditioned by the forms of language. At first Wittgenstein toyed with various sorts of things the atoms of the world might be, but in the *Tractatus* such considerations are absent because he intended to dissolve in an essentially Kantian manner the epistemological problem that any such account would prompt. Russell never took this step. For him the atoms logically proper names refer to are the entities with which we have direct acquaintance. What matters here is not what he took these entities

---

[2]'Review of *Principia Mathematica*, 2nd edn.', 506.

to be — usually sense-data — but the fact that he thought his account had to settle this question at all.

Several things follow from this. First, and most directly, we must abandon the assumption that the atomic propositions are independent of one another. For even if the entities we treat as simple really are physically irreducible, it is an empirical question whether natural laws further constrain the arrangement of these entities. It follows that we must abandon Wittgenstein's conception of the rôle of language as being to express the range of possibilities as to how the world is.[3]

But if the task of language is not to express possibilities, what is it? Without Wittgenstein's notion of the sense of a proposition, which is merely the range of possibilities the proposition allows, Russell had to fall back on a subjective conception according to which meanings are mental entities which we by convention associate with particular sentences. There is no longer, of course, any place for Wittgenstein's construction of the self as what converts signs into symbols, since there is no longer any distinction between signs and symbols in play. Instead Russell attempted to construct a complex self out of the mental entities he called meanings.

Russell unselfconsciously kept the word 'tautology', but without an objective notion of sense it could not mean the same for him as it had done for Wittgenstein: a tautology, in Russell's usage, expresses the fact that two signs have the same meaning, and is therefore a significant statement about the conventions of language rather than a degenerate statement about the world.

Once we accept that the atoms are particular sorts of thing in the world, it becomes at best an empirical conjecture that whatever we take them to be are genuinely simple. It will of course be true that from within our language they will *appear* simple, but that is only because we lack the resources to express their complexity, not because there is anything absurd about supposing them to be complex. This inevitably leads us to admit a metalinguistic perspective from which to express the fact that what language treats as simple may not be.

7.2 The hierarchy of propositional functions

The treatment of elementary propositions as non-linguistic that makes the first edition of *Principia* so hard for the modern logician to understand had disappeared by the time of the second edition. Now Russell

[3]Cf. *The Analysis of Matter*, ch. xvii.

copied Wittgenstein's conception of propositions as extensionally dependent upon the atomic (i.e. elementary, in Wittgenstein's terminology) propositions and accepted, albeit hesitantly, Wittgenstein's suggestion that those elementary propositions that appear not to be truth-
functional combinations of atomic propositions could in fact be analysed
so as to be extensionally dependent on their parts. Russell therefore
concluded that every elementary proposition (in the sense of the first
edition of *Principia*) is a truth-functional combination of atomic propositions, and affirmed moreover the axiom of extensionality,

$$\phi x \equiv_x \psi x \supset f(\phi \widehat{x}) \equiv f(\psi \widehat{x}).$$

Much of what is new in the second edition is involved in what is from
a philosophical point of view an unimportant technical matter, namely
the replacement of two logical constants $\sim$ and $\vee$ with a single constant
$|$, which Russell called the *stroke*. He rendered the meaning of $p \mid q$
as 'p and q are incompatible', which suggests a modal or inferential
force that the stroke does not have: $p \mid q$ is the truth-function that
is false just when p and q are both true. Thus the stroke is the dual
of Wittgenstein's N, which is intended to stand for joint denial (so
that $N(p, q)$ is true just when p and q are both false). The choice
between the two is a matter of indifference: either can serve as a basis
for propositional calculus. Where Wittgenstein and Russell differed was
in their understanding of how these connectives function: Wittgenstein,
as we saw in the last chapter, treated N as an operation acting at
the level of sense; Russell saw the stroke function as applying at the
level of symbols. The significance of this difference lies in the fact
that if symbols can only be finitely complex, then the stroke function,
understood in Russell's way, can take only a finite number of arguments.
In order to go beyond the elementary we need quantifiers, which are
distinct from the stroke and act in a different way. The application of
the stroke function to the atomic propositions leads us to precisely the
class of elementary propositions.

The hierarchy of propositional functions is not at all the same in the
second edition as it is in the first. We shall for simplicity's sake concentrate here on functions $\phi(\widehat{x})$ of one individual variable. We find, just as
in the text of the first edition, a hierarchy of *elementary functions*, i.e.
functions that can be expressed without the use of quantifiers. Such
functions we denote $\phi!\widehat{x}$, $\psi!\widehat{x}$, etc. So if, for instance, Ra and Sab are
among the atomic propositions, then $R\widehat{x} \vee Sa\widehat{x}$, $\sim S\widehat{x}b$, $S\widehat{x}a \supset Ra$, etc.
will be first-order elementary functions. Similarly we can form second-
order elementary functions such as $\widehat{\phi}!\widehat{x}$, which can be represented by
the second-order variable $f!(\phi!\widehat{z}, \widehat{x})$.

So far we are dealing with what is recognizably the hierarchy of matrices of the first-edition text. But now Russell introduces a new sort of variable ϕ_1, ψ_1, etc. to range over what in the Introduction to the first edition he called predicative functions of an individual variable, i.e. first-order functions such as $(\exists y)S\hat{x}y$, $(y)Ry . \supset . R\hat{x}$, etc. In the text of the first edition there was of course no bar on such variables, but they never occurred bound. Now they are permitted to occur bound in such expressions as $(\phi_1)\phi_1\hat{x}$, which is a second-order function having functions such as the ones we just listed as instances. In the same way Russell now introduces a variable ϕ_2 to range over second-order functions, and permits it too to occur bound in such third-order functions as $(\phi_3)\phi_3\hat{x}$. And so on.

The introduction of these new types of bound variables complicates the hierarchy significantly. In the first edition there was only one way to form a second-order function of an individual, namely to bind a first-order matrix variable to form an expression such as $(\phi)\phi!\hat{x}$ or $(\exists\phi)\phi!\hat{x}$; now in the second edition there is another way, namely to bind a first-order predicative variable to form an expression such as $(\phi_1)\phi_1\hat{x}$ or $(\exists\phi_1)\phi_1\hat{x}$. The number of ways of forming new functions increases further at each succeeding order. Thus the functions of an individual, which in the first edition were arranged simply in a linear hierarchy, now form a pyramidal structure which becomes more and more elaborate as the order increases.

Another instance of the complexity of the new hierarchy emerges if we widen our attention to include second-level functions. Suppose that we define a function $f(\hat{\phi})$ by writing $f(\phi) = \phi(a)$. In the first edition we would have to interpret the variable here as a matrix, thus making $f(\hat{\phi})$ into a second-order matrix $\phi!a$. But in the second edition $f(\hat{\phi})$ ambiguously expresses a whole sequence of functions $\phi!a$, ϕ_1a, ϕ_2a, ϕ_3a, etc., each of which has a different range of significance.

7.3 Mathematical induction

But at this point we have to confront the most profound difference between the two editions of *Principia*: in the second edition Russell tried to do without the axiom of reducibility. I mentioned earlier that under Wittgenstein's influence Russell in 1919 thought reducibility an empirical statement which might be false, in contrast to the basic axioms of *Principia*, which he took to be logically necessary. But since by the time of the second edition Russell rejected the notion of necessity, he correspondingly rejected Wittgenstein's account of a way the axiom of reducibility could be false. Instead we find him reaffirming both the regressive method and Frege's claim to have shown arithmetic to be analytic 'at least in the obvious interpretation'.[4] So even if Wittgenstein's argument to show that reducibility is not a tautology which we mentioned earlier (§ 5.18) influenced Russell, he did not refer to it in the second edition as his reason for doing without reducibility.

Now the principle of mathematical induction is plainly fundamental to arithmetic, and in the first edition of *Principia* its proof depends crucially on the axiom of reducibility, as we saw in § 5.15. But the hierarchy described in the second edition is different, and Russell thought he had a method[5] of arriving at arbitrary instances of induction in the new system without reducibility. His idea was to define an ancestral relation R_{*n} for each order n by writing $xR_{*n}y$ to mean

$$z\ R\ w.\supset_{z,w}.\phi_n z \supset \phi_n w :\supset_{\phi_n}: \phi_n x \supset \phi_n y,$$

i.e. y has every hereditary property of order n possessed by x. By an elaborate argument Russell purports to show that

$$R_{*n} = R_{*5} \text{ for } n \geq 5,$$

i.e. that every application of induction may be reduced to an instance of induction of order at most 5. Russell's argument was in fact fallacious, as Gödel[6] noticed, but Landini[7] has recently contended that his error can be repaired, so that his system (including the axiom of infinity) is an adequate basis for the development of arithmetic.

Even if Russell's proof can be repaired, can the second edition of *Principia* be said to represent a reduction of arithmetic to logic? Its conception of logic is very different from that in the first edition: there, and throughout the period leading up to it, Russell drew no distinction between logic and the world. The world could not consist merely of individuals, because if it did there would be no structure in the world for language to describe. (What else there is other than individuals and what the logical relationships are between them are questions on which Russell changed his mind frequently.) In the second edition, on the other hand, the limits of the world are much more tightly drawn. Russell supposes that the relationships between individuals that we wish to describe can be expressed in language by means of atomic sentences. These sentences can be combined logically in various ways to form complex sentences. There are parts of this conception that are close to the *Tractatus*, but Russell rejected Wittgenstein's notion of the unsayable

---

[4] *Papers*, IV, 163.   [5] *PM*, Appendix B.   [6] *Works*, II, 135.   [7] 'The definability of the set of natural numbers in the 1925 *Principia*'.

and instead adopted the conception, absent also in the first edition of *Principia*, of a metalanguage in which the logical theory could be described.

The adoption of a metalanguage was in fact essential if Russell was to try, as he did, to do without anything corresponding to Wittgenstein's notion of sense. This is because any logic of types plainly needs some external source of regulation. In the *Tractatus* the hierarchy is supposed to fall naturally out of the meanings of the expressions involved: a string of signs is type-theoretically well formed if and only if it has a structure that enables it to be read as expressing a sense. In the second edition of *Principia*, by contrast, it is the stipulations in the metalanguage that decree which strings of signs are to count as well formed.

The most ingenious feature of the second edition is undoubtedly its argument to show that all arithmetical proofs can be converted, by a constructive method, into formal proofs in the system (albeit possibly much longer ones) in which the orders of the uses of mathematical induction have been reduced to no more than 5. This demonstration presages many technical results in logic that have come since: Gödel himself compared it to his own demonstration that every constructible set of integers is definable at a level $< \omega_1$ in the transfinite hierarchy. But it seems to have raised in Russell's mind the spectre of Poincaré's old objection that logicism could not establish mathematical induction without making use of induction to do so. To evade this objection Russell did not present his demonstration as an inductive proof, but simply appealed to our ability to 'see' from our metalinguistic perspective that it works. In fact, however, this concern is less important than it might seem since we have no need to rely absolutely on the validity of the demonstration. Once we have obtained any particular proof by induction involving a property of higher order, we can, if Russell's procedure is correct, use it to reduce the proof explicitly to order 5, after which the general argument that such reductions are always possible becomes irrelevant.

7.4 The definition of identity

In his Introduction to the *Tractatus* Russell wrote that

the conception of identity is subjected by Wittgenstein to a destructive criticism from which there seems no escape. The definition of identity by means of the identity of indiscernibles is rejected, because the identity of indiscernibles appears to be not a logically necessary principle. According to this principle x is identical with y if every property of x is a property of y, but it would, after all, be logically possible for two things to have exactly the same properties. If this does not in fact happen that is an accidental characteristic of the world, not a logically necessary characteristic, and accidental characteristics of the world must, of course, not be admitted into the structure of logic.[8]

It is a surprise, therefore, to find that in the Introduction to the second edition of *Principia* the definition of identity is taken over unaltered from the first edition. We may deduce that Russell had changed his mind about the 'destructive criticism from which there seems no escape' and no longer found it suasive. This is confirmed by Ramsey's diary entry for 3 February 1924, when he met Russell to discuss a draft of the new Introduction:

To lunch with Russell, and afterwards for a walk with him, he is nice and amusing, discussed partly types partly identity. He rather good against W[ittgenstein]'s identity, poor on types; doubts Dedekindian section as he can't prove it though he can Math[ematical] Induction without Axiom of Reducibility.[9]

What were Russell's 'rather good' arguments against Wittgenstein on identity? They are not contained in the Introduction to *Principia*, which is silent on the matter (an omission to which Ramsey drew attention in a review).[10] Only some years later did Russell say any more about his change of mind:

Wittgenstein eliminates identity altogether by the convention that different letters are always to represent different objects. This is possible, but very inconvenient, and makes it impossible to find a defining concept for a finite set of objects given by enumeration. Stated in traditional terms, the question is as to the identity of indiscernibles. Ramsey says: 'Take two things, *a* and *b*. Then there is nothing self-contradictory in *a* having any self-consistent set of properties, nor in *b* having this set, nor therefore, obviously, in both *a* and *b* having them, nor therefore in *a* and *b* having all their elementary properties in common.' But this begs the question in its opening clause 'take *two* things, *a* and *b*'. This assumes that numerical diversity is a primitive idea, whereas I should maintain that to say that *a* and *b* are two *means* that they have different properties.[11]

On the face of it Russell is here doing no more than reasserting the definition of identity in *Principia*, but this is not mere cussedness on Russell's part. It was permissible for him to deny Wittgenstein's objection to his definition because he denied the conception of possibility that underpins it — denied, indeed, that there could be *any* notion of possibility applicable to propositions about the world. 'Propositions

[8] *TLP*, intro., 16–17. [9] King's College Library, Cambridge. [10] 'The new *Principia*'.
[11] *Papers*, X, 110.

which are not analytic', he said, 'can only be true or false; a true synthetic proposition cannot have a further property of being necessary, and a false synthetic proposition cannot have the property of being possible.'[12] Russell's definition of identity is in perfect order when it is applied to things as they actually are since, as Russell pointed out, different things do indeed differ. Wittgenstein's objection to the definition only arises when we apply it to things not as they are but as they might be, but this is precisely what Russell now denied that we can do.

Russell's definition of identity presents a significant technical challenge in the absence of the axiom of reducibility: we have work to do in order to arrive at the indiscernibility of identicals since if x and y share all their predicative properties it no longer follows trivially from reducibility that they share all their higher-order properties too.

Russell's argument for this conclusion is in two stages. The first stage is to show that from $x = y$, i.e.

$$(\phi)\phi!x \equiv \phi!y, \tag{1}$$

we can deduce

$$(\phi_1)\phi_1 x \equiv \phi_1 y.$$

In order to do this, however, Russell needed a restricted form of the axiom of reducibility, namely

$$(\phi).\, f!(\phi!\hat{z}, x, y)\,.\supset.\, f!(\phi_1\hat{z}, x, y), \tag{2}$$

which Russell took as a primitive proposition in the second edition. If we assume this, the conclusion follows straightforwardly: just take $f!(\phi\hat{z}, x, y)$ to be $\phi x \equiv \phi y$.

In the second stage Russell had to show that

$$(\phi_2)\phi_2 x \equiv \phi_2 y, \tag{3}$$

also follows if $x = y$. (If he could do this, the succeeding steps to

$$(\phi_3)\phi_3 x \equiv \phi_3 y,$$

etc. would then follow similarly.) Russell's method was to claim that any $\phi_2 x$ will be of the form $(\phi).\, f!(\phi!\hat{z}, x)$ or $(\exists\phi).\, f!(\phi!\hat{z}, x)$; but from (1) it follows that

$$f!(\phi!\hat{z}, x) \equiv f!(\phi!\hat{z}, y)$$

---

[12] *The Analysis of Matter*, 170.

by the principle of extensionality; hence we may deduce (3) for the two sorts of $\phi_2\hat{x}$ in question. (The fact that there are only two sorts of $\phi_2\hat{x}$ to consider marks the contrast between this argument and the justification of the first stage, where there were infinitely many forms of $\phi_1\hat{x}$ to consider.)

In view of Wittgenstein's demonstration that the axiom of reducibility is not a tautology we need an argument to show that the restricted form used in the first part of the proof just sketched can legitimately be taken as a primitive proposition. The argument Russell provided is based on a general method of reducing predicative variables to elementary ones: predicative variables, he said,

can be replaced by an infinite conjunction or disjunction. Thus e.g.

$$(\phi_1).\,\phi_1 x. \equiv: (\phi):\phi!x : (\phi,y).\,\phi!(x,y) : (\phi) : (\exists y).\,\phi!(x,y) : \text{etc.},$$
$$(\exists\phi_1).\,\phi_1 x. \equiv: (\exists\phi).\,\phi!x : \vee : (\exists\phi) : (y).\,\phi!(x,y) :$$
$$\vee : (\exists\phi,y).\,\phi!(x,y) : \vee : \text{etc.}^{13}$$

So to demonstrate the restricted axiom of reducibility,

$$(\phi).\,f!(\phi!\hat{z},x,y) . \supset . f!(\phi_1\hat{z},x,y),$$

it is enough to prove, on the hypothesis $(\phi).\,f!(\phi\hat{z},x)$, that each of

$$(\phi).\,f!(\phi\hat{z},x), \; (\phi,y).\,f!(\phi(z,y),x), \; \text{etc.}$$

holds. Now the first of these is just the premiss of the argument. Russell sketches what is in effect a proof of the second by induction on the complexity of the pseudo-matrix f and observes that all the others can be proved similarly.

The use Russell makes here of infinite conjunctions and disjunctions is a surprise for which the reader is unprepared. There is nothing up to this point to suggest that formulae might be infinitely long. Indeed, if infinitely long formulae are permitted, the structure of his hierarchy, in which the lowest level consists only of finite truth-functional combinations of atomic functions, makes no sense whatever. It is clear, therefore, that Russell's words are not to be understood as an argument within the formal system. They are intended only to justify the restricted axiom of reducibility (2) which Russell proposes to take as a primitive proposition.

This is why Russell remarks

---

[13] *PM*, 2nd edn., p. xxxiii.

that, in practice, an infinite conjunction or disjunction such as the above cannot be manipulated without assumptions *ad hoc*. We can work out results for any segment of the infinite conjunction or disjunction, and we can 'see' that these results hold throughout. But we cannot prove this, because mathematical induction is not applicable. We therefore adopt certain primitive propositions, which assert only that what we can prove in each case holds generally. By means of these it becomes possible to manipulate such variables as ϕ_1.[14]

So in order to accept certain of the primitive propositions of Russell's system, we therefore have to be able to 'see' that certain results hold for the manipulation of infinitely long symbols of the system. But the structure of these infinitely long symbols is at least as elaborate as that of the natural numbers.

Thus Russell's argument involves an appeal to our intuitions about the behaviour of infinite conjunctions and disjunctions, but he has provided us with no clue as to how these intuitions are to be explained. As Gödel observed,[15] if we are permitted to appeal to intuitions about infinitely long disjunctions in our account of arithmetic, we might as well just define *number* by means of the propositional function

$$\hat{x} = 0 \vee \hat{x} = 1 \vee \hat{x} = 2 \vee \ldots,$$

and then appeal to intuition to 'see' all its properties.

[14]Ibid., p. xxxiv. [15]*Works*, II, 134.

8

Ramsey

While he was still an undergraduate at Cambridge, Frank Ramsey was involved in preparing the English translation of the *Tractatus*. When he graduated in the summer of 1923, he went to visit Wittgenstein, who was by then a primary school teacher in Lower Austria, and discussed the *Tractatus* with him in detail. He then set about developing an account of the theory of types which avoided the difficulties associated with the axiom of reducibility by following what he took to be Wittgensteinian principles. After another visit to Austria (to be psychoanalysed) he wrote up his work in December 1924 as an entry for a Cambridge mathematical prize. Although it did not win the prize (presumably because it was not mathematical enough), the essay was eventually published under the title 'The foundations of mathematics'. The material in the essay that is relevant here falls into three distinct parts: in the first Ramsey showed how to develop a theory of types on Wittgensteinian principles that has no need of the problematic axiom of reducibility; in the second he dealt with the derivation of the theory of classes from the theory of types; and in the third he addressed the problematic dependence of the theory on the axiom of infinity.

8.1 Propositions

In the *Tractatus* Wittgenstein gives two complementary ways of generating a conception of the domain of propositions. In § 6.5 we discussed the first of these, the notion of the sense of a proposition as the expression of agreement or disagreement with truth-possibilities of elementary propositions. The significance of this notion is that it permits an unstratified conception of the domain of propositions. Ramsey's analysis of the reason for this is that the elementary propositions form an objectively fixed totality and the notion of sense provides a circumscription of a domain of entities to act as possible values for propositional symbols to express. The propositional paradoxes which led Russell to stratify the domain of propositions arise when vicious circularities in the order of formation of symbols enable us to construct ever more symbols expressing new propositions, causing an explosion in the domain of propositions. Such paradoxes cannot occur in any system in which propositions are individuated at the level of Wittgensteinian sense, rather than at the level of symbols, because Wittgensteinian sense is explained without reference to the process of formation of new symbols from the objectively given elementary propositions.

But if the domain of senses is circumscribed by means of an explanation which does not depend on symbolization, we nevertheless need an account of how symbols can be constructed to express these senses. This is the second way Wittgenstein gives of conceiving of the notion of a proposition: if there is a class $\bar{\xi}$ of symbols expressing senses, there is also a symbol $N(\bar{\xi})$ expressing the joint denial of the members of $\bar{\xi}$; and every proposition we can symbolize is obtainable from elementary propositions by a finite number of iterations of this process.[1] Wittgenstein lists three ways in which the class $\bar{\xi}$ of symbols occurring as argument to the N operation can be specified:

1. Direct enumeration. ... 2. Giving a function fx, whose values for all values of x are the propositions to be described. 3. Giving a formal law, according to which those propositions are constructed.[2]

But he is otherwise silent as to what range of specifications is permitted. This is of a piece with the general indifference he exhibits towards the practicalities of the construction of a workable symbolic language. In particular, Wittgenstein is silent on whether every sense that the earlier account independent of symbolization allows can actually be symbolized; whether, in other words, the general form of proposition $[\bar{p}, \bar{\xi}, N(\bar{\xi})]$ is adequate to express every possible arrangement of truth-possibilities of elementary propositions. If there are only finitely many elementary propositions, then it certainly is adequate: this is just another way of saying that the N operation is adequate to express all finite truth-functions. But if there are infinitely many elementary propositions, a simple cardinality argument shows that it will not be adequate unless we allow there to be symbols which cannot be expressed by means of finite signs.

Now what Ramsey saw was that the question whether we should allow finitely inexpressible symbols has nothing to do with the avoidance of the propositional paradoxes. As long as we individuate propositions at the level of sense, we can allow any means of expression we like and still not introduce paradox into Wittgenstein's system, because we are

[1] See *TLP*, 6.0. [2] Ibid. 5.501.

merely devising new ways of expressing items — senses — belonging to a domain we have already circumscribed independently.

When we speak of propositions we shall generally mean the types of which the individual symbols are instances, and we shall include types of which there may be no instances. This is inevitable, since it cannot be any concern of ours whether anyone has actually symbolized or asserted a proposition, and we have to consider all propositions in the sense of all possible assertions whether or not they have been asserted.[3]

But this decoupling of the symbols from the finite signs we ordinarily use to symbolize them comes at a price. Now that the notion of a symbol had floated free of whether it ever has been or ever could be expressed, Ramsey had little choice but to remove signs from his account as irrelevant. Now of course the mathematical languages which concerned Ramsey are all of the logically perfect sort in which a single sign does not in different places express different symbols. So the fact that he did not now have the sign/symbol distinction available as a means of explaining ambiguities did not concern him. But I suggested in § 6.1 that this was not the primary point of that distinction: it is in reading a sign as a symbol that the self plays its part in Wittgenstein's logic. Since in Ramsey's account there are no longer signs to be read, it follows that Ramsey must locate the self elsewhere; quite where will emerge later.

8.2 Predicating functions

The *Tractatus* conceives of propositional functions as falling into a hierarchy, but goes into no detail as to what that hierarchy is. This, we said, is because it plays no central rôle in his system. Ramsey, on the other hand, intended to base mathematics on a theory of classes derived from the hierarchy in a broadly Russellian manner, and therefore could not afford to be so casual about its structure. Ramsey's idea was that if Wittgenstein's notion of sense solved the propositional paradoxes without requiring a stratification of the domain of senses, it should correspondingly solve the paradoxes of propositional functions without requiring a ramification of the hierarchy of functions. So he defined the notion of a propositional function in a manner as far as possible analogous to his Wittgensteinian explanation of the notion of a proposition. A propositional function of individuals, he said, is

[3] *FoM*, 33.

a symbol of the form '$f(\hat{x}, \hat{y}, \hat{z}, \dots)$' which is such that, were the names of any individuals substituted for '$\hat{x}$', '$\hat{y}$', '$\hat{z}$', $\dots$ in it, the result would always be a proposition. ... Two such symbols are regarded as the same function when the substitution of the same set of names in the one and in the other always gives the same proposition [i.e. a proposition with the same sense].[4]

In thus defining the notion of a function of individuals Ramsey made use of a variable ranging over individuals. He regarded this as unproblematic because individuals form 'an objective totality which there is no getting away from'.[5] Before we can form second-level functions, though, we must first identify the range of first-level functions which can be arguments to such functions, and here there is an important difference from the previous case: 'whereas functions are symbols, individuals are objects'.[6] So the range of first-level functions is a range of symbols and 'this range of symbols, actual or possible, is not objectively fixed, but depends on our methods of constructing them and requires more precise definition.'[7] A propositional function of individuals, we might say, is the symbol we obtain when we replace a name in a propositional symbol with a variable. But what if the propositional symbol in question contains a quantifier ranging over first-level propositional functions? In that case by forming the propositional function from it we create a new symbol lying in a domain over which we have already quantified. This is just the sort of circumstance where the risk of paradox lurks. To avoid it we have to specify a range of first-level functions that does not depend in this manner on how they are symbolized.

The procedure of defining a propositional function to be what we obtain if we replace a name in a proposition with a variable is not, we said, in general unproblematic. Ramsey starts, though, by considering the one case where it *is* wholly unproblematic, namely where the proposition in question is *atomic*, i.e. what Wittgenstein calls 'elementary'. Ramsey defines an *atomic function of individuals* to be 'the result of replacing by variables any of the names of individuals in an atomic proposition expressed by using names alone.'[8] The reason the procedure is in no danger of leading to paradox in this restricted case is that symbols which express atomic propositions do not contain quantifiers and hence *a fortiori* a function formed from such a proposition cannot lie in any domain over which we have already quantified.

So far Ramsey's method is recognizably similar to Russell's in the second edition of *Principia*. But at this point they diverge. As we saw in the last chapter, Russell adopted neither Wittgenstein's notion of sense nor his conception of the self as a limit of language. He therefore

[4]Ibid. 35. [5]Ibid. 36. [6]Ibid. [7]Ibid. 36–7. [8]Ibid. 38.

had no alternative to treating propositional functions as signs (which is why his appeal to 'seeing' the properties of infinitely long formulae comes as such a surprise). The first stage in the formation of Russell's hierarchy after the atomic functions is the first-order elementary functions, i.e. truth-functions of any *finite* number of atomic functions. He then proceeds to construct ever more elaborate propositional functions of higher orders. His difficulty was then to either justify or eliminate the axiom of reducibility, which asserts that all these more elaborate propositional functions are extensionally equivalent to elementary functions and can therefore (since the logic is now assumed to be extensional) be treated as if they are of the same logical type.

Now propositional functions and propositions are assigned orders according to the highest level of quantification occurring in them. What Ramsey noticed was that these orders are attributes only of the symbols and not of their senses, since symbols of different orders can express the same sense: if $\phi\hat{x}$ is an elementary function of an individual, for example, then 'ϕa' is of order 0, but '$\phi a : (\exists x)\phi x$', which expresses the same sense, is of order 1. Ramsey illustrates this with the analogy of the numerator of a fraction: '$\frac{1}{2}$' denotes the same number as '$\frac{2}{4}$', but the numerators of the two fractions are different; so the numerator of a fraction must be an attribute only of the sign used to denote it and not of the number itself.

Ramsey describes Russell's method of constructing a hierarchy of signs as *subjective*. Ramsey's own method, by contrast, is what he called *objective*, by which he meant that he considered propositions to be individuated at the level of sense. The significance of this is that from Ramsey's objective perspective the notion of the order of a proposition drops away since, as we have just noted, it is a property of the symbol rather than of its sense. Nor is there any rationale whatever from this perspective for limiting the first stage in the hierarchy to elementary functions, since whether a function is elementary is similarly a property not of the function, objectively regarded, but of how it is expressed. Ramsey therefore moves directly to functions of individuals which are truth functions 'of arguments which, whether finite or infinite in number, are all either atomic functions of individuals or propositions.'[9] Ramsey called such functions 'predicative', but this usage invites confusion with Russell's use of the term for another purpose, so here I shall call them *predicating* functions.

Ramsey's procedure for obtaining the range of predicating functions from the atomic functions thus precisely mimics that for obtaining symbols for propositions from symbols for atomic propositions. If we write

[9]Ibid. 39.

$\overline{p}(x)$ for the class of all atomic functions of an individual variable x, the predicating functions of x can be said to have the general form $[\overline{p}(x), \overline{\xi}, N(\overline{\xi})]$, in precise analogy with the general form of proposition $[\overline{p}, \overline{\xi}, N(\overline{\xi})]$. In other words, a predicating function can be thought of as a symbol expressing a sense — agreement or disagreement with the truth-possibilities of atomic functions — in a way that generalizes straightforwardly the Wittgensteinian notion of sense for propositions discussed in the previous section.

By individuating propositional functions at the level of sense Ramsey was thus able to solve the extensional paradoxes without resorting to a ramified hierarchy, but this leaves still to be dealt with the intensional paradoxes, which speak of the relationship between symbols and what it is they express. We have seen three attitudes to intensions in the preceding chapters. Wittgenstein held that they are inexpressible. Russell rejected this because it put them out of the reach of logic, and at first thought that when correctly analysed they would turn out to be expressible in the original language; but in the end he rejected this view too and concluded that they should be expressed in a more inclusive (but extensional) metalanguage. Ramsey's position was different again. He rejected, like Russell, the notion that the relationship between signs and senses might be ultimately inexpressible, but he did not think that this places an obligation on the logician to explain the relationship in formal terms. He said in a review of the second edition of *Principia* that the assumption that any function of functions $F(\phi!\hat{z})$ can be constructed from the values of $\phi!z$ by truth-operations and generalization could, even if it is false,

be made a mere matter of definition, by deciding that in mathematics 'all functions of functions' is to include only such as fulfil the required condition. Nevertheless [Appendix C of the second edition of *Principia*] is devoted to the gratuitous inquiry into whether the assumption is in fact true.[10]

This seems at first to display a remarkably casual attitude to the problem Russell was addressing, but his reason emerges in 'The foundations of mathematics', where he states that the intensional paradoxes

are not purely logical, and cannot be stated in logical terms alone; for they all contain some reference to thought, language, or symbolism, which are not formal but empirical terms. So they may be due not to faulty logic or mathematics, but to faulty ideas concerning thought and language. If so, they would not be relevant to mathematics or to logic, if by 'logic' we mean a symbolic system, though of course they would be relevant to logic in the sense of the analysis of thought.[11]

[10]'Review of *Principia Mathematica*, 2nd edn.', 506. [11]*FoM*, 20–21.

So Ramsey did not, as Russell had done in the first edition of *Principia*, treat intensions as part of the apparatus of a formal logic, but neither did he, like Wittgenstein, regard them as being wholly inexpressible. He regarded them instead as a legitimate subject of informal logic, whose study was to be conducted within what we now call the metalanguage, which was to be the language of ordinary discourse. Since it is in the metalanguage that Ramsey permits talk of the meaning of the signs in the formal language, it is here that we must look for what corresponds in Ramsey's account to Wittgenstein's notion of the self.

Within the informal metalanguage, of course, the intensional paradoxes arise as before. Ramsey's resolution of them is a straightforward adjustment of Russell's. The solution to Weyl's heterological paradox, for instance, is that there is within our language a hierarchy of meanings of 'means': the way in which a first-order sign symbolizes is not the same as that in which a second-order sign does. Suppose that we write 'means$_1$', 'means$_2$', etc. for the various meanings of 'means'. We can then define $\mathrm{Het}_1 \hat{z}$ to mean

$$(\exists \phi).\, x \text{ means}_1 \phi\hat{z}.\sim\phi x,$$

but the sense in which $\mathrm{Het}_1 \hat{z}$ has meaning cannot be the first-level one that is used in defining it. This blocks the paradox since the most we can say about this second-level meaning is that

$$\text{'Het}_1\text{' means}_2 \mathrm{Het}_1 \hat{z},$$

which is not sufficient to deduce the contradiction.

As we noted in § 5.16, the ramification of the hierarchy in the first edition of *Principia* is wholly obliterated by the axiom of reducibility where extensional functions are concerned. What Ramsey did was to restrict the scope of formal logic to extensional functions by fiat, so that the need for the ramification in the formal part of logic was removed. But although it was removed, it did not disappear completely: the ramification was merely relocated to the metalanguage and emerged there as a hierarchy of meanings of 'meaning'. Ramsey presented his account as Wittgensteinian in origin, and so for the most part it is, but his solution to the paradoxes is by contrast highly unWittgensteinian. If the Tractarian self is to be found in the reading of signs as symbols, what are we to make of the idea that there is a hierarchy of different ways of doing this? This is of course just a variant of Russell's proposal considered earlier (§ 6.3) of a hierarchy of ever more inclusive selves. Putting the point another way, to describe meaning$_1$, meaning$_2$, etc. as all being meanings of 'meaning' is to concede that there is one concept, namely *meaning*, of which they are all special cases, which is in turn to dissolve the distinction Ramsey needed in order to block the intensional paradoxes in the first place. If, on the other hand, we insist that meaning$_1$, meaning$_2$, etc. are genuinely distinct concepts with only a verbal similarity to unite them, then I seem to be speaking not one language but infinitely many.

8.3 Extending Wittgenstein's account of identity

Ramsey evidently discovered his theory of predicating functions quite soon after his first meeting with Wittgenstein. Only four months later he was telling Moore that he had 'got on W[ittgenstein]'s principles a new theory of types without any doubtful axiom, which gives all the results of Russell's one, and solves all the contradictions.'[12] But although Ramsey's theory does indeed obviate the need for the 'doubtful' axiom of reducibility, it does not in itself suffice to ground a satisfactory logicist reduction of mathematics, because it leaves the problem of identity unaddressed.

That problem, let us recall, was that if we reduce all talk about classes to talk about predicating functions in the Russellian manner we synthesize only what I earlier called the accidental notion of class — classes of the form $\{x : \phi x\}$ derived from predicating functions $\phi\hat{x}$. We can, sure enough, get a class whose only member is in *fact* an object a, but we are unable to synthesize the class $\{a\}$ which not only has in fact just one member a but would have just that member even if the world were disposed differently. We cannot, in other words, retrieve what I called the essential notion of class — classes with particular objects as members irrespective of what properties the objects may have. Without essential classes Russell's reduction of arithmetic to the theory of classes works, if at all, only by accident, as it were. To see why, let us prescind for the moment from the difficulties associated with the axiom of infinity and suppose that there are as many objects as one could wish for. Then there are one-element classes. But there might not be: each object *might* share all its properties with at least one other, in which case the Russellian number one, which is the class of all one-element classes, would be empty.

The difficulty, then, is that we cannot reduce essential classes to predicating functions. Another way of putting the point is that on Wittgenstein's account there is no such relation as identity between objects. That this is so is a direct consequence of Wittgenstein's atomism. If

---

[12]Letter to Moore, 6 Feb. 1924, in Rothhaupt, 46.

objects are atoms, they are necessarily distinct from one another. If there were a genuine relation of identity, there would be a possibility, even if an unrealized one, that two objects are equal, in which case they would not really be atoms.

In order to reflect this the sign of identity '=' does not occur in the primitive vocabulary of Wittgenstein's system, but is replaced by a notational convention, namely that distinct names are never used to denote the same object, and correspondingly for variables. At first Ramsey suspected that this notation has a flaw, namely that 'something other than a has f' is inexpressible. 'Have you noticed', he wrote to Wittgenstein, 'the difficulty in expressing without = what Russell expresses by $(\exists x) : fx . x \neq a$?'[13] If Ramsey had been right that this is inexpressible, Wittgenstein's notation would have been seriously flawed. 'Something other than a has f' is not a pseudo-proposition whose inexpressibility would be a virtue, but a genuine proposition: to see why it is a genuine proposition we merely have to observe that if, say, 'a', 'b', and 'c' are the only names in the language, what we want is just '$fb \vee fc$', which is undoubtedly a Wittgensteinian proposition. However, Ramsey was wrong: the proposition in question *is* expressible in Wittgenstein's notation. Indeed Wittgenstein himself responded to Ramsey's query with the correct translation

$$fa . \supset . (\exists x, y)' . fx . fy : \sim fa \supset (\exists x)' fx.$$

Ramsey, concerned not to let Wittgenstein think him a logical dunce, hastily replied:

I didn't think there was a real difficulty about $\exists x : fx . x \neq a$, i.e. that it was an objection to your theory of identity, but I didn't see how to express it, because I was under the silly delusion that if an x and an a occurred in the same proposition the x could not take the value a. I had also a reason for wanting it not to be possible to express it.[14]

What Ramsey had not until then grasped, since there is no indication if it in the *Tractatus*, was Wittgenstein's rule as to the scope of the convention in respect of quantifiers. Ramsey was now able to formulate the rule as follows:

Two different constants must not have the same meaning. An apparent variable cannot [have] the value of any letter occurring in its scope unless the letter is a variable apparent in that scope.[15]

Even this is ambiguous, however. The notion of a letter *occurring in* a propositional function does not mean the same at the level of symbols

---

[13] *Cambridge Letters*, 191. [14]Ibid. 194. [15]*Notes*, 159.

and at that of sense. The name 'a' occurs in the symbol '$f\hat{x} \; . \; fa \lor \sim fa$' but not in '$f\hat{x}$', for instance; yet both symbols express the same sense, in which 'a' does not occur.

But it is quite unworkable to interpret the convention at the level of sense because this would make it in general undecidable what the meaning of a quantified sentence is. In the example just quoted it was clear that $fa \lor \sim fa$ was a tautology and thus expressed agreement with all truth-possibilities: the object a therefore did not occur in it. But in more elaborate cases than this we have in general no way of knowing whether a proposition is a tautology or not and hence whether its sense contains a or not.

So we are forced to interpret the convention at the level of symbols. '$(x).\,fx$', for instance, must therefore mean 'for all x, fx', whereas '$(x) : fx \; . \; fa \lor \sim fa$' must mean 'for all x other than a, fx' since an 'a' occurs in the scope of the quantifier. Thus interpreted the convention is, as Ramsey eventually realized, 'workable, although generally inconvenient':[16] what makes it inconvenient is that we cannot safely introduce abbreviations by definition unless the notation we use for the *definiendum* contains all the names occurring in the *definiens*.

But the fact that Wittgenstein's convention is impractical does not remove our interest in determining its scope. In fact, it is not hard to devise rules to translate between Wittgenstein's notation and Russell's; so the two notations are of equal strength provided that we restrict our attention to what count as genuine propositions in Wittgenstein's account.

So Wittgenstein's convention is adequate to express all the quantifications of genuine propositions that the Russellian notation can express. But Wittgenstein's account has it that arithmetical equations are pseudo-propositions. So even if its dependence on the axiom of infinity can be dealt with, the account still leaves quantification over natural numbers, and *a fortiori* the rest of mathematics, wholly unexplained. This may not have bothered Wittgenstein, who was not a mathematician, but it certainly bothered Ramsey, who was. Ramsey therefore decided to try an account of quantification that extended Wittgenstein's treatment without supplanting it:

W[ittgenstein] and I think it wrong to suppose with R[ussell] that mathematics is more complicated formal logic (tautologies); and I am trying to make definite the vague ideas we have of what it does consist of.[17]

We cannot simply reduce quantified statements in arithmetic to schematic genuine propositions, but what if we treat the pseudo-

[16] *FoM*, 32. [17] Letter to Moore, 6 Feb. 1924, in Rothhaupt, 46.

propositions of arithmetic — equations such as '7 + 5 = 12' — *as if* they were genuine propositions? We have, that is to say, a collection of pseudo-propositions which we treat as the atomic propositions of a new language. We can then form a hierarchy of quantified expressions — let us call them *formal* propositions — in just the same way that we formed the hierarchy of genuine propositions.

Ramsey spent some time considering this possibility, but he had eventually to reject it for the by now familiar reason that it does not explain the application of arithmetic. What we have is two distinct hierarchies, connected at the base by the fact that the atomic formal propositions are equations whose meaning consists in certain schematic propositions of the genuine hierarchy. But we have no way of coping with cases where propositional functions of the genuine hierarchy occur within the scope of quantifiers from the formal hierarchy. Ramsey considered the example of the proposition 'The square of the number of ϕ's is greater by two than the cube of the number of ψ's'.

This proposition we cannot, I think, help analysing in this sort of way:

$$(\exists m, n) . \hat{x}(\phi x) \in m . \hat{x}(\psi x) \in n . m^2 = n^3 + 2.$$

It is an empirical not a mathematical proposition, and is about the ϕ's and ψ's, not about symbols; yet there occurs in it the mathematical pseudo-proposition $m^2 = n^3 + 2$.[18]

The rules which enable us to translate from Russell's notation into Wittgenstein's break down in the face of examples such as this because they involve terms for numbers: the problem is that Wittgenstein's convention cannot be extended to number terms occurring inside the scope of quantifiers.

8.4 Propositional functions in extension

The failure of Ramsey's investigation of the possibility of quantifying over formulae treated as pseudo-propositions convinced him that we simply cannot do without the theory of classes. Rather than extend Wittgenstein's system piecemeal to cover particular cases, Ramsey decided that

the only practicable way is to do it as radically and drastically as possible; to drop altogether the notion that ϕa says about a what ϕb says about b; to treat propositional functions like mathematical functions, that is, extensionalize them completely.'[19]

---

[18]*FoM*, 18.   [19]Ibid. 52.

Thus Ramsey introduced the notion of a *propositional function in extension*,

that is to say, a correlation, practicable or impracticable, which to every individual associates a unique proposition, the individual being the argument of the function, the proposition its value.[20]

Ramsey introduced the variable ϕ_e to range over propositional functions in extension and then defined '$x = y$' to mean

$$(\phi_e) . \phi_e x \equiv \phi_e y.$$

According to this definition identity is thus 'a function in extension of two variables. Its value is tautology when x and y have the same value, contradiction when x, y have different values.'[21] This is enough to give us the essential notion of class, since we can replace any class α with the function in extension which is the logical sum of the functions $\hat{x} = a$ for all $a \in \alpha$.

On Ramsey's account the three notions of class, identity, and propositional function in extension therefore form a job lot, to be accepted or rejected together. The hierarchy which these notions allow us to construct contains the hierarchy of predicating functions, and the containment is strict unless identity is itself a predicating function. This could happen only if no two names could ever occur in the same position in an atomic proposition, i.e. if there were no atomic proposition $\phi(a)$ such that $\phi(b)$ was also meaningful. In such circumstances every object would be *sui generis* and generalization over objects, although possible, would be pointless.

Thus identity is not, except in the most unlikely circumstances, a predicating function. Indeed, the point of Ramsey's notion of propositional function in extension is that it represents a genuine expansion of what the language can express. Ramsey's claim about this expansion is twofold: first, it is necessary in order to express uses of mathematics in ordinary propositions; second, it is an 'intelligible notation'. If we grant that the notion of a propositional function in extension *is* intelligible, we are thus able to develop an account of classes exactly after the manner of *Principia*. Results in the theory of classes that are provable in the system of *Principia* will also be provable in Ramsey's system. Moreover, this will show that they are tautologies in Wittgenstein's sense. By adopting the notion of a propositional function in extension Ramsey was thus able to conclude, contrary to the view he had inherited from Wittgenstein, that mathematics is indeed merely more complicated tautologies.

[20]Ibid. [21]Ibid. 53.

8.5 *Wittgenstein's objections*

But was Ramsey right to think that the notion of a propositional function in extension is intelligible? One worry that needs to be addressed
straightaway is that Ramsey's account might be viciously circular. He
treats propositional senses as forming an objective totality, and then introduces a new kind of symbol for functions from objects to senses. The
concern is that he allows these symbols to appear in further propositions: this seems on the face of it to introduce just the sort of circularity
that is wont to end up in contradiction since it is in danger of generating
a vicious enlargement of the totality of senses. The difficulty evaporates,
though, when we notice that at the level of propositional sense Ramsey
has introduced nothing new, because all the senses we can refer to by
means of the newly introduced symbols belong to the objective totality previously characterized. What *is* true is that the introduction of
propositional functions in extension, if it is indeed intelligible, greatly
extends the range of subjective propositions, i.e. the range of senses we
can *express* in our symbolism. That was, as we have already noted,
precisely its point. But these propositions will always be new ways of
expressing old senses. The proposition '$a = a$', for example, which was
banned in Wittgenstein's symbolism but is now available to us, is just a
new way of expressing tautology; and '$a = b$' is a new way of expressing
contradiction.

There is, however, a deeper worry. Ramsey's account will not do as
it stands, for it is guilty of an elementary confusion between use and
mention.[22] If ϕ_e is a propositional function in extension, i.e. a function
from objects to senses, then for any object x the symbol '$\phi_e(x)$' is a
name of a sense; as is $\ulcorner\phi_e(x) \equiv \phi_e(y)\urcorner$. So '$(\phi_e).\ulcorner\phi_e(x) \equiv \phi_e(y)\urcorner$',
which is Ramsey's proposed way of expressing that $x = y$, is nonsense
since it attempts to quantify over names of senses when it ought to be
quantifying over propositions.

We might try correcting the definition so as to read

$$x = y. =_{\text{Df}}. (\phi_e)(\ulcorner\phi_e(x) \equiv \phi_e(y)\urcorner \text{ is true}).$$

But if this corrects the confusion between use and mention, it does not
yet follow that we have introduced an 'intelligible notation'. We now
have the difficulty of explaining in general the relation between a sense
p and the proposition 'p is true'. The analogy with Russell's difficulty
about the relation between the meaning of a denoting phrase and its
denotation is striking. Here, too, we have the problem that there is

[22]See Sullivan, 'Wittgenstein on *The Foundations of Mathematics*, June 1927'.

no backwards road from the sense to the proposition. A given sense may be expressed by many different symbols (or by none). And the problem is not merely one of selecting, for each sense p, a privileged symbol expressing that sense and deciding by fiat that 'p is true' is to name that symbol, since we wanted 'p is true' to *express* a sense, not to name a symbol, so we should be reduced to using ' "p is true" is true' in an evidently futile regress of attempts to express what we want.

The problem, then, is that a proposition containing a propositional function in extension does not express its sense in anything like the way the previously admitted propositions do. We are therefore owed an explanation of this, and it is hard to see how such an explanation should go 'because here the rules for functions in the old sense of the word don't hold at all'.[23]

The effect of Ramsey's definition was, as we have noted, to make '$x = x$' always a tautology and '$x = y$' always a contradiction. So we might try to short-circuit the problem by simply prescribing that '$x = x$' should be a tautology and '$x = y$' a contradiction, but if we do this just the same difficulty recurs in a more direct form. Wittgenstein put the point as follows:

It is remarkable that in the case of a tautology or a contradiction you actually could speak of a sense and reference in Frege's sense.

If we call its property of being a tautology the reference of a tautology, then we may call the way in which the tautology comes about here the sense of the tautology. And so for contradiction.

If, as Ramsey proposed, the sign '=' were explained by saying that $x = x$ is a tautology, and $x = y$ a contradiction, then we may say that the tautology and the contradiction have no 'sense' here.

So, if a tautology shows something through the fact that just *this* sense gives *this* reference, then a tautology à la Ramsey shows nothing, since it is a tautology by definition.[24]

The point is one we met in connection with Frege's attempt to give meaning to the formal language of *Grundgesetze*. We observed then that we cannot give a language meaning simply by prescribing which signs in it name truth and which falsity, because if we could it would be possible to assert the truth without asserting any particular truth, which is absurd. In the same way the strangeness of the account of identity we have been considering here is shown by observing that it gives us no indication of what it *means* for '$x = y$' to be true or false.

Wittgenstein expressed his criticisms of Ramsey's notion of propositional function in extension first of all in a letter to Schlick in 1927,

---

[23]Wittgenstein, *Phil. Grammar*, 317. [24]*Phil. Remarks*, 141–2.

reformulated them in *Philosophical Remarks*, and repeated them in
Philosophical Grammar:

Now what exactly is the specification of a function by its extension? Obviously, it is a group of definitions, e.g.

$$fa = p \quad \text{Def.}$$
$$fb = q \quad \text{Def.}$$
$$fc = r \quad \text{Def.}$$

These definitions permit us to substitute for the known propositions 'p', 'q', 'r' the signs 'fa', 'fb', 'fc'. To say that these three definitions determine the function $f(\xi)$ is either to say nothing, or to say the same as the three definitions say.

For the signs 'fa', 'fb', 'fc' are no more function and argument than the words 'Co(rn)', 'Co(al)' and 'Co(lt)' are. (Here it makes no difference whether or not the 'arguments' 'rn', 'al', 'lt' are used elsewhere as words).[25]

The point Wittgenstein is making rather neatly here is just the one we considered in connection with Wittgenstein's generalized adjectival strategy, namely that defining a complete symbol does not allow us to regard part of the symbol as a variable. The definition gives meaning to each of the signs 'fa', 'fb', and 'fc' separately, but does not license the transition to a function $f\xi$ in which ξ is a variable capable of being quantified over.

Wittgenstein puts the point again slightly differently:

Ramsey's theory of identity makes the mistake that would be made by someone who said that you could use a painting as a mirror as well, even if only for a single posture. If we say this we overlook that what is essential to a mirror is precisely that you can infer from it the posture of a body in front of it, whereas in the case of the painting you have to know that the postures tally before you can construe the picture as a mirror image.[26]

This is an objection to what Ramsey saw as precisely the point of propositional functions in extension, namely that they do not say the same thing about different objects of which they are 'predicated'. In more detail, the consequence of Ramsey's definition is that '$x = x$' turns into a tautology and '$x = y$' turns into a contradiction (remembering Wittgenstein's convention that he expresses 'difference of the objects by difference of the signs').[27] Thus each of the signs '$a = a$', '$b = b$', etc. is a way of denoting tautology. But 'each of the signs "$a = a$", "$a = c$", etc. in the definitions $(a = a). =_{\text{Def}}$. Taut. etc. is a *word*.'[28] In other words, we are back at precisely the difficulty we considered before, when we noted that Wittgenstein's account of numbers did not license

[25] *Phil. Grammar*, 317. [26] Ibid. [27] *TLP*, 5.53. [28] *Phil. Grammar*, 317.

the replacement of a numeral by a variable. The mistake we make, according to Wittgenstein, is to think that our definition of '$a = a$', '$b = b$', etc. allows us then to introduce a variable and consider, for example, the propositional function '$\hat{x} = a$'.

It is here that the omission of the distinction between sign and symbol harms Ramsey's account. He needed to appeal additionally to some such device as a function '$\hat{x}$ is true' which takes any name 'p' of a propositional sense to a proposition 'p is true' which expresses that sense. We cannot, of course, understand '$\hat{x}$ is true' as a function on a level with any that can be expressed in our language. But in that case it is quite obscure how we can understand it at all.

8.6 The axiom of infinity

In Chapter 6 we considered the following transcendental argument that there are infinitely many objects. Let $T\hat{x}$ be a propositional function expressing a tautology for each x (such as $f\hat{x} \vee \sim f\hat{x}$) and consider the sign

$$(\exists x_1)' \ldots (\exists x_n)'.\, Tx_1 . \cdots . Tx_n.$$

If there are exactly N objects, this sign expresses a true proposition for each $n \leq N$ but does not express anything at all for $n > N$. A language which represented only finitely many objects would thus be unable to express the proposition that there are infinitely many — a proposition which seems significant even if it is not true. Wittgenstein might have questioned the premiss of the argument — that we *can* significantly say that there may be infinitely many objects — but could not object to the argument itself. Once we allow Ramsey's definition of identity, though, another way of expressing what we want becomes possible. The proposition $(\exists x, y).\, x \neq y$

is the logical sum of the propositions $x \neq y$, which are tautologies if x and y have different values, contradictions if they have the same value. Hence it is the logical sum of a set of tautologies and contradictions; and therefore a tautology if any one of the set is a tautology, but otherwise a contradiction. That is, it is a tautology if x and y can take different values (i.e. if there are two individuals), but otherwise a contradiction.[29]

As Ramsey observes, 'this will hold not merely of 2, but of any other number.'[30] That is to say, we can form a proposition p_n for each n in

[29] *FoM*, 60. [30] Ibid.

such a way that if N is the number of objects, p_n is a tautology for $n \leq N$ and a contradiction for $n > N$, but always significant.

So we can no longer deduce the truth of the axiom of infinity from its significance. Rather the position is that the falsehood of the axiom would imply its absurdity. But if the axiom of infinity is absurd, then so is most of mathematics. So if the axiom is not true, the higher parts of mathematics, which Ramsey wished to justify, are self-contradictory.

The axiom of infinity in the logic of the whole world, if it is a tautology, cannot be proved, but must be taken as a primitive proposition. And this is the course which we must adopt, unless we prefer the view that all analysis is self-contradictory and meaningless.[31]

When he wrote this, Ramsey evidently intended the last sentence to be no more than a rhetorical flourish: mathematics is obviously not self-contradictory, he thought, so the axiom of infinity must be true. (Ramsey's suggestion that analysis is *meaningless* if the axiom of infinity is false is surely a slip on his part, a mistaken survival from the Wittgensteinian view of identity he had by now rejected.) Very soon after publishing his paper, though, Ramsey began, if not quite to doubt the consistency of analysis, then at least to see that we cannot simply use it in its own justification. What he had shown was that in his system the consistency of the axiom of infinity implies its truth. That would be a genuine advance if there were a method of establishing its consistency that did not depend on its truth, but, as Ramsey pointed out, 'it is generally accepted that the only way of demonstrating that postulates are compatible is by an existence theorem showing that there actually is and not merely might be a system of the kind postulated.'[32] If the point of the project is to show that mathematics is true, appealing to its truth as a premiss is not so much an interesting transcendental argument as a straightforward circularity. The only way out would be if there were a way of 'demonstrating that postulates are compatible' other than by an existence theorem. In the next chapter we shall discuss Hilbert's attempt to find such a demonstration.

[31] Ibid. 61.   [32] Ibid. 79.

9

Hilbert's programme

By the time his first period of published research in the foundations of mathematics came to an end in about 1904, Hilbert had formulated but not solved the problem of finding, for a formal system of arithmetic such as that supplied by Peano, a proof of consistency not reliant on the construction of a model. But we saw when we discussed this problem in Chapter 3 that even if he succeeded in obtaining such a non-semantic proof, there would remain two substantial objections to placing any philosophical significance on the result. First there is Frege's objection that the consistency of a list of axioms does not in itself ensure the existence of anything satisfying them: we need to explain the features of the mathematical domain that allow mere positing to ensure existence there when it manifestly fails to do so in the domain of rugby players; and we need to explain how there can be individually consistent but mutually incompatible pairs of posits. Then there is Poincaré's objection that the proof of consistency must make use of the principle of mathematical induction and is therefore inherently circular; more generally, *any* absolute consistency proof for mathematics is itself a piece of mathematics and hence, if the justification it provides is not to be wholly circular, cannot depend on mathematical existence claims at all. In this chapter we shall study how in the work he published from 1918 onwards Hilbert maintained the centrality to his project of finding a consistency proof for arithmetic while adopting a sort of formalism that transformed the significance of such a proof so as to answer these two objections.

9.1 Formal consistency

One of the most important elements in Hilbert's later philosophy is the distinction between the object language whose consistency is to be proved and the metalanguage in which the proof is to be conducted. Drawing this distinction does not in itself commit us to formalism: Frege, for instance, intended to specify the syntax of the object language only as a prelude to laying down the senses of the expressions in it; once he had done this, the object language would be a *language* in just as full-blooded a sense as the metalanguage, and might in appropriate cases be capable of expressing just the same range of thoughts. But even if it does not force us to conclude that there is no more to the operation of language than its syntactic rules, the distinction between object language and metalanguage does at least allow us to separate matters of syntactic combination from the underlying thoughts expressed. This in turn permits us (for a time, at least) to evade Poincaré's objection that a proof of the consistency of induction which itself makes use of induction is inherently circular, for the principle whose consistency we are proving is strictly speaking to be thought of at this stage as no more than a syntactic rule with a formal similarity to the contentful induction rule of the metalanguage. But although this answers Poincaré's objection as originally posed, it can hardly be said to draw its sting: if we come to see that the formal rule whose consistency we have proved *does* express the induction principle we have made use of in the metalanguage, we are back at the same circularity as before.

To avoid this circularity we must abandon the Fregean attempt to see the expressions of the object language as expressing thoughts already in principle expressible in the metalanguage: we must, in other words, adopt a species of formalism. By doing this, though, we at once rule out Hilbert's earlier account of the significance of the consistency proof. That account allowed us to introduce a new name and make a stipulation involving it: provided that the stipulation was consistent, Hilbert held that we were entitled to assume the existence of an object referred to by the name. But this procedure requires the stipulation to make sense, and if we treat the matter at the level of syntax we are not yet entitled to assume this. So formalism forces us to seek a different explanation of the significance of the formal consistency of a set of axioms. If mathematical theories are games played with signs, why is a formally consistent game preferable to an inconsistent one?

Note that when we refer here to the possibility of inconsistency in a formal system, it is not conflicts between rules that are in question. There would certainly be a genuine difficulty if the rules of our game were incompatible, i.e. if one rule allowed a move that another rule forbade, but that is not what is in question here. It is not hard to lay down the rules of a formal system such as Peano Arithmetic in such a way as to render it is quite obvious that inconsistencies of this sort — conflicts between rules — cannot arise. (The simplest way of achieving this is by the strategy of including in the system *only* permissive rules and not restrictive ones.)

The sort of inconsistency that concerns us, then, is one that is wholly internal to a formal system, such as an arithmetical proof whose last line is the string '0 = 1'. What is wrong with a system in which such a proof can arise? Since we are treating the signs of the theory as meaningless, there is on the face of it no reason to regard a proof which has the string '0 = 1' as its last line with any greater suspicion than one which has the string '0 = 0'. One common response is to say that a system in which '0 = 1' is provable is trivial since once we have a proof of '0 = 1' we can (assuming that the logical rules of the system are fairly standard) obtain a proof of any other sentence in two steps by application of the rule *ex falso quodlibet*. But as an explanation of the superiority of consistent over inconsistent games this response is quite inadequate. The flaw in it was well expressed by Wittgenstein in a conversation with members of the Vienna Circle.

WITTGENSTEIN: If I arrived in a calculus at the formula '0 ≠ 0' would the calculus be uninteresting because of that?
SCHLICK: Yes, a mathematician would say that such a thing does not interest him.
WITTGENSTEIN: But excuse me! It would be tremendously interesting that just that was the result! In a calculus you are surely always interested in results! How strange! Here this is the result — and there that! Who would have thought so![1]

The attempt to equate consistency with non-triviality fails because it tacitly assumes that the point of the game we play with our formal system is to find out which sentences are provable in it. If this is the case, a system in which every sentence is provable will indeed be trivial, but why should this be the point? It is possible to imagine many possible reasons for manipulating strings of signs in adherence with the rules of Peano Arithmetic. One might, for example, wish to use the resulting patterns to decorate one's walls. The example may seem fanciful, but according to the version of formalism we have been considering it is as good a reason to do arithmetic as any other.

What we have to do, then, if we wish to resurrect formalism is to explain the point of the game we play when we prove mathematical theorems without appealing directly to the notion of meaning. Hilbert took his inspiration for this from the use of ideal elements in mathematics. Consider projective geometry. There is an elegant method of proving theorems in affine plane geometry that involves adding a line at infinity to the plane so as to convert the proposition of affine geometry to be proved into a proposition of projective geometry. Very often the projective proposition has a short, elegant proof and the affine proposition only a much longer, less elegant one. It is never the case, however, that the projective result is provable and the affine one is not.

---

[1] Waismann, *Wittgenstein and the Vienna Circle*, 139.

Projective geometry is thus what is called a *conservative* extension of affine geometry.

What Hilbert now began to express, although not at first with any great clarity, was the idea that a proof of the formal consistency of a system might be a route to establishing its conservativeness.

> There is just one condition, albeit an absolutely necessary one, connected with the method of ideal elements. That condition is a *proof of consistency*, for the extension of a domain by the addition of ideal elements is legitimate only if the extension does not cause contradictions to appear in the old, narrower domain, or, in other words, only if the relations that obtain among the old structures when the ideal structures are deleted are always valid in the old domain.[2]

What marks a radical shift in Hilbert's thinking here is that the notion of conservativeness, unlike that of consistency, is essentially a relative one. From now on his account involved a partition of arithmetic into two parts, the *real* and the *ideal*, and the ideal theory I is supposed to be couched in a formal language that contains that of the real theory R. The real theory is then said to be *conservative* over the real theory if every real sentence provable in the ideal theory is provable in the real theory too. This is what Hilbert meant by his requirement that 'the relations that obtain among the old structures when the ideal structures are deleted are always valid in the old domain.' The objective of what I shall call *axiomatic formalism* is thus a proof that I is conservative over R. The link between consistency and conservativeness is easily established by the twin observations that any conservative extension of a consistent theory is consistent; and that any consistent extension of a complete theory is conservative. In particular, if the real theory is complete the constraint that the ideal theory should be conservative over it simply reduces to its formal consistency. Nonetheless, shifting the explanatory weight from the absolute notion of consistency to the relative notion of conservativeness provided Hilbert with ways of answering both the objections to his earlier theory that we considered earlier, Frege's and Poincaré's.

Since the usefulness of the ideal part was to be explained by its ability to prove things in the real part, the link between consistency and existence was broken, and so the account of the ideal part could no longer be described as axiomatic structuralism. It was rather a version of formalism, since there was no longer any need to argue that the sentences of the ideal part express genuine thoughts about mathematical entities at all. It did not, however, suffer from the defects of pure formalism,

---

[2]In Benacerraf and Putnam, 199.

since the conservativeness result would, if it could be proved, provide the axiomatic formalist with precisely the explanation of the applicability of mathematics that the pure formalist lacked. Moreover, although the sentences of the ideal theory were not now to be seen as expressing genuine thoughts, Hilbert nevertheless considered it to be possible to treat them as if they did: if we have a choice between different ideal theories, each of which is conservative over the real theory, one of the considerations he took to be relevant to the choice between them was the extent of their similarity to the language of everyday thought; and the reason for this was that Hilbert took it that if we used a theory which is similar to our everyday language, we would find ourselves able to reason with it, since the psychological moves involved would be ones we are familiar with from the everyday case.

The partition of mathematics into a real and an ideal part also made it comprehensible how a consistency proof for the ideal part might be achieved. The problem with the old theory had been that the axiomatic structuralist had to provide a consistency proof for mathematics that is in a sense content-free, since it depends on no mathematical existence assumptions: this would be possible only if the problem of consistency were trivial. On the new account the axiomatic formalist has the resources of the real theory at his disposal when he comes to construct the proof that the ideal theory is conservative.

The idea of regarding part of mathematics as no more than an idealization, justified solely on the basis of its consequences, was not Hilbert's. Leibniz, for example, commented that

if someone does not admit infinite and infinitely small lines as real objects with metaphysical rigour, he can nevertheless make use of them as ideal notions which shorten arguments.[3]

It is particularly instructive to note the similarity between Hilbert's programme and Russell's regressive method. In both cases an ideal theory I is to be justified solely on the ground that it is conservative over a real theory R. But Russell faced two related difficulties. If the real theory was to be one that could be given an empiricist grounding, it would not contain enough of arithmetic to constrain the ideal theory: it might force the ideal theory to deliver the equation $7 + 5 = 12$ (which has been empirically confirmed often enough), but not the equation $10^{10^{10}} + 1 = 1 + 10^{10^{10}}$ (which has not). And if our only ground for believing that the ideal theory *is* conservative over the real theory is the inductive one that no conclusion contradicting a truth of the real theory has yet been derived by its means, then the validity this gives to

---

[3] Letter to Varignon, 2 Feb. 1702, in *Schriften zur Logik*, 252.

the ideal methods is at best a defeasible one: we have not yet succeeded in proving in the system of *Principia* something we believe for other reasons to be false, but we might succeed in doing so tomorrow.

If he was to overcome these weaknesses in Russell's account, Hilbert needed to provide a non-formalist justification for a real theory large enough to contain all the numerical equations of conventional arithmetic; and then to give a proof that the ideal theory is conservative over this real theory. We shall consider Hilbert's treatments of both these problems in turn.

9.2 Real arithmetic

The first challenge, then, is to identify and ground the real theory. When we have done so, there will remain with respect to it our original problem of explaining both its necessity and its applicability, but the hope is that they will be relatively easy to solve because the real theory will not involve the quantifications over infinite totalities that complicate the other accounts we have been considering. Nevertheless, Hilbert was clear that he could not expect the real theory to vanish completely: it would have to appeal to *some* irreducible content.

Kant taught — and it is an integral part of his doctrine — that mathematics treats a subject matter which is given independently of logic. Mathematics, therefore, can never be grounded solely on logic. Consequently, Frege's and Dedekind's attempts to so ground it were doomed to failure.[4]

In lectures as early as 1905 Hilbert identified quantifier-free elementary arithmetic as belonging to the contentful part, contrasting it in this respect with the part of arithmetic that involves quantification over all numbers:

The simplest example would be

$$1 + n = n + 1$$

as a statement for 'every' whole number. This proposition has no content which one can write down on paper in finitely many signs, unlike a proposition such as

$$1 + 7 = 7 + 1$$

which *does* have such a content. Rather the content for the first of these appears at first as infinitely large in a certain way, and the primary task is to transform this content into one that *can* be written down.[5]

---

[4] In Benacerraf and Putnam, 192. [5] In Hallett, 'Hilbert and logic', 169.

In the first published writings of his second period, in which Hilbert began to report the results of his foundational research programme, we find the place of quantifier-free elementary arithmetic in the contentual core confirmed. At first he took as canonical a notation in which the names are '1', '1+1', '1+1+1', etc., but later he simplified it and used as his names simply the finite strings of strokes '|', '||', '|||', etc. He then presented contentful arithmetic as consisting primarily in the study of the behaviour of such finite strings of strokes under various defined operations. If a and b are numerals (i.e. finite strings of strokes), $a + b$ is defined as the result of appending a copy of b to a copy of a, and ab is defined as the result of concatenating a copy of a for each copy of b. We can then establish any numerical equation or inequation of $\mathbf{EA_0}$ by directly expanding each side into the stroke symbol it abbreviates. Thus, for example,

$$1 + 7 = | + ||||||| = |||||||| = ||||||| + | = 7 + 1.$$

What is the significance of these finite strings of strokes? Hilbert's answer was that they do not at first have any significance beyond the signs themselves.

The objects of number theory are for me — in direct contrast to Dedekind and Frege — the signs themselves, whose shape can be generally and certainly recognized by us — independently of space and time, of the special conditions of the production of the sign, and of insignificant differences in the finished product. The solid philosophical attitude that I think is required for the grounding of pure mathematics — as well as for all scientific thought, understanding, and communication — is this: *In the beginning was the sign.*[6]

But if 'the objects of number theory are ... the signs themselves', how does Hilbert's account avoid the objections that led us to reject reflexive formalism earlier? That, let us recall, was the view that the numerals are names of themselves, and it foundered because it could not explain either the applicability of arithmetic or the existence of different numerical notations none of which has a privileged status except by our stipulation. And whether or not Hilbert intended his stroke numerals to be names of themselves, it is clear that unless it is supplemented his account faces just the same objections. What Hilbert needed to do, therefore, was to provide an account of how 'the signs themselves', which he took to be the objects of number theory, could have a wider significance that would enable contentful arithmetic to be applicable.

Earlier we found Hilbert making an appeal to Kantian authority to rule out as pointless any attempt to ground mathematics on logic. So

[6]In Mancosu, 202.

far as it goes here, this appeal is essentially negative, but it suggests the idea of giving a positive Kantian account of how an arithmetic grounded on the combinatorial properties of finite stroke strings is applicable. But that is to make arithmetic dependent on the a priori structure of sensibility, which for Kant was spatio-temporal. The difficulty with this was that Hilbert regarded the structure of space and time as a question for physicists to settle, not philosophers, and therefore felt obliged to abandon space and time as a priori conditions of experience. By doing this Hilbert took himself to be merely responding to modern physics, which had shown the classical conception current in Kant's time to be untenable.

Physics teaches that a homogeneous continuum that would allow continued divisibility and would thus realize the infinitely small is nowhere encountered in reality. The infinite divisibility of a continuum is an operation that only exists in thought — is only an idea, which is refuted by our observations of nature and the experiences of physics and chemistry. On the other hand, in astronomy there are grave doubts about the existence of infinite space, and thus of the infinitely large. And all our action is finite; the infinite has no place in it. The infinite is realized nowhere; it does not exist in nature, nor is it admissible as a foundation of our rational thought.[7]

So the a priori attitude which structures our experience cannot be spatio-temporal. 'The Kantian theory of the a priori', he said, 'still contains anthropological dross from which it must be liberated.'[8] What is left when we have stripped away this 'anthropological dross' is the finitary viewpoint. But will this do? Hilbert certainly thought that the sign combinations on which contentful arithmetic is based are 'extra-logical concrete objects given in intuition prior to all thoughts', and that finitary intuition was a third source of knowledge besides deduction and experience, but this is not enough for his purpose. What is needed if stroke arithmetic is to be applicable to experience is an argument to show that experience conforms to the structure which the finitary viewpoint imposes.

In Chapter 1 I suggested that Kant might have flirted briefly in his *Inaugural Dissertation* with the idea that arithmetic is a third form of pure intuition alongside space and time, but that he had certainly come in the end to think it could be derived from the other two. Now Hilbert reversed the order of reduction: space and time become on his account no more than theoretical constructs whose utility is ultimately explained by the consistency proof his proof theory is intended to supply. All our experience is of finite numbers of concrete objects in combination. Although we routinely think of these concrete objects as spatio-temporal,

---

[7]Ibid. 268–9.   [8]In Ewald, 1163.

we have no reason to suppose that this spatio-temporality occurs either in the objects themselves or in the mode by which they are presented to our senses as raw data. It is enough to suppose that what are presented are objects in finite combinations: all the rest is a theory we use to conceptualize the particular sorts of finite combinations that as a matter of fact we experience.

The question that faces us now, though, is how much of Kant's account survives if we simply replace space and time with finitary combination in the structure of sensibility. But we do not have to look far for an answer: the *Tractatus* is, after all, an attempt to answer just this question. So we might expect that in the end these two explanations of the applicability of arithmetic to the world, Wittgenstein's and Hilbert's, would not prove so very dissimilar. It turns out, though, that neither account suffices without supplementation to ground the application to the world of arithmetic as standardly practised.

In the case of the *Tractatus* we have seen this already: the account of arithmetic in the *Tractatus* does not deliver an indefinite supply of distinct numbers unless we supplement it with something such as Ramsey's 'Kantian argument' that our language contains the possibility of indefinitely many symbols. 'This', Ramsey remarked, 'would give an idea of mathematics very like Hilbert's.'[9] Ramsey was right. Once we can individuate operations at the level of symbols, our grasp of the application of the general form of proposition within the domain of symbols will be sufficient to ground a conception of arithmetic corresponding to the system we have called **EA**. In other words, Wittgenstein's account thus supplemented will map onto Hilbert's.

On the other hand, what Hilbert's more explicitly Kantian account of arithmetic as based on intuitions of finite arrangements of concrete objects lacks is an explanation of the applicability of arithmetic to everything we experience, and it is here that it in turn must borrow from the *Tractatus*. As we saw in Chapter 1, Kant made arithmetic dependent on sensibility: this both guaranteed and limited its applicability to what we experience via sensibility, i.e. to everything we intuit. Wittgenstein's account places language in the rôle of sensibility, so that arithmetic is applicable to all and only what can be expressed propositionally. Hilbert, on the other hand, adopted Kant's account but limited the pure form of intuition to the structure exhibited by finite arrangements of concrete objects. Hence for Hilbert's account to parallel Kant's it would have to be the case that this is the *only* form of intuition available to us, so that all our experience would be subject to this structure. Contentful arithmetic would then once more be

---

[9] *Notes*, 179.

applicable to everything we experience.

The difficulty with this, however, is that it is not immediately clear how arithmetic would then be applicable to anything abstract. Wittgenstein's account does not share this limitation since nothing in it compels us to suppose that the objects we refer to in a Wittgensteinian language are concrete. For Hilbert's account to achieve the generality of Wittgenstein's, therefore, we need to add to it an argument to show that *all* our thought, even about abstract things, is subject to the structure of this finitary conception of sensibility. The notion of sensibility that is now in play seems too distant from Kant's for *his* argument to this conclusion to be directly applicable. The crucial step occurs when Hilbert says that the finitary mode of thought is 'necessary for mathematics and for all scientific thought, understanding, and communication, and without [it] mental activity is not possible at all.'[10] Hilbert's argument is thus that arithmetic is applicable because it is based on a structure which grounds all our mental activity. It is evident, I hope, how close this has now come to the central thesis of the *Tractatus*.

9.3 Schematic arithmetic

What Hilbert came to see as distinctive about higher mathematics was its use of the concept of the infinite, a concept which we find nowhere instantiated in nature. Hilbert's task was to show how the mathematics of the infinite can be grounded on our intuitions of finite arrangements of concrete objects. So far, though, the mathematics we have considered as contentful gives us little reason even to bother with higher mathematics. As Ramsey pointed out,

any statement of elementary arithmetic can be easily tested or proved without using higher mathematics, which if it be supposed to exist solely for the sake of simple arithmetic seems entirely pointless.[11]

The technical way of putting the matter is to say that $\mathbf{EA}_0$ is both complete and decidable. So no extension of $\mathbf{EA}_0$ could allow us to prove anything in it that we could not prove already by entirely mechanical means. The best we could hope for would be that the proofs by means of higher mathematics were shorter or more elegant than those provided by our mechanical decision procedure.

The question we need to address, then, is whether $\mathbf{EA}_0$ exhausts the part of arithmetic that is contentful from a finitary standpoint. Let us

[10]In Mancosu, 267.   [11]*FoM*, 71.

consider in particular whether it is possible for us to assert contentfully
a schema of the form

$$f(\mathfrak{a}) = g(\mathfrak{a})$$

where f and g are elementary number-theoretic functions, the letter 'a'
being understood as standing for an arbitrary numeral. Hilbert in 1905
denied that such a schema has a 'content which one can write down
on paper in finitely many signs'. Later, though, he came to think that
expressions in which letters occur standing schematically for numerals
can be treated as contentful. There was, as we shall see, a practical
reason for Hilbert to do this: if expressions containing schematic letters
could never be contentful, it would be impossible genuinely to express
— let alone prove — the formal consistency result which guarantees
the usefulness of the ideal theory. But the use of schematic letters
here is in any case nothing new. Although the *theorems* of $\mathbf{EA}_0$ do
not contain either variables or schematic letters, the definitions do.
For example, we earlier defined the sum of two numerals $\mathfrak{a}$ and $\mathfrak{b}$ to
be the numeral obtained by placing a copy of the numeral $\mathfrak{b}$ after a
copy of the numeral $\mathfrak{a}$. Since there are indefinitely many numbers, we
cannot understand this definition unless we can understand a certain
kind of generality, namely the notion of a rule to be applied in different
cases. The involvement of schematic letters cannot in itself, then, be
a reason not to regard an expression as contentful: *some* degree of
generality is built into the very idea of applying a rule, and so whatever
grounds our grasp of $\mathbf{EA}_0$ must already ground our understanding of
general schematic claims about numbers. It would in any case be odd
if the appearance of schematic letters represented in itself a significant
extension here, since such letters already occur in the expressions of
propositional calculus, and we have seen that they fall within the scope
of the Kantian analytic.

What is harder to adjudicate is Hilbert's claim that we can establish
the *truth* of a schema by wholly contentful methods. Consider, for
example, his proof that $\mathfrak{a} + \mathfrak{b} = \mathfrak{b} + \mathfrak{a}$:

If, as we are entitled to assume, $\mathfrak{b} > \mathfrak{a}$ (that is, the number-sign $\mathfrak{b}$ extends
beyond $\mathfrak{a}$), then $\mathfrak{b}$ can be decomposed in the form $\mathfrak{a} + \mathfrak{c}$, where $\mathfrak{c}$ serves to
communicate a number; then one need only show that $\mathfrak{a} + \mathfrak{a} + \mathfrak{c} = \mathfrak{a} + \mathfrak{c} + \mathfrak{a}$,
that is, that $\mathfrak{a} + \mathfrak{a} + \mathfrak{c}$ is the same number-sign as $\mathfrak{a} + \mathfrak{c} + \mathfrak{a}$. But this is
the case as long as $\mathfrak{a} + \mathfrak{c}$ is the same sign as $\mathfrak{c} + \mathfrak{a}$, i.e. $\mathfrak{a} + \mathfrak{c} = \mathfrak{c} + \mathfrak{a}$.
But here, in contrast to the original communication, at least one 1 has been
removed by the decomposition of $\mathfrak{a}$, and this procedure of decomposition can
be continued until the summands that are to be exchanged agree with each
other. For every number-sign $\mathfrak{a}$ is built up in the manner described from

the signs 1 and +; it can therefore also be decomposed by the splitting and cancellation of the individual signs.[12]

Hilbert was insistent that proofs such as this do not depend on the principle of mathematical induction:

When we develop number theory in this way, there are no axioms, and no contradictions of any sort are possible. We simply have concrete signs as objects, we operate with them, and we make contentual statements about them. And in particular, regarding the proof just given that $\mathfrak{a} + \mathfrak{b} = \mathfrak{b} + \mathfrak{a}$, I should like to stress that this proof is merely a procedure that rests on the construction and deconstruction of number-signs and that it is essentially different from the principle that plays such a prominent role in higher arithmetic, namely, the principle of complete induction or of inference from n to $n + 1$. This principle is rather, as we shall see, a formal principle that carries us farther and that belongs to a higher level; it needs proof, and the proof can be given.[13]

Hilbert seems here to be suggesting that the proof of the schema $\mathfrak{a} + \mathfrak{b} = \mathfrak{b} + \mathfrak{a}$ can itself be regarded schematically. What he sketches is indeed a schematic proof, but only of the *induction step* of the proof that $\mathfrak{a} + \mathfrak{b} = \mathfrak{b} + \mathfrak{a}$. It shows, that is to say, that the equation $\mathfrak{a} + \mathfrak{b} = \mathfrak{b} + \mathfrak{a}$ follows from another equation $\mathfrak{c} + \mathfrak{b} = \mathfrak{b} + \mathfrak{c}$, where $\mathfrak{c}$ is some numeral such that $\mathfrak{c} < \mathfrak{a}$. In order to complete the proof we must repeat this step an indeterminate (but finite) number of times until we have reduced the problem of establishing that $\mathfrak{a} + \mathfrak{b} = \mathfrak{b} + \mathfrak{a}$ to the trivial case $0 + \mathfrak{b} = \mathfrak{b} + 0$. We therefore cannot represent the *whole* proof that $\mathfrak{a} + \mathfrak{b} = \mathfrak{b} + \mathfrak{a}$ in schematic form since the number of applications of the induction step we should have to include depends on $\mathfrak{a}$ and is unbounded.

It seems unavoidable, then, that in order to establish theorem schemas of the sort we are discussing we need the principle of mathematical induction. Hilbert's suggestion to the contrary is surely wrong. He was, however, right to distinguish the principle involved here from the principle of mathematical induction in **PA**: there quantifiers are allowed to appear in the induction predicate, whereas here only quantifier-free predicates are permitted. A proof of the consistency of **PA** using this restricted induction principle would thus not be straightforwardly circular.

Although it is significantly weaker than the full induction principle, the restricted induction principle nevertheless vastly extends the scope of what can be proved in schematic arithmetic. What we obtain when we make use of it to establish a theorem schema is not in fact a schematic proof as such, but may be thought of as specifying a method for constructing proofs of particular instances of the theorem schema. In the typical case we have a proof of $\phi(0)$ and a schematic proof of $\phi(\mathfrak{a} + 1)$

---

[12]In Mancosu, 203. [13]Ibid.

from $\phi(\mathfrak{a})$. In order to prove $\phi(\mathfrak{b})$ we simply string together the proof of $\phi(0)$, the instance of the schematic proof proving $\phi(1)$ from $\phi(0)$, the instance proving $\phi(2)$ from $\phi(1)$, ... , and the instance proving $\phi(\mathfrak{b})$ from $\phi(\mathfrak{b} - 1)$.

This way of explaining matters does not, of course, give us a non-circular route to a *justification* of induction — I shall come back to that question shortly — but there is a further difficulty we have not yet addressed as to whether the restricted induction principle is even finitistically *statable*. What we did was to take a proof of $\phi(0)$ and a schematic proof of $\phi(\mathfrak{a} + 1)$ from $\phi(\mathfrak{a})$ as given and outline a procedure for producing from them, given any numeral $\mathfrak{b}$, a proof of $\phi(\mathfrak{b})$. If we tried to state the general conclusion of this procedure as a rule, we should naturally write

$$\frac{\phi(0) \qquad \phi(\mathfrak{a}) \supset \phi(\mathfrak{a} + 1)}{\phi(\mathfrak{b})}$$

But this rule has infinitely many premisses and is therefore not finitistically acceptable. Our mistake is that our earlier argument did not in fact establish a conclusion as strong as the rule we have just attempted to state. It is not part of what is asserted by the premiss $\phi(\mathfrak{a}) \supset \phi(\mathfrak{a}+1)$ of the new rule that there should be a schematic proof, involving the schematic letter $\mathfrak{a}$, of $\phi(\mathfrak{a} + 1)$ from $\phi(\mathfrak{a})$. Even if any finitistically acceptable proof of $\phi(\mathfrak{a}) \supset \phi(\mathfrak{a} + 1)$ is reducible to this form, it is not finitistically deducible that this is so.

But things are not quite as bad as they might seem. The principle of induction is not, when thought of in this way, wholly infinitistic, since for any particular numeral $\mathfrak{a}$ only finitely many premisses of the form $\phi(\mathfrak{b}) \supset \phi(\mathfrak{b}+1)$ are needed to deduce $\phi(\mathfrak{a})$. The difficulty is simply that the number of such premisses required varies with $\mathfrak{a}$. To express the rule in such a way that it involves only finitely many premisses, therefore, it seems unavoidable that we must introduce quantifiers $(\forall x < \mathfrak{a})$ and $(\exists x < \mathfrak{a})$. With these available to us we can represent the induction rule as follows:

$$\frac{\phi(0) \qquad (\forall x < \mathfrak{a}).\, \phi(x) \supset \phi(x + 1)}{\phi(\mathfrak{b})}$$

Let us pause now to consider the point we have reached. Hilbert based his account of elementary arithmetic on an appeal to our intuitions of finite arrangements of concrete objects. We operate with finite strings of strokes, and thus obtain results that express combinatorial features of any arrangements we might experience with these finite numbers of elements. But we noted that in order to be able to grasp the rules for adding and multiplying strings of strokes we need a general grasp of the notion of a finite string and not merely an individual grasp of any particular finite string.

This is, of course, a thoroughly Kantian conclusion: to reason generally about numbers it is not sufficient to represent them schematically by means of letters; we need also to recognize the numbers as finite — to represent them, in other words, as having the structure of finiteness. But once we do that, we have the resources to grasp the restricted principle of mathematical induction, since what is involved in grasping a numeral *as* finite is precisely that it is obtainable by repeated addition of strokes to a string and hence that the induction rule is applicable to it. Moreover, we must also understand the bounded quantifiers $(\forall x < \mathfrak{a})$ and $(\exists x < \mathfrak{a})$, since if we grasp the numeral $\mathfrak{a}$ as finite, we presuppose all the numerals less than it.

The conclusion we have reached, then, is that by reflecting on whatever understanding is needed to ground our grasp of $\mathbf{EA}_0$ we can ground schematic reasoning using bounded quantifiers and instances of induction involving them. What we cannot achieve by such direct reflection, though, is a grasp of arbitrary primitive recursive functions. To see why not, let us compare the recursive definitions of two familiar functions.

The first function we shall consider is $f(\mathfrak{a}) = \mathfrak{a}\mathfrak{b}$, which can be given a recursive definition as follows:

$$f(0) = 0$$
$$f(x + 1) = f(x) + \mathfrak{a}$$

Our grasp of the acceptability of this definition can be explained in the same manner as Hilbert's proof that $\mathfrak{a} + \mathfrak{b} = \mathfrak{b} + \mathfrak{a}$: we cannot provide a single schema which represents the process of calculating $f(\mathfrak{a})$ from the recursive definition for an arbitrary numeral $\mathfrak{a}$, since the number of steps in the process depends on $\mathfrak{a}$, but we can represent schematically the process which has to be iterated $\mathfrak{a}$ times, namely that of adding $\mathfrak{b}$ to a number.

Consider now by contrast the recursive definition of the exponential function $g(\mathfrak{a}) = \mathfrak{b}^{\mathfrak{a}}$:

$$g(0) = 1$$
$$g(x + 1) = f(g(x))$$

This is superficially similar, but when we try to represent schematically the process which has to be iterated $\mathfrak{a}$ times in order to calculate $g(\mathfrak{a})$

— that of multiplying by $\mathfrak{b}$ — we have to invoke our description of the function f, which, as we have seen, in turn involves iteration of a schematic process. So what is involved here is a nested recursion. In order to be in a position to see that the outer recursion process terminates, we must *already* see that the inner one does. If we express the matter in terms of the inductive argument we would give to establish that the outer recursion terminates, the difficulty is that the steps in that induction are now not instances of a single schematic argument but calculations of steadily increasing complexity whose correctness can be established by means of another inductive argument. So to validate the introduction of symbols for arbitrary primitive recursive functions into arithmetic we need to be in a position to argue inductively on sequences of objects — in this case calculations — which, although they can be generated by means of a rule, are not given to us directly as finite.[14]

Some have argued[15] that the finitist perspective should be interpreted in this more liberal manner, and certainly there were others in Hilbert's school who did so, but there is nothing in Hilbert's writings before 1930 to support an attribution of this view (which I shall call *broad* finitism) to him. Hilbert is undoubtedly vague at key points in his discussion of the limits of the finitary standpoint, but insofar as he delineates the scope of finitist reasoning at all, it seems to be the *narrow* conception, which outlaws nested induction, that is in play.

9.4 Ideal arithmetic

Reflection on the intuitions that ground $\mathbf{EA_0}$ also grounds schematic reasoning involving addition and multiplication but not, I have argued, schematic reasoning involving arbitrary primitive recursive functions, for which further reflection is required. But schematic arithmetic is inherently non-formal; if we try to formalize it, we have to recognize that the syntactic objects involved are at base not the schemas, which are metalinguistic, but their instances, so it collapses once more into a formalization of the contentful part $\mathbf{EA_0}$.

If we are to formalize the process involved, we must evidently turn the schemas from metalinguistic forms into object language sentences: for each predicate ϕ we include in the object language a sentence $(x)\phi(x)$; we then add to the rules of the system all instance of the induction

---

[14]Cf. Parsons, 'Finitism and intuitive knowledge'.   [15]See e.g. Tait, 'Finitism'.

scheme

$$\frac{\phi(0)}{(y)\phi(y)} \quad (x)(\phi(x) \supset \phi(x+1))$$

in which ϕ is quantifier-free. I shall call the resulting formal system Elementary Arithmetic or **EA**. Note, though, that we are now engaged in what is from the narrow finitist standpoint adopted by Hilbert already an idealization since the expressions of **EA** such as '$(x)\phi(x)$' are not themselves meaningful from that standpoint. In order to obtain contentful assertions from them we need a further rule of inference warranting instantiation of generalizations:

$$\frac{(x)\phi(x)}{\phi(\mathfrak{a})}$$

So although the expressions of **EA** are not themselves meaningful, they correspond to expressions which we used meaningfully when we argued metalinguistically. For example, the expression '$(x)\phi(x)$' can be thought of as going proxy in **EA** for the form '$\phi(\mathfrak{a})$' which we used when arguing schematically. For that reason the argument we gave earlier to ground schematic arithmetic can be converted into an argument that **EA** is conservative over **EA₀**: proofs in **EA** may be reliably used to deduce numerical equations and inequations. We shall in general say that a formal arithmetical theory I is *outer consistent* if it obeys this narrow conservativeness constraint, i.e. if for every sentence $(x)\phi(x)$ of Goldbach type provable in I the instance $\phi(\mathfrak{a})$ is true for each numeral $\mathfrak{a}$. With this terminology the conclusion we have just reached is that anyone who reflects on their own grasp of **EA₀** should agree that **EA** is outer consistent.

The expressions of **EA** are what Wittgenstein would have called pseudo-propositions, as is illustrated by the fact that there are generally no contentful expressions of finitistic arithmetic that we can make correspond to their negations. For this reason the formation rules of **EA** do not permit the negation of a generalization to be constructed. Now as long as we adhere strictly to the doctrine that the sentences of **EA** are ideal, their lack of negations should not worry us, but for Hilbert one of the points of the ideal theory was that it should be possible for us to *reason* with it. Classical logic is a convenient tool for reasoning about the world, and we have a great facility with it. It is therefore natural, if only for psychological reasons, for us to want to make the expressions of our formal mathematical system obey rules which are formally the same as those of classical logic. We therefore extend the language of **EA** by permitting the use of the negation operator and decree that the new expressions we obtain are to obey the familiar logical rules. Finally (and crucially) we also extend the scope of the induction rule to apply to all the formulae of the extended language. The result is the formal system known as Peano Arithmetic or **PA**.

But the argument we gave to show that **EA** is outer consistent, and hence reliable as a means of deriving numerical equations and inequations, does not extend to **PA**, since the sentences of **PA** cannot be seen as going proxy for metalinguistic schemas in the same way. If we are to make use of **PA** in deriving numerical equations and inequations, therefore, we must prove that it is outer consistent or, equivalently, that it is consistent.

9.5 Metamathematics

How is Hilbert's proof of the consistency of **PA** to proceed? I mentioned earlier that Frege at one time thought the only way to prove the consistency of a theory was to construct a model of it. In this he was wrong: the compactness theorem, for example, provides us with a way of proving the consistency of a theory by constructing separately a model for each finite list of axioms of the theory. Nevertheless, the compactness theorem would not have filled Hilbert's need since its proof depends on non-constructive methods. Since the point of the programme was to license the use of infinitary — in particular, non-constructive — methods, Hilbert needed to be able to prove consistency in a way that did not appeal to such methods. Indeed consistency proofs that proceed by means of the construction of models will generally be ruled out as involving infinitary methods since in the cases that interest us the theories in question will not have any finite models.

Hilbert thus needed another method. The one he hit on was to exploit a striking analogy between the proofs that make up a formal theory and the number-signs of arithmetic.

The axioms, formulae, and proofs that make up this formal edifice are precisely what the number-signs were in the construction of elementary number theory ... ; and with them alone, as with the number-signs in number theory, contentual thought takes place — i.e. only with them is actual thought practised.[16]

---

[16] In Mancosu, 204.

What gives elementary number theory its content is the fact that it has as its subject matter the number-signs themselves, i.e. finite strings of strokes. In metamathematics the subject matter consists once again of finite string of signs, only this time they are the formulae and proofs of the theory under investigation.

Frege had objected that global formalism is impossible because even if mathematics is a formal game without content, metamathematics cannot be viewed in the same way: if we prove that it is impossible to mate in chess with only a king and a knight, we have thereby learnt something about chess. Hilbert here grants Frege's objection and turns it to his own purposes. The aim of his proof theory is to show that certain sorts of game (i.e. proofs) are impossible. The statement that these proofs are impossible has genuine content for the same reason that the statements of quantifier-free arithmetic have content: the analogy between the two spheres is sufficiently close that a justification for one can easily be converted into a justification for the other.

In fact, the analogy in question can be made quite precise by means of the technique of arithmetization of syntax. All the formulae, axioms, and proofs that make up the apparatus of a formal theory can be represented as finite strings of signs drawn from a fixed stock. Let us assign a natural number $n(\alpha)$ to each sign α in the stock: we do this more or less arbitrarily except that distinct signs are assigned distinct numbers. The technique is then to give any finite string α a number $\ulcorner\alpha\urcorner$ called its *Gödel number*. If α is $\alpha_1\alpha_2\ldots\alpha_k$, its Gödel number is defined as

$$\ulcorner\alpha_1\alpha_2\ldots\alpha_k\urcorner = p_1^{n(\alpha_1)}p_2^{n(\alpha_2)}\ldots p_k^{n(\alpha_k)},$$

where $p_1, p_2, p_3, \ldots$ are the prime numbers written in ascending order. Under this correspondence every finite string in the language of our theory has a natural number associated with it. Moreover, the procedure is reversible: the fundamental theorem of arithmetic tells us that every natural number is expressible uniquely as a product of powers of primes; so given any number there is at most one string of symbols whose Gödel number it is, and we can work out explicitly what it is.

Hilbert cannot have been wholly unaware of the technique of arithmetization of syntax when he set out his proof-theoretic programme: it was certainly known to Leibniz two centuries earlier and in any case it is hardly sophisticated mathematics. He did not mention it explicitly, though, because the exact equivalence between the two theories is not in fact essential to his project. Arithmetic is needed as the real theory over which the ideal theory is to be proved conservative; metamathematics is the theory in which the proof of conservativeness is to be conducted. Both theories must be seen as having content, but for different reasons: arithmetic, in order to explain the ultimate applicability of higher mathematics; metamathematics, in order that we can treat the conservativeness result, once proved, as genuinely true.

9.6 Hilbert's programme

Specifically, then, the object of the programme Hilbert was engaged in was to formalize an ideal theory I which extends **EA** and prove that this theory is outer consistent, i.e. that whenever we can use it to prove a sentence of the form $(x)f(x) = 0$ each of the instantiations $f(a) = 0$ is true. If this could be done, there would be no need to regard the strings of signs occurring in the ideal theory as meaningful at all. Indeed the general method by which the proof of outer consistency was to be conducted involved treating such strings as objects on a par with numerals. This parallelism can be developed by the method of arithmetization of syntax. In order to avoid an infinite regress it is plainly necessary for the proof of outer consistency to be genuinely contentful and not dependent for its validity on a further consistency proof. Since the only part of mathematics which Hilbert took to be epistemologically secure was finitist arithmetic, the proof of outer consistency had thus to be finitistically acceptable.

Hilbert no doubt hoped eventually to be able to supply such a finitistic consistency proof for the theory of types including the axioms of infinity and reducibility, and hence justify the whole of mathematics at one stroke. But at first he and his co-workers concentrated on the more modest goal of proving the consistency, and hence the outer consistency, of Peano Arithmetic. Several times, starting in 1921, Hilbert announced in published lectures that he had indeed succeeded in proving arithmetic to be consistent. What he was referring to was presumably the work of his doctoral student, Ackermann, who in his thesis claimed to prove by finitistic means the consistency not only of arithmetic but of analysis. By the time he published the material[17] Ackermann had realized that there was a gap in his proof, although he still thought he had proved the consistency of **PA**. Then in 1927 von Neumann[18] noticed that in fact the proof is valid only for arithmetic with quantifier-free induction. The more general result depended in addition on what Hilbert described as 'an elementary finiteness theorem that is purely arithmetical',[19] and everything hinged on proving this 'purely arithmetical' result.

[17]'Begründung des "Tertium non datur" ...'. [18]'Zur Hilbertischen Beweistheorie'. [19]In Mancosu, 229.

Influenced, no doubt, by the failure of their attempts to bridge this gap, some of the members of Hilbert's school began around this time to contemplate extending the scope of the methods to be considered as finitistic. Bernays, for example, had said in 1922 that the restricted form of induction which 'can be applied as a tool of contentual inference' relates 'only to something completely and concretely given',[20] whereas by 1930 he was content to apply recursion to processes in order to argue that exponentiation is finitistically acceptable. He first of all gives a finitistic description of the process of multiplication by ten. From this, he says,

we arrive at the process of transition from a number a to 10^a as follows. We let the number 10 correspond to the first 1 in a and to every affixed 1 we apply the process of multiplication by 1, and we keep going until we exhaust the figure a. The number obtained by means of the last process of multiplication by ten is denoted by 10^a. This procedure offers basically no difficulty at all for the intuitive view.[21]

It is hard to see how the *process* of multiplication by ten could be said to be 'completely and concretely given'. What Bernays says here therefore represents an extension of the finitary standpoint beyond what he envisaged in 1922. If followed through, this broader conception of finitism will license not only exponentiation but primitive recursive functions in general. The formal system which bears the same relation to this broad conception of finitism as **EA** bears to the narrow conception is called Primitive Recursive Arithmetic or **PRA**.

The pressure which drove Bernays to widen his conception of the form of induction which the finitistic standpoint can underwrite was that of proving the consistency of arithmetic; even on the broader conception of finitism that he now recommended, though, a demonstration of the 'elementary finiteness theorem' that would close the gap in Ackermann's proof remained elusive. But Hilbert himself evidently remained confident. When he was installed as a freeman of his home city of Königsberg in September 1930, Hilbert gave a speech in which, in conscious homage to another of Königsberg's famous sons, he outlined the Kantian grounding for mathematics which I have been discussing here. He ended with a declaration which became his epitaph: in mathematics there are no unsolvable problems. Instead of the foolish *ignorabimus*, our answer is on the contrary

We must know,
We shall know.

---

[20]Ibid. 221. [21]Ibid. 249, modified.

10

Gödel

On 7th September 1930, the day before Hilbert received the freedom of Königsberg, Gödel announced at a conference in the same city that 'one can even give examples of propositions (and in fact of those of the type of Goldbach or Fermat) that, while contentually true, are unprovable in the formal system of classical mathematics.'[1] Hilbert himself probably did not attend the conference session in question, but von Neumann — one of his co-workers in the programme of proving the consistency of classical mathematics — did. Alone among those present, perhaps, von Neumann realized immediately the significance of what Gödel had said and talked to him about it afterwards. Over the next few weeks von Neumann continued to think about its implications and soon discovered that the true unprovable sentence could be devised in such a way as to express the consistency of the system itself. On 20 November he wrote to tell Gödel this, but Gödel had got there before him: displaying a readiness to publish that deserted him in later life, he had submitted on 23 October an abstract[2] announcing both the incompleteness of the formal system of *Principia* and — what von Neumann had discovered independently — the unprovability of the consistency of the system by methods formalizable within it.

It is worth noting the similarities between these events and those of 1902. Then Russell wrote to Frege informing him of a simple technical result which destroyed the logicist programme that Frege thought he had virtually completed. Now Gödel announced a technical result which von Neumann at least evidently accepted as demonstrating the impossibility of the formalist programme that had seemed to be on the brink of success. Russell later paid eloquent tribute to Frege's generosity of spirit on receiving the letter which informed him of Russell's paradox:

As I think about acts of integrity and grace, I realise that there is nothing in my knowledge to compare with Frege's dedication to truth. ... Upon finding

---

[1] Dawson, 'Discussion on the foundations of mathematics'. [2] *Works*, I, 140.

that his fundamental assumption was in error, he responded with intellectual pleasure clearly submerging any feelings of personal disappointment.[3]

Whether Hilbert was as generous is more open to doubt: according to Bernays his first reaction was fury.

But as we have seen logicism did not quite die in 1902: Russell spent the next ten years trying to keep it alive. And Gödel at first went as far as to deny expressly that his theorems killed off Hilbert's programme.[4]

Three doubts were salient. First, Gödel's theorems apply only to theories that are formal, in the sense that 'reasoning in them, in principle, can be completely replaced by mechanical devices'.[5] Gödel was the first to give a precise mathematical characterization of this property, but he needed to be convinced that his definition correctly captures the intended class of theories. Second, in order to demonstrate that the consistency of a formal system cannot be proved by methods formalizable in the system itself it was necessary to appeal to certain features of the method of formalization: a consistency proof formalizable by methods not sharing these features therefore remained a possibility. Third, what Hilbert had demanded was a finitary proof of consistency: Gödel's theorem does not rule that out unless all finitary methods are formalizable in the system in question. Eventually, Gödel overcame his doubts on all three counts, but to see why, we need to investigate his reservations in detail. The matter is one of some technical complexity since the versions of his two results which Gödel announced in 1930 are not quite those on whose philosophical consequences he later came to rely.

10.1 Incompleteness

It was central to Hilbert's project that both the language in which the ideal theory was couched and the ideal theory itself should be what he called formal. He did not define this term precisely, but evidently he meant by it that both language and theory should be amenable to treatment by contentful methods. What the arithmetization of syntax does is to give us a way of making this precise. Finitary arithmetic is limited, at its broadest, to primitive recursive functions. So we shall say that a syntactic operation is *formal* if the function that corresponds to it under arithmetization is primitive recursive; and a theory is *formal* if the Gödel numbers of its proofs can be specified by means of a primitive recursive function. It will be useful to have a notation for the function that picks out the proofs of our ideal theory: I is formal just in case it

---

[3] See van Heijenoort, 127. [4] *Works*, I, 195. [5] Ibid.

is possible to define a primitive recursive function prf_I of two variables such that $\text{prf}_I(m, n) = 1$ if m is the Gödel number of a proof in I of the sentence whose Gödel number is n; and $\text{prf}_I(m, n) = 0$ otherwise.

The incompleteness theorem that Gödel proved in the summer of 1930 involved a notion that he called ω-consistency. The result that is nowadays generally referred to as Gödel's first incompleteness theorem is a stronger version due to Rosser, who showed that the condition of ω-consistency may be weakened to mere consistency. The method of proof exploits the idea of arithmetization of syntax mentioned in the last section and depends on the following key lemma.

Lemma 1. *Given any coding of a formal language, there is a primitive recursive function* $\text{sub} : \mathbb{N}^2 \to \mathbb{N}$ *such that if* $\alpha(x)$ *is a formula in the language with one free variable* x *and* f *is a primitive recursive function, then* $\text{sub}(\ulcorner\alpha\urcorner, \ulcorner f\urcorner) = \ulcorner\alpha(f(\ulcorner f\urcorner))\urcorner$.

The proof of this lemma is tedious and technical, but what it asserts is a case of a highly plausible general claim, namely that the operations one carries out on strings of signs correspond under arithmetization to primitive recursive functions.

Lemma 2. *If the formal language contains that of arithmetic, then with each formula* $\alpha(x)$ *with one free variable* x *we can effectively associate a term* τ *such that* $\tau = \ulcorner\alpha(\tau)\urcorner$.

Proof. Let $f(x) = \text{sub}(\ulcorner\alpha\urcorner, x)$. So f is primitive recursive by lemma 1. If τ is the term $f(\ulcorner f\urcorner)$,

$$\tau = f(\ulcorner f\urcorner) = \text{sub}(\ulcorner\alpha\urcorner, \ulcorner f\urcorner) = \ulcorner\alpha(f(\ulcorner f\urcorner))\urcorner = \ulcorner\alpha(\tau)\urcorner.$$

Q.E.D.

Gödel's incompleteness theorem. *If* I *is a consistent formal theory extending* **PRA$_0$***, there is a primitive recursive function* f *such that* $f(n) = 0$ *for each natural number* n *but* $I \not\vdash (x)\, f(x) = 0$.

Proof. Apply lemma 2 in the case where $\alpha(y)$ is the formula

$$(x)\, \text{prf}_I(x, y) = 0$$

to obtain a term τ such that

$$\tau = \ulcorner(x)\, \text{prf}_I(x, \tau) = 0\urcorner,$$

and let f be the primitive recursive function defined by

$$f(x) = \text{prf}_I(x, \tau),$$

so that

$$\tau = \ulcorner (x)f(x) = 0\urcorner.$$

Now if $(x)\,f(x) = 0$ is provable in I and n is the Gödel number of some proof of it, then

$$f(n) = \mathrm{prf}_I(n,\tau) = \mathrm{prf}_I(n,\ulcorner(x)f(x) = 0\urcorner) = 1,$$

and so $I \vdash f(\mathfrak{b}) = 1$, which makes I inconsistent. So we conclude that $I \nvdash (x)f(x) = 0$. But now it follows that for each n

$$f(n) = \mathrm{prf}_I(n,\ulcorner(x)f(x) = 0\urcorner) = 0.$$

Q.E.D.

A sentence $(x).\,f(x) = 0$ of Goldbach type that is not provable in I even though each of its numerical instances is true is called a *Gödel sentence* for I. With this terminology the theorem asserts that every consistent formal theory extending $\mathbf{PRA_0}$ has a Gödel sentence.[6]

10.2 Formal theories

What gives Gödel's first incompleteness theorem its importance in the philosophy of arithmetic is above all its ineluctability: it applies to any formal theory whatever that is strong enough to prove all the results of quantifier-free arithmetic. The definition of formality that is involved here was conceived by Gödel for the purpose of proving the incompleteness theorem, and he did not at first commit himself to the view that his definition encompassed all systems we should intuitively regard as formal. So Gödel's theorem leaves open the possibility that we could obtain a complete system for arithmetic by adding a rule which is not formal in the precise sense Gödel gave to this term. And indeed very soon after Gödel announced his result Hilbert did just this. He proposed to add to arithmetic variants of what is nowadays called the ω-rule:

$$\frac{\phi(\mathfrak{a})\ \text{for every numeral } \mathfrak{a}}{(x)\phi(x)}$$

First, in a lecture delivered in December 1930, he considered what is essentially the system $\mathbf{EA}^\omega$ obtained from $\mathbf{EA}$ by adding the ω-rule for

---

[6]This treatment of Gödel's theorems is heavily indebted to Jeroslow, 'Redundancies in the Hilbert-Bernays derivability conditions...'.

the case in which the formula $\phi(x)$ is quantifier-free. He proved that this system is complete on the assumption that **EA** is consistent (which he thought Ackermann had virtually proved). In a later paper he went on to consider the system **PA**$^\omega$ obtained by adding the ω-rule for an arbitrary formula $\phi(x)$.

What Hilbert's completeness result for **EA**$^\omega$ shows, given Gödel's theorem, is of course that the ω-rule cannot be formal in Gödel's sense. Yet Hilbert casually described the rule without argument as 'finite'. Was he right? This hinges on what we wish to regard as the application of a rule. Ever since Frege the guiding idea behind the process of formalization had been that of distinguishing the rules of proof from their application. The controversy about whether a proof was correct was then to focus entirely on the acceptability of the rules, which should have been formulated with sufficient clarity that the question whether the proof was indeed a correct application of those rules became wholly trivial and subject to no possible doubt. If this were not so, we should simply have arrived at a regress, since a proof at the metalevel would now be required to show that the purported proof was indeed a proof in the sense previously stipulated.

Gödel eventually became convinced that his initial caution about his definition of what were formal proofs was unwarranted, but he did so only when Turing demonstrated that they coincided precisely with those proofs whose correctness can be checked by means of a very simple kind of computer called a *Turing machine*. 'A formal system', Gödel concluded, 'can simply be defined to be any mechanical procedure for producing formulas, called provable formulas.'[7] The significance of this notion lies in the fact that it isolates precisely the property that is of interest to us here: a Turing machine (or a digital computer more generally) may be characterized by its capacity to follow a finite sent of rules slavishly without having any reflective grasp on the operations it is carrying out.

As we have already noted, the fact that arithmetic with the ω-rule is complete shows that the ω-rule cannot be formal in Gödel's sense. We can now locate the difficulty with it more precisely. If it is stated in the form

$$\frac{\phi(0), \phi(1), \phi(2), \ldots}{(x)\phi(x)}$$

the rule has infinitely many premises and is therefore quite obviously not finitistic. Hilbert thought that he could circumvent this difficulty

---

[7] Ibid., II, 370.

by stating the rule in the form

$$\frac{\phi(\mathfrak{a}) \text{ for every numeral } \mathfrak{a}}{(x)\phi(x)}$$

In other words, if we have by finitary methods established $\phi(\mathfrak{a})$ with $\mathfrak{a}$ a schematic numeral, we may then conclude that $(x)\phi(x)$. What Hilbert had failed to realize was that he had not delineated the scope of the finitary methods in question with any precision. Once we allow this restricted ω-rule into our reasoning, it is presumably permissible to use it in deriving the premiss to an application of the rule itself. The scope of what is to count as the finitary part of arithmetic is therefore inherently unformalizable: there is therefore no mechanical test which will decide for an arbitrary numerical predicate $\phi(x)$ whether the schematic proposition $\phi(\mathfrak{a})$ has been established by finitary methods. This is why Hilbert's version of the ω-rule is non-formal.

10.3 The unprovability of outer consistency

Among the many syntactic operations that are involved in forming the strings of signs that constitute ideal mathematics there is one that will arise in our discussion sufficiently often to deserve a notation of its own. We state it in the form of a lemma without proof:

Lemma. *It is possible to define a primitive recursive function* inst : $\mathbb{N}^2 \to \mathbb{N}$ *such that for each primitive recursive function* f

$$\mathbf{PRA} \vdash (x)(y)(\text{inst}(\ulcorner(x)f(x) = 0\urcorner, y) = f(y)).$$

Once we have the functions inst and prf_I at our disposal, it is quite easy to construct a sentence in the language of **PRA** that will be true if and only if I is outer consistent. For instance, let Outercon_I be the sentence

$$(x)(y)(z)(\text{prf}_I(x, z) = 0 \lor \text{inst}(z, y) = 0). \tag{1}$$

This has as instances the sentences of the form

$$(x)(y)(\text{prf}_I(x, \ulcorner(w)f(w) = 0\urcorner) = 0 \lor \text{inst}(z, y) = 0),$$

and this is provably equivalent in **PRA** to

$$(x)(y)(\text{prf}_I(x, \ulcorner(w)f(w) = 0\urcorner) = 0 \lor f(y) = 0).$$

This last sentence has as its instances sentences of the form

$$\mathrm{prf}_I(\mathfrak{a}, \ulcorner (w)f(w) = 0 \urcorner) = 0 \vee f(\mathfrak{b}) = 0,$$

which will all be true if and only if whenever $(w)\,f(w) = 0$ is provable in I all the instances $f(\mathfrak{b}) = 0$ are true. Thus $\mathrm{Outercon}_I$ expresses that any sentence of Goldbach type provable in I has all its instances true, i.e. that I is outer consistent.

The form of the Gödel sentence constructed in the proof of Gödel's theorem depends not only on I but on the choice of Gödel numbering for the language of I, and even then many different constructions of Gödel sentences for I are possible, but $\mathrm{Outercon}_I$ is one that has particular relevance in the context of our discussion of Hilbert's programme. We shall restrict our attention from now on to theories whose logic unproblematically represents inferential reasoning with generalized equations, so that if, for instance, $I \vdash (x)\,f(x) = g(x)$ and $I \vdash (x)\,g(x) = h(x)$, then $I \vdash (x)\,f(x) = h(x)$

Gödel's outer consistency theorem. *If I is a consistent formal theory extending* **PRA**, *the sentence* $\mathrm{Outercon}_I$ *expressing the outer consistency of I is not provable in I.*

Proof. Suppose on the contrary that $\mathrm{Outercon}_I$ is provable in I, i.e.

$$I \vdash (x)(y)(z)(\mathrm{prf}_I(x, z) = 0 \vee \mathrm{inst}(z, y) = 0).$$

Let τ and f be as in the proof of Gödel's theorem given earlier, so that

$$I \vdash \tau = \ulcorner (x)f(x) = 0 \urcorner.$$

Now because I extends **PRA**,

$$I \vdash (x)(y)(\mathrm{prf}_I(x, \ulcorner (w)f(w) = 0 \urcorner) = 0 \vee f(y) = 0).$$

But from the definition of f we can show that

$$I \vdash (x)(f(x) = \mathrm{prf}_I(x, \ulcorner (w)f(w) = 0 \urcorner)),$$

and so

$$I \vdash (x)(y)(f(x) = 0 \vee f(y) = 0),$$

from which it follows that

$$I \vdash (x)f(x) = 0,$$

contradicting Gödel's theorem established earlier.   Q.E.D.

10.4 The demise of Hilbert's programme

If Hilbert's programme is to succeed we must provide a contentful proof of the outer consistency of some formal theory I containing arithmetic. What we have now shown is that this is impossible provided that I is strong enough to represent all contentful methods. But Gödel's first theorem already tells us that no formal theory is strong enough to prove every sentence of Goldbach type all of whose instances are true. So the theorem on the unprovability of outer consistency does not on its own refute the Hilbertian: there remains to be considered the possibility that there might be proofs that are finitary in Hilbert's sense but cannot be formalized in I. Gödel himself emphasized just this point in his 1931 paper: such unprovability results do not, he said,

contradict Hilbert's formalistic viewpoint. For this viewpoint presupposes only the existence of a consistency proof in which nothing but finitary means of proof is used, and it is conceivable that there exist finitary proofs that *cannot* be expressed in the formalism of [the system in question].[8]

Now it was central to Hilbert's project that the methods employed in metamathematical proofs should be justifiable from a finitist viewpoint, i.e. directly on the basis of the content supplied to us a priori by the structure of our experience of finite arrangements of concrete objects. So Gödel's suggestion that finitary methods might outrun any given formalism is flatly at variance with the last chapter, where we concluded that even when finitism is broadly conceived, its methods can always be represented within the formalism of **PRA**. The discrepancy is easy to explain, however: Gödel had correctly realized that the incompleteness theorem does not apply to the methods accepted by intuitionism; what he had not done was to distinguish intuitionism from finitism. This is hardly surprising since in the 1920s the two terms were used almost interchangeably. Herbrand, for example, throughout his writings referred to the methods usable in Hilbert's metamathematics as 'intuitionistic'. But in 1933 Gödel obtained a simple intuitionistic consistency proof for **PA**: no doubt what enabled him to clarify the distinction between finitism and intuitionism was the process of analysing where this proof used non-finitary methods. Then in 1936 Gerhard Gentzen supplied another constructive consistency proof for **PA** by a radically different method, employing induction as far as the transfinite ordinal

$$\varepsilon_0 = \omega^{\omega^{\omega^{\cdot^{\cdot^{\cdot}}}}} \; ;$$

[8]Ibid., I, 195.

Gentzen's method can be adapted to prove the corresponding result for **PRA**, using induction as far as ω^ω.

These two consistency proofs, Gödel's and Gentzen's, illustrate in somewhat different ways the point that the theorem in the last section is very far from preventing a proof of the outer consistency of **PA** from being genuinely informative, since each of them could be used to convince someone that classical arithmetic is consistent who was previously ignorant of that fact. Gödel's proof could be used to convince an intuitionist that the law of the excluded middle cannot in itself be responsible for introducing a contradiction into arithmetic, but it does nothing to address worries someone might have concerning the impredicativity of the unrestricted principle of mathematical induction. Gentzen's proof, on the other hand, avoids the standard accusation of circularity since the induction formulae which occur in it are always quantifier-free, but the proof nevertheless remains on its natural interpretation evidently non-finitary since it makes use of transfinite ordinals: it is plain that we cannot arrive at a conception of all the ordinals $< \omega^\omega$, far less all those $< \varepsilon_0$, directly from intuitions of finite arrangements of concrete objects.

But, as Gentzen himself showed in his paper, it is possible to arrive at such a conception indirectly by means of an extension of the device of arithmetization that we considered earlier. That is to say, we can represent every ordinal $< \varepsilon_0$ by a finite symbol of a recursively specifiable kind. The issue we should address, then, is whether we can arrive constructively at the correctness of the principle of transfinite induction for such symbols. Gentzen himself gave a rather indirect argument intended to establish that we can.

Most somehow constructivistically oriented authors place special emphasis on *building up constructively* (up to ω^ω, for example) an *initial segment* of the transfinite number sequence. ... I fail to see, however, at what 'point' that which is constructively indisputable is supposed to end, and where a further extension of transfinite induction is therefore thought to become disputable. I think, rather, that the reliability of the transfinite numbers required for the consistency proof compares with that of the first initial segments, say up to ω^2, in the same way as the reliability of a numerical calculation extending over a hundred pages with that of a calculation of a few lines: it is merely a considerably *vaster* undertaking to convince oneself of this certainty from beginning to end.[9]

On this view, then, quantifier-free induction as far as an ordinal α becomes gradually less reliable as α increases, but there is no definite point at which it requires for its justification any essentially new idea. It

[9] *Collected papers*, 286.

should be clear from what I said in the last chapter about the distinction between the narrow and broad conceptions of finitism that I disagree with Gentzen's view. It will be instructive to consider one coding of the ordinals in detail in order to see whether we can isolate a definite point at which the justification of transfinite induction does make use of a new idea.

Let us start with the case of transfinite induction as far as ω^ω. Since this suffices to prove a formalization of the outer consistency of **PRA**, we can be sure that its formalization cannot be proved in **PRA** itself. What we wish to do is to analyse what else is required. Our first task is to code every ordinal $< \omega^\omega$. To do this we use the fact that every such ordinal α can be written uniquely in *Cantor normal form*, i.e. as

$$\alpha = \omega^{n_1} + \omega^{n_2} + \cdots + \omega^{n_k} \quad (n_1 \geq n_2 \geq \cdots \geq n_k).$$

We can thus represent α by means of the finite sequence $(n_1, n_2, \ldots, n_k)$. This coding, which converts every ordinal $< \omega^\omega$ into a finite sequence of natural numbers, converts the usual ordering of the ordinals into a lexicographic ordering of such finite sequences.

The proof of the outer consistency of **PRA** proceeds by attaching to each proof in **PRA** an ordinal $\alpha < \omega^\omega$ and hence via the coding a finite sequence $(m_1, \ldots, m_k)$: an explicit method is then given of converting any proof of a false equation in **PRA** with ordinal α into another such proof whose associated ordinal β is less than α. The outer consistency of **PRA** follows if we know for any such α that the ordinals $< \alpha$ are well ordered. It is worth comparing this procedure with Hilbert's proof of the commutative law for addition which we quoted in the last chapter. That proof can be thought of as depending on the fact that for any numeral $\mathfrak{a}$ the numbers $< \mathfrak{a}$ are well ordered by the usual ordering. Our general grasp of this fact depends in turn on the notion of finiteness: in order to grasp a numeral $\mathfrak{a}$ *as* a numeral it is necessary to grasp it as finite and therefore implicitly to realize that there are only finitely many numerals less than it. The current case is different. Here we have to consider the finite sequence $(m_1, \ldots, m_k)$ which codes an arbitrary ordinal $\alpha < \omega^\omega$, and provide an argument to show that it cannot be the start of an infinite descending chain. We can show this for any particular $(m_1, \ldots, m_k)$ by means of an induction formalizable in **PRA**. The difficulty is that in order to prove it in general we find ourselves having to perform a second induction within which the first induction is nested.

We already know, of course, that this nested induction cannot be formalized in **PRA**, since otherwise we should be able to obtain a proof in **PRA** of its own outer consistency, contrary to Gödel's theorem.

What causes the trouble is that whichever way we try to represent the ordering of the ordinals $< \omega^\omega$ so as to make apparent that it is a well-ordering we find ourselves having to visualize an array that is infinite in two distinct respects, for instance a tree that is both infinitely deep and infinitely wide.

When we turn to Gentzen's proof for **PA**, the standard coding becomes even more elaborate. Any ordinal $\alpha < \varepsilon_0$ can be written in Cantor normal form as

$$\alpha = \omega^{\alpha_1} + \omega^{\alpha_2} + \cdots + \omega^{\alpha_k} \quad (\alpha > \alpha_1 \geq \alpha_2 \geq \cdots \geq \alpha_k).$$

Now write each of the exponents $\alpha_1, \alpha_2, \ldots, \alpha_k$ in Cantor normal form. Then write each of the exponents in these expressions in Cantor normal form. And so on. The procedure eventually terminates, at which point we have arrived at a representation of α by means of a finite sequence of finite sequences of ... of finite sequences of natural numbers.

The difficulty involved in seeing that these finite sequences are well-ordered by the appropriate ordering is that no bound on the complexity of the sequences is available in advance. So when we try to formalize the proof we find ourselves requiring an indefinite number of nested inductions. As Gödel observed,

one cannot grasp at one glance the various structural possibilities which exist for decreasing sequences, and there exists, therefore, no immediate concrete knowledge of the termination of every such sequence. But furthermore such concrete knowledge (in Hilbert's sense) cannot be realized either by a stepwise transition from smaller to larger ordinal numbers, because the concretely evident steps, such as $\alpha \rightarrow \alpha^2$, are so small that they would have to be repeated ε_0 times in order to reach ε_0.[10]

Much more recently Daniel Isaacson[11] has developed an argument that there is a stable notion of the arithmetical which coincides with what can be formalized in **PA** and hence suffices to license use of induction as far as any ordinal $< \varepsilon_0$ but not as far as ε_0 itself.

As we saw in the last chapter, it was not Hilbert's intention that a formal system of arithmetic could be given a purely logical proof of consistency and hence justified without any appeal to intuition. He thought rather that the proof could be based on our grasp of the structure of the finite arrangements of concrete objects that we encounter. He correctly saw that the consistency property he needed to prove could be expressed as a combinatorial theorem about such finite arrangements of objects, but his mistake was to think that this combinatorial theorem could be proved on the basis of our grasp of this structure on its own,

[10] *Works*, II, 273.   [11] 'Arithmetical truth and hidden higher-order concepts'.

without any appeal to infinitary properties, and hence that instances of the principle of induction in which the induction formula is of arbitrary logical complexity could be justified as consistent by appeal to the quantifier-free case alone. What Gödel's theorems demonstrate is that if the structure we use to ground arithmetic is that of the natural numbers then any increase in the logical complexity of the induction formulae is a genuine increase in the strength of the system and cannot be justified on that basis alone.

But basing arithmetic on a structure isomorphic to the natural numbers is not the only possibility. By the device of coding we can unwind infinite sets of natural numbers onto the transfinite ordinals in such a way that an induction of some logical complexity on the natural numbers converts into a quantifier-free induction as far as some transfinite ordinal. For any formal theory of arithmetic the upper bound of these ordinals is a measure of strength known as the proof-theoretic ordinal of the theory: the proof-theoretic ordinal of **EA** is ω; that of **PRA** is ω^ω; and that of **PA** is ε_0. What I have argued here, *contra* Gentzen, is that these three ordinals mark stable boundaries, in each case requiring a new concept to advance beyond them. The narrow finitist account will only justify induction as far as ordinals less than ω; the broad finitist account only as far as those less than ω^ω; and the account canvassed by Isaacson only as far as those less than ε_0.

10.5 The unprovability of consistency

There are many ways of expressing the consistency of a formal system of arithmetic within the system itself. We shall use here for convenience one that is fairly similar to the statement of outer consistency given earlier. Let Con_I be the sentence

$$(x)(y)(z)(w)(\mathrm{prf}_I(x,z) = 0 \vee \mathrm{prf}_I(w, \ulcorner \mathrm{inst}(z,y) \neq 0 \urcorner) = 0). \qquad (2)$$

This has as instances sentences of the form

$$(x)(y)(w)(\mathrm{prf}_I(x, \ulcorner (x)f(x) = 0 \urcorner) = 0$$
$$\vee \mathrm{prf}_I(w, \ulcorner \mathrm{inst}(\ulcorner (x)f(x) = 0 \urcorner, y) \neq 0 \urcorner) = 0),$$

which is provably equivalent in **PRA** to

$$(x)(y)(w)(\mathrm{prf}_I(x, \ulcorner (x)f(x) = 0 \urcorner) = 0 \vee \mathrm{prf}_I(w, \ulcorner f(y) \neq 0 \urcorner) = 0).$$

The instances of this are of the form

$$\mathrm{prf}_I(\mathsf{a}, \ulcorner (x)f(x) = 0 \urcorner) = 0 \vee \mathrm{prf}_I(\mathsf{c}, \ulcorner f(\mathsf{b}) \neq 0 \urcorner) = 0,$$

and these are all true if and only if whenever $(x) f(x) = 0$ is provable in I no inequation $f(\mathfrak{b}) \neq 0$ is also provable. Thus Con_I expresses that no sentence of Goldbach type that is provable in I has an instance whose negation is also provable in I, which is evidently a form of formal consistency for I.

At this point an unexpected complication emerges, though. It is the outer consistency of the ideal theory that ensures its reliability in drawing conclusions about quantifier-free arithmetic, but Hilbert generally couched the goal of his programme as being to prove only its consistency. This difference may hardly seem worth remarking on at first since, as we have already noted, consistency and outer consistency are equivalent for the theories we are considering. So we might expect the theorem on the unprovability of $\mathrm{Outercon}_I$ proved in § 10.3 to carry over straightforwardly to a theorem on the unprovability of Con_I. But a difference between the two emerges when we try to formalize in I the proof that Con_I and $\mathrm{Outercon}_I$ are equivalent. In order to do this we must impose a further condition on the proof function for I. It is not enough that the proof function should be extensionally adequate to represent which strings of signs are proofs of which sentences. When we proved Gödel's theorem on outer consistency we assumed that the theory I extends $\mathbf{PRA}_0$, and hence that every true numerical equation $f(n_1, \ldots, n_k) = 0$ and every true inequation $f(n_1, \ldots, n_k) \neq 0$ is provable in I. Moreover, by further assuming that I extends $\mathbf{PRA}$ we ensured that the obvious methods of proving such equations and inequations by direct calculation from the defining equations for the functions involved will count as proofs in I. But we did not rule out the possibility that the fact that these obvious methods do count as proofs in I might depend on some further condition which, although true, is non-trivially so. We need to rule this out by supposing that the provability function obeys — and can be shown in I to obey — a sort of uniformity condition which we shall call 'well-presentedness'. Informally the idea of describing I as well presented is that for each primitive recursive function there should be a mechanical method of calculating the values of f whose validity can be demonstrated within I. More formally, we say that a provability function prf_I is *well presented* if for every primitive recursive function f there is a primitive recursive function d such that

$$I \vdash (x)(f(x) = 0 \supset \mathrm{prf}_I(dx, \ulcorner f(x) = 0 \urcorner) \neq 0)$$

and

$$I \vdash (x)(f(x) \neq 0 \supset \mathrm{prf}_I(dx, \ulcorner f(x) \neq 0 \urcorner) \neq 0)$$

We shall show now that the well-presentedness of the provability function is the condition we need if we are to formalize in I the deduction of outer consistency from consistency.

Lemma. *If I is a formal theory and prf_I is a well presented provability function for I, then $I, \mathrm{Con}_I \vdash \mathrm{Outercon}_I$.*

Proof. Recall that Con_I is the sentence

$$(x)(y)(z)(w)(\mathrm{prf}_I(x, z) = 0 \vee \mathrm{prf}_I(w, \ulcorner \mathrm{inst}(z, y) \neq 0 \urcorner) = 0).$$

Now since prf_I is well presented there is a primitive recursive function d such that the sentence

$$(y)(z)(\mathrm{inst}(z, y) = 0 \vee \mathrm{prf}_I(d(z, y), \ulcorner \mathrm{inst}(z, y) \neq 0 \urcorner) \neq 0)$$

is provable in I. If we combine these two sentences, we can easily obtain by first-order logic

$$(x)(y)(z)(\mathrm{prf}_I(x, z) = 0 \vee \mathrm{inst}(x, y) = 0),$$

i.e. $\mathrm{Outercon}_I$.   Q.E.D.

Gödel's second incompleteness theorem. *If I is a consistent formal theory which extends* **PRA** *and prf_I is a well presented provability function for I, then Con_I is not provable in I.*

Proof. This follows at once from the above lemma and the theorem on the unprovability of outer consistency in § 10.3.   Q.E.D.

We have not shown here how to construct a proof function for any of the standard theories such as **PA** . If we had done so, we should now have the further task of showing that our proof function is indeed well presented, so that we could then conclude from the theorem just established that the corresponding consistency sentence is unprovable in the system.

Of course the fact that we have used the well-presentedness of prf_I in establishing Gödel's second theorem does not in itself establish that it — or indeed *any* extra condition on prf_I — is necessary, but in fact it is. It is possible to construct examples of non-well-presented proof functions for which the theorem fails. To see how such examples come about let us first try to analyse in more detail what the well-presentedness of I amounts to.

Roughly speaking, the idea is that **PRA** should not only be contained in I but should be embedded in it in a straightforward manner. Suppose that f is a primitive recursive function. There is an obvious method available to us within **PRA** of testing for any n whether $f(n) = 0$ or not: simply calculate $f(n)$ using the defining equations for f. Such a calculation will always constitute a proof in **PRA** either of the equation $f(n) = 0$ or of the inequation $f(n) \neq 0$. Let $\phi(n)$ be whichever of these two the calculation proves. Since I is an extension of **PRA**, the calculation will constitute a proof in I of $\phi(n)$ too. Let the Gödel number of this proof be $d(n)$. Now calculate $\mathrm{prf}_I(d(n), \ulcorner \phi(n) \urcorner)$. Since $d(n)$ is the Gödel number of a proof in I of the sentence whose Gödel number is $\ulcorner \phi(n) \urcorner$, it is plain that $\mathrm{prf}_I(d(n), \ulcorner \phi(n) \urcorner) \neq 0$.

Now the point of going through this in detail is to note that it is in almost every respect a finitistically acceptable argument. Therefore we would expect it to be formalizable in **PRA** and hence in I, so that

$$I \vdash (x)(\phi(x) \supset \mathrm{prf}_I(d(x), \ulcorner \phi(x) \urcorner) \neq 0),$$

i.e. prf_I is well presented. So how can prf_I ever fail to be well presented? The only way this is possible is if the fact I described as 'plain', namely that $\mathrm{prf}_I(d(n), \ulcorner \phi(n) \urcorner) \neq 0$, depends for its truth on some feature of I that is not formalizable in I.

Suppose, for instance, that $\mathrm{prf}_{\mathbf{PA}}$ is a well presented proof function for **PA**. Now define a new function $\mathrm{prf}'_{\mathbf{PA}}$ so that $\mathrm{prf}'_{\mathbf{PA}}(x,y) = 1$ if and only if x is the Gödel number of a proof of the sentence whose Gödel number is y and this sentence does not contradict any sentence whose proof has a lower Gödel number than x. Now by Gödel's second theorem $\mathrm{Con}_{\mathbf{PA}}$ is not provable in **PA**; but the sentence $\mathrm{Con}'_{\mathbf{PA}}$ obtained from $\mathrm{Con}_{\mathbf{PA}}$ by replacing $\mathrm{prf}_{\mathbf{PA}}$ with $\mathrm{prf}'_{\mathbf{PA}}$ throughout is easily seen to be provable in **PA**, and it follows that $\mathrm{prf}'_{\mathbf{PA}}$ cannot be well presented. What this example shows very clearly is that whether a provability function is well presented does indeed depend on how it is presented and not solely on the values it takes, for $\mathrm{prf}_{\mathbf{PA}}$ and $\mathrm{prf}'_{\mathbf{PA}}$ do in fact take the same values for all arguments because **PA** is consistent.

The importance of this example and others like it for assessing Hilbert's programme is, however, largely historical. When Gödel stated his second incompleteness theorem in his 1931 paper, he couched it in terms of consistency rather than outer consistency and restricted it to the particular (well presented) provability function defined in that paper; but he did not give the proof, which was to have been included in a second part of the paper that never appeared. The first to publish a proof of the second incompleteness theorem were Hilbert and Bernays in 1939,[12] who gave it in a more general form that applied to all proof

---

[12] *Grundlagen der Mathematik*, II, § 5, no. 1(c).

functions satisfying what have become known as Hilbert's derivability conditions. These conditions are somewhat more restrictive than is necessary: they imply but are not implied by the condition of well-presentedness given here. But examples such as the one just considered make it plain that *some* condition on what can be proved in the theory about the proof function is needed if it is to be impossible for the consistency sentence to be provable in the theory itself. As a result some of the subsequent discussions of whether Gödel's second theorem refutes Hilbert's programme have been diverted into considering whether Hilbert's derivability conditions embody a reasonable restriction on the notion of a proof function.

It was Gödel himself who made the discovery that no such extra conditions are needed in order to guarantee that the outer consistency sentence is unprovable, but he did not publish this result until 1967.[13] He described it a few years later as 'the best and most general version of the unprovability of consistency in the same system' and suggested that 'perhaps it has not received sufficient notice'.[14] Its importance lies precisely in the fact that it demonstrates the issue of the derivability conditions to be irrelevant to the assessment of whether Hilbert's programme is feasible: whether or not its provability predicate is well presented, the outer consistency of a formal theory extending **PRA** cannot be proved finitistically.

10.6 Axiomatic formalism

The unprovability of outer consistency thus suffices to refute Hilbert's programme narrowly conceived. But Hilbert's idea of distinguishing between the real and the ideal parts of a theory could be applied more widely. The original programme was to justify the use of ideal methods by showing that numerical equations and inequations proved by their means must be true, but, as we saw in the last chapter, this programme had two strands which Hilbert developed in response to two quite distinct sorts of criticism of his use of the axiomatic method in mathematics. On the one hand Frege's criticism of Hilbert's idea that consistency implies existence drove him in the 1920s towards his distinctive version of formalism according to which ideal methods could be shown to be reliable by a metamathematical proof of conservativeness. On the other, his search for an epistemologically secure source of content that could ground the real part of mathematics a priori without

[13] *Works*, I, 235. [14] Ibid., II, 305.

depending on questionable assumptions about the structure of space and time led him to the finitary viewpoint. It is these two strands taken together that Gödel's theorem on the unprovability of outer consistency shows to be incompatible. It is worth pausing, therefore, to consider what becomes of the first of these strands if it is disentangled from the second. And it is here that the stronger claim of the unprovability of consistency, which requires the condition that the provability function be well presented, becomes relevant.

The idea, then, is that we could justify the use of a formal theory by showing that it is entirely dispensable. That is to say, our aim in general is to show that an ideal theory I is *conservative over* a real theory R. The case Hilbert considered was one where R is quantifier-free arithmetic, but there are many others that might be fruitful. For instance, R might simply be a formalization of the non-mathematical language we use to describe the world ordinarily, together with the logical apparatus of the ramified theory of types, and I might be the result of adding to R the problematic axioms of infinity and reducibility: if in this case I could be shown to be conservative over R we could apply the results of *Principia* without having to respond to Wittgenstein's doubts over the validity of the extra axioms. Another notable case is that in which R contains second-order logic and I adds Frege's numerical equivalence to it: if in this case I could be shown to be conservative over R, Frege's concern to supply an argument that the two sides of the numerical equivalence have the same sense would drop away as redundant. A third case is the programme outlined by Hartry Field in *Science Without Numbers*. There R is a scientific theory that counts by his lights as nominalistic; I contains a significant part of mathematics. Field's view of mathematics is not on its face formalist, for he regards it as containing genuinely meaningful sentences which would, if true, refer to abstract objects such as numbers. But since he does not believe that we could know anything about such objects, he does not think we are ever entitled to treat sentences referring to them as true or false. So the only justification possible for making use of the ideal sentences in reasoning about the real ones is just the Hilbertian one that I can be shown to be conservative over R. The meanings of the ideal sentences are thus idle wheels in Field's account.

Although Gödel's theorem on the unprovability of outer consistency allowed us to circumvent all discussion of the well-presentedness of the provability function where it was only Hilbert's original programme that was in question, in the more general setting now under consideration it becomes a live question once more whether it is ever possible to give an informative proof that an ideal theory I is conservative over a real theory R using only resources that were already available in R. We have already seen an example of a theory which proves its own consistency, so it seems possible in principle that if I were such a theory a proof of conservativeness might be possible. In all the cases just outlined the ideal theory certainly extends **PRA**. So if we are to have a chance of proving that any of them is conservative over the corresponding real theory by methods that the real theory validates, Gödel's theorem tells us that the provability function cannot be well presented.

The method of axiomatic formalism is so general that I doubt if there is any argument to show that the constraint of well-presentedness is justified in all cases. In the current context, though, where what concerns us is the grounding of arithmetic, it surely is. As I have argued above, a theory which is not well presented must be one in which the validity of the method of direct calculation of the values of primitive recursive functions from their defining equations is not provable within the theory. I said at the start that our task would be to justify arithmetic as standardly practised. That must mean that the ideal formal theory I is constrained to be one which validates not only the *results* of ordinary arithmetical calculations but the calculations themselves, and hence cannot prove its own formal consistency.

11

Carnap

The *Tractatus*, as we presented it in Chapter 6, is an attempt to reconfigure the self. Kant had conceived of it as supplying the spatial and temporal structure through which we experience the world. Wittgenstein, by contrast, conceived of it as constituted by, or at any rate knowable by us only through, the relationship between language and the world. The self is thus for Wittgenstein the paradigm of what is unsayable. (Indeed in the widest sense the unsayable just *is* the self.) In Vienna during the 1920s there emerged a group of philosophers — the logical positivists — who wished to deny that any metaphysical questions are meaningful. In particular, although they held much of the *Tractatus* in high regard, they took the parts of it which gesture towards the unsayable — especially the mystical sections near the end of the book — to embody a straightforward mistake on Wittgenstein's part. If they accepted the Tractarian conception of language, even in outline, their position thus amounted to a denial of the concept of the self. What will interest us here, in light of the suggestion already made that our grasp of arithmetic is located in the relationship between the self and the world, is the extent to which the positivists' account of arithmetic, the *locus classicus* for which is Carnap's *Logical Syntax of Language*, survives their denial of metaphysics.

11.1 Language and symbolism

Logical Syntax of Language contains detailed descriptions of the syntax of two formal languages (imaginatively entitled Language I and Language II). Although Carnap's descriptions of these languages are original in certain respects, what will interest us here is rather the account that follows of the features of formal languages in general. Even tough it is in the end profoundly unTractarian, Carnap took his account to be one whose general outlines the *Tractatus* endorsed. The phrase 'logical syntax' which he uses as his title occurs repeatedly in the *Tractatus*, and he quotes with approval Wittgenstein's admonition:

In logical syntax the meaning of a sign ought never to play a rôle; it must admit of being established without mention being thereby made of the *meaning* of the sign: it ought to presuppose *only* the description of the expressions.[1]

One of the features of formal languages that Carnap was much struck by was the fact that by means of arithmetization their formation rules (what Carnap called their *definite* syntax) can be precisely described in a relatively weak metalanguage such as Carnap's Language I. Since all the languages that interest us are at least as strong as this, we may conclude, Carnap said, that

in every language S, the syntax of any language whatsoever — whether of an entirely different kind of language, or of a sub-language, or even of S itself — can be formulated to an extent which is limited only by the richness in means of expression of the language S.[2]

There is no doubting the importance Carnap attached to the realization that the definite syntax of a language is expressible within it. He later described how

the members of the Circle, in contrast to Wittgenstein, came to the conclusion that it is possible to speak about language and, in particular, about the structures of linguistic expressions. On the basis of this conception, I developed the idea of the logical syntax of a language as the purely analytic theory of the structure of its expressions.[3]

Carnap underlines this 'contrast to Wittgenstein' in *Logical Syntax of Language* itself,[4] but his way of putting the point misrepresents Wittgenstein's position. Wittgenstein certainly thought that the syntax of a language could not be regulated by means of formal rules; but the reason for this was that 'the rules of logical syntax must follow of themselves, if we only know how every single sign signifies.'[5] If we have read the signs as symbols, we are powerless to limit by formal rules the combinations of these symbols that are meaningful: that is determined not by us or by our conventions but by the shape of logical space. If, on the other hand, we have not yet read the signs as symbols, we do not in Wittgenstein's view have a language at all: we simply have a row of signs. Nothing Wittgenstein says in the *Tractatus* suggests that he thought one could not formulate formal rules for manipulating signs, or indeed that one could not do so within the language in question. But insofar as these rules are arbitrary, they are invalid; and insofar as they are not, they go without saying.

Carnap's misrepresentation of Wittgenstein is instructive because it is just here that the difference between their conceptions lies. For

---

[1] *TLP*, 3.33.   [2] *Syntax*, § 18.   [3] 'Intellectual autobiography', 53.   [4] § 73.   [5] *TLP*, 3.334.

Wittgenstein a system of signs could not be a language without being *someone's* language; and it becomes someone's language when its propositional signs are read as propositions, i.e. as bearers of sense. It is this part of Wittgenstein's conception that is wholly absent from Carnap's. The consequences of this will emerge as we progress.

11.2 *The rejection of the* Tractatus

I mentioned in § 6.6 that in the *Tractatus* elementary propositions are to be taken as independent of each other: if a logical dependency exists between two propositions, that is to be taken simply as evidence that the propositions in question are not yet fully analysed. The example Wittgenstein considers is that of colours:

For two colours ... to be at one place in the visual field, is impossible, logically impossible, for it is excluded by the logical structure of colour. ... (It is clear that the logical product of two elementary propositions can neither be a tautology nor a contradiction. The assertion that a point in the visual field has two different colours at the same time, is a contradiction.)[6]

The conclusion, therefore, is that the statement that a point in the visual field is red cannot be an elementary proposition: it must be further analysable into other, simpler propositions. Now the *Tractatus* contains, as we have seen, an outline of the features a language must have in order to be a language. What it does not contain is any of the details of how to analyse actual languages into Tractarian form. In it Wittgenstein displays a striking insouciance as to what the elementary propositions of language actually are. In particular, he does not trouble to say what the 'logical structure' of colour is that shows the presence of two colours at the same place in the visual field to be logically impossible. This vagueness as to detail was antithetical to the aim of the Vienna Circle, which was to apply to philosophy the methods of precise scientific enquiry. (Several of its members had a predominantly scientific background.) As a result this difficulty over the analysis of colour words was for the Circle a serious objection to Wittgenstein's account. And although Wittgenstein never shared their view of philosophy as science — Carnap described his attitudes as 'more similar to those of a creative artist than to those of a scientist'[7] — he did come to accept that the practical problems of analysing natural language were relevant to assessing the success of the *Tractatus*. In 1929 he published an article (his only one) in which he addressed the problem of analysing colour words. This led him to make what he described as his 'first definite

[6]Ibid. 6.3751.   [7]'Intellectual autobiography', 25.

remark on the logical analysis of actual phenomena', namely 'that for their representation numbers (rational and irrational) must enter into the structure of the atomic propositions themselves.'[8] In the article itself this remark is presented as if it were no more than a minor adjustment of his former view, but if it is right it has two consequences which refute entirely the Tractarian account of mathematics. First, by allowing that number terms may occur in elementary propositions he admitted numbers as objects, even though the adjectival strategy he had adopted in the *Tractatus* is quite unable to explain the substantival occurrences of number terms that he now countenanced. Second, by allowing that both rational *and* irrational numbers might be necessary for the correct analysis of the grammar of colour words he admitted the need for an account of mathematics that goes beyond quantifier-free arithmetic, an account which the *Tractatus* simply cannot supply.

Wittgenstein's own response to these two inadequacies in his earlier account of mathematics led him rapidly to views too far removed from our current narrative to be considered here. The positivists, on the other hand, tried at first to adhere quite closely to the account of logic presented in the *Tractatus*, according to which language is designed to fit the world it attempts to describe and the tautologies of logic are merely a by-product of this attempt. If numbers are objects, as Wittgenstein's views now made them seem to be, arithmetic presumably consists of propositions, not pseudo-propositions as in the *Tractatus*. The necessity of these propositions must therefore consist in their being tautologies, since the *Tractatus* allows no other sense in which a proposition *can* be necessary. The positivists thus hoped to show that mathematics too consists of tautologies — if they were to accept Wittgenstein's framework it was essential to their project that this should be so — but they did not know how to go about the task. It was natural, therefore, that they should study Ramsey's work with great interest, even though in the end they did not accept it. (Indeed in an article he wrote in 1930 Ramsey's is almost the only account of mathematics Carnap decisively rejects.) The positivists may well have been influenced in this by Wittgenstein's conviction that Ramsey's notion of propositional function in extension, and hence his definition of identity, is incoherent. Certainly members of the Vienna Circle — Waismann and Schlick (and Carnap until Wittgenstein excluded him) — met Wittgenstein frequently between 1928 and 1931 to discuss the philosophy of mathematics, and Wittgenstein's objection to Ramsey was one of the topics discussed. But it is not entirely clear that Carnap understood Wittgenstein's point; the nearest he came to criticizing

[8]'Some remarks on logical form'.

Ramsey's notion of propositional function in extension in print was to dub it 'theological'.[9]

Whatever his reasons, though, Carnap came to believe that mathematics is not tautological in Wittgenstein's sense. What this suggested to him was that he should replace Wittgenstein's notion of tautology with a notion of analyticity that was — at least potentially — richer, but retain what he regarded as Wittgenstein's fundamental insight that the propositions of logic are devoid of content. To achieve this Carnap added to his requirements for the specification of a language that in addition to formal rules of syntax to determine which strings of signs are to count as sentences there should also be defined a relation of consequence between sentences. His great insight was that once the consequence relation is in place, other notions such as that of analyticity can be defined in terms of it. The key notion is that of determinacy: a sentence is *determinate* if its truth or falsity is settled by the consequence relation alone. Which parts of the vocabulary of the language are to count as *logical* is defined so that any sentence formed solely from logical vocabulary is determinate: the logical vocabulary is defined to be the largest set of vocabulary elements that has this property, if such a set exists; if there is no unique largest set, we take as the logical vocabulary the intersection of all the maximal sets with the property. Any vocabulary that is not logical is called *descriptive*. Sentences which are consequences of the empty set, and remain so under all substitutions of descriptive vocabulary, are called analytic; those of which anything is a consequence, and which retain this property under all substitutions of descriptive vocabulary, are called contradictory.

Carnap's account thus turns Wittgenstein's conception of language upside down. According to Wittgenstein we fashion language to describe the world. 'The *application* of logic decides what elementary propositions there are.'[10] Logic — tautologies — is a by-product, albeit an inevitable one, of this process. According to Carnap it is the notion of consequence that is primary. The part of language that we use to describe the world — the descriptive vocabulary — is the by-product since it consists of elements which contribute to form sentences whose truth or falsity the language does not determine.

11.3 Conventionalism

By separating the syntactic description of a language from the question of its meaning, in contrast to Wittgenstein, Carnap committed himself

[9]'Die Mathematik als Zweig der Logik', 307. [10]*TLP*, 5.557.

to a species of formalism. But as we saw in Chapter 3, formalism faces powerful objections. It is a delicate matter to construct a position that evades them all. To see this we shall consider in some detail a position that Carnap in fact came to reject.

We have seen that Carnap placed the notion of consequence at the centre of his conception. It might seem natural at this point to say that in order for a formal system of the kind Carnap discusses to be genuinely a *language* what is needed is that the notion of consequence we define in it should conform to certain constraints that entitle it to be regarded as instantiating the notion of logical consequence. What these constraints are would be a matter for investigation by means which, even if they could no longer conform to the details of those employed in the *Tractatus*, would at any rate be recognizably analogous to them.

Logical consequence would thus be conceived as a language-transcendent concept which fashions logical space and limits all languages in a uniform way. Carnap's position would then be a case of axiomatic structuralism. It would, however, be a degenerate case because Carnap accepted that mathematics is part of logic. There would thus be no need for any axioms: everything would be loaded onto the consequence relation.

Because of its degeneracy the position would evade the objections to axiomatic structuralism considered earlier. The Julius Caesar problem would not arise, because the account would now be applied in the most thoroughgoing manner possible, not merely to arithmetic but to the whole of language. There would, moreover, be no problem about formal consistency since there would be no axioms. The consistency of the consequence relation itself would not be an issue once it was established that it was indeed *logical* consequence that was in question.

A substantial problem would remain, though, namely to determine for any particular formal language the scope of the relation of consequence. This would be delimited by means of various rules of inference within the language. Instances of what is involved were supplied by Carnap in his descriptions of Language I and Language II. The old debates as to the logical validity of the axiom of infinity and the axiom of reducibility or the coherence of Ramsey's notion of propositional function in extension would arise just as before, but slightly relocated.

The position just described may be regarded as unifying logicism with formalism. It is superficially attractive, and towards the end of the 1920s Carnap advocated something that approximates to it.[11] It is, however, completely incoherent. The position diagnoses the standard

---

[11] 'Die Mathematik als Zweig der Logik'.

objections to axiomatic structuralism as demonstrating the futility of attempting to attach a formal language to an already existing interpreted language. It avoids those objections by conceiving of the *whole* of language as formal, but just by doing so it renders the notion of *logical* consequence inapplicable to it. If a sentence contains some logical vocabulary, we cannot tell what its logical consequences are until we know what the logical vocabulary means. But since we are now being recommended to conceive of the logical vocabulary as having no meaning other than that given to it by the rules that define the notion of consequence, we have evidently arrived at a stalemate.

What the stalemate demonstrates is that the notion of logical consequence has no application to meaningless strings of signs. Compromise formalism will not work. If we are to regard our language as formal, we must go the whole hog and claim that no sense can be given to the notion of a language-transcendent concept of logical consequence. The rules that implicitly define the notion of consequence for a language cannot therefore be answerable to any external constraints on their coherence: they are mere conventions, just as the formation rules for the language are.

This position, which we shall refer to as *conventionalism*, is the one Carnap adopted in *Logical Syntax of Language* under the guise of what he encapsulated as the 'Principle of Tolerance' or, as he once suggested it should more exactly be called, 'principle of the conventionality of language forms': this is the proposal that 'it is not our business to set up prohibitions, but to arrive at conventions';[12] or, more catchily but less precisely, 'In logic there are no morals.'[13]

Even before *Logical Syntax* Carnap was attempting to conciliate between rival accounts of the philosophy of mathematics by adopting elements of each of them. The Principle of Tolerance enabled him to take this conciliatory approach to the extreme by accepting on their own terms *all* of the apparently conflicting positions, and denying the existence of a perspective from which to arbitrate between them on any but practical grounds. When we discussed the axiomatic structuralist view of geometry, we remarked that it leaves the word 'triangle' as it occurs in the axioms of Euclidean and of non-Euclidean geometry without any but a verbal similarity to connect them and therefore makes it puzzling how the difference between the two geometries can be understood as hinging on whether the angles of a triangle sum to two right angles. Carnap's view, by extending formalism to logic itself, draws exactly the same conclusion for the logical connectives. If classical logic accepts, and intuitionistic logic rejects, the law of excluded middle, for

---

[12] *Syntax*, § 17. [13] Ibid.

example, this only serves to show that the sign 'V' does not mean the same in the two calculi. We therefore cannot formulate the difference between them as a difference in the properties of disjunction. It is thus on this account an illusion to suppose that there is a unitary notion of disjunction whose properties the intuitionist and the classical logician disagree about, and with their disagreement thus disarmed neither can be pronounced right or wrong:

Once the fact is realized that all the pros and cons of the Intuitionist discussions are concerned with the forms of a calculus, questions will no longer be put in the form: 'What is this or that like?' but instead we shall ask: 'How do we wish to arrange this or that in the language to be constructed?' or, from the theoretical standpoint: 'What consequences will ensue if we construct a language in this or that way?' On this view the dogmatic attitude which renders so many discussions unfruitful disappears.[14]

Indeed what is striking is just how many of the discussions in the philosophy of mathematics become on the basis of the Principle of Tolerance quite pointless. If Carnap's account is right, Ramsey should not have wasted his time explaining why on his view the primitive propositions of type theory were tautological: all he needed to do was state the rules and shut up, since the decision whether to accept the theory is to be made solely on practical grounds.

11.4 Completeness

According to the Principle of Tolerance, then, there are no theoretical constraints that the consequence relation of a language must satisfy. In particular, each of the formal theories that have arisen in our discussion (**PRA**, **PA**, etc.) determines a consequence relation in an obvious way. Now we mentioned before that Carnap's division of the vocabulary of a language into a logical and a descriptive part depends on the consequence relation for the language in such a way that every logical sentence is automatically either analytic or contradictory. The logical part of a Carnapian language is thus always trivially complete. But there is no magic here: if the consequence relation is one determined by an incomplete theory, it must follow that some of the vocabulary of the language does not count as logical under Carnap's definition.

Two contrasting examples will make this plain. The theory $\mathbf{PRA}_0$ of quantifier-free arithmetic is complete: so when we regard it as a Carnapian language all its vocabulary will count as logical. Since it has no descriptive vocabulary at all, it cannot be used to talk about the world

---

[14]Ibid., § 16.

and Carnap's conventionalism reduces, when applied to it, to precisely the crude formalism considered in §0.5. Now **PRA**, by contrast, is incomplete, as Gödel's first incompleteness theorem shows, and so its vocabulary cannot be wholly logical. But **PRA** contains $\mathbf{PRA}_0$, and the only vocabulary that it adds is the universal quantifier. So in **PRA** the universal quantifier must count (bizarrely) as descriptive. Nor is the difficulty particular to **PRA**. Because of its generality Gödel's theorem presents Carnap with a dilemma: every Carnapian language strong enough to contain quantified arithmetic must either have a non-effective consequence relation or make some arithmetical vocabulary count as descriptive.

However bizarre it may seem for a quantifier that is intended to range over the natural numbers to come out as descriptive even though all the numerals are logical, there is from the syntactic perspective no principled objection that can be mounted against the idea. It is therefore only in order to conform to familiar usages that Carnap arranged for each of the two languages he defined in detail in *Logical Syntax of Language* to have a consequence relation that makes the universal quantifier logical and not descriptive. His Language I, for instance, is the Carnapian analogue of the theory $\mathbf{PRA}^{\omega}$ obtained from **PRA** by adding the ω-rule:

$$\frac{\phi(\mathfrak{a}) \text{ for every numeral } \mathfrak{a}}{(x)\phi(x)}$$

The difficulty with this rule, as we have already observed (§ 10.2), is that it has infinitely many premisses and is therefore not finitistic. So $\mathbf{PRA}^{\omega}$ is not a formal theory and the consequence relation it determines is not effective: in Carnap's parlance it is *indefinite*. In Language II, which corresponds to the simple theory of types recommended by Ramsey, Carnap's definition of consequence mimics what we should nowadays recognize as the *semantic* notion of consequence for the system: it is saved from being a semantic definition, however, by replacing all mention of individuals with use of their names. It is therefore extensionally the same as the corresponding semantic notion provided that we assume all individuals have names in the language. The definition is once again, of course, in Carnap's sense indefinite, i.e. non-effective.

11.5 Consistency

We have already noted in §9.1 that on a formalist view of arithmetic there is no reason to be any more alarmed by a proof of the string

'0 = 1' than of '0 = 0'. Quine made a similar point in lectures he gave at Harvard in 1934:

Let us now consider the protest ... that our freedom in assigning truth by convention is subject to restrictions imposed by the requirement of consistency. ... Consistency in the assignment of truth is nothing more than a special case of conformity to usage. If we make a mark in the margin opposite an expression '− − −', and another opposite '∼ − − −', we sin only against the established usage of '∼' as a denial sign. Under the latter usage '− − −' and '∼ − − −' are not both true; in taking them both by convention as true we merely endow the sign '∼', roughly speaking, with a meaning other than denial. Indeed, we might so conduct our assignments of truth as to allow no sign of our language to behave analogously to the denial locution of ordinary usage; perhaps the resulting language would be inconvenient, but conventions are often inconvenient. It is only the objective of ending up with our mother tongue that dissuades us from marking both '− − −' and '∼ − − −', and this objective would dissuade us also from marking 'It is always cold on Thursday'.[15]

On Carnap's conventionalist view consistency is thus downgraded from an absolute constraint on any language to a matter of mere convenience. Arthur Prior once famously suggested adding to logic a connective 'tonk' with the following inference rules:

$$\frac{P}{P \text{ tonk } Q} \qquad \frac{P \text{ tonk } Q}{Q}$$

He called 'tonk' a runabout inference ticket because it allows us to infer any sentence from any other in two simple steps. There is on Carnap's view nothing theoretically askew with a language containing this connective.

In an article called 'Is mathematics syntax of language?',[16] which went through numerous drafts but was not published in his lifetime, Gödel attempted to argue that this is a mistake: consistency is an absolute constraint on language and not a matter of mere convenience since, as 'tonk' illustrates, if we adopt an inconsistent convention we can make anything whatever true, but the empirical world is plainly not thus beholden to linguistic conventions. Gödel's argument does not even get off the ground when applied to Carnap, however, because Carnap did not accept the language-independent notion of the empirical which Gödel's argument depends on.[17] The partition of the vocabulary of a language into the logical and the descriptive is defined by Carnap *in terms of* the prior definition of consequence for the language. Moreover,

[15] *The Ways of Paradox*, 96–7. [16] *Works*, III, 334–63. [17] Cf. Ricketts, 'Carnap's principle of tolerance ... '.

the definition is constructed in such a way that the requirement Gödel placed on the language simply cannot be stated. Gödel wanted to be assured that the mathematical axioms do not entail empirical assertions to which the language is not independently committed already, but this way of shearing off the mathematical part of a language is simply not available to Carnap. The only way of shearing off mathematics is to change our definition of consequence, but this is to adopt an entirely new language, within which the partition into logical and descriptive will be different. There is no reason to expect any principled way of mapping the descriptive sentences of the old language onto the new language in order to be able to formulate the claim Gödel wanted to settle.

11.6 Semantics

A Carnapian language derived from an incomplete mathematical theory will make some of the mathematical vocabulary count as descriptive. If the theory is inconsistent, on the other hand, the embarrassment is in the opposite direction: since every sentence is derivable, every sentence is determinate, and the language has no descriptive vocabulary at all. However bizarre such languages may seem, though, *Logical Syntax of Language* gives us no theoretical justification for ruling them out. The reason is that the book contains no theory of semantics. When he wrote it, indeed, Carnap thought that a rigorous account of semantics was impossible. It is true that he referred frequently to the notion of a material interpretation for a language, but he was at pains to point out that this is inexact and non-formal:

If a material interpretation is given for a language S, then the symbols, expressions, and sentences of S may be divided into logical and descriptive, i.e. those which have a purely logical, or mathematical, meaning and those which designate something extra-logical — such as empirical objects, properties, and so forth. This classification is not only inexact but also non-formal, and thus not applicable in syntax.[18]

So when I described Carnap's definition of the consequence relation in Language II as mimicking the corresponding semantic notion, that is to be seen as merely an informal motivational remark. Carnap did not suppose that a semantic notion of consequence is available to underpin the syntactic definition.

This entirely syntactic account did not last long: even before *Logical Syntax of Language* appeared in German in 1934, Tarski's account of

[18] *Syntax*, § 50.

semantics[19] had already appeared in Polish. Thereafter Carnap hurried to revise his theory to take account of the new science of semantics. By 1939 Carnap was writing that the syntactical rules

can be chosen arbitrarily and hence are conventional if they are taken as the basis of the construction of the language system and if the interpretation of the system is later superimposed. On the other hand, a system of logic is not a matter of choice, but either right or wrong, if an interpretation of the logical signs is given in advance.[20]

In other words, the introduction of a theory of semantics is to be seen as a constraint on the Principle of Tolerance.

Now from any perspective not embedded in the somewhat obsessively scientific outlook of the Vienna Circle it may seem odd not to take a constraint seriously until one has a theory about it, and it is hard to see what point there could be in studying languages that are incapable of interpretation. The issues that concern us here do not in any case depend on any particular theory of semantics. All we need to suppose is that an interpretation of a language involves mapping all the descriptive sentences of the language onto claims about the world. What these claims are need not concern us greatly. Indeed the more loosely we interpret this notion the better, since if we were to presume a precisely delineated domain of facts existing independent of language, we should be in a position to resurrect precisely the language-independent notion of logical consequence that Carnap rejected.

The constraint of interpretability now allows us to expose the difficulty with the first horn of the dilemma mentioned earlier, namely that a consequence relation derived from a mathematical theory either makes some of the mathematical vocabulary descriptive or is non-effective. The difficulty with supposing that some of the mathematical vocabulary is descriptive is that some mathematical sentences will then have to be interpreted as making claims about the world.

It is plain that no logical positivist could tolerate this. But even a diehard platonist, who thinks that the world has an abstract as well as a physical part and that mathematics makes claims about the abstract part just as physics does about the physical part, will find the position uncomfortable. What is odd about such a language is that it will typically make only *some* of the mathematical vocabulary descriptive. In the case we considered earlier of a language derived from **PRA** we saw that the numerals came out as logical but the universal quantifier did not. So the Gödel sentence $(x)\phi(x)$ has its truth or falsity determined by how things are in the realm of numbers, but its instances $\phi(0)$, $\phi(1)$,

[19] *Pojecie prawdy w jezykach nauk dedukcyjnych.*   [20] *Foundations of logic and mathematics*, 48.

etc. are all true by dint of linguistic convention alone. This is scarcely what the platonist had in mind.

It seems, then, that once we take the need for interpretation into account we shall all, of any metaphysical stripe or none, be forced onto the other horn of the dilemma and restrict ourselves to languages whose consequence relation is non-effective. The difficulty with this horn will not emerge until we widen the scope of our enquiry a little further.

The constraint that descriptive sentences should have real-world correlates also allows us to revivify Gödel's view that consistency must act as a constraint on any formally specified language. If we adopt an inconsistent language, we do not, as Gödel feared, force cups to move by dint of mere convention. On the contrary, we become unable to say that they move or that they don't.

To see why this is it may be helpful here to consider a very limited case of language change. Imagine someone who claims that all intelligent people vote Tory, but is untroubled when taxed with the example of Stephen Fry, the well-known Labour voter: Mr Fry cannot be intelligent, she explains, if he votes Labour. Now this woman's language is in perfect order. There is nothing wrong with defining 'intelligent' to mean what *we* mean by 'intelligent and right wing'. The only weakness of this aberrant language (apart of course from its very aberrance) is that it lacks expressive power: its speaker is unable to express the thought which we would express by saying that all intelligent people vote Tory. When applied to this example Carnap's Principle of Tolerance seems quite correct: it is purely a pragmatic matter to choose between the two languages in question on the basis of whether the lack of expressive power in the aberrant one is important; if (as seems plausible) we never find ourselves wanting to express the thought that all intelligent people vote Tory, then it may not be.

But our concession to the linguistically aberrant right-winger that there was nothing wrong with her language did not force us to concede that all intelligent people really do vote Tory: that claim is one that she was unable even to express, let alone persuade us of. In the case of concern to us now, namely that of an inconsistent language, the same is true in spades. Because, as we saw earlier, such a language has no descriptive vocabulary, it cannot be interpreted as saying anything whatsoever (even anything trivial) about the world. It is a purely formal construct.

So once we take into account the need for semantics, the requirement of formal consistency acts as a genuine constraint on the languages we can adopt. This is not yet an objection to Carnap's account, however, since the languages Carnap proposed — Language I and Language II

— may very well be consistent. If so, they will contain sentences that make claims about the world. The difficulty with this, as with the non-effectiveness of the consequence relation, emerges only once we turn to what Carnap called the pragmatics of language use.

11.7 Pragmatics

This is the point at which the self, so long absent from Carnap's account, finally makes its presence felt. For we have said nothing yet to explain what it is for someone to use a sentence of the language to express the meaning the semantics allocates to it. The way Carnap expressed the matter was to divide the theory of signs and languages, which he called semiotic, into three parts, syntax, semantics, and pragmatics: only in this last part is reference to a speaker of the language permitted. Even after Carnap had adopted this taxonomy, though, he continued for some time to consider pragmatics to be relevant only to the empirical investigation of historically given languages. In pure semiotic, the study of languages as formal systems, Carnap continued to maintain that pragmatics had no regulatory rôle, belonging rather to psychology than to logic. But if we now add the requirement that a language must have a user as a further constraint on the Principle of Tolerance, Carnap's position comes under strain because of both of Gödel's theorems.

We have already seen that the first theorem forced Carnap, once the interpretational constraint was in place, to limit himself to languages with non-effective consequence relations. If I am a user of such a language, the mathematical theorems are held to be analytic for me as a consequence of my adoption of the linguistic conventions embodied in the definition of this consequence relation. But since the definition is non-effective, it cannot be embodied in a finite set of rules.

An objection sometimes made against conventionalism with respect to natural language is that it is trivially false since competent speakers of such languages may well be ignorant of the grammatical rules governing their speech. This is not a fatal objection, but to circumvent it we have to grant that it makes sense to attribute an *implicit* grasp of a set of rules to anyone who is regularly disposed to act in accordance with them, whether or not they are aware of the rules. An appeal to the notion of implicit grasp will not save us, though, when we are dealing with a non-effective definition, as in the current case. The competence we ascribe to someone whom we credit with an implicit grasp of a finite set of rules is nonetheless a finite competence: it is describable in finite terms. To say that the grasp is implicit is only to recognize that someone can be unaware of the exact limits of their own competence. If the competence in question cannot be finitely described at all, on the other hand, it is hard to see why it should be thought explanatory to describe it as a grasp of a set of rules at all.

When we turn to the problems raised by Gödel's second theorem, on the other hand, the question we need to address is whether there is any need for a proof of the consistency of a formal language in order to ensure that the language is usable. It may be convenient to approach the point by contrasting it with an objection often made to the conventionalist's claim that all the propositions of logic follow from linguistic conventions. The objection is that we must presuppose a certain amount of logic in order to be able to deduce the propositions from the conventions: to play the game of logic we must be, at least in a minimal sense, logical reasoners already. We have already noted repeatedly the difficulties that beset compromise versions of formalism. The current objection suggests that conventionalism, which was intended to evade these objections by its rejection of a language-independent notion of consequence, is still not sufficiently extreme: it must in turn be replaced with a *radical conventionalism* that regards each individual proposition of logic as a linguistic convention.

There is a great deal that can be said about this objection to Carnap's more moderate conventionalism, but this is not the place to say it. I have mentioned the objection only in order to draw from it the simple moral that anyone who uses a Carnapian language, constituted as it is by a set of rules, must be presumed competent to follow these rules in practice. Indeed it is fundamental to the notion of the self that it should have the capacity to follow such rules. Or, to put the point less allusively, the metalanguage in which we describe the formal language must already contain a certain amount of logic.

If what concerned us now were only that the proof of the consistency of mathematics must make use of mathematics in the metalanguage, this would merely be another version of the same point. To require that the syntactic rules be consistent is not to require that we should know they are consistent, and it is only the latter which is barred to the conventionalist. After all, Gödel's second theorem tells us that a formal system cannot informatively prove its own consistency, not that it cannot *be* consistent. In *Logical Syntax of Language* Carnap does indeed provide a proof of the consistency of Language II, for instance. That proof is not genuinely informative since it is conducted in a metalanguage that is essentially stronger than Language II itself, but perhaps this lack of informativeness should not trouble us, since the aim of the account is merely to explain the conventional nature of mathematics to someone who already grasps mathematics, not to provide a justification that would convince someone *ab initio*. There is indeed a regress, the thought runs,

but it is not obviously circular or vicious unless one thinks that some foundational work must be done by the syntactical description of a language. If no such task is at issue, then the upshot is simply that we can never make the conventional nature of mathematics fully explicit in any framework. The structure of Carnap's view is then coherent. Given the distinction between issues within a linguistic framework and issues between linguistic frameworks — a distinction that is always central to Carnap's thought — then the position is not circular so much as self-supporting at each level. If the mathematical part of a framework is analytic, then it's analytic; and so invoking mathematical truths at the level of the metalanguage is perfectly acceptable, since they flow from the adoption of the metalanguage.[21]

But what is at issue is whether Carnap's account in *Logical Syntax of Language* even permits a plausible picture of our grasp of language as meaningful. In fact it does not, and the reason is ultimately that its holism fails to leave room for the transparency of the grasp of meaning to the language user himself. Imagine the case of a language which has been used for many years with apparent success despite the existence within its mathematical part of an abstruse and as yet undiscovered contradiction (the Burali-Forti paradox, say). We seem to be forced by Carnap's account to say that despite appearances this language is not succeeding in saying anything about the world. If the contradiction is eventually discovered, the language must be rejected wholesale and a new one constructed. It does not even seem possible to salvage the descriptive sentences of the discredited language by translating them into descriptive sentences of the new one (rather like salvaging a computer disk which has been corrupted by a virus) because we are now in a position to see that the old language did not in fact possess any descriptive sentences at all: there just is not anything there to salvage.

The conventionalist could try to resist this highly implausible story on the basis that its premiss is false. Mathematics is not in fact inconsistent: if we assume counterfactually that it is, we shall of course arrive at wildly implausible conclusions, of which the story we have just told is merely one example. However, the only ground the conventionalist has for insisting that the premiss is false is the inductive one that we have not found a contradiction in mathematics so far. Moreover, the nature of the implausibility in the story we have been describing leads on to a further thought. However much we are tossed about on the seas of

---

[21] Goldfarb and Ricketts, 'Carnap and the Philosophy of Mathematics', 71.

language by indeterminacy of translation or the private language argument, one datum seems to be constant, namely that the ultimate point of language is to say things about the world. It is this fundamental point which is threatened by Carnap's account. Even if the syntax of my language is in fact sound with respect to its semantics, if I do not know that it is sound then according to Carnap I cannot know that 'The table is black' makes the empirical claim that the table is black. But I do know this. It follows on Carnap's account that I must know mathematics is consistent. This is not knowledge that I can have. So his account is wrong.

The conventionalist might demur on the ground that it is possible to be mistaken about the meaning of what one says. Even if this is so, it is not enough, however. In order for the argument against Carnap to go through there need only be one sentence in my language which I am indefeasibly sure I can use to express an empirical claim. According to Carnap there must always remain a lurking doubt that my language might turn out inconsistent and hence not refer to the world, a doubt which on his view I have no more than inductive evidence to dispel. This is plainly absurd. Even if I am capable of conceiving of things non-linguistically, I do not have any non-linguistic conception of the empirical distinct from and set against my linguistic conception of it. So Carnap's view makes it an experimental fact that I have a conception of an empirical world at all. That is as close to a straightforward contradiction as one is likely to encounter in philosophy.

Conclusion

Two questions, I said. Can we give an account of arithmetic which does not make it depend for its truth on the way the world is? And if so, what constrains the world to conform to arithmetic? I warned the reader at the outset not to expect any of the answers to these questions discussed in this book to be altogether satisfactory. And so, I think, it has proved. All the accounts we have considered have turned out to be flawed. But it is striking how often we have had to reject an account not for philosophical reasons but for technical ones. We have been principally concerned with the fifty years following Frege's publication of the *Grundlagen* in 1884, and the pattern that emerges most forcibly from that period is the persistent tendency for philosophical aspirations to outrun technical feasibility. It is time now to see whether there are any morals to be drawn from this pattern of failure.

Aristotelian logic, strictly understood, recognizes objects only as faceless place-holders for the application of concepts. In such a logic we cannot even make sense of the idea of counting. Since the extent of the Kantian analytic coincides with what can be proved in this restricted logic, arithmetic is not analytic in Kant's sense. To go beyond this restricted logic we need the general notion of an object. But do we have access to any such general notion independent of a particular structure within which we can conceive of the object as occurring? It was essential to the coherence of Kant's system as a whole to say that we do not, but to insist that the only way we can be affected by an object is via sensibility, which imposes a structure to which we conceive of the object as conforming. The difficulty with this is that it makes not just arithmetic but quantified logic dependent on the spatio-temporal structure of the world as we experience it, which seems implausible.

Treating sensibility as schematic, so that quantified logic is what all beings with *any* sort of sensibility have in common, helps only until its incoherence is pointed out (§ 2.4): viewed in this way there would not really be anything the beings had in common. The alternative is to deduce the notion of an object from that of a concept: purely conceptual thought is impossible since the notion of a concept presupposes that of an object to which it may or may not apply. If we adopt this idea, quantified logic will be applicable to objects just because objects are the subject matter of propositions. What this account leaves unclear, though, is what the relations are between objects thus conceived. Indeed it remains to be explained how there can be relations such as those of identity and difference between objects at all.

But even if this matter can be settled, and we agree that quantified logic with identity can be regarded as analytic in a suitably extended sense of Kant's term, we can hardly expect it to deliver on its own the content of arithmetic as standardly understood. This is because arithmetic refers to infinitely many objects, and although opinions differ on whether it is analytic that there is at least one thing, it clearly cannot be analytic that there are infinitely many. Is there any way out?

One possibility is to abandon our commitment to numbers as objects in the full sense which gives them independent aspects, and accept instead that they are mere place-holders in arguments. This proposal has much to recommend it. After all, Frege's own argument in the *Grundlagen* that numbers are objects is extremely weak; and he himself cautions us against assuming uncritically that the surface grammar of our use of number terms must always be a reliable guide to the underlying form. The most natural way to develop the idea is by means of numerically definite quantifiers, which can be defined using only the resources of quantified logic: we can, for instance, express that there are two Fs by the proposition that

$$(\exists x, y)(Fx \, . \, Fy \, . \, x \neq y \, . \, (z)(z = x \lor z = y \lor \sim Fz)).$$

Indeed we can generalize this by writing

$$\mathbf{0}(F) =_{\mathrm{Df}} \sim(\exists x)Fx,$$
$$s(\mathbf{n})(F) =_{\mathrm{Df}} (\exists y)(Fy \, . \, \mathbf{n}(\lambda x(Fx \, . \, x \neq y)),$$

and defining '**m** is a number' to mean

$$(F)((F\mathbf{0} \, . \, (\mathbf{n})(F\mathbf{n} \supset F(s(\mathbf{n})))) \supset F\mathbf{m}).$$

These definitions will allow us to derive the equations of elementary arithmetic such as $2+2 = 4$. Unfortunately, though, we cannot similarly derive inequations such as $2 + 2 \neq 5$, which are just as much part of arithmetic as standardly practised, unless we assume that there are infinitely many objects. Since this is the assumption we were hoping to avoid in the first place, and by its nature the proposal has nothing to say on whether it is true, we must seek the answer to our question elsewhere.

Another account that seeks to free arithmetic of ontological commitments modalizes its claims, so that arithmetical propositions are taken to assert not what is true but what is possible. We have not considered this treatment in any detail here, because the authors we have been discussing did not propose it, but it is very hard to see how it can solve our problem since proving that arithmetic is possible is not obviously easier than proving that it is true. In any case, as Ramsey pointed out, we should then 'have to make large alterations in our system of logic in order to validate proofs depending on constructions in terms of things which might exist but don't.'[1] Nor does talk of possible worlds help much: if we were puzzled how numbers are applicable to the world, it scarcely helps to shift the problem so that the numbers are in a different world from the things they are supposed to be applied to.

The account in the *Tractatus* is a great improvement on the modal treatment because it presents arithmetic as a by-product of language and therefore applicable just as widely. But since it lies in the same territory as the treatment in terms of numerically definite quantifiers that Frege rejected, we should not be surprised if Wittgenstein's account suffers the same technical limitation of being unable to account for any part of arithmetic beyond the most elementary. Does this matter? If we insist on justifying the unrestricted principle of mathematical induction, for instance, we are evidently going beyond the arithmetic not only of the Guaranies and the Aranda but of most educated Western adults, who are unlikely ever to have come across a proof that makes use of nested induction. Nevertheless, it is difficult simply to maintain that the narrow objective of grounding elementary arithmetic will suffice, since once we have formulated the question of the validity of unrestricted induction, it is hard to deny that we ought to have an answer to it.

In any case, lest we suppose that this is the only problem the philosophy of arithmetic has to face, it is worth noting, too, that even if there are in fact infinitely many objects, both the account via numerically definite quantifiers and Wittgenstein's via exponents of operations will still be inadequate, since although they will then explain how we count objects, they will still be unable to deal with how we count numbers themselves.

Not only may we be forced, then, to engage in the search for a source of content which can provide us with the infinitely many objects we conceive of arithmetic as discussing, but at this point, too, there begins to emerge a second aspect to our problem. The philosophy of arithmetic

---

[1] *FoM*, 79–80.

is not merely a matter of finding the source of its content, but has to enquire into the source of the concepts which apply to that domain. The distinction between these two aspects of the problem is hinted at by Kant when he suggests that arithmetic depends on postulates but has no need of axioms, but it took much longer for the significance of the second aspect to be recognized. Indeed impredicativity was at first seen as a difficulty for analysis and set theory rather than for arithmetic. Let us now review what we have learnt about the two aspects of the problem in turn. Content first.

The search for a source of the content of arithmetic is heavily constrained by our insistence that we should aim to explain the applicability of arithmetic to the world. In the Introduction I remarked that since the problem of arithmetic participates in the larger puzzle of the relationship between thought, language, experience, and the world, we can distinguish accounts that look to each of these to supply the content we require: those that involve the structure of our experience of the world; those that explicitly involve our grasp of a 'third realm' of abstract objects distinct from the concrete objects of the empirical world and the ideas of my private *Gedankenwelt*; those that appeal to something non-physical that is nevertheless an aspect of reality in harmony with which the physical aspect of the world is configured; and finally those that involve only our grasp of language.

The first sort of account gives sensibility the original Kantian rôle of structuring experience. In Kant's conception this structure is spatio-temporal. Whether Kant saw arithmetic as dependent on the temporal part of this structure alone or on both space and time is largely irrelevant since the principal difficulty with Kant's account is that it seems implausible for arithmetic to depend on either space *or* time. Yet despite this implausibility the account has the undoubted merit of providing an explanation of applicability that serves as a benchmark for its rivals: arithmetic applies to experience because it is derived from the structure of experience. Moreover, since that structure is supplied by us, and is not itself part of experience, the applicability is a priori.

Hilbert's alternative conception of sensibility as providing a way of experiencing the world as constituted by finite arrays of concrete objects is at first sight more promising since it does not commit us to supposing that the particular structure our current physical theories ascribe to the spatio-temporal world is a priori. Now instead of arithmetic depending on space and time, space and time depend on arithmetic. But for the account to inherit Kant's explanation of the applicability of arithmetic we need the further premiss that all our thought conforms to the same structure as finite arrangement of concrete objects such as stroke strings. This is evidently at least a close relative of the thesis that all thought is computational. Its principal drawback is that Hilbert gives us no reason to think it is true.

Frege's account of arithmetic was of the second sort. He derived arithmetic from the numerical equivalence and hoped to show that this was a purely logical principle. He thought this could be done indirectly via an explicit definition of numbers as extensions of concepts, but that depended on Basic Law V, which is plainly not a logical law since it is contradictory. To do it directly instead we should have to establish a notion of content for which the left-hand side of the numerical equivalence could be seen as doing no more than recarving the content expressed by the right-hand side. Frege did not supply any such notion of content, and the difficulty involved in doing so is severe since we know that the syntactically similar Basic Law V cannot be viewed in terms of such a recarving.

But in any case Frege's appeal to the notion of content at this point establishes that the numerical equivalence is not logical in the narrow sense which the word commonly has today. In the same way Dedekind's construction of the natural numbers goes beyond logic because it appeals to entities which, although created by the intellect, are nevertheless objectively available to it. Of course, for Dedekind's proof that there are infinitely many objects to be valid the 'thoughts' referred to in it must be thoughts available to me rather than thoughts I shall actually have. What Dedekind does not supply, however, is an argument to show that our experience must conform to the structure of thoughts so conceived. Kant, of course, never considered this matter because he thought intellectual intuitions of the kind Dedekind appeals to were possible only for God and not for finite beings such as ourselves. In any case the step in Dedekind's treatment that is quite unmotivated is the formation of a system with all these thoughts as members.[2] This lacuna is understandable — Dedekind was writing without any awareness of the paradoxes — but that does not make it any easier to fill.

One way out of this impasse might be to follow Russell in looking to the world itself for the content of arithmetic, since this makes the applicability of arithmetic to the world wholly unproblematic. Alone among the accounts we have been considering it makes arithmetic truly independent not only of me but of all of us; but it is hard to see how the world could supply the infinite content we require unless there are in fact infinitely many things. The trouble with this is that it is, as Russell himself observed, an empirical hypothesis which there seems

[2]Cf. Hilbert, *Natur und mathematisches Erkennen*, 33.

no good reason to believe. Indeed, as we have seen, one of Hilbert's principal motivations for his work in the foundations of arithmetic was that modern physics seemed to him to have made the finitude of the physical world a wholly plausible hypothesis.

But the reason Russell saw arithmetic as stemming from the world is that arithmetic is part of logic and logic is the study of an aspect of the world. So it might seem to be open to him to argue that even if Hilbert was right to suppose the physical world finite, the world as a whole contains infinitely many things of another sort, universals such as the logical constants and variables. The difficulty now, though, is to explain how we can know that there are infinitely many such abstract entities. At one time Russell thought we could infer their existence as an hypothesis which explains numerical equations, rather as a theory of electricity explains the read-out on a voltmeter, but that just pushes the epistemological question back one step to the numerical equations which are acting as a constraint on our logical theorizing. How do we come to know *them*?

The fourth sort of explanation gives the rôle of sensibility to the structure of language. Wittgenstein's account in the *Tractatus* makes numerals a notational representation of the general feature of language that it essentially involves operations, i.e. transitions from one proposition to another which may be applied repeatedly. But our grasp of language has two parts — the general form of proposition, on which the notion of an operation depends, and the range of elementary propositions that form the base from which other propositions are obtained. If we interpret Wittgenstein's operations as acting strictly at the level of sense, his account may generate equations well enough, but it will not generate inequations unless there are infinitely many elementary propositions. And on purely conceptual grounds there seems no reason to insist on such a language.

One way out is to observe that languages with only finitely many elementary propositions, although feasible, do not allow us to say significantly (what would in such a case be false) that there are infinitely many things. Since in our language it seems that we *can* significantly say this, we may deduce transcendentally that our language has infinitely many elementary propositions at its base. This is progress, but only of a sort: it makes our grasp of arithmetic no more puzzling than our ability to talk about the infinite in general; but it does not offer an obvious route to an explanation of *that*, and it is hostage to the possibility that what appears to be talk about the infinite might turn out on analysis to be representable in finite terms.

Another way out involves the fact that even if there are only finitely many elementary propositions, there will be infinitely many signs. That our language works, that all these infinitely many signs symbolize, shows, we might argue, that there is an essential feature of our language which is inevitably infinite. But it is far from clear that this *is* an essential feature of language: if there were indeed only finitely many elementary propositions, we could very well express every sense in a finite notation.

Both these attempted transcendental arguments were mentioned by Ramsey, but they depend on features of Wittgenstein's account which he soon abandoned: once he regarded identity as an 'intelligible notation', the axiom of infinity became for him either a contradiction or a tautology but always significant, thus destroying the first argument; and by abandoning symbols and recognizing only signs and their senses he barred the way to the second. Briefly Ramsey thought the possibility that all of analysis should be contradictory sufficiently absurd that he was happy to treat the tautologousness of the axiom of infinity as obvious. But quite soon he realized that as a justification for mathematics this argument is no better than Russell's regressive one.

Carnap's account stands in the same Wittgensteinian tradition of making the sensibility linguistic, but viewed in this light his Principle of Tolerance amounts to a denial that our sensibility imposes any particular structure at all. It is the structure our sensibility imposes that determines the sort of beings we are. If we are, as Carnap claimed, free to adopt any structure at all, it is hard to see what connection there can be between the self that adopts one structure and the self that adopts another.

This point corresponds precisely to the objection we made earlier to treating the sensibility as schematic in a Kantian account of polyadic logic. Any account that attempts to base arithmetic on a subject matter treated as schematic, abstracting from the particular features of our sensibility or our language, loosens the binding between us that explains how we communicate with one another, and hence risks descending into solipsism.

So much for the existence of numbers. What about their properties? Kant thought that arithmetic, unlike geometry, has no need of axioms: there is no more to it than can be derived directly from the numerical equations and inequations that form its base. Insofar as he had an argument for this, it seems to have been that the concepts of arithmetic arise in the understanding and are not regulated by the structure of sensibility: intuition is needed to supply us with the objects of arithmetic, but once these are given to us their properties follow by reason alone. And as long as it is only numerical equations and inequations that are in question, this view is very plausible. But as a general account of arithmetic it is wrong, for reasons due to Gödel of which Kant could not have had the slightest conception. The problem which Gödel's theorems expose is that the concepts of arithmetic are not as easily separable from the objects as Kant supposed. If the numbers are given to us as a totality, we can use our grasp of that totality to form new concepts applicable to numbers but not available to us independently.

Hilbert, too, was caught out by a failure to realize that a grasp of a domain of entities is not the same as a grasp of the range of properties of that domain. He thought he could evade Poincaré's objection to circular justifications of the principle of induction by giving a proof that the principle is consistent while using only a much restricted version of induction in the proof. But the ordinal analysis of the proof-theoretic strength of systems of arithmetic shows clearly the flaw in this approach: the principle of induction employed in Peano Arithmetic is a genuinely stronger assumption than the quantifier-free induction principle of Elementary Arithmetic: accepting the latter involves no commitment to accepting even the bare consistency of former.

The accounts presented by Frege and Dedekind face an analogous difficulty: the appeal to a realm of thoughts may supply us with infinitely many objects, but this still does not deliver any more than the quantifier-free arithmetic of equations and inequations unless we can take the further step of regarding the numbers — whether obtained by Frege's route via the numerical equivalence or Dedekind's via intellectual abstraction — as lying in the domain of the quantifiers. And as soon as we take this step, our account is evidently impredicative. We have two choices, both of which seem unattractive: if we say that thoughts occupy a realm quite distinct from the empirical things we normally talk about, we need to explain why what we say about one realm can be used in reasoning about the other; if we say instead that they occupy the same realm, of which we have a single, unified grasp, we seem to have lapsed into idealism, since there is no reason to suppose that anything real belongs to this realm at all.

The impredicativity of induction emerges most clearly in Russell's account. For even if the physical world supplies enough objects for arithmetic, Gödel's theorems show that it cannot supply on its own a structure rich enough to ground the unrestricted induction scheme any more than Hilbert's concrete intuition could. In order to make up this deficit Russell had to posit other entities — universals of some kind or other — which participate in the world and lend it structure. But, in the first edition of *Principia* at least, he could not derive the principle of complete induction without assuming that these other entities obey the axiom of reducibility, and it is hard to see what possible way there could be of telling whether this is so. Russell was eventually reduced to treating the axiom as an empirical hypothesis, but it is an odd sort of empirical hypothesis that cannot, even in principle, have any evidence for or against it.

Although the background to Carnap's account is different from, and more explicitly linguistic than, Russell's, it reaches a similar conclusion, at least if we add to it the premiss that any language I can grasp is recursively describable. For then it will turn out that although the numerals all belong to the logical part of the vocabulary, the universal quantifier ranging over the natural numbers counts as descriptive. In other words, some at least of the properties of numbers are empirical even though the numbers themselves are not.

Both Russell and Carnap came eventually to realize that an account which makes numbers logical but their properties empirical has little to recommend it, but in order to overcome the difficulty they each ended up ascribing to us the capacity to grasp features of the infinite directly. Russell in the second edition of *Principia* tried to prove induction correct without using the axiom of reducibility but had instead to appeal to the properties of infinitely long formulae, which we 'see' directly. Carnap, on the other hand, adopted a language with a consequence relation which cannot be described by means of a finite list of formal rules. At this point, therefore, both had simply given up on the attempt to explain how a finite intelligence can grasp arithmetical truths which appear to refer to an infinite domain of objects.

If we try to justify the principle of induction within Wittgenstein's account, we find that what plays the corresponding intuitive rôle is another layer of content beyond what can be obtained from individual propositions, namely our awareness of the general concept of proposition. If we allow operations to apply at the level of symbols, thus in effect ascribing to ourselves an explicit awareness of the structure of our own language, we can obtain Elementary Arithmetic, just as in the Hilbertian account, but not the theory of classes or complete induction. Wittgenstein, unlike Hilbert, was not troubled by the fact that he had failed to justify the whole of mathematics. 'In life it is never a mathematical proposition which we need.'[3] This seems hard to maintain. Although it is true that nothing in life seems to turn on the truth or falsity of Goldbach's conjecture, we frequently act on beliefs dependent on arithmetical generalizations, quite apart from the myriad applications of higher mathematics.

---

[3] *TLP*, 6.211.

What we need if we are to pursue the idea of placing language in the Kantian rôle of structuring experience is therefore an extension of Wittgenstein's system that will ground higher mathematics. Ramsey's account was intended to meet this challenge. He provided a definition of identity, and hence a theory of classes, by means of the notion of a propositional function in extension, i.e. any mapping from objects to propositions. Ramsey was concerned principally with avoiding contradictions: his notion achieved this aim because the domains of objects and senses have been delineated in advance, independent of the construction of symbols for expressing them, and so the introduction of propositional functions in extension cannot lead to any vicious explosion in these domains. Moreover, if we combine this notion with the simple theory of types already considered we do (at least if we assume the axiom of infinity) obtain a system that is adequate for mathematics. But the difficulty now is that of explaining our grasp of the notion of a propositional function in extension. If we try to explain it on anything like the model of our previous understanding of propositional functions as extracted from propositions by replacing constant constituents of them with variables, we run into total perplexity, as Wittgenstein realized. What we are dealing with has now lost all contact with the notion of a language, and hence with applicability. If, on the other hand, we simply appeal to a primitive grasp of the notion, as Ramsey was inclined to do, this primitive grasp seems to be an idle wheel which, once more, cannot have anything to do with the application of mathematics to the world.

What is clear, then, is that arithmetic is not logic, if by logic is meant the laws to which our thought should conform simply by virtue of being propositional. Arithmetic has a content that logic, so conceived, cannot supply. It is senseless to look for that content in the world, for we, being finite, are incapable of experiencing the world directly as infinite, whether it is so or not. But the world and our configuration of it seem to be the only sources of content available to us, so we are driven to look for a feature of the structure of our experience of the world that can provide us not only with the infinite, which the accounts we have considered already can supply, but with an ability to impose on the infinite a further structure not implicit in the notion itself.

Where is such a further structure to be sought? The discussion so far makes it plausible that it cannot be derived directly from the structure of any of the four sources — experience, thought, the world, and language — considered so far. Moreover, the similarities that have emerged between the scopes of the various approaches are surely suggestive. What these similarities show, I believe, is that in order to grasp the part of arithmetic that goes beyond the mechanical calculations of numerical sums we have to appeal to higher-order concepts, i.e. what Gödel describes as concepts which do not have as their content properties or relations of concrete objects (such as combinations of symbols), but rather of thought structures or thought contents (e.g. proofs, meaningful propositions, and so on), where in the proofs of propositions about these mental objects insights are needed which are not derived from a reflection upon the combinatorial (space-time) properties of the symbols representing them, but rather from a reflection upon the meanings involved.

The issue here is one that has already arisen in our discussion of Ramsey's account of the theory of types. We saw that in order to avoid paradox he had to adopt a hierarchy of languages. The danger, of course, is that if my self is constituted by my capacity to invest the language I speak with meaning, then a hierarchy of languages with different meaning relations is really a hierarchy of selves. In order to avoid this fragmentation of the self I need to assume a further relation that binds together this hierarchy of meaning relations into one. What could that further relation be? If I regard it as yet another meaning relation, I am simply iterating the process into the transfinite — I am treating meaning as what Michael Dummett calls an indefinitely extensible concept — but I am only postponing the difficulty, not resolving it. (If it is possible to form the union of the hierarchy, the paradox forces me to treat the meaning relation for that union as part of a further language not yet included; if it is not possible, I have a fragmented self again.)

The only way out is evidently to treat the self as a distinct item bearing to each of these languages a relation that makes it my language. But in saying this I am beyond the limit of sense, for the relation that the self bears to each of these languages cannot be expressed in language; nor — crucially — can I simply adopt the Tractarian solution of treating the relation as shown by my successful use of the language even though it cannot be expressed within it. That way works for a single language but makes no sense for an infinite number since I cannot as a finite being show my successful grasp of infinitely many different languages at once.

So the way out that I am recommending seems unavoidably to involve repeated appeal to the very confusion that Wittgenstein (following Kant) warned us against, namely that between the self of empirical psychology and the self as metaphysical subject: I have to conceive of myself empirically as an object in the world insofar as I conceive of myself as bearing determinate relations to the languages in the hierarchy; but I must also conceive of myself metaphysically insofar as these relations are ultimately inexpressible. This is an uncomfortable conclusion to reach: it would indeed be alarming if the whole of higher mathematics depended on such a confusion. But I cannot for the moment think what else to say.

Bibliography

Ackermann, W., 'Begründung des "Tertium non datur" mittels der Hilbertischen Theorie der Widerspruchsfreiheit', *Math. Ann.*, **93** (1924), 1–36

Benacerraf, Paul, 'What numbers could not be', in Benacerraf and Putnam, *Philosophy of mathematics: Selected readings*, 272–94

—————— and Hilary Putnam (eds.), *Philosophy of mathematics: Selected readings*, 2nd edn. (Cambridge University Press, 1983)

Berkeley, George, *A Treatise concerning the Principles of Human Understanding*, 2nd edn. (Dublin, 1734)

——————, *The Analyst, or, A discourse addresed to an infidel mathematician* (London: Tonson, 1734) (repr. in Ewald, *From Kant to Hilbert*, pp. 60–92)

Boolos, George, *Logic, Logic, and Logic*, ed. by Richard Jeffrey (Cambridge, Mass.: Harvard University Press, 1998)

Broad, C. D., 'Kant's mathematical and philosophical reasoning', *Proc. Arist. Soc.*, **42** (1942), 1–24

Carnap, Rudolf, 'Die Mathematik als Zweig der Logik', *Blätter deutsche Phil.*, **4** (1930), 298–310

——————, *Foundations of logic and mathematics*, International Encyclopaedia of Unified Science, I (University of Chicago Press, 1939)

——————, *The Logical Syntax of Language* (London: Routledge & Kegan Paul, 1937)

——————, *Logische Syntax der Sprache*, Schriften zur wissenschaftlichen Weltauffassung, 8 (Vienna: Springer, 1934) (trans. as *Logical Syntax of Language*)

——————, 'Intellectual autobiography', in *The philosophy of Rudolf Carnap*, ed. by P. A. Schilpp, Library of living philosophers (La Salle, Ill.: Open Court, 1963), 1–84

Carroll, Lewis, *Through the looking glass: and what Alice found there* (London: Macmillan, 1872)

Copi, Irving M., 'The inconsistency or redundancy of *Principia Mathematica*', *Phil. Phenom. Res.*, **11** (1950), 190–9

Dawson, Jr., John W., 'Discussion on the foundations of mathematics', *Hist. Phil. Logic*, **5** (1984), 111–29

Dedekind, R., *Gesammelte mathematische Werke*, ed. by R. Fricke, E. Noether, and O. Ore, 3 vols. (Braunschweig: Vieweg, 1932)

————, *Was sind und was sollen die Zahlen?* (Braunschweig: Vieweg, 1887) (trans. in Ewald, *From Kant to Hilbert*, pp. 787–832)

Dobrizhoffer, Martin, *An account of the Abipones, an equestrian people of Paraguay*, 3 vols. (London: Murray, 1822)

Dummett, Michael, *Frege: Philosophy of Language*, 2nd edn. (London: Duckworth, 1981)

————, *Frege: Philosophy of mathematics* (London: Duckworth, 1991)

————, 'Neo-Fregeans: In bad company?', in Schirn, *Philosophy of Mathematics Today*, 369–87

Euclid, *Elements*, ed. by Sir T. L. Heath (Cambridge University Press, 1928)

Ewald, William B. (ed.), *From Kant to Hilbert: A Source Book in the Foundations of Mathematics* (Oxford, 1996)

Field, Hartry, *Science Without Numbers: A defence of nominalism* (Oxford: Blackwell, 1980)

Fine, Kit, *Reasoning With Arbitrary Objects*, Aristotelian Society Series, 3 (Oxford: Blackwell, 1985)

Frege, Gottlob, *Begriffsschrift, eine der arithmetischen nachgebildete Formelsprache des reinen Denkens* (Halle: Nebert, 1879)

————, *Funktion und Begriff* (Jena: Pohle, 1891) (trans. in *Philosophical Writings*, 21–41)

————, *Grundgesetze der Arithmetik*, 2 vols. (Jena: Pohle, 1893–1903) (partially trans. in *Philosophical Writings*, 117–224)

————, *Die Grundlagen der Arithmetik* (Breslau, 1884) (trans. as *The Foundations of Arithmetic*)

————, *Translations from the Philosophical Writings of Gottlob Frege*, ed. by Peter Geach and Max Black, 3rd edn. (Oxford: Blackwell, 1980)

————, *Philosophical and Mathematical Correspondence* (Oxford: Blackwell, 1980)

————, *Posthumous Writings*, trans. by Peter Long and Roger White (Oxford: Blackwell, 1979)

————, *The Foundations of Arithmetic*, trans. by J. L. Austin, 2nd edn. (Oxford: Blackwell, 1953)

————, 'Kritische Beleuchtung einiger Punkte in E. Schröders Vorlesungen über die Algebra der Logik', *Archiv für systematische Philosophie*, **1** (1895), 433–56 (trans. in *Philosophical Writings*, 86–106)

————, 'Über Begriff und Gegenstand', *Vierteljahrsschrift für wiss. Phil.*, **16** (1892), 192–205 (trans. in *Philosophical Writings*, 42–55)

Gasking, D. A. T., 'The analytic-synthetic controversy', *Austral. J. Phil.*, **50** (1972), 107–23

Gentzen, Gerhard, *Collected papers*, ed. by M. E. Szabo (Amsterdam: North-Holland, 1969)

Gödel, Kurt, *Collected Works*, 4 vols. (Oxford University Press, 1986–)

Goldfarb, Warren, and Thomas Ricketts, 'Carnap and the Philosophy of Mathematics', in *Science and Subjectivity*, ed. by David Bell and Wilhelm Vossenkuhl (Akademie Verlag, 1992), 61–78

Grassmann, Hermann, *Lehrbuch der Arithmetik für höhere Lehranstalten* (Berlin: Enslin, 1861) (repr. in *Werke*, II.1, 295–349)

————, *Gesammelte mathematische und physikalische Werke*, ed. by Friedrich Engel, 3 vols. (Leipzig: Teubner, 1894–1911)

Grattan-Guinness, I., *Dear Russell — Dear Jourdain. A commentary on Russell's logic, based on his correspondence with Philip Jourdain* (London: Duckworth, 1977)

Hale, Bob, 'Grundlagen § 64', *Proc. Arist. Soc.*, **97** (1997), 243–61

Hallett, Michael, 'Hilbert and logic', in *Logic, Mathematics, Physics and History of Science*, ed. by M. Marion and R. S. Cohen, Québec Studies in the Philosophy of Science (Dordrecht: Kluwer, 1996), 135–87

Heck, Richard, 'Finitude and Hume's principle', *J. Phil. Logic*, **26** (1997), 589–617

————, 'The development of arithmetic in Frege's *Grundgesetze*', *J. Symb. Logic*, **58** (1993), 579–601

Hilbert, David, *Natur und mathematisches Erkennen: Vorlesungen gehalten 1919–1920 in Göttingen*, ed. by David E. Rowe (Basle: Birkhäuser, 1992)

————, 'Mathematische Probleme', *Nachr. Königl. Gesell. Wiss. Göttingen*, (1900), 253–97

———— and Paul Bernays, *Grundlagen der Mathematik*, 2 vols. (Berlin: Springer, 1934–9)

Hume, David, *A Treatise of Human Nature*, ed. by Páll S. Árdal, 2 vols. (Collins, 1962–72)

Husserl, Edmund, *Philosophie der Arithmetik*, Gesammelte Schriften, 1 (Hamburg: Meiner, 1992)

Isaacson, Daniel, 'Arithmetical truth and hidden higher-order concepts', in *The Philosophy of Mathematics*, ed. by W. D. Hart (Oxford University Press, 1996), 203–24

Jeroslow, R. G., 'Redundancies in the Hilbert-Bernays derivability conditions for Gödel's second incompleteness theorem', *J. Symb. Logic*, **38** (1973), 359–67

Kant, Immanuel, *Critique of Pure Reason*, trans. by Norman Kemp Smith (London: Macmillan, 1929)

————, *Inaugural dissertation and early writings on space*, trans. John Handyside (Königsberg: Open Court, 1929)

————, *Kritik der reinen Vernunft* (Riga: Hartknoch, 1781; B edn. 1787) (trans. as *Critique of Pure Reason*)

————, *Logic*, trans. by John Richardson (London: Simpkin & Marshall, 1819)

————, *Logic*, trans. by Robert S. Hartman and Wolfgang Schwarz (New York: Dover, 1988)

————, *Philosophical Correspondence, 1759–99*, ed. and trans. by Arnulf Zweig (University of Chicago Press, 1967)

————, *Prolegomena zu einer jeden künstigen Metaphysik die als Wissenschaft wird auftreten können* (Riga: Hartknoch, 1783) (trans. as *Prolegomena*)

————, *Prolegomena to any future metaphysics that will be able to come forward as science*, trans. by Paul Carus, rev. by James W. Ellington (Indianapolis: Hackett, 1977)

Kripke, Saul, *Naming and Necessity*, rev. edn. (Oxford: Blackwell, 1980)

Landau, Edmund, *Foundations of Analysis*, trans. by F. Steinhardt, 2nd edn. (New York: Chelsea, 1960)

————, *Grundlagen der Analysis (das Rechnen mit ganzen, rationalen, irrationalen, komplexen Zahlen): Ergänzung zu den Lehrbüchern der Differential- und Integralrechnung* (Leipzig: Akademische Verlagsgesellschaft M.B.H., 1930) (trans. as *Foundations of Analysis*)

Landini, Gregory, 'The definability of the set of natural numbers in the 1925 *Principia*', *J. Phil. Logic*, (1996), 1–19

Leibniz, G. W., *New Essays on Human Understanding*, trans. and ed. by Peter Remnant and Jonathan Bennett (Cambridge University Press, 1981)

————, *Schriften zur Logik und zur philosophischen Grundlegung von Mathematik und Naturwissenschaft*, Philosophische Schriften, 4 (Frankfurt am Main: Suhrkamp, 1996)

Lewy, Casimir, 'A note on the text of the *Tractatus*', *Mind*, **76** (1967), 416–23

Locke, John, *An Essay Concerning Human Understanding*, ed. by J. W. Youlton (London: Dent, 1961)

Makin, Gideon, 'Making sense of "On denoting" ', *Synthese*, **102** (1995), 383–412

Mancosu, Paolo (ed.), *From Brouwer to Hilbert: The debate on the foundations of mathematics in the 1920s* (Oxford University Press, 1998)

Marion, Mathieu, *Wittgenstein, Finitism and the Foundations of Mathematics* (Oxford University Press, 1998)

Martin, Gottfried, *Arithmetic and Combinatorics: Kant and His Contemporaries*, trans. and ed. by Judy Wubnig (Carbondale, Ill.: Southern Illinois University Press, 1985)

McGuinness, Brian, 'Wittgenstein's pre-*Tractatus* manuscripts', in *Wittgenstein in focus — Im Brennpunkt: Wittgenstein*, ed. by Brian McGuinness and Rudolf Haller, Grazer philosophische Studien (Amsterdam: Rodopi, 1989), 35–47

Menger, Karl, 'On Intuitionism', in *Selected Papers*, Vienna Circle Collection, 10 (Dordrecht: Reidel, 1979), 46–58

Monk, Ray, *Ludwig Wittgenstein: The Duty of Genius* (London: Cape, 1990)

Myhill, John, 'The undefinability of the set of natural numbers in the ramified *Principia*', in *Bertrand Russell's philosophy*, ed. by George Nakhnikian (London: Duckworth, 1974), 19–27

Nelson, Edward W., *Predicative Arithmetic* (Princeton University Press, 1986)

Parsons, Charles, *Mathematics in Philosophy: Selected Essays* (Ithaca, NY: Cornell University Press, 1983)

———, 'Finitism and intuitive knowledge', in Schirn, *Philosophy of Mathematics Today*, 249–70

———, 'The structuralist view of mathematical objects', *Synthese*, **84** (1990), 303–46

Plato, *Laws*, trans. by Benjamin Jowett, 4th edn. (Oxford University Press, 1954)

———, *Philebus*, trans. by J. C. B. Gosling (Oxford: Clarendon Press, 1975)

Putnam, Hilary, 'The thesis that mathematics is logic', in *Mathematics, Matter and Method*, Philosophical Papers, 1, 2nd edn. (Cambridge University Press, 1979), 12–42

Quine, W.V., *The Ways of Paradox and Other Essays*, rev. and enlarged edn. (Cambridge, Mass.: Harvard University Press, 1976)

———, 'On Frege's way out', *Mind*, **64** (1955), 145–59

Ramsey, F. P., *The Foundations of Mathematics and other logical essays*, ed. by R. B. Braithwaite (London: Kegan Paul, Trench, Trubner, 1931)

———, *Notes on Philosophy, Probability and Mathematics*, ed. by Maria Carla Galavotti, History of Logic, 7 (Naples: Bibliopolis, 1991)

———, 'Review of *Principia Mathematica*, 2nd edn.', *Mind*, **34** (1925), 506–7

———, 'The new *Principia*', *Nature*, **116** (1925), 127–8

Ricketts, Thomas, 'Carnap's Principle of Tolerance, Empiricism, and Conventionalism', in *Reading Putnam*, ed. by Peter Clark and Bob Hale (Oxford: Blackwell, 1994), 176–200

Rothhaupt, Josef G. F., *Farbthemen in Wittgensteins Gesamtnachlass: philologisch-philosophische Untersuchungen im Längschnitt und in Querschnitten*, Monografien Philosophie, 273 (Weinheim: Beltz, 1996)

Russell, Bertrand, *Essays in Analysis*, ed. by Douglas Lackey (London: Allen & Unwin, 1973)

——, *Introduction to Mathematical Philosophy* (London: Allen & Unwin, 1919)

——, *Logic and Knowledge: Essays 1901–1950*, ed. by Robert Charles Marsh (London: Allen & Unwin, 1956)

——, *Collected Papers*, 13 vols. (London: Routledge, 1983–)

——, *The Principles of Mathematics* (London: Allen & Unwin, 1903; 2nd edn. 1937)

——, *Selected Letters*, ed. by Nicholas Griffin, 2 vols. (Harmondsworth: Allen Lane, 1992–)

——, *The Analysis of Matter* (London: Kegan Paul, Trench, Trubner, 1927)

Schirn, Matthias (ed.), *Philosophy of Mathematics Today* (Oxford University Press, 1998)

Schlick, Moritz, *Philosophical Papers*, ed. by Henk L. Mulder and Barbara F. B. van de Velde-Schlick, 2 vols. (Dordrecht: Reidel, 1978–9)

Schröder, Ernst, *Lehrbuch der Arithmetik und Algebra* (Leipzig: Teubner, 1873)

Schultz, Johann, *Erläuterungen über des Herrn Professor Kant Kritik der Reinen Vernunft*, 2nd edn. (Königsberg: Hartung, 1791) (trans. as *Exposition*)

——, *Exposition of Kant's* Critique of Pure Reason, Philosophica, 47 (University of Ottawa Press, 1995)

——, *Prüfung der Kantischen Critik der reinen Vernunft*, 2 vols. (Königsberg, 1789–92)

Sinisalo, M. K., 'Checking the Goldbach Conjecture up to 4×10^{11}', *Math. Comput.*, **61** (1993), 931–4

Sullivan, Peter M., 'The sense of a name of a truth value', *Phil. Quart.*, **44** (1994), 476–81

————, 'Wittgenstein on *The Foundations of Mathematics*, June 1927', *Theoria*, **61** (1995), 105–42

Swift, Jonathan, *Gulliver's Travels* (Oxford University Press, 1986)

Tait, W. W., 'Finitism', *J. Phil.*, (1981), 524–46

Tarski, Alfred, *Pojecie prawdy w jezykach nauk dedukcyjnych* (Warsaw, 1933)

Thomae, J., *Elementare Theorie der analytischen Functionen einer complexen Veränderlichen*, 2nd edn. (Halle: Nebert, 1898)

van Heijenoort, Jean (ed.), *From Frege to Gödel: A Source Book in Mathematical Logic, 1879–1931* (Cambridge, Mass.: Harvard University Press, 1967)

von Neumann, John, 'Zur Hilbertischen Beweistheorie', *Math. Zeit.*, **26** (1927), 1–46

von Wright, G. H., *A portrait of Wittgenstein as a young man: From the diary of David Hume Pinsent 1912–1914* (Oxford: Blackwell, 1990)

Waismann, Friedrich, *Wittgenstein and the Vienna Circle*, ed. by Brian McGuinness and trans. by Joachim Schulte and Brian McGuinness (Oxford: Blackwell, 1979)

Wallis, John, *Opera mathematica* (Oxford, 1693–9)

Whitehead, Alfred North, and Bertrand Russell, *Principia Mathematica*, 3 vols. (Cambridge University Press, 1910–13; 2nd edn. 1925–7)

Wiener, Norbert, 'A simplification of the logic of relations', *Proc. Camb. Phil. Soc.*, **17** (1914), 387–90 (repr. in van Heijenoort, *From Frege to Gödel*, 224–7)

Wittgenstein, Ludwig, *Cambridge Letters: correspondence with Russell, Keynes, Moore, Ramsey, and Sraffa*, ed. by Brian McGuinness and G. H. von Wright (Oxford: Blackwell, 1995)

————, *Notebooks, 1914–1916*, ed. by G. H. von Wright and G. E. M. Anscombe, 2nd edn. (Oxford: Blackwell, 1979)

————, *Philosophical Grammar*, ed. by Rush Rhees and trans. by Anthony Kenny (Oxford: Blackwell, 1974)

————, *Philosophical Remarks*, ed. by Rush Rees and trans. by Raymond Hargreaves and Roger White (Oxford: Blackwell, 1975)

————, *Prototractatus: An early version of Tractatus Logico-Philosophicus*, ed. by B. F. McGuinness, T. Nyberg, and G. H. von Wright, trans. by D. F. Pears and B. F. McGuinness, intro. by G. H. von Wright (London: Routledge & Kegan Paul, 1971)

————, *Tractatus Logico-Philosophicus* (London: Kegan Paul & Trubner, 1922; corrected edn. 1933)

————, 'Some remarks on logical form', *Proc. Arist. Soc., Supp. Vol.*, **9** (1929), 162–71

Wright, Crispin, *Frege's Conception of Numbers as Objects*, Scots Philosophical Monographs, 2 (Aberdeen University Press, 1983)

Index